Rex Ambler

1992

Perspectives on World Politics

Perspectives on World Politics

A Reader edited by
MICHAEL SMITH, RICHARD LITTLE
AND MICHAEL SHACKLETON
at the Open University

R

ROUTLEDGE
in association with
THE OPEN UNIVERSITY PRESS

First published 1981 by Croom Helm Ltd
Reprinted 1981, 1982, 1984, 1985 and 1987
Reprinted by Routledge 1989, 1990
11 New Fetter Lane, London EC4P 4EE

Printed and bound in Great Britain by
Biddles Ltd, Guildford and King's Lynn

British Library Cataloguing in Publication Data

Perspectives on world politics: a reader
  1. Foreign relations
  I. Smith, Michael, *1947 Apr. 1.–*
  II. Little Richard, *1944–*
  III. Shackleton, Michael
  327
  ISBN 0-415-03976-2

CONTENTS

ACKNOWLEDGEMENTS

The compilation of this Reader involved a number of exacting and time-consuming tasks and the editors would like to acknowledge that they would have been unable to hand over the completed manuscript on time without the cheerful and unstinting efforts of Debbie Curtis. A debt of thanks is also owed to other members of the Open University and to colleagues elsewhere for their help in the selection of some of the articles. The opinions expressed here are not necessarily those of the course team nor of the University.

INTRODUCTION

The Study of World Politics

World politics as an area of academic inquiry and practical activity holds at one and the same time immense promise and immense potential difficulty. Its promise — and a major reason for its attractiveness to students at all levels as well as to politicians and other 'practitioners' — lies in its focus on phenomena which are heavy with implications for the continued existence and flourishing of humankind. Questions of security and prosperity, order and justice, war and peace, and ultimately life and death, have always formed a major preoccupation of those engaged in the field: indeed, the emergence of an identifiable field of study, known widely as International Relations, was one of the less apocalyptic consequences of the First World War, and the growing awareness throughout the twentieth century that international events have important implications for political life at all levels has been accompanied by the expansion and diversification of international studies.

The difficulties and problems which have attended studies of world politics are in many ways the mirror image of its appeal. A focus on global problems, at a time when the ramifications of political activity have extended almost daily, carries with it the problem of complexity and change. Scholars in the field, no less than diplomats and other officials with more direct involvement, become hardened to the fact that many areas of inquiry grow, disappear or are transformed as they are studied. Likewise, the assertions that a comprehensive description of the world political scene ought logically to include the whole of human knowledge, or that the really important elements in global developments are precisely those which are likely to be least accessible, should act as a warning to those who enter the field. A warning, maybe, but not by any means a discouragement: it can be argued that the problems inherent in a study of world politics make of it one of the most challenging fields of inquiry or action available to scholars or practitioners.

There are several major dimensions to the challenge of world politics, which can briefly be noted here. Firstly, there is a challenge of *organization* and *ordering:* how are the phenomena of such a complex field to be moulded into some kind of coherent, ordered description? One expression of this problem can be found in the so-called 'level-of-analysis' problem which has beset international studies and aroused periodic debate. At its simplest, this dilemma reduces itself to a choice of the unit to be studied in any inquiry: is it to be the whole system of world politics, or a particular geographical area, or a set of specific problems, or a particular social or political grouping, or the individual? Such difficulties of choice and discrimination relate closely to the second challenge which can be noted here: the challenge of *theory*. How is it possible to formulate viable and testable theories about an area of complexity and diversity such as world politics? This question especially preoccupies those who conceive of world politics as the concern of social science and who envisage a gradual accumulation of theory and evidence rather akin to that experienced by the natural sciences. The social sciences as a whole have encountered difficulty in attempts to formulate laws of human behaviour, and world politics confronts them with a singularly intractable field. As a result, a third challenge, that of *explanation*, has proved extremely resistant to the assaults of scholarship and analysis: in an area where there is little tried and tested theory, and in which it is a considerable achievement to produce an ordered and coherent description of events, the relationship of cause and effect, of motivation and action, presents a daunting obstacle. These predominantly academic problems spill over into a final area of difficulty: the gap between scholarly investigation and practical politics. It is all too easy to conclude that the challenges of the field are likely to render useless all but the most basic exercises of description, and that attempts at theory are likely to have no practical relevance in the day-to-day conduct of affairs.

Not surprisingly, in the light of such challenges to a growing field of study, the development of world politics as an area of inquiry has been marked by some heated debates. Partly these have been debates over method – the most notable example being furnished by the disputes between so-called 'classical' and 'scientific' schools in the 1960s. Partly also they have been debates over questions of value – over what ought to be the case in world politics, as opposed to what seems to be the case – and here the debates between 'realists' and 'idealists' in the early post-war years provide a major illustration. These debates have been notable for their overwhelming concentration within one academic community – that of the United States – and for their reflections of some at least of the dominant concerns of American policy makers. In the 1970s, however, it became clear that there was more than one version of the 'world' within which world politics occurred: almost simultaneously, American views became less certain and more questioning, and new or existing approaches from other traditions emerged.

The readings in this book are intended directly to attack the questions which arise as soon as it is allowed that there may be more than one version of world politics. In one way, the approach taken has a good deal in common with that implied by a study of the 'level-of-analysis' problem, which alerts the student to the fact that his initial orientation or preconceptions can colour the questions he asks, the methods he employs and the answers he arrives at. Here, however, the focus is not simply on different facets of an agreed 'world' but rather on different versions of the 'world' as a whole, which colour and at the same time reflect issues of method, values and action. The approach is based on the conviction that there exist in the study of world politics certain definable perspectives, which shape the forms of academic activity and practical politics where they are implicitly or explicitly adopted. Three such perspectives form the core of the material assembled here: there may be others which could be identified, and it is not always clear where the boundaries of each perspective lie, but this does not affect the basic premise outlined above. To illustrate the approach in more detail, the next section of this Introduction assesses each in turn, in relation to some central concerns of world politics.

Three Perspectives on World Politics

The three perspectives on world politics which provide the framework for the selections of material in this Reader stem from widely differing temporal and political contexts. After what E.H. Carr has described as the initial 'utopian' phase of the study of world politics, there developed during the late 1930s and 1940s a definable focus on *the politics of power and security*. In this first perspective, the stress is laid on the quasi-anarchical nature of the world political system and the consequent concern of states with national security. During the 1960s and 1970s, it became evident that a second perspective had emerged − not to supplant the first in its entirety, but to offer a radically different view based on *the politics of interdependence and transnational relations*. Here, the stress was upon the coexistence and interaction of a mass of politically active groups in the world system and on the consequent problems of bargaining and regulation. At the same time, and from fundamentally different historical and philosophical roots, there had emerged a third perspective based on *the politics of dominance and dependence*. In many ways, this perspective predated the others, since it drew on the work of Marx, Lenin and others in the nineteenth and early twentieth centuries; but it experienced a resurgence with the process of decolonization in the 1950s and 1960s and with the associated problem of economic and social development in new states. How could the poor and weak of the world orientate themselves towards and operate within a global system which seemed to place them at a perpetual disadvantage?

From this discussion, it should be apparent that the problems raised by these perspectives have concrete historical roots, and that they concern not only academic theory but also political action. Some of the implications of these relationships are brought out by the selections in the final section of the Reader, which have been chosen to provide a 'perspective on perspectives'. A good way of exploring these problems further here, and of highlighting the distinctive concerns of each perspective, is by comparing their approach to three central questions of substance in world politics. Firstly, what appear as the significant *actors* in world politics in each case? Secondly, what view of the global political *process* is implied by each perspective? Finally, what kinds of *outcomes* are emphasized by each approach, and what kind of world do they see as emerging from the actors and processes dealt with?

The Politics of Power and Security

Since this perspective could also be described in terms of 'state-centric politics', there can be no confusion over its assumption of state dominance. This is not to deny that other groups can operate in world politics; rather, it is to assert that the state is dominant to such an extent that other groups gain influence only in so far as they can affect the policies of states. International organizations, economic groupings and other bodies are part of the context within which states operate, but they play an essentially subordinate or contingent role. Perhaps the central attribute which marks the state off from other bodies is its assumed monopoly of the legitimate use of force: as a result of this, states are enabled to pursue their other claims in the international system. Among these claims are those to control of a defined territory, to external sovereignty, and to recognition through exchange of diplomatic missions and admission to international organizations such as the United Nations. The problem is that, although states to this extent form an exclusive 'club', there is also intense competition between the members of the 'club' for scarce resources. In this context, the idea of 'resources' denotes not simply raw materials for the generation of wealth, nor simply the territory which may furnish raw materials, but also things which are much less tangible, such as security. Security — based on territory or other assets — is seen as a limited resource which is central to the concerns of all states but which none can enjoy completely. Nor can all enjoy it in equal measure: at the core of a 'power and security' approach is the assumption that there is an international hierarchy in which military might and economic capacity define the rank of any given state.

The actors in a 'power and security' approach are thus defined as states, commonly seeking to assure their own security and prosperity within the limits of scarce resources. Such a definition is important to a view of the significant processes in world politics, since their importance is clearly derived from the involvement of states. At the level of the state itself, foreign policy can be seen clearly as the process by which national (state) interests are pursued within an insecure world. The assumption is made that states act: in other words, the state moves as a single unit in pursuit of unified objectives. These objectives – and the exertion of power in pursuit of them – constitute the product of a process of rational choice in which the interests and resources of the state in question and of other states are assessed, the implications of particular choices are weighed and action is taken. Foreign policy is a matter of high secrecy and involves only a very restricted elite working on behalf of the state. This follows logically from the assumption that foreign policy is overwhelmingly concerned with matters of national security (both military and economic); in an insecure world, could it be otherwise? Such being the case, it is clear that success or failure in foreign policy is a matter of the appropriate application of power. In any given relationship, the state which most effectively and appropriately wields its power will prevail, with almost mathematical certainty.

A view of foreign policy as being concerned with national security and defence of national interests virtually dictates that the international political system (that is to say, the interstate system) will be characterized by competition and conflict. This is especially likely given the inevitable absence of any institutions accepted by and binding on all members of the system. The interstate system is an 'insecurity community' in which war is an ever-present 'contingent liability', and in which the axiom 'might is right' applies. That it does not apply universally is due to the existence of a core of practices which produce a minimum of international order: international law, the balance of power, the fear of war itself. On the whole, however, the outcome of the 'politics of power and security' is an international system which operates according to a power hierarchy, and in which there is a continuing tension between the concerns and activities of individual states and the demands of the system as a whole. States cannot escape the demands of the system, although it is possible to deflect or balance them in advantageous ways.

The Politics of Interdependence and Transnational Relations

Although the state remains a significant — if not the most significant — actor in the second perspective, its role undergoes a transformation. There is a central paradox here — between the growing concern of most states, especially those in industrialized countries, with what goes on in other societies, and the limited ability of many states to achieve their objectives in their ever-broadening area of concerns. The state itself — partly as a consequence — becomes penetrated, by other states or by a variety of other actors, and can no longer lay claim in many cases to the control of territory and the external sovereignty which are the building blocks of the 'politics of power and security'. Notions of power and of a power hierarchy are undermined, since it becomes clear that a state which is 'powerful' or well endowed in one area can be extraordinarily weak in others and vulnerable to its apparent inferiors. Alongside the state emerges a whole range of new, non-state actors which have distinctive areas of concern and arenas of activity. 'Subnational' actors with a base in one state can develop activities which significantly affect the policies of that state in other states or which bypass the state machinery completely. 'Supranational' actors — of which the European Economic Community is the most highly developed example — can in limited areas achieve the ability to override the authority of the state and produce policies which entail a diminution of state sovereignty. 'Transnational' actors, headed by the multinational corporations (MNCs) can establish operations with a multinational base, giving them in theory at least the ability to transfer activities and resources across state boundaries on a large scale. Within this perspective, there are variations in the extent to which the 'death of the state' is predicted or diagnosed: what is clear, however, is that it is no longer taken for granted as the dominant actor in the international sphere, nor is it seen as the uniform building block of a privileged 'club'. How could it be, when the financial resources of the largest MNCs exceed those of all but a handful of states?

Although the state is no longer, in the 'politics of interdependence and transnational relations', seen as the sole gatekeeper for international political processes, foreign policy does still matter. In this perspective, however, foreign policy is difficult to separate from wider political processes at home and abroad, since its subject matter is of much more immediate impact. The foreign policy system itself thus becomes penetrated, with action emerging not as the result of rational calculation by a unitary decision-making body, but rather as the outcome of complex political and organizational processes. We become aware not only that public and special-interest groups are involved in foreign policy questions, but also that the foreign policy machinery itself is an arena for political competition and dissent. The state becomes disaggregated, and so does the foreign policy process. Externally, the proliferation of channels for action and interaction accompanies the proliferation of issues and their increasing politicization to make foreign policy a matter of delicate management and coalition building rather than the comparatively simple safeguarding of national positions. New actors can intervene to complicate processes, and it is no longer the case that the hierarchy conditions outcomes. Indeed, there is no clear and uncontested hierarchy in newly politicized issue areas, and much activity has to be devoted to the building of rules and institutions to regulate the new agenda.

The international system in these conditions 'explodes'. A system of 'mixed actors' creates the potential for a multitude of coalitions and balances, corresponding to the intersection of novel and existing issues and the absence of a clear or unified global hierarchy. Although it could be said that a global military hierarchy, based especially on nuclear weapons, still exists, such an assertion becomes debatable in conditions where, firstly, nuclear weapons do not constitute a rational policy instrument and, secondly, the proliferation of nuclear capacity threatens to complicate the picture and create new instabilities. World politics became simultaneously more diffuse, penetrating new regions and activities, and more interconnected, with linkages between a variety of actors. The resulting conditions of interdependence − between actors and states − increase both the mutual sensitivity of those engaged in world politics and, in many cases, their mutual vulnerability to new forces. The response of those who espouse the second perspective is to call for enhanced mechanisms of management: in a way, they are calling for the *construction* of a system of behaviour of rules and standards (often termed a *regime*) to constrain the actors, whereas in the 'politics of power and security' the hierarchy and the imperatives of national security form a perpetual constraint. For the rather primitive imperatives of the first perspective are substituted a set of beliefs in managerial procedures and the fruits of multilateral negotiation which have to prove themselves in conditions of polyarchy where the sources of power are widely dispersed.

The Politics of Dominance and Dependence

An analysis of world politics based on the examination of dominance and dependence structures implies yet a third view of the role of the actors and of processes which take place in the global system. Although the state still acts as a focus of activity and coercive power, it stands in a particular structural relationship to dominant economic and political interests, which use it as a channel or a support for the pursuit of their aims. The state achieves less autonomy as an actor in world politics, since in many ways it is merely the recruit or the representative of other, more fundamental interests. Where the state is adequate to the task of supporting dominant interests — chiefly those of big capital — then it will be used, but where it fails to match up to the increasingly global needs and activities characteristic of large corporations, then it will be discarded or ignored.

Such a view implies that the real actors in world politics are dominant class or economic interests. It also implies that those in dependent positions within the global structure are systematically prevented from achieving any kind of capacity for autonomous action. A critical stage in the analysis of any actor within this perspective is therefore an assessment of its location within the global structure. In terms of classical imperialist theories, such a location is largely determined by relations between metropolitan powers and colonial areas, which are formalized by territorial occupation and administrative dominance. Where formal territorial imperialism does not exist, as it has not to any marked degree in the 1970s outside the Soviet bloc, new concepts become important in the study of relations between dominant and dependent groups. One of the most fruitful of these concepts has been that of centre-periphery relationships, in which the major determinant of international action has been seen as the confrontation between the dominant 'centre' of developed capitalism and the dependent 'periphery' of the less developed areas. The ideas of 'centre' and 'periphery' are not identical with particular groups of *states*, since it is part of this perspective's argument that relations between centre and periphery exist within, as well as between, nations. From this situation emerge a host of cross-cutting relationships, in which the common interests of those at the 'centre of the centre' and the 'centre of the periphery' form a major source of exploitation for peripheral groups.

It is apparent from this discussion that the systematic and structural patterns of dominance and dependence within the international system define the 'actorness' of groups within the system. The processes by which the structure is sustained and developed are equally a reflection of the fundamental imbalance between elements of the system. In the days of the great colonial empires, the mechanisms were formal and institutional as well as social and political in nature: the very rules of international life sanctioned armed intervention and division of territory between the metropolitan European powers. The decline of the nineteenth-century empires during the first two-thirds of the twentieth century was dramatic, but it did not imply that the processes of dominance and dependence had disappeared. In fact, it was possible to discern a distinctive process of 'underdevelopment' which consolidated the continuing dominance of the centre at the expense of the periphery. Such a process in specific cases is sustained by a number of mechanisms: by exploitation, in which the balance of benefits from international processes of exchange is biased towards the centre; by penetration, in which the forms and standards of the centre are pursued by 'recruits' among the elite of peripheral nations at the expense of the mass; and by fragmentation, through which a policy of 'divide and rule' dilutes the potential influence of dependent areas in their struggle against dominant forces. Although there may seem to be changes, and a process of 'development' may seem to take place in dependent areas, this does not alter the brutal basic fact of systematic disadvantage which gives 'structural power' to certain groups at the expense of others.

The outcome of these processes can only be described as a vicious circle. The rich get richer and the poor, in relative terms, can only get poorer as the structures of dominance and dependence are consolidated. In contrast to the view implied by the 'politics of interdependence and transnational relations', attempts at management and reform within the existing structure are ultimately futile; indeed, they are themselves the weapons of those whose central interest is in the continuation of the existing system and of the benefits it confers upon the privileged. In the final analysis, the contradictions and conflicts of interest produced by the prevailing structure can only be resolved by its collapse and its replacement by a more equitable global system. Given that the privileged cannot be expected to connive at their own destruction, such an outcome can only be the result of a traumatic upheaval, possibly induced by the growing internal contradictions of the advanced societies or by the upsurge of revolutionary discontent in the periphery.

An Overall View

The preceding discussion has uncovered at least some of the central features of the three perspectives examined. More particularly, it appears that it is possible to distinguish between them according to their approaches to the three questions posed earlier: who are the *actors* in world politics, what are the characteristics of the global political *process*, and what kinds of *outcomes* express the nature of the world system? Although it is wise to be cautious, and to be aware of the dangers inherent in the drawing of boundaries between approaches, the kinds of contrasts which have emerged can be crudely summarized as in Figure 1.

It should be clear that the three perspectives examined express broad differences of philosophy and of emphasis in the study of world politics. They may intersect or overlap at particular points, but it would be difficult

Figure 1: The Three Perspectives on World Politics

	Power and Security	Interdependence and Transnational Relations	Dominance and Dependence
Actors	States	State and non-state organizations	Economic classes and their representatives
Processes	Competitive pursuit of national interest	Management of global problems	Exploitation and dependency
Outcomes	Limited order within an anarchical society	Rule-governed behaviour in a polyarchical society	Struggle within a centre-periphery structure

to argue that they are simply special cases of one broader 'reality'. Three major areas of divergence can be mentioned here in support of such a judgement. Firstly, it is apparent that each perspective embodies a distinctive view of the relationship between the whole and the parts in the world political arena. A view based on the 'politics of power and security' postulates a constant tension between the interests of states and the dynamics of the state system, which creates an atmosphere of insecurity and the possibility of violence. An approach in terms of 'interdependence and transnational relations', on the other hand, enshrines a view of the world as a pluralistic political system within which there is a constant process of mutual and multilateral adaption to events. The 'politics of dominance and dependence', finally, centre upon a world in which the existing structure conditions all political action, and in which the actions and interests of the parts are reflections of the relationships built into the system as a whole.

A second area of divergence, linked to the first, concerns the possibilities for change or reform in the world system. Whereas the 'politics of power and security' is in many ways a conservative approach to world politics, basing its analysis on the existing distribution of global power, it does admit the possibility of macro-political change as the potential of particular states grows or declines. It does not, however, contemplate a change in the dominant role of the state in general, of the type which is almost a precondition for the 'politics of interdependence and transnational relations'; in this second perspective, the state becomes a variable capable of reform or transformation, and the global system itself is seen as demanding effective management. Such a reformist view, implying that political actions can enable the existing system more effectively to meet the demands of its members, is denied by the 'politics of dominance and dependence'.

Since the system embodies structural dominance and dependence, reform is out of the question and the only way of achieving fundamental change is through fundamental transformation.

As a consequence of divergences over the relationship between whole and parts, and over the possibility of reform or change, the three perspectives finally diverge in terms of their relationship to values and political action. The watchword of those who espouse the 'politics of power and security' is 'political realism', in which the sober and rational calculation of interests and capabilities is a central activity and the means of action should be carefully matched to the demands of particular circumstances. Whilst the need for appropriateness and calculation is by no means denied by the 'politics of interdependence and transnational relations', a major place is accorded to other values based on the possibility of progress and the development of new norms and conventions of behaviour. The 'politics of dominance and dependence' focus far less on the capacity for progress by adaptation and far more on the need for radical political action to exacerbate the contradictions of a system which systematically oppresses some of its members.

With these contrasts, the argument comes almost full circle. At the beginning of this Introduction it was remarked that the study of world politics poses particular challenges for scholar, student and practitioner alike, in terms of description, theory and explanation and in terms of the links between academic endeavour and political actions. None of the three perspectives presented here and in the remainder of this Reader can be seen in isolation from each other or the world in which they have emerged. They offer, to at least a modest degree, an illustration of the ways in which perspectives can shape the form of academic activity and practical politics in a complex world.

A Note on the Selection and Arrangement of Material

A number of criteria have influenced the selection of material for this Reader. Firstly, in line with the framework outlined in this Introduction, each section is intended to represent as fairly as possible the assumptions shared by authors writing within the perspective; in the case of the final section, the aim was to include material which explicitly assessed the implications of perspectives for the study and practice of world politics. Secondly, and as a consequence of these initial aims, it has been the concern of the editors to ensure that each individual selection reflects as fully as possible, within the inevitable constraints of space, the chief arguments of its author. Thirdly, wherever possible, the editors have made selections which illustrate the application of ideas within a perspective to particular examples, although no case studies as such have been included. Finally, although it has not been possible, for obvious reasons, to adhere rigidly to an approach based on 'actors, processes and outcomes' within each perspective, such an orientation was implicit in the collection of material.

Each section is preceded by a general introduction to the selections it contains, and each selection by a short introductory summary of content. Since in some cases the original material was accompanied by extensive footnotes and references, the editors decided to edit these in accordance with a uniform set of criteria. Thus notes are included where either there is a quotation in the text, or an author is referred to by name, or direct reference is made to a particular body of literature. It is hoped that this approach combines the maximum of economy in notes with as accurate a reflection as possible of the original author's intentions.

This Reader has been produced as part of the package of materials accompanying an Open University Course, *World Politics*, first presented in 1981. As well as forming part of the set reading for the course, and reflecting its general organization and approach, it is designed to represent trends in the study of world politics which will be of interest and use to students in higher education and the informed reader more generally.

Part 1

THE POLITICS OF POWER AND SECURITY

INTRODUCTION

The nine articles in this section have all been written since the Second World War. This reflects a bias in the choice, because this perspective has always dominated the way political thinkers have conceived of world politics. It would not, in fact, have been difficult to cover many of the ideas found in this section by taking extracts from Thucydides, *The Peloponnesian War*, Machiavelli, *The Prince*, and Hobbes, *Leviathan*. The advantage of doing this would have been to stress that there is a tendency for adherents of this perspective to believe that there are eternal verities which underlie world politics. The disadvantage would have been to move the focus away from the contemporary international arena. Thucydides was talking about Greek city states, Machiavelli was concerned with the ruler of an Italian city state and even Hobbes's Leviathan had little in common with today's nation-state. We have chosen, therefore, to restrict the selection to modern writers who nevertheless remain convinced that the age-old concepts of power and security still form the bed-rock upon which any analysis of world politics must be built.

All the articles rest on a common, critical assumption which dominates the perspective: that transactions among nation-states form the essential substance of world politics. The nation-state can be defined by a number of common features and these are catalogued by Stoessinger (1.1). He goes on to show, however, that, although the nation-state forms the basic building block of world politics, when it comes to analyzing relations among states, a distinction must be drawn in terms of their power resources. Rejai and Enloe (1.2) also stress that nation-states need to be distinguished, but in terms of their mode of development. For the most part, states in the Western world, such as Germany and Italy, emerged as a response to nationalism, whereas 'nation building' — the attempt to unify a group of people living within the boundaries of a common state — remains one of the major tasks confronting leaders in developing countries. In the remaining articles, however, this important distinction is not pursued. Instead 'power' is used as the critical variable which distinguishes states and underlies transactions in the international system.

When world politics was established as an academic discipline, after the First World War, attention was focused upon international law and international organizations which were viewed as instruments capable of preventing future wars. Analysis was, as a consequence, deflected away from the role of power in world politics. This period — subsequently dubbed 'utopian' or 'idealist' — gave way, after the Second World War, to a period dominated by the 'realists' who acknowledged the primacy of power in world politics.

Morgenthau (1.3), one of the prime movers, believes, as his contribution on the national interest reveals, that the crucial factor which faces every state is the need to survive. For him, survival constitutes the 'irreducible minimum' of state policy. However, although this interest may underpin all others, it is clear that states pursue a wide variety of goals, and Legg and Morrison (1.4) argue that the pursuit of these goals is based upon a rational strategy.

Since the Second World War, it has frequently been argued that with the development of nuclear weapons, among other factors, this rational strategy excludes the use of force. Garnett (1.5) strenuously resists this line of argument, insisting that the utility of military power remains one of the most distinctive features of world politics. Yet, even if this argument is accepted, it remains the case that states have other means for achieving their goals and, as Knorr (1.6) demonstrates, in the modern world, economic power is a major weapon which can be used to affect the behaviour of other states.

So far the articles concentrate on the nation-state as the unit of analysis. In the last three articles in this section attention is centred on the international system, where nation-states interact. Jervis (1.7) examines the consequences of each state developing its military potential in an effort to overcome a sense of insecurity. In the international system, states observing the military preparations of others experience a further desire to increase armaments. This spiral of insecurity represents a security dilemma which cannot be resolved in the anarchic international system.

Nevertheless, states have developed ways of preserving an element of order in the international system, despite the presence of the security dilemma, and Bull (1.8) shows that the balance of power represents the principal mechanism whereby states attempt both to preserve their independence and to maintain order in the international system.

Security has always been the major focus of attention for the realist but, in recent years, there has been a growing recognition that the study of world politics needs to accommodate the economic dimension of state behaviour. As Krasner (1.9) reveals, however, for the realist, even in the area of international trade, state power remains the crucial variable in explaining behaviour in the international system.

1.1

THE ANATOMY OF THE NATION-STATE
AND THE NATURE OF POWER

John Stoessinger

Source: *The Might of Nations*, 4th edn (Random House, New York, 1973), pp. 7-27.

Stoessinger first identifies a set of components (primarily sovereignty and nationalism but also territorial and economic ties, common language, culture and religion) which combine to establish the structure of the nation-state and help to maintain its cohesion. He then examines a set of tangible (geography, natural resources, population and government) and intangible (national character, morale, ideology and leadership) sources of power available to the nation-state.

The Anatomy of the Nation-State

Our world is made up of over one hundred political units called nation-states. There is hardly a place on this planet that is not claimed by a nation-state. Only a century ago the world still abounded with frontiers and lands that remained unpre-empted. But in our time, man can no longer escape from the nation-state system — unless he migrates to the frozen polar zones or to the stars. The nation-state has become ubiquitous. And everywhere it is the highest secular authority. It may decree that a man die; and, with no less effort, it may offer him the protection that enables him to live. When no state wants him — when man is naked in his humanity and nothing but a man — he thereby loses the very first precondition for his fellows even to be able to acknowledge his existence. Whether it be to be born, to live, or to die, he cannot do without official recognition — the recognition of a nation-state.

This modern-day fact of life is astounding when one considers that the nations that possess this inescapable power of life and death are in many ways only abstractions, figments of the human imagination. For though the power that is brought to bear to implement a nation's will is ultimately physical, the will itself is chiefly the result of human images, images about what a nation is and about why and how its will should be expressed and obeyed.

25

There are two principal aspects of this universal political image. In the first place, man has endowed the nation-state with a quality that it shares with no other human association — the attribute of *sovereignty*. It is indeed no coincidence that the theory of sovereignty was first formulated in the sixteenth century, at a time when the nation-state system was in process of emerging from the universalism of the medieval world. Its first systematic presentation was contained in the writings of the French political thinker Jean Bodin. Bodin's definition of sovereignty as 'the state's supreme authority over citizens and subjects', set forth in his *De La République* in 1576, is still largely valid today. The nation remains the final arbiter over the lives of its citizens, leaving them recourse to no higher law. And while this is true in peacetime, it is even more totally and dramatically the case in times of war. For in the latter eventuality, the sovereign state has the right to send its citizens to their death and, through its sanction, to transform even the most brutal forms of killing into acts of patriotic heroism. [...] It is sovereignty, more than any other single factor, that is responsible for the anarchic condition of international relations. Bodin conceived of sovereignty as essentially an *internal* phenomenon, 'the state's supreme authority over citizens and subjects'. While the advent of democratic government has rendered this power far less than absolute, no government, democratic or totalitarian, has been willing to yield major portions of its sovereignty in its relations with *other* nation-states. Hence, it would seem that sovereignty in our time is fundamentally a phenomenon of *international* relations, a fact of life in political intercourse among nations. Over three hundred years ago man created the image of Leviathan. In some parts of the world Leviathan is man's servant; in others, he remains the master. But no Leviathan yields to another except by its own consent. Sovereignty, originally no more than a political construct defining man's relationship to the state, has taken on a life of its own on the international scene. In the internal affairs of states, sovereignty has often created political order and stability. In international relations it has led to anarchy.

The second key component that has come into the making of nations has been the phenomenon of *nationalism*. In the broadest terms nationalism may be defined as a people's sense of collective destiny through a common past and the vision of a common future. In a very real sense, a nation's 'personality' is its common past, or history. Empirically, a nation is merely a group of people occupying geographic space. But nations exist much more in time than in space. The history of common triumphs and suffering evokes powerful bonds of solidarity for nations large and small. Common suffering seems to be more important in this respect than are victories. [...]

The vision of a common future constitutes the second ingredient of nationalism. Here, too, man's aspirations as an individual are often projected onto the larger stage of politics and international relations. The unconscious realization that one's personal future may be bleak and devoid of larger meaning is often unbearable. Hence, as Erich Fromm has brilliantly demonstrated in his *Escape from Freedom*, man may seek compensation for his lack of personal future in the reflected glory of the nation's collective future. This form of identification may manifest itself in socially constructive ways; it may also lend itself to nationalism of a more destructive kind, as it did, for example, in Nazi Germany. The process whereby the identification is generated takes place largely in the 'illogical, irrational, and fantastic world of the unconscious'.[1] [. . .]

It would, of course, be a mistake to claim that the psychological phenomenon of nationalism and the legal institution of sovereignty are the sole foundations of a nation. There are also a number of more 'objective' ingredients that play an essential part. Most prominent among these are territorial and economic ties and the presence of common language, culture, and religion.

Clearly the very first requirement of a nation is that it possess a *geographical base*, a territory of its own. Yet it does not necessarily follow from this that attachment to the soil of the homeland primarily explains the fact of national unity. The insights of social psychology would seem to indicate that an individual may remain attached to a much more specific and limited location, such as his place of birth or the countryside where he was raised. In fact, a person may feel more 'at home' in a spot in a foreign land that reminds him of his youth than in an unfamiliar locale in his own country. Moreover, powerful emotional ties to specific locales may even divide a nation. When this is the case, the nation in question tends to be vulnerable to serious disunity and, frequently, internecine strife. Yet even when strong local attachments are not present, a really active attachment to the national territory as a whole usually results only from powerful nationalistic propaganda.

Another major contributing factor to the existence and unity of a nation lies in its common and interdependent *economic patterns*. Especially has this come to be the case since the advent of modern technology and mass production, with their need for vast national markets. Yet this same economic logic has also tended to undermine the nation-state system. For why limit production and distribution to nationally protected markets? And significantly, the only genuinely 'supranational' organizations in existence in our time are of a primarily economic character. It is therefore incorrect to assert that economic ties reinforce the nation exclusively.

Modern technology and the enlargement of markets work equally for the development of economic patterns that reach far beyond national boundaries.

It is similarly difficult to generalize about the part that is played in the making of a nation by the presence of a *common language*. In many countries, as for example the United States, a common tongue is an important integrative factor. In other nations, the fact that the same common language may be spoken in many different versions definitely constitutes a divisive influence. This is very notably the case with the Chinese language, for instance, which consists of hundreds of dialects. Thus, if a native of Shanghai wants to communicate with a Cantonese, he can do so only by falling back on written Chinese or by resorting to some foreign language that both may know. Switzerland, on the other hand, with its three major languages, has achieved a very high degree of national unity. Still other nations have hoped to increase national cohesion by resurrecting a dead language. The revitalization of the Hebrew language in Israel is a case in point. But it is safe to assume that language is a relatively minor factor in Israeli unity. At times the quest for a national language has caused endless internal friction. The attempt to make Urdu the national language of Pakistan met with bitter resistance from that part of the Pakistani population which spoke Bengali. And India, after independence, had to accept English, a 'foreign' language, as its temporary *lingua franca*. Hence the role of language in the life of nations is clearly a rather ambiguous one.

Surely one of the most perplexing concepts is that of *'national character'*. Few social scientists would deny that certain cultural patterns occur more frequently and are more highly valued in one nation than in another. But it is almost impossible to find agreement among scholars on precisely what these common patterns are. In other words, we are faced with the paradox that 'national character' seems to be an indisputable factor but that no one knows exactly what it is. This confusion probably stems from the fact that cultural patterns continue to live as stereotypes. For example, the stereotypes of the 'volatile Frenchman' and of the 'materialistic American' are strictly time-bound. Only a century ago almost opposite images were current. Moreover, patterns may differ from region to region in the same country. And it is never difficult to find exceptions to the prevailing images. On the whole, it would therefore appear that though national character patterns are a fact, their uniqueness and their significance in supporting national unity vary from nation to nation.

The role of *religion*, finally, is equally two-edged. In the United States, religion has neither substantially contributed nor detracted from national unity. In other countries, Israel for example, religion has proved a very significant factor in making for unity in national terms. Yet in certain other cases religion has played a key part in preventing national unity. Thus it was chiefly the religious friction between Moslems and Hindus that in 1947 made necessary the partition of the Indian subcontinent into two separate nations – India and Pakistan. Religions have probably tended as much to keep nations divided as to aid their unity.

In summary, then, what constitutes a nation in our time may be characterized as follows. First and foremost, it is a sovereign political unit. Second, it is a population that in being committed to a particular collective identity through a common image of past and future shares a greater or lesser degree of nationalism. And finally, it is a population inhabiting a definite territory, acknowledging a common government, and usually – though not always – exhibiting common linguistic and cultural patterns.

Having examined the structure of the nation-state, we can now focus our attention on the heart of our subject matter – the behavior *among* nations. As a first step in this larger analysis, we must devote some attention to that most crucial of all the concepts in the study of international relations, the concept of *power*.

The Nature of Power

The nature of a nation's power *vis-à-vis* other nations is one of the most elusive aspects of international relations. It is frequently suggested that a nation's *power* is simply the sum total of its *capabilities*. Yet such a definition fails to do the concept of power full justice. For though power always involves capabilities, it concerns other dimensions as well. Most importantly, while capabilities are objectively measurable, power must in every case be evaluated in more subtle psychological and relational terms.

The psychological aspect of power is crucial, since a nation's power may depend in considerable measure on what other nations think it is or even on what *it thinks* other nations think it is. The relational aspect of power can be illustrated as follows. Let us assume that two nations, for example the United States and the Soviet Union, are approximately balanced in their capabilities. To the extent that this condition prevails, the power of either nation *vis-à-vis* the other is almost nil, even though their capabilities might suffice to wipe each other from the face of the earth. Hence, because power is a relational thing, whereas capabilities are not, there may upon occasion be no correlation whatsoever between the two. Indeed, when capabilities are equal, as in a stalemate, power tends to disappear altogether. To put it crassly, when everybody is somebody, nobody may be anybody. By the same token, of course, even a small increase in the capabilities of one of the two nations might mean a really major advantage in terms of its power. [. . .]

Coming now to the analysis of the anatomy of power as a whole, including its tangible capability aspects, we find it frequently asserted that 'the most stable factor upon which the power of a nation depends is geography'. In the words of Hans J. Morgenthau:

> The fact that the continental territory of the United States is separated from other continents by bodies of water three thousand miles wide to the east and more than six thousand miles wide to the west is a permanent factor that determines the position of the United States in the world.[2]

In the opinion of other scholars, however, the advent of the atomic age and the development of intercontinental ballistic missiles have brought about the obsolescence of 'territoriality'. As John H. Herz has put it, 'now that power can destroy power from center to center, everything is different'.[3]

It would be difficult to agree with Morgenthau that *geography* is always and necessarily a crucial factor in the power of nations. No doubt the enormous land mass of the Soviet Union prevented that country from being conquered by three different invaders in three succeeding centuries. Yet there may also be circumstances in which geographical considerations are much less relevant. Thus the same Russia whose vast expanses proved the undoing of Charles XII of Sweden, Napoleon, and Hitler, was in 1904 brought low in a naval battle by tiny Japan. It would be misleading, however, to go all the way with Professor Herz and suggest that the role of geography has drastically declined. Even the coming of nuclear weapons and intercontinental missiles may be less significant in this regard than is often claimed. As many military strategists have pointed out, mutual nuclear deterrence on the part of the superpowers may result in the wars of the future being 'limited' to weapons and strategies not much different from those that have been used in the past. And to the extent that this might be the case, facts of national geography, location, and topography would continue to retain very considerable importance in the balancing of international power. [. . .]

A second major element in a nation's international power is usually considered to be its possession of *natural resources*. Yet though this factor is always significant it, too, is in itself by no means decisive. For it is not primarily the possession of raw materials that makes a nation powerful; it is above all the *use* that nation is able to make of the resources it has available. Though the Arab states of the Middle East, for example, have grown rich and been extensively courted because of their large oil deposits, they have not, by virtue of this fact, become powerful nations.

What use a nation is able to make of the raw materials it possesses depends primarily on the extent of its economic and industrial development. To develop a powerful military establishment, nations today must first command an advanced technological base. How vital this requirement may be can be seen from the examples of Germany, Italy, and Japan in World War II. In the possession of strategic raw materials, all three of these countries are relatively poor. Yet because of their highly developed industry and technology, they proved able to build military machines that almost succeeded in bringing about an Axis victory. That the power of the Allies triumphed in the end is largely attributable to the fact that the latter possessed *both* an abundance of essential raw materials *and* an advanced industrial apparatus. [. . .]

The same point that has been noted in regard to geography and natural resources is also true of a third major element of national power, *population*. Once again, though a nation's population is certain always to be important as a factor in its power, the actual extent of its significance depends on many other considerations as well. Though both very populous, neither China nor India was in the past considered very powerful. Indeed, as the case of China illustrates, population is primarily *potential* power. As a result, it has been possible for nations with large populations to be weak, but impossible for nations without large populations to be powerful. Though the advent of atomic weapons may diminish the importance of manpower in warfare, the Vietnamese War would seem to have shown that the foot soldier has by no means been superseded. In the future as in the past, large populations are likely to remain an important military advantage. Hitler found it necessary to import slave labor from Eastern Europe to make up for manpower shortages in Germany. An armed conflict with a nation as populous as China would prove a struggle of the most overwhelming proportions. Even though it at the time had little else but its vast population, China was at the end of World War II accorded greatpower status in the United Nations.

Population becomes most important of all as a power factor when it is combined with industrialization. It is common knowledge that those countries now going through the process of industrialization are also the ones that are growing most rapidly in population. This fact, known as the 'demographic transition', significantly affects a nation's power.

Industrialization leads to an increase in population, which in turn may make possible further industrialization. As the case of China demonstrates once again, the potential power of population is actualized only when it is *used*, most profitably in the development of a modern industrial base which in turn makes possible a first-rate military establishment. In the view of many observers, once China succeeds in harnessing its immense population, it may in time become the most powerful nation on earth. [. . .]

A fourth element of national power, whose effects it is difficult to assess concerns the nature of a country's *government*. It is tempting to assume that a democratic form of government provides greater national strength than a dictatorship. Yet though the historical record does not invalidate this assumption, it certainly places it in question. The victory of Sparta over Athens is only one of many instances in which dictatorship emerged triumphant. But any analysis of this issue must remain inconclusive. There are simply too many imponderables involved to permit any easy conclusion. [. . .]

Many observers point out that democracy has a great advantage because it rests on the consent and voluntary support of the governed, where dictatorship requires coercion. While there is much truth in this oft-repeated assertion, it has been overdone. Modern totalitarianism has developed highly effective means of psychological indoctrination. Nazi Germany, Fascist Italy, the Soviet Union, and Communist China each developed a highly organized youth movement for this express purpose. In addition, 'brainwashing' − a kind of psychoanalysis in reverse − was widely applied to 'reactionary elements' in Communist China during the Cultural Revolution. These techniques, when coupled with the fact that modern totalitarianism deprives a population of standards of comparison in both time and space, have made possible the emergence of a new type of government: 'totalitarianism with the consent of the governed'; at times, totalitarian governments do not have to create popular support through these methods. The Nazi dictatorship, for example, enjoyed the fanatical support of most of the German population before 1941. Hence, a broad base of popular support as a source of power is not a monopoly of the democracies. [. . .]

It appears from the above that the objective or 'capability' attributes of a nation's power depend, above all, on the *use* which its government makes of such physical factors as geography, population, and natural wealth. In the hands of a resourceful government, democratic or totalitarian, geography is turned to strategic advantage, and population and natural resources become twin pillars of power − military preparedness and industrialization. But as we have stated at the outset, despite their great importance these objective bases of national power are by no means the whole story. Of no less importance for a nation's power arsenal are its image of itself and, perhaps most crucial of all, the way it is viewed by other nations. To understand the latter dimension of power we must consider chiefly the factors of national character and morale, ideology, and national leadership.

We have seen earlier that the concept of *national character* is highly elusive, and that it refers to something that is constantly changing. Its relevance to power does not lie so much in its objective existence, which is still disputed by many scholars, but in the persistence of stereotypes that are imputed by one nation to another. The instability of these stereotypes themselves denies the permanence of national character. Yet that they vitally affect a nation's power nevertheless can be seen from the following situation. Before the United States had established any physical contact with Japan, the American image of the Japanese was that of a quaint, romantic, and picturesque society, almost rococo in its fragility. Hence when the Americans decided to 'open' Japan to the West in the mid-nineteenth century, they simply sent Commodore Perry and a few warships to force the door. Actually, the Japan of 1850 was a rigidly stratified society that had been ruled for over two hundred years by an authoritarian military clan, the Tokugawa. Under the Western impact, Japan modernized with astounding rapidity. [. . .]

Americans' image of Japan had also changed rapidly. The 'sweet and doll-like' Japanese of Perry's day had become 'leering, bespectacled sadists' who raped and murdered innocent women and children. By the late 1930s, the Japanese image of the West, especially of the United States, became that of a decadent, corrupt, and spineless society which would disintegrate in the wake of a determined military attack. This distorted perception of America was matched by a Japanese self-image of absolute superiority and invincibility. In other words, a high *national morale* now became a major power factor. If the Japanese in 1941 had perceived themselves and the United States as they really were, there would have been no Pearl Harbor. It would have been obvious that Japan could not possibly win a war against the United States; that, in short, the objective fact of vastly superior capabilities was bound to overwhelm her. It was the power of an image that precipitated the Japanese attack. The incredible feats of little Japan during World War II cannot be explained in terms of its meager objective resources, but must be attributed above all to the existence of a self-image that was translated into superior national morale. This national morale became an immense storehouse of power. [. . .]

We have seen earlier that the very essence of nationalism is a nation's image of a common past and a common future. Hence it goes without saying that nationalism vitally affects a nation's power. Under certain conditions, moreover, the vision of a common future may become an *ideology*. This occurs when a nation's image of the future includes *the notion of a dynamic evolution toward some universal utopia*. Ideology has largely become the monopoly of totalitarian nations. Napoleon's vision of universal empire was rationalized by the ideology of the French *'mission civilisatrice'*. The ultimate vision of Nazi Germany was the enthronement of the 'Aryan race'. To accomplish this end, it became necessary for Germany to expand into ever wider areas of *Lebensraum* or 'living space'. The Japanese 'Co-Prosperity Sphere' was based on similar assumptions. The Communists, in turn, have their own blueprint for the world, which predicts the growing influence of the Soviet Union and China. In all these cases, the nation is seen as the dynamic instrument for world-wide dominion.

It would be too simple to assert, as does Morgenthau, that ideology is simply 'a flattering unction' for the concealment of imperialist expansion:

> It is a characteristic aspect of all politics, domestic as well as international, that frequently its basic manifestations do not appear as what they actually are — manifestations of a struggle for power. Rather, the element of power as the immediate goal of the policy pursued is explained and justified in ethical, legal, or biological terms. That is to say: the true nature of the policy is concealed by ideological justifications and rationalizations. . . .
>
> Politicians have an ineradicable tendency to deceive themselves about what they are doing by referring to their policies not in terms of power but in terms of either ethical and legal principles or biological necessities. In other words, while all politics is necessarily pursuit of power, ideologies render involvement in that contest for power psychologically and morally acceptable to the actors and their audience.[4]

Not only is it an exaggeration to claim that *all* politics is a pursuit of power, but the relationship between power and ideology is a much more complex and multifaceted one. In the first place, a widespread belief in the 'truth' of an ideology may hasten its realization and thus become a power factor. For example, the ideological conviction of many Communists that the victory of Communism is ordained by history has added immensely to the power of the Soviet Union and Communist China. This faith in a metaphysical determinism has tended to inspire Communism with a self-image of invincibility. Second, ideology may assume an authority all its own, precisely because its adherents are convinced of its metaphysical validity. Power, in the last analysis, must rest on the capacity of physical force. Authority, on the other hand, may attain similar compliance because it is accepted as legitimate or 'true'. Ideology serves the peculiar function of 'justifying power and transforming it into authority, thus diminishing the amount of power which must be applied to achieve compliance or to produce the desired effect'.[5] [...]

Ideology as a source of power is largely a monopoly of totalitarianism. A democracy may have goals or ideals but not an ideology. Since the very essence of a democracy is the principle of the right of disagreement on substantive goals, such a nation lacks the fanaticism and uniformity that lend an ideology its coherence and drive. The citizens of the United States may disagree on America's 'national purpose'. A totalitarian society, on the other hand, has only one official ideology. This does not mean, of course, that democracy has no resources to marshal against the aspirations of a universal ideology. As we have seen, it has other great sources of power. Besides, ideology is not *only* a source of power. It is the great overreacher of international relations. By definition, its goals are boundless and its horizons of conquest unlimited. The time must come, as it always has, when the image of a universal ideology is thwarted by an unyielding reality — when power encounters concerted counter-power. Hence each ideology carries within itself the seed of its own destruction, the hubristic assumption that power can expand without limit.

Finally, the quality of a nation's *leadership* and the image which it projects upon the world are important sources of power. If leadership is defective, all other resources may be to no avail. No amount of manpower or industrial and military potential will make a nation powerful unless its leadership *uses* these resources with maximum effect on the international scene. If the tangible resources are the body of power, and the national character its soul, leadership is its brains. It alone can decide how to apply its nation's resources. For example, the United States before World War II possessed virtually every single attribute of a powerful nation. But it played a relatively minor role in international relations because its leadership was committed to a policy of isolation. Hence as far as American power was concerned, the advantages of geography, natural resources, industrial and military potential, and size and quality of population might as well not have existed at all, for though they did in fact exist, American leadership proceeded as if they did not.

In concluding our analysis of power, we must take note of a striking paradox: while the power gap between big and small states has never been greater, never have big states been less able to impose their will upon lesser countries. The conflicts between the United States and North

Vietnam, France and Algeria, and the Soviet Union and Yugoslavia are cases in point. Part of the reason for this is, of course, the fact that whenever one superpower is engaged against a lesser state, the other superpower tends to be arrayed on the other side. Yet, the French experience in Algeria and both the French and American experiences in Indochina demonstrate that power also has a great deal to do with a nation's willingness to accept punishment. American policy in Southeast Asia failed because the threshold of suffering for North Vietnam and the Vietcong was much higher than Washington had assumed, while the American threshold was considerably lower. The United States dropped more bombs on North Vietnam than she dropped on the Axis powers during the entire period of World War II. Yet that little nation virtually fought the United States to a standstill. It seems that, with the coming of the atomic age, the power of big states has diminished while the power of small states has increased. At any rate, power can no longer be calculated simply by adding up a nation's physical capabilities. Psychology and will must be given as much weight as resources and hardware.

Now that we have analyzed the anatomy of power, we may propose the following definition: *power in international relations is the capacity of a nation to use its tangible and intangible resources in such a way as to affect the behavior of other nations.*

Notes

1. Louis L. Snyder, *The Meaning of Nationalism* (Rutgers University Press, New Brunswick, NJ, 1954), p. 89.

2. Hans J. Morgenthau, *Politics Among Nations*, 4th edn (Knopf, New York, 1967), p. 106.

3. John H. Herz, *International Politics in the Atomic Age* (Columbia University Press, New York, 1959), p. 108.

4. Morgenthau, *Politics Among Nations*, pp. 83-4.

5. Zbigniew K. Brzezinski, *The Soviet Bloc: Unity and Conflict* (Harvard University Press, Cambridge, Mass., 1960), pp. 386-7.

1.2

NATION-STATES AND STATE-NATIONS

Mostafa Rejai and Cynthia H. Enloe

Source: *International Studies Quarterly*, vol. 13, no. 2 (International Studies Association/Sage, 1969), pp. 140-58.

Rejai and Enloe argue that the interaction between 'nation' and 'state' in developed countries has taken a different form from that outside the Western world. In the latter, authority and sovereignty have tended to precede a sense of national identity, whereas in the former the pattern has been reversed, with structures of political authority running behind cultural integration.

Nationalism takes a variety of forms and carries with it a variety of political consequences. A major variable distinguishing one pattern of nationalism from another has been the interplay between 'nation' and 'state'. At bottom, this is a relationship between national identity and political autonomy, between national integration and political sovereignty.

In many of the developed countries of the post-World War II world the sense of national identity evolved prior to the crystallization of the structures of political authority. By contrast, in most of the currently underdeveloped, newly independent countries this sequence is reversed: authority and sovereignty have run ahead of self-conscious national identity and cultural integration. To this extent it can be said that Europe produced nation-states, whereas Asia and Africa have produced state-nations. [...] For our purposes, we shall define a nation as a relatively large group of people who *feel* that they belong together by virtue of sharing one or more such traits as common language, religion or race, common history or tradition, common set of customs, and common destiny. As a matter of empirical observation, none of these traits may actually exist; the important point is that a people believe that they do. Although the variable of size is necessarily imprecise, it is intended to suggest that a nation is larger than a village, clan, or city-state. [...]

'Nation', it is clear, is not the same as 'state'. The latter refers to an independent and autonomous political structure over a specific territory, with a comprehensive legal system and a sufficient concentration of power to maintain law and order. 'State', in other words, is primarily a political-legal concept, whereas 'nation' is primarily psycho-cultural. Nation and state may exist independently of one another: a nation may exist without a state, a state may exist without a nation. When the two coincide, when the boundaries of the state are approximately coterminous with those of the nation, the result is a *nation-state*. A nation-state, in other words, is a nation that possesses political sovereignty. It is socially cohesive as well as politically organized and independent.

Nations and states, then, do not necessarily evolve simultaneously; nor is it possible to say, as an inflexible rule, which one comes first. The argument has been made that in nineteenth century Europe the nation preceded and created the state, whereas in the developing countries today this relationship has been reversed, so that the state is creating the nation. While the distinction between nation-states and state-nations on this basis is relevant and useful, both sequences and formations are to be found in the West as well as in the developing areas. The emergence of a degree of national and cultural consciousness preceded the formation of the state in Germany, for example, whereas in France the situation was reversed and the monarchical state preceded national consciousness. Similarly in the non-Western world, Turkey and Iran, for example, may be viewed as nation-states, whereas most of the African countries are (at least potentially) state-nations. It is true, in general, however, that state-nations have tended to predominate in the non-Western world where the processes of cultural integration frequently gain momentum under the impetus of political unification. The reasons are not difficult to identify. Political independence necessarily involves demarcation of territorial boundaries and the subjection of a given people to a single government. This in turn encourages the adoption of a common administrative structure, a common educational system, a common body of law, a common language, and a common system of communications. [. . .]

Nationalism is a distinctive phenomenon of the nineteenth century. The development of political thought from the Greek thinkers through Machiavelli, Grotius, Hobbes, and Rousseau is an intellectual prelude to the emergence of nationalism. The ideas of the secular state and political sovereignty had to be wedded to the concept of 'mass politics' before nationalism could crystallize. It is the 'mass' quality which distinguishes the French Revolution and which implies a pooling of energies and loyalties of an entire citizenry. Overnight, as it were, France — for long a monarchical state — became a nation; and the nation assumed responsibility for the destiny of its citizens, demanding loyalty and devotion in return.

The French Revolution spread the idea that the nation has a right and an identity of its own. Sovereignty was lodged squarely in the nation. The Declaration of the Rights of Man and Citizen (1789) boldy proclaimed that 'sovereignty resides essentially in the nation; no body of men, no individual, can exercise authority that does not emanate expressly from it'. With the French Revolution nation and state merged. [. . .]

The rise of nationalism coincided with the growth of some democratic ideas and sentiments. 'Liberty, Equality, Fraternity' were not accidental slogans of the French Revolution. The middle classes were demanding new rights, including the rights of representation and participation in public affairs. This in turn suggests a relationship between nationalism and industrialism: only industrialism could have produced the new classes which rose to assert their new powers and demand new rights. Indeed, without the advances in transportation, communication, trade, and commerce afforded by the Industrial Revolution, it would not have been possible for modern nations to come into being.

National honor, national self-determination, popular and national sovereignty were inescapable components of the doctrine of nationalism. A nation, it was felt, should choose its own form of government; it should decide for itself the course of action that it wishes to follow. Monarchy, tyranny, and absolutism no longer would be tolerated. Equally remarkable is the fact that all this was seen as a right, not only of France, but of all peoples and nations. Although nationalism would benefit every nation, however, the spreading and propagation of the new order was seen as a special mission of the French people. Michelet, for example, saw France as the center of universal history. The French people would bring enlightenment and freedom to all nations of the world: upon France depended the salvation of mankind. Inspired by the example of France, all peoples were to rise and overthrow privilege and dictatorship. If they refused 'Liberty, Equality, Fraternity', the French would take it upon themselves to accomplish this task for them — by military force, if necessary. From early in its beginning, in short, nationalism became associated with messianism, militarism, and war. This war, however, was seen as a new type of conflict which put, not peoples against peoples, but peoples against tyrants and despots. [. . .]

German nationalism of the nineteenth century — initially a response to Napoleonic expansionism — departed from its French counterpart. Long before 1789, there had existed among the German principalities a sense of social and cultural unity. The French Revolution intensified this.

Johann Gottfried von Herder (1744-1803) had expounded what in effect might be called a cultural nationalism. He had conceived of humanity as made up of a series of cultures each consisting of a group or a 'folk'

(Volk) with its own tradition, custom, literature, music, language, and even 'soul' *(Volksgeist)*. To Herder each culture represented natural and organic growth. He used a biological analogy in describing cultural groups as living organisms that are born, grow, and mature. He advocated a comparative 'physiognomy' of the peoples of the world.

Herder did not call for the creation of nation-states. For him, nationalism was a romantic conception looking towards humanity rather than states; it was devoid of political imperatives. It was Georg Wilhelm Friedrich Hegel who succeeded in giving Herder's cultural nationalism a firm political grounding. What Hegel had done in theory and philosophy, Otto von Bismarck and Heinrich von Treitschke accomplished in practice.

At the hands of Hegel, the state was turned into a God-like creature capable of commanding the unquestioned loyalty of all Germans as a step toward final unification. The state was seen as the supreme repository of all moral and spiritual values, the supreme object of man's devotion.

Bismarck and Treitschke employed the teachings of Hegel to maximum advantage. Together, the two Prussians propagated the cult of the state as the embodiment of might and power.

The overriding and urgent task was still German unification, but now under Prussian leadership. Bismarck and Treitschke argued that Prussia should constitute the nucleus of a unified Germany, conquering and controlling the smaller principalities. The unification of Italy had preceded and inspired that of Germany. Bismarck and Treitschke watched developments in Italy with great interest and stressed the affinities of the Prussian and Sardinian regimes. They thought, in fact, that the two regimes should collaborate to break French predominance on the Continent.

Bismarck's successes in the war of 1866, in which Prussia fought Austria, Saxony, and most other German principalities, and in the war of 1870 against France, confirmed his (and Treitschke's) belief in Prussia's mission and destiny. The new German Reich, proclaimed by Bismarck on January 18, 1871, was in effect an expanded Prussia. It symbolized the union of militarism and nationalism.

This brief examination of French and German nationalism would seem to indicate that the relationship between 'nation' and 'state' is a complex one. In Germany, the nation preceded the state; in France, the state preceded the nation.

[The authors go on to discuss the effect of the rapid extension of nationalism outside the Western world in the twentieth century.]

Non-Western nationalism is largely a consequence of the spread of Western

civilization, that is to say, Western ideas, techniques, and institutions —
even though non-Western countries have frequently taken a stance militantly
resentful of Westernization. At the same time, the 'paradox of colonialism'
or 'irony of imperialism' refers to the proposition that the colonial powers,
by introducing these ideas and institutions, forged the instruments for
their own destruction. The colonial peoples, in other words, seized upon
these very instruments in their efforts to uproot imperialism. One of the
processes running through most non-Western nationalism is an attempt to
integrate foreign values and practices without sacrificing the essential
distinctiveness which justifies the practice of colonial peoples calling
themselves 'nations'. Most Western nations did not suffer the traumas of
this ordeal in their development. 'Integration' has even more profound
implications, therefore, in the non-Western nationalist experience.

Non-Western nationalism is, at least initially, a protest movement. The
doctrinal and attitudinal content of non-Western nationalism is largely
negative, signifying a reaction against foreign domination. Thus Coleman
has defined nationalism in Nigeria, for example, as 'sentiment and activity
opposed to alien control'.[1]

A related feature of non-Western nationalism lies in the extremely
important role played by the intellectual elite. This is not to suggest that
the intellectuals have not played a critical role in all nationalism. But in
the non-Western world in particular, nationalism has been almost exclusively
the handiwork of the intellectuals. Non-Western intellectuals have in fact
served as intermediaries between Western and non-Western cultures.

In the underdeveloped countries, where as a rule the state has preceded
the nation, nationalism exerts two kinds of pressures on the political system,
pressures not as apparent in the development of European nationalism.
First, anticolonial nationalism poses a greater challenge to political legitimacy than did nationalism in the earlier-developing societies. Second, due
to the fortunes of timing, nationalism in the postwar countries has been
more visibly associated with growth, not just autonomy. The twin pressures
of *legitimation* and *growth* have given nationalism in the underdeveloped
world its distinctive character. More than was the case in Western Europe
in its nationalist heyday, nationalism in twentieth century Asia and
Africa is being employed to sustain preexistent state authority and to
accelerate state-directed modernization.

Throughout most of Africa and Asia the state, with its formal institutions,
its explicit codes of law, its fixed territorial jurisdiction, was already in
existence when nationalism emerged as a political force. It was colonialism,
more than any other single factor, which determined this state-nation
sequence: colonialism initially fashioned and entrenched the structures of

political authority and then, later, provided the stimulus which provoked the nationalist movements. In other words, not only did the state precede the nation but it played a crucial role in creating and mobilizing it.

The European powers perceived their colonies as essentially administrative units. They were more intent upon establishing an efficient civil service and a legal code than they were in fostering a popular allegiance to collectivities beyond the parochial village or clan. No state is merely an administrative phenomenon, but certainly administration is close to the core of any state. When the imperial powers withdrew and granted autonomy to their former colonies, what they left behind were skeletal states: frameworks for political decision-making.

Where there were popular nationalist movements they usually either moved into the abandoned skeletal structure or had to share occupancy with those Westernized indigenous civil servants who continued to man the ministries, courts, and police forces. The Indonesian civil servant who still preferred to speak Dutch at the office and the Nigerian judge who continued to don wig and robe in the courtroom — these were witnesses to the state-before-nation pattern of sequence.

Having occupied the deserted structures of the state and having begun to formulate and implement policies in the name of the state's formal authority, the new indigenous rulers discovered that their authoritative sanction was extremely vulnerable because it lacked a grounding in popular identification. The former colonial rulers were subject to the same vulnerability, but it was less of an immediate threat because the colonialists, clearly outsiders, could more openly rely on coercive authority. The latent vulnerability became manifest when authority passed to the indigenous rulers. They possessed the instruments of coercion but based their claims of legitimacy on popular acceptance. Their efforts to expand the function of the state beyond administration and maintenance of peace also shed harsh light on the flimsiness of their authority. In their attempts to reduce their vulnerability in this new situation, the indigenous rulers have looked to nationalism as the means of vitalizing and conserving the authority of the state.

The condition of the state in a postcolonial country is roughly analogous to a castle — a repository of rules and orders — which in the past had dominated a territory without actually resting upon it, held up instead by stilts representing coercive superiority, technological and organizational innovation, and indigenous deference. The end of colonial rule either weakened or cut through these supporting stilts, leaving the castle precariously hovering above the ground. The task of the castle's new occupants is to construct a first story or, better, a basement to the castle. Nationalism is the material most commonly employed in this post-independence construction.

This metaphor, if at all valid, implies that in the countries which have gained political autonomy since the mid-1940s nationalism will be cultivated at the top and filtered downward. This process is the reverse of that experienced in the eighteenth and nineteenth centuries in France, where nationalism developed from the bottom upward toward the formal institutions which it eventually transformed. The nationalism which finally resulted was not necessarily more genuine because it emerged out of an upward (rather than a downward) process. But the direction of instigation does affect the overall impact that nationalism will have on a given political system. Furthermore, this dichotomy between upward and downward-cultivated nationalism usually is modified in practice. There were powerful nationalist sentiments in parts of Africa and Asia even prior to the exodus of the colonial powers and the conferring of political autonomy. Nevertheless, what nationalism there was then was frequently confined to a relatively small percentage of the indigenous society, to those who were most highly politicized. Most often it was a nationalist *movement* which either seized or negotiated the occupancy of the state's structures, and this is not the same as there being a society-wide feeling of commonality, the character of which often molded the vehicles of authority.

In countries where nationalism is instigated at the top there is a suspicion of any nationalist sentiment which appears to emerge at the mass level. In other words, in the state-nations the downward process is due in part to the preexistence of the state which is trying to bolster its own legitimacy, but it is also due to a deliberate squelching of upward-developing nationalism. The reason for viewing grassroots sentiments with suspicion lies in the heterogeneity of these countries. Even if labeled 'nationalist' by its advocates, a grassroots collective self-consciousness is likely to be exclusivist and divisive. Thus upward-cultivated nationalism is feared by the officialdom because it may exacerbate tribalism or communalism at the expense of societal integration; it may undermine rather than reinforce the state's authority.

When nationalism precedes and shapes the state it is probable that the resultant jurisdiction of the state will embrace a citizenry which is relatively homogeneous in terms of historical experience, language, religion, custom — though by no means all of these. On the other hand, when the legal and territorial definitions are set prior to the existence of a notion of national identity, the state is more apt to include within it disparate, even mutually hostile, linguistic, religious, and racial groups. A cursory glance at the histories of India, Indonesia, Sudan, Vietnam, or the Congo underlines this likelihood. The administrative and commercial preoccupations of the imperialist powers made cultural homogeneity relatively unimportant in the drawing up of state jurisdictions. As a result, ethnic and tribal communalism has plagued most of the former colonies and has produced a bias toward downward-generated nationalism, a definition of identity and allegiance which is worked out at the most general, all-embracing level of society.

A sense of nationhood which can bind the fragmented society together under the state's authority will have to be of a sort that does not depend heavily on linguistic and other cultural affinities. In addition, the nationalism prevalent in the postcolonial countries will be shaped by the perceived needs of the state. Thus it will be more self-consciously politicized. In short, whereas in most of the developed countries states have had cohesive nations corresponding to them, in the developing countries this has been rare.

The first question for the architects of the new nations is what integrative cement can serve as a substitute for cultural affinity. The very mixed success of national language acts (e.g., in India and Malaysia) and state religion establishments (e.g., in Burma) casts doubt on the ability of authorities to create cultural affinities by fiat. Therefore, the substitutes have been most frequently political and economic rather than cultural — even though the national language act may remain on the books for symbolic reasons.

There is nothing strikingly new about political and economic dimensions to nationalism. All nationalisms have led to the assertion of one group's autonomy from other groups. But in countries such as Ghana or Indonesia the assertion is particularly exclusivist; it is a rejection of domination or infringement by any 'outsider' emanating from an abhorrence of subjugation rather than from a sense of cultural identity which separates the outsider from the insider. It is difficult to sustain the vitality of this highly exclusivistic nationalism once formal external domination has been removed. The concept of 'neo-colonialism' offers one means for preserving its relevance after independence.

There also has been an economic fiber running through most nationalism, but, here again, it becomes more important in countries marked by cultural fragmentation. Advocates of economic development projects in underdeveloped countries often support their arguments by contending that economic interdependence can foster a sense of common interest and common focus within an otherwise divided society. If citizens do not speak a mutually intelligible language or hold similar beliefs about the supernatural, they still may participate in a common marketing and production system. Investment of skill, capital, and labor will create a stake in a common enterprise, and eventually the development of a distinctive economic system will produce common attributes (consumer tastes, productive skills, etc.) which can outweigh cultural diversity. This economic system (which is to generate a new sense of national identity) will be controlled largely by the state, or at least indirectly guided to fit the state's long-range goals.

This reliance on economic bonds in lieu of cultural bonds makes modernization crucial to the realization of nationalism in the postcolonial countries. In Europe nationalism spurred modernization; in most of Africa and Asia modernization is looked to as a means of promoting nationalism. In the latter there has been a running parallel to the state-before-nation sequence: the precedence of the modernizing drive before nationhood.

The ingredients encouraging national integration usually include such things as common language, common values, common religion, territorial contiguity, communications media, common markets, and racial affinity. Some of these ingredients are 'givens', others can be manipulated. The postcolonial countries suffer from a shortage of the 'givens' and so depend especially on the manipulable ingredients. Moreover, because national integration is being stimulated from above by the state, there is further inclination toward concentrating on the types of bonds that are susceptible to manipulation and innovation. Intrajurisdictional bonds such as telephone lines, railroads, postal systems, schools, production schemes, price controls − are precisely the sorts of linkages which authorities governing a non-nation-state can employ in constructing a foundation to support their state 'castle'.

There is a subtle irony in this formulation, however. These manipulable, culturally detachable links are the products of modernization. Modernization depends on mobilization of all available resources. Mobilization in the past has frequently depended on the existence of nationalism. In other words, the very instrumental linkages on which the authorities of the new states are wont to rely are those which require nationalism for their production. [. . .]

The result is that in the state-nations of Africa and Asia nationalism is translated into 'nation-building'. The prevalence of cultural heterogeneity and the pressures for modernization put a premium on organization and on authoritative guidance. In France the emergence of nationalism was analogous to a maturing personality; in Burma or Nigeria the more appropriate analogy is architectural construction. [. . .]

The evolution of nationalism currently appears to have confronted a paradox: a tendency toward the subordination of nationalism is being accompanied by the simultaneous tendency toward its reassertion in both Western and non-Western countries. For over two decades unprecedented efforts have been invested on behalf of a united Europe, a political community capable of bridging the national divisions. While not without lapses and digressions, the overall trend seems to be toward greater, not lesser, crossnational interaction. On the other hand, Belgium and Great Britain, for example, are currently experiencing the growing internal strains generated by indigenous groups claiming nationalism for themselves; the Flemings and Walloons each have powerful advocates calling for some sort of organizational separateness to embody their 'national' identity, while in Great Britain the Welsh and the Scottish nationalist parties are more prominent and politically emboldened today than they have been in generations.

The same paradox appears to be operating in the non-Western world. At the same time as nationalist credentials are the *sine qua non* of political authority, there is evidence of an increasing range of supranational exchange and cooperation in the newly independent countries (including those with Communist regimes). The Asian Development Bank, the Association of Southeast Asian Nations, and the Organization of African Unity are institutional embodiments of this regionalism. Furthermore, perhaps to an even more alarming extent than in Europe, the state-nations are marked by persistent and growing secessionist movements: Burma, India, Nigeria, and Tanzania are only a few instances of such sub-state nationalist fragmentation.

To this extent, the developed and the underdeveloped countries are exhibiting striking similarities; the paradox of nationalism's simultaneous waxing and waning characterizes all areas. This in turn may indicate a gradual closing of the political developmental gap lying at the heart of the dichotomy we have assumed throughout this essay. The distinction between nation-state and state-nation is still valid, but it may be less relevant in the future. [. . .]

Note

1. James S. Coleman, *Nigeria: Background to Nationalism* (University of California Press, Berkeley and Los Angeles, 1958), p. 169.

ANOTHER 'GREAT DEBATE': THE NATIONAL INTEREST OF THE US

Hans J. Morgenthau

Source: *The American Political Science Review*, vol. XLVI, no. 4 (American Political Science Association, 1952), pp. 971-8.

Morgenthau wishes to reopen the 'Great Debate' between realism and utopianism (or idealism) in the context of American foreign policy and he argues that foreign policy should be defined in terms of the national interest rather than utopian ideals. He believes that the national interest provides an essential guide for policy makers. It contains two elements: a logically necessary element – state survival; and a variable element – the form of which depends upon changing circumstances.

It has been frequently argued against the realist conception of foreign policy that its key concept, the national interest, does not provide an acceptable standard for political action. This argument is in the main based upon two grounds: the elusiveness of the concept and its susceptibility to interpretations, such as limitless imperialism and narrow nationalism, which are not in keeping with the American tradition in foreign policy. The argument has substance as far as it goes, but it does not invalidate the usefulness of the concept. [. . .]

Any foreign policy which operates under the standard of the national interest must obviously have some reference to the physical, political, and cultural entity which we call a nation. In a world where a number of sovereign nations compete with and oppose each other for power, the foreign policies of all nations must necessarily refer to their survival as their minimum requirements. Thus all nations do what they cannot help but do: protect their physical, political, and cultural identity against encroachments by other nations.

It has been suggested that this reasoning erects the national state into the last word in politics and the national interest into an absolute standard for political action. This, however, is not quite the case. The idea of interest is indeed of the essence of politics and, as such, unaffected by the circumstances of time and place. Thucydides' statement, born of the experiences of ancient Greece, that 'identity of interest is the surest of bonds whether between states or individuals' was taken up in the nineteenth century by Lord Salisbury's remark that 'the only bond of union that endures' among nations is 'the absence of all clashing interests'. The perennial issue between the realist and utopian schools of thought over the nature of politics, to which we have referred before, might well be formulated in terms of concrete interests vs. abstract principles. Yet while the concern of politics with interest is perennial, the connection between interest and the national state is a product of history. [. . .]

The national state itself is obviously a product of history and as such destined to yield in time to different modes of political organization. As long as the world is politically organized into nations, the national interest is indeed the last word in world politics. When the national state will have been replaced by another mode of organization, foreign policy must then protect the interest in survival of that new organization. For the benefit of those who insist upon discarding the national state and constructing supranational organizations by constitutional fiat, it must be pointed out that these new organizational forms will either come into being through conquest or else through consent based upon the mutual recognition of the national interests of the nations concerned; for no nation will forego its freedom of action if it has no reason to expect proportionate benefits in compensation for that loss. This is true of treaties concerning commerce or fisheries as it is true of the great compacts, such as the European Coal and Steel Community, through which nations try to create supranational forms of organization. Thus, by an apparent paradox, what is historically relative in the idea of the national interest can be overcome only through the promotion in concert of the national interest of a number of nations.

The survival of a political unit, such as a nation, in its identity is the irreducible minimum, the necessary element of its interests *vis-à-vis* other units. Taken in isolation, the determination of its content in a concrete situation is relatively simple; for it encompasses the integrity of the nation's territory, of its political institutions, and of its culture. Thus bipartisanship in foreign policy, especially in times of war, has been most easily achieved in the promotion of these minimum requirements of the national interest. The situation is different with respect to the variable elements of the national interest. All the cross currents of personalities, public opinion, sectional interests, partisan politics, and political and moral folkways are brought to bear upon their determination. In consequence, the contribution which science can make to this field, as to all fields of policy formation, is limited. It can identify the different agencies of the government which contribute to the detemination of the variable elements of the national interest and assess their relative weight. It can separate the long-range objectives of foreign policy from the short-term ones which are the means for the achievement of the former and can tentatively establish their rational relations. Finally, it can analyse the variable elements of the national interest in terms of their legitimacy and their compatibility with other national values and with the national interest of other nations. We shall address ourselves briefly to the typical problems with which this analysis must deal.

The legitimacy of the national interest must be determined in the face of possible usurpation by subnational, other-national, and supranational interests. On the subnational level we find group interests, represented particularly by ethnic and economic groups, who tend to identify themselves with the national interest. Charles A. Beard has emphasized, however one-sidedly, the extent to which the economic interests of certain groups have been presented as those of the United States.[1] Group interests exert, of course, constant pressure upon the conduct of our foreign policy, claiming their identity with the national interest. It is, however, doubtful that, with the exception of a few spectacular cases, they have been successful in determining the course of American foreign policy. It is much more likely, given the nature of American domestic politics, that American foreign policy, insofar as it is the object of pressures by sectional interests, will normally be a compromise between divergent sectional interests. The concept of the national interest, as it emerges from this contest as the actual guide for foreign policy, may well fall short of what would be rationally required by the overall interests of the United States. Yet the concept of the national interest which emerges from this contest of conflicting sectional interests is also more than any particular sectional interest or their total sum. It is, as it were, the lowest common denominator where sectional interests and the national interest meet in an uneasy compromise which may leave much to be desired in view of all the interests concerned.

The national interests can be usurped by other-national interests in two typical ways. The case of treason by individuals, either out of conviction or for pay, needs only to be mentioned here; for insofar as treason is committed on behalf of a foreign government rather than a supranational principle, it is significant for psychology, sociology, and criminology, but not for the theory of politics. The other case, however, is important not only for the theory of politics but also for its practice, especially in the United States.

National minorities in European countries, ethnic groups in the United States, ideological minorities anywhere may identify themselves, either spontaneously or under the direction of the agents of a foreign government, with the interests of that foreign government and may promote these interests under the guise of the national interest of the country whose citizens they happen to be. The activities of the German-American Bund in the United States in the 'thirties and of Communists everywhere are cases in point. Yet the issue of the national interest vs. other-national interests masquerading as the national interest has arisen constantly in the United States in a less clear-cut fashion.

A country which had been settled by consecutive waves of 'foreigners' was bound to find it particularly difficult to identify its own national interest against alleged, seeming, or actual other-national interests represented by certain groups among its own citizens. Since virtually all citizens of the United States are, as it were, 'more or less' foreign-born, those who were 'less' so have frequently not resisted the temptation to use this distinction as a polemic weapon against latecomers who happened to differ from them in their conception of the national interest of the United States. Frequently, this rationalization has been dispensed with and a conception of foreign policy with which a writer happened to disagree has been attributed outright to foreign sympathy or influence or worse. British influence and interests have served as standard arguments in debates on American foreign policy. Madison, in his polemic against Hamilton on the occasion of Washington's Neutrality Proclamation of 1793, identified the Federalist position with that of 'the foreigners and degenerate citizens among us, who hate our republican government, and the French revolution',[2] and the accusation met with a favorable response in a majority of Congress and of public opinion. However, these traditional attempts to discredit dissenting opinion as being influenced by foreign interests should not obscure the real issue, which is the peculiar vulnerability of the national interest of the United States to usurpation by the interests of other nations.

The usurpation of the national interest by supranational interests can derive in our time from two sources: religious bodies and international organizations. The competition between church and state for determination of certain interests and policies, domestic and international, has been an intermittent issue throughout the history of the national state. Here, too, the legitimate defense of the national interest against usurpation has frequently, especially in the United States, degenerated into the demagogic stigmatization of dissenting views as being inspired by Rome and, hence, being incompatible with the national interest. Yet here, too, the misuse of the issue for demagogic purposes must be considered apart from the legitimacy of the issue itself.

The more acute problem arises at the present time from the importance

which the public and government officials, at least in their public utter-
ances, attribute to the values represented and the policies pursued by
international organizations either as alternatives or supplements to the
values and policies for which the national government stands. It is frequently
asserted that the foreign policy of the United States pursues no objectives
apart from those of the United Nations, that, in other words, the foreign
policy of the United States is actually identical with the policy of the
United Nations. This assertion cannot refer to anything real in actual
politics to support it. For the constitutional structure of international
organizations, such as the United Nations, and their procedural practices
make it impossible for them to pursue interests apart from those of the
member-states which dominate their policy-forming bodies. The identity
between the interests of the United Nations and the United States can
only refer to the successful policies of the United States within the United
Nations through which the support of the United Nations is being secured
for the policies of the United States. The assertion, then, is mere polemic,
different from the one discussed previously in that the identification of a
certain policy with a supranational interest does not seek to reflect discredit
upon the former, but to bestow upon it a dignity which the national
interest pure and simple is supposed to lack.

The real issue in view of the problem that concerns us here is not
whether the so-called interests of the United Nations, which do not exist
apart from the interests of its most influential members, have superseded
the national interest of the United States, but for what kind of interests
the United States has secured United Nations support. While these interests
cannot be United Nations interests, they do not need to be national
interests either. Here we are in the presence of that modern phenomenon
which has been variously described as 'utopianism', 'sentimentalism',
'moralism', the 'legalistic-moralistic approach'. The common denominator
of all these tendencies in modern political thought is the substitution for
the national interest of a supranational standard of action which is generally
identified with an international organization, such as the United Nations.
The national interest is here not being usurped by sub- or supranational
interests which, however inferior in worth to the national interest, are
nevertheless real and worthy of consideration within their proper sphere.
What challenges the national interest here is a mere figment of the imagination, a product of wishful thinking, which is postulated as a valid norm
for international conduct, without being valid either there or anywhere
else. At this point we touch the core of the present controversy between
utopianism and realism in international affairs.

The national interest as such must be defended against usurpation by non-national interests. Yet once that task is accomplished, a rational order must be established among the values which make up the national interest and among the resources to be committed to them. While the interests which a nation may pursue in its relation with other nations are of infinite variety and magnitude, the resources which are available for the pursuit of such interests are necessarily limited in quantity and kind. No nation has the resources to promote all desirable objectives with equal vigor; all nations must therefore allocate their scarce resources as rationally as possible. The indispensable precondition of such rational allocation is a clear understanding of the distinction between the necessary and variable elements of the national interest. Given the contentious manner in which in democracies the variable elements of the national interest are generally determined, the advocates of an extensive conception of the national interest will inevitably present certain variable elements of the national interest as though their attainment were necessary for the nation's survival. In other words, the necessary elements of the national interest have a tendency to swallow up the variable elements so that in the end all kinds of objectives, actual or potential, are justified in terms of national survival. Such arguments have been advanced, for instance, in support of the rearmament of Western Germany and of the defense of Formosa. They must be subjected to rational scrutiny which will determine, however tentatively, their approximate place in the scale of national values.

The same problem presents itself in its extreme form when a nation pursues, or is asked to pursue, objectives which are not only unnecessary for its survival but tend to jeopardize it. Second-rate nations which dream of playing the role of great powers, such as Italy and Poland in the interwar period, illustrate this point. So do great powers which dream of remaking the world in their own image and embark upon world-wide crusades, thus straining their resources to exhaustion. Here scientific analysis has the urgent task of pruning down national objectives to the measure of available resources in order to make their pursuit compatible with national survival.

Finally, the national interest of a nation which is conscious not only of its own interests but also of that of other nations must be defined in terms compatible with the latter. In a multinational world this is a requirement of political morality; in an age of total war it is also one of the conditions for survival.

In connection with this problem two mutually exclusive arguments have been advanced. On the one hand, it has been argued against the theory of international politics here presented that the concept of the national interest revives the eighteenth-century concept of enlightened self-interest, presuming that the uniformly enlightened pursuit of their self-interest by all individuals, as by all nations, will of itself be conducive to a peaceful and harmonious society. On the other hand, the point has been made that the pursuit of their national interest by all nations makes war the permanent arbiter of conflicts among them. Neither argument is well taken.

The concept of the national interest presupposes neither a naturally harmonious, peaceful world nor the inevitability of war as a consequence of the pursuit by all nations of their national interest. Quite to the contrary, it assumes continuous conflict and threat of war, to be minimized through the continuous adjustment of conflicting interests by diplomatic action. No such assumption would be warranted if all nations at all times conceived of their national interest only in terms of their survival and, in turn, defined their interest in survival in restrictive and rational terms. As it is, their conception of the national interest is subject to all the hazards of misinterpretation, usurpation, and misjudgment to which reference has been made above. To minimize these hazards is the first task of a foreign policy which seeks the defense of the national interest by peaceful means. Its second task is the defense of the national interest, restrictively and rationally defined, against the national interest of other nations which may or may not be thus defined. If they are not, it becomes the task of armed diplomacy to convince the nations concerned that their legitimate interests have nothing to fear from a restrictive and rational foreign policy and that their illegitimate interests have nothing to gain in the face of armed might rationally employed.

Notes

1. Charles A. Beard, *The Idea of National Interest: An Analytical Study in American Foreign Policy* (New York, 1934).

2. James Madison, 'Helvidius, in Answer to Pacificus, on President Washington's Proclamation of Neutrality', in *Letters and other Writings of James Madison* (Philadelphia, 1867), vol. 1, p. 611.

THE FORMULATION OF FOREIGN POLICY OBJECTIVES

Keith R. Legg and James F. Morrison

Source: *Politics and the International System: An Introduction* (Harper and Row, New York, 1971), pp. 140-50.

Legg and Morrison discuss the requirements of a rational foreign policy. They suggest that it is the task of top decision makers to identify the political, economic and psychological needs of their country, to recognize the limitations involved in their pursuit and to work out 'a well-defined and well-ordered set of foreign policy objectives'.

Whatever the decision-making structure of a given state, some individual or institution must resolve conflict within the state, make collective decisions about the general needs and goals of the state and work out strategies for attaining them, including a determination of which goals can be attained only through interaction with other states in the international system. The process of formulating foreign policy objectives is by no means a simple one. In the first place, it is a fallacy to assume that a foreign policy decision — any more than a domestic policy one — affects all members of a state in the same way especially in the short run. The costs and benefits of most foreign policy decisions are unevenly distributed, and consequently, as noted, there is usually considerable internal conflict over what foreign policy should be. In the United States, for example, East European political refugees and those who profit from a high level of military expenditure are often less anxious to see a Soviet-American entente than are pacifists, businessmen who see opportunities to trade with Eastern Europe if agreement can be reached, or those who would prefer to see more money available for domestic welfare programs. Those of draft age or those who live in vulnerable cities may be less anxious to get involved in a war than those who live in rural areas and are in less danger of being directly involved. Manufacturers who sell to a domestic market and must compete with foreign imports are likely to be more favorable toward a protective tariff than those whose living depends on exports and who might suffer from retaliation. While all conflicting interests are not necessarily represented, the top decision-making authorities in a state must make some order out of the conflicting demands presented — integrating them with the decision-making elites' own beliefs about what is in their own interest and in the long-range interest of the state collectively. Although foreign policy goals in practice are seldom completely explicit, well-defined, stable, internally consistent, or ranked according to priority, a rational foreign policy model requires the decision-making authority of a state to work out such a well-defined and well-ordered set of foreign policy objectives as well as a strategy for attaining them.

A word must be said at this point about the relation between objectives and strategy (or between ends and means). In practice this distinction is largely analytical. In the first place, the distinction depends primarily on the objective on which one happens to be focusing. Few things we think of as objectives are ends in themselves, but are rather means, in turn, for the achievement of still more abstract or distant ends (e.g., happiness, security, success, prestige). The United States objective of winning the war in Korea or Vietnam, for example, is really only a means to contain Communism. This in turn is only a means to protect the stability of the international system and to preserve a balance of power in the world favorable to the United States, and this, in turn, is a means to protect American security. In other words, there is no such thing as ends and means, only a complicated ends-means chain or an even more complicated intertwining ends-means net.

In the second place, objectives which originated entirely as a means of attaining some more distant end often take on a life of their own and become valued for their own sake, or because they become intertwining with other goals (originally not involved at all) such as prestige or self-respect. Although the objective of winning the war in Vietnam originated as a means of containing communism, in time winning became an end in itself — particularly for those most directly and emotionally involved in fighting or for those whose reputations as policy-makers depend on victory. The drive to win continued, despite growing doubts about whether it was possible or whether continuing to fight would in fact weaken and contain the communist movement and despite increasing evidence that continuing the fight might actually strengthen the Communists and weaken the United States at home and her position in other parts of the world.

In the third place, experience and tradition over time — in combination with basic values and norms — create a set of relatively inflexible principles which also at least in part originated as means to achieving certain objectives. These principles, too, take on a life of their own and tend to persist even after they have ceased to serve as effective means, or principles. Examples of such general historical principles of United States foreign policy are the idea that Communism must be contained at all costs, that the United States will never strike the first blow in a war, that only liberal-democratic states should be recognized or supported.

In the fourth place, there are often unintended consequences of the means one selects — i.e., the means may prove totally ineffective or even produce the opposite results than those intended, or they may produce both the desired ends and unintended consequences.

In the fifth place, every state, like every individual, has many objectives — and some of these objectives are bound to be in conflict with one another; therefore, the means necessary to achieve one objective may require a sacrifice of some other objective.

Despite these limitations, the distinction between ends and means is still useful. The rational foreign policy-making process to a large extent is the process of organizing clear and reliable (i.e., the means actually do lead to the desired end) means-ends chains, controlling the tendency of means to become ends in themselves and seeing that the original and more fundamental objectives are kept in perspective.

It is also important to remember that the goals or objectives of states — or even of each individual state — differ considerably not only in substance but also in a number of other ways:

1. The number, scope and mutual compatibility of the goals.
2. The intensity with which they are held, i.e., their relative importance *vis-à-vis* domestic goals and one another, and the cost the state is willing to pay in terms of the expenditure of capabilities or the sacrifice of other goals.
3. The urgency with which they must be achieved.
4. The flexibility with which they are pursued (i.e., the degree to which one goal can be substituted for another or modified in response to pressures for compromise, as long as the long-range goals are not impaired).
5. The risk the state is willing to run in the attempt to achieve its goals.
6. The state's expectations that the goals can actually be attained.

Sources of Foreign Policy Objectives

The most fundamental source of foreign policy objectives is perhaps the universally shared desire to insure the survival and territorial integrity of the community and state. Military security against invasion or bombardment is the minimum objective of every state's foreign policy. A related and also universal need is the preservation of the state's economy. These are usually purely defensive objectives, but under some circumstances internal or external conditions may require offensive action to insure the survival of the community and/or the state.

Perhaps the single most important set of domestic sources of foreign policy are the economic needs of the community. These needs, however, are by no means static. Changing technology, growing population, economic development, new organizations and classes, changing values, beliefs, and expectations, and a changing political system will very much affect economic needs and their expression. At any given moment, however, the top decision-makers of a given state and the specialized foreign policy-making bureaucracy must consider a wide variety of factors: overpopulation and the consequent pressure for new cultivable land to increase food supplies, the need for industrial raw materials and investment capital as well as other imports necessary for the population's well-being and for economic development, the need for foreign markets for the goods produced in the state (particularly if the state must import to survive), the related need to preserve the state's balance of payments and to protect its currency, the need to protect or procure essential lines of communication and transportation, the need to protect investments in other states, ships and overseas installations, and one's citizens and nationals outside the country. (This latter need is often less an economic need than it is a matter of prestige or a cultural need.)

It is important to emphasize that economic needs are fundamental sources of a state's foreign policy. First, there are strong pressures generated in the state's political system to satisfy individual or group economic needs through foreign policy. Second, the economy of a state is fundamental to a state's capabilities and therefore to its power *vis-à-vis* other states, i.e., its ability to get other states to do what it desires. No top decision-maker in any state can be rational and ignore the problem of maintaining and, if possible, increasing capabilities to the point where they are adequate to achieve the state's objectives.

Another major domestic source of foreign policy is what we might call the political needs of a state and its leaders. If the state has serious internal political conflict or the political system has low legitimacy, the top decision-makers of the political system are likely to emphasize the foreign policy goals of preventing foreign intervention on the side of the dissenting or dissident groups and may seek aid in preserving the system or their own place in it (e.g., the USSR in 1918-1924, South Vietnam at present [in the early 1970s]). Alternatively, the political leadership may take advantage of or even try to create foreign threats in order to distract the attention of a dissatisfied population from domestic problems or from the role of the élite in creating the problems. In general, even in stable political systems, the continued viability of the system rests on the ability of the top decision-makers to respond to politically significant domestic demands. This means that demands for foreign policy decisions from all quarters for any other cause also fall into this category.

Still another major domestic source of foreign policy is the cultural, psychological, and/or ideological needs of the state for prestige and status in the world: identity or meaning in life, needs for fulfilment of religious or sacred ideological imperatives, needs to follow moral principles or fulfill obligations (e.g., to come to the aid of victims of aggression or unjust oppression), and the like. Here we might also mention such psychological needs as relief for the population from tension, strain, uncertainty, anger, and frustration, which may generate strong pressures on foreign policy-makers to alter goals or even to take action immediately. Theoretically, this may not have a place in rational foreign policy-making, but it is clearly a fact of life in actual foreign policy-making and execution, and no national policy-maker can ignore such pressures completely.

One other domestic source of foreign policy might be termed the capability requirements of the state. Although most capability needs are met through decisions made in the area of domestic policy (e.g., decisions regarding investment rates, resource allocation, education, propaganda, government, military expenditures, draft calls), there is also an important area of capabilities determined by foreign policy decisions. Most obvious are decisions regarding the use of diplomacy to create alliances; acquire foreign air, naval, and other installations; to gain control over strategic land and waterways; or secure sources of raw materials. Decisions to recruit, train, and deploy intelligence-gathering units and clandestine operations teams and decisions to use force to increase one's capabilities are other examples. Somewhat less obvious are decisions regarding the recruitment and training of diplomats and career foreign service men. Least obvious, perhaps, is the long-range impact of the success or failure of foreign policy decisions on capabilities: if, for example, a diplomatic or military threat is made but not carried out (because of inadequate capabilities, planning, or willingness to run risks), then in the future when that state makes a similar threat, it is likely to go unheeded, even if the state has sufficient military capabilities or the will to act. In other words, a failure of foreign policy at one time may reduce the very important capability of credibility – a capability which, if successfully used, may avoid the expenditure of many irreplaceable capabilities in open warfare.

Capability considerations of this kind are also important sources of foreign policy for rational decision-makers. On the other hand, the successful carrying out of a threat, though costly at the time, may increase one's credibility and increase the probability that making a similar threat in the future will itself be sufficient to achieve compliance.

Some writers (most notably Hans Morgenthau) have argued that capability considerations ('power' in Morgenthau's terminology) are the most important sources of foreign policy, and that states above all seek to increase their capabilities (power), as capabilities (power) are the key to all other objectives and therefore become the overriding objective for their own sake. This seems to us a very oversimplified theory, yet nevertheless one which contains more than a little truth.

There are also important external sources of foreign policy which the top foreign policy decision-makers and relevant general population alike must take into account. We have already mentioned external threats of military intervention and economic ruin. By implication, many of the domestic sources of foreign policy also have an external counterpart which has to be taken into account. If raw materials must be imported or foreign buyers found for one's products to pay for needed imports, the reality of the international economic and political system must be considered before policy is formulated. The external opportunities and limitations of trade are just as important determinants of a policy objective as are the actual domestic needs. The domestic needs are meaningless for foreign policy unless there is an external possibility of meeting those needs. Most foreign policies, in other words, involve a domestic need of one state which can be met only by enlisting active cooperation or at least the acquiescence of another state. The foreign policies of two states must interact to meet the domestic needs of each.

Nevertheless, there are also needs that arise primarily from external sources, such as a threat of invasion, subversion, or economic discrimination or blockade by another state. They create foreign policy needs for protection that can be met by alliance with a third state or by membership in a supranational or international organization. Likewise, by the very creation of a common market, or alliance, or international organization, neighboring states may create a threat to one's economic well-being or military security, if the activity is ignored, but it can also create an opportunity to cooperate and reap benefits otherwise unavailable. Another type of external source of foreign policy are opportunities created by events outside one's state: two neighboring states at war with one another; the disintegration of a neighboring empire; the discovery of new continents or mineral resources; two states on the verge of war in need of a mediator;

and other similar changes create opportunities for a state to increase its power, size, wealth, or prestige by responding with a creative foreign policy. (In the same way that domestic sources of foreign policy have a foreign counterpart; likewise, such foreign sources of foreign policy require their domestic counterpart.)

Which of these various internal and external sources of foreign policy will be most important in a given case depends on the individual situation. By and large, among the domestic sources of foreign policy, the political system (the institutions and rules of the game) and the relative power of the contending groups will be among the major determinants.

The Limitations of the Formulation of Objectives

It is important to keep in mind that there are some important limitations which come into play in the rational formulation of foreign policy objectives. The internal limitations on goal formulation include limited capabilities or a limited ability to mobilize them for foreign policy objectives. This may mean an inability to mobilize adequate popular support or acquiescence for policies even among top decision-makers. There may also be cultural limits on policy objectives.

No rational attempt at foreign policy formulation can set forth serious objectives which exceed the ability of the state to achieve them. Every state's capabilities are limited, and one of the basic problems of rational foreign policy formulation is to keep the objectives of the state within the limits of the capabilities to achieve them. The possession of objective capabilities, of course, does not necessarily mean the ability to mobilize them for foreign policy purposes. The relevant population and institutions may be willing to utilize the capabilities which they control for some purposes (e.g., fighting off an invasion of home territory) but not for others (e.g., fighting in a distant land, for objectives that are not entirely clear). Despite the best efforts of specialized foreign policy élites, it may simply prove impossible to persuade the domestic policy élites (or even the chief executive) to expend the necessary resources or run the risks necessary to achieve the objectives (or use the means) that the specialists think most desirable.

A failure to achieve announced objectives can be costly not only in terms of prestige, but can also be expensive in terms of the wasted economic and military capabilities which could have been put to better use. Moreover, failure also means a loss of political capabilities, such as reduced morale and loss of self-confidence and will. Even if one backs down from announced objectives, there is still the danger of lost prestige and credibility. All these things decrease the overall capabilities of a state and increase its vulnerability to other states. It is, of course, not easy to judge just how many capabilities one has available or what a given set of capabilities can accomplish. There are always unforeseen circumstances. Other states may suddenly join together to form a new alliance. There may be sudden advances in weapons technology (e.g., the atomic bomb). The weather may affect military operations unexpectedly (e.g., Napoleon's disastrous invasion of Russia). Internal economic or political crises may unexpectedly limit the ability to mobilize capabilities (e.g., the United States' experience in Vietnam). Moreover, there is no way to evaluate with any degree of precision the effects of given policies or weapons. Different types of weapons systems (e.g., armored weapons, airpower, guerrilla warfare tactics) are often used against one another and the effects of each against the others are not easy to measure accurately. In addition, there are factors of strategy, morale, and luck to consider even when opponents use similar weapons systems. At best, then, an evaluation of a given state's capabilities − even in relation to another state or a given set of objectives − is only a rough estimate. Incorrect analyses of the probable effectiveness of one's capabilites are among the important causes of war, e.g., World War II, Vietnam, the Arab-Israeli war of 1967.

For these reasons, rational decision-making requires the careful limitation of objectives to well within the range of state capabilities in order that possible errors of calculation can be sustained. Capabilities can also be underestimated and the state that is willing to run the greatest amount of risk − especially in relation to cautious states that are less willing to run risks − has a great advantage over adversaries because of the ability to bluff and force concessions. The irrational state in a world of rational states, in other words, often is at an advantage, at least in the short run and for limited gains that do not threaten what the other states consider to be their core values.

Another important domestic limit on foreign policy objectives is the need to mobilize sufficient support for a given objective. Enough people have to be persuaded that a given policy objective is worth the cost and risk involved. What constitutes adequate support, of course, depends on the nature of the political system, but even in highly authoritarian states the problem of mobilizing adequate support among the top decision-making élite remains. Lack of consensus over goals in either decentralized or highly centralized decision-making systems can lead to paralysis and an inability to take decisive action. It goes without saying that if a policy objective does not have adequate support it cannot be adopted. Problems of paralysis arise where there is a fairly even division between supporters and opponents of a given policy, a nearly even balance of support for different but conflicting policies, or where support is divided among three or more conflicting objectives with no single policy commanding adequate support. In such circumstances even if one faction is victorious over the others and a given policy is adopted, the lack of real consensus provides only precarious support for the decision, and there is always a good chance that the victorious faction or coalition will be overturned. Such continual crises not only make foreign policy irrational but also endanger the achievement of domestic goals and weaken the general capabilities of the state. Under such conditions objectives are often modified to accommodate enough individuals and groups to form a firmer base for the policy or the objectives are abandoned.

Finally there are domestic cultural limits on a state's objectives. Obviously the culture of a state affects the mobilization of support for objectives in general. It affects what people value and how much they are willing to pay or risk to achieve a given objective. Over and above this, however, there is another kind of limitation: namely, the body of norms and general principles which specify legitimate state objectives, strategies, and foreign policy instruments. A state holding to the norm of self-determination of peoples or anti-imperialism will find it more difficult to adopt an imperialist policy than states without such principles, even when great economic benefits could be derived from such a policy.

There are also important external limits to a state's goals, and in some ways these are also only counterparts of the domestic limitations. The capabilities of other states, for example, determine the probability that one's own will be sufficient to secure a given objective. The limits created by international organizations and norms operate effectively either because a state shares the norms itself (i.e., they are a part of its own cultural limitations) or because they are shared by others who consequently will be able to mobilize more capabilities to counter the initiatives of the state that does not share them.

THE ROLE OF MILITARY POWER

John Garnett

Source: *Contemporary Strategy* (Croom Helm, London, 1975), pp. 50-64.

Garnett examines a series of arguments which suggest that military power has become irrelevant in the modern world. He counters each argument and reasserts the continuing importance of military power. He concludes, moreover, that the evidence indicates that most political actors will continue in the future to see military power as an essential ingredient of world politics.

At its simplest, the term military power refers to the capacity to kill, maim, coerce and destroy, and although occasionally this power may be possessed by individuals within the state — as the feudal barons possessed it during the Middle Ages and as the IRA possesses it today — nowadays military power tends to be monopolized by states and used primarily by *governments* to protect their countries from external aggression and internal subversion. Military power, therefore, is the legally sanctioned instrument of violence which governments use in their relations with each other, and, when necessary, in an internal security role.

Underlying the above definition is the assumption that military power is a purposive, functional thing — one of the many instruments in the orchestra of power which states use at an appropriate moment in the pursuit of their respective national interests. Since Clausewitz it has been fashionable to regard military power as but one of the many techniques of statecraft, taking its place alongside diplomacy, economic sanctions, propaganda and so on. But of course even Clausewitz recognized that war is not always an instrument of policy, a purposive political act. Sometimes war is a kind of madness, an explosion of violence which erupts not as a result of political decisions but in spite of them.

[Garnett goes on to stress, however, that he is only concerned with the use of military power as a rational technique for pursuing foreign policy.]

Clearly, military power does not come into being by accident. It cannot be acquired without enormous effort in terms of manpower and industrial resources, and its very existence is a source of worry for the governments which control it. Democratically elected governments feel uneasy about military power for at least two reasons. First, because it is so incredibly expensive that its acquisition is bound to be unpopular with the electorate, particularly during a period of prolonged peace. In modern, welfare-orientated societies there is a tendency to see the acquisition of military power as a misallocation of resources. President Eisenhower spelt out the 'opportunity cost' of modern weapons very clearly when he said, 'the cost of one modern bomber is this: a modern brick school in more than thirty cities. It is two electric power plants each serving a town of 60,000 popu-lation. It is two fine, fully equipped hospitals. It is some fifty miles of concrete highway.'[1] In short, military power is regarded by many not as a means to economic well-being, but as an alternative to it. [...]

But there is an even more fundamental reason why democratic societies feel uneasy about the existence of large amounts of military power in their midst. Their unease stems from a real dilemma; while it is widely ack-nowledged that military power is necessary to protect democratic states from aggression and subversion, it is also recognized that the mere existence of this power in the hands of a few represents an inherent threat to the very democratic values it is supposed to protect. The problem of reconciling or striking a balance between the need to concentrate military power in the hands of a few and the need to preserve democratic values is a funda-mental one for any democratic state. The political control of the military is almost taken for granted in the United Kingdom where there is a long tradition of political neutrality in the armed services, and where the threat of military rule is quite unreal. But not all states are as fortunate in their constitutional arrangements. In post-war years, even the United States has experienced growing tension between its large military establish-ment and its liberal democratic principles. The 'Industrial Military complex', as President Eisenhower called it, is a very real symptom of this problem. Once 'Big Business' and 'the Military' became inextricably entwined, an enormous and frightening pressure group was created which, according to some critics, is now so powerful that it dominates large areas of American life and is beyond democratic civilian control.[2]

If military power is electorally unpopular and inherently difficult to control, one is tempted to ask why governments do not abolish it. And the answer, of course, is that the serious worries which are caused by the acquisition of military strength are quite dwarfed by the worries of trying to manage without it. Given the kind of world in which we live, military power is regarded by most statesmen as a prerequisite for national survival.

Even neutral states, with no great ambitions, have found it necessary to remain armed, and many states have found that, over the years, their prosperity and influence have been directly related to their military power. In a world of independent sovereign states which, by definition, acknowledge no authority higher than themselves, and which are in constant and unceasing competition for scarce resources, military power has been an indispensable instrument of the national interest. Life in international society has been likened to life in Hobbes' 'state of nature'. To survive in that tough, ruthless, ungoverned environment is a difficult business, and military power has proved a useful weapon. Its use frequently determines not who is right, but who is going to prevail in the constant jockeying for prosperity, prestige and security. Its acquisition represents an attempt by statesmen to control as far as possible the dangerous and unpredictable environment in which they have to make their way, and it is difficult to imagine what international politics would be like in its absence. It is perfectly true that there are groupings of states within which war is unthinkable — the Common Market is one such 'security community' — but it is dangerous to assume either that relations between Common Market countries are unaffected by military power or that such relations could ever be extended to the world as a whole.

Michael Howard has suggested that 'the capacity of states to defend themselves, and their evident willingness to do so, provides the basic framework within which the business of international negotiations is carried on'. Military power is an intrinsic part of the rather fragile international order associated with the international system, and as Howard says, 'it is not easy to see how international relations could be conducted and international order maintained, if it were totally absent'.[3] Until the world is radically transformed and the system of sovereign states replaced by a quite different international order, military power, and the capacity for violence which it implies, are bound to play a significant part in international politics.

Because military power is an intrinsic part of a world of sovereign states, there is a sense in which criticism of it is irrelevant. Of course it would be nice if the world was ordered differently; but it is not, and schemes to change it invariably founder on grounds of practicality. Over the years there have been many proposals to rid the world of armed power, to disarm and to build a better organized world community, but none of them have been practical politics. Henry IV's reputed comment on one such scheme is still appropriate. 'It is perfect', the king said, 'perfect. I see no single flaw in it save one, namely, that no earthly prince would ever agree to it.' Hedley Bull has rightly condemned such solutions as 'a corruption of thinking about international relations and a distraction from its proper concerns'.[4] Constructive criticism accepts military power as a fact of life. It seeks not to abolish that which cannot be abolished; but to manage it successfully so that wars, both inter-state and internal, become less rather than more frequent occurrences in international politics.

Traditionally, of course, neither statesmen nor political theorists have queried the utility of military power, and even today its value is self-evident in many parts of the world. It is very doubtful, for example, whether the Israelis or the Arabs or the Indians or the Chinese hold any illusions about the continuing importance of military power. Nor are there many signs of Soviet disenchantment. Many statesmen would consider it preposterous to question the value of military power given the dangerous world in which we all live and given the historical record of violence in the twentieth century. The authors of the recent volume of the *Cambridge Modern History* dealing with the twentieth century entitled it 'The Age of Violence', and this grim description is perhaps some sort of indication of the importance of military power in contemporary international politics.

Nevertheless, a number of American commentators — not all of them left-wing radicals — have in recent years questioned the importance of military power. One of the reasons that they have been able to do this with any degree of plausibility at all is that from the perspective of the United States and Western Europe, the international environment seems less dangerous than at any time since the Second World War. After all, the USA has managed to extricate itself from Vietnam, the politics of Cold War have given way to the easier atmosphere of *détente*, there have been *rapprochements* with China, and the crises which threatened world peace throughout the 1950s and early 1960s have melted into history. All this has produced, in L.W. Martin's words, 'a diffused feeling of greater safety' in which military force seems less necessary and, hence, less useful. As Martin puts it, 'For many Western taxpayers, the military are on the way to becoming latter-day remittance men, given a small slice of the family income on condition that they go off and pursue their unsavoury activities quietly where they will not embarrass decent folk.'[5]

It remains to be seen, however, whether these optimistic features of the international environment reflect long-term changes in state behaviour or whether they reflect a much more transient and fortuitous juxtaposition of circumstances. It is possible to speculate that if the world economic crisis deepens and the competition for energy, raw materials and markets intensifies, then states may once again find it expedient to pursue their interests by the age-old techniques of intimidation, war and conquest.

Many of the critics of military power have emphasized the uselessness of weapons of mass destruction for all practical purposes. American writers, soured by their country's experiences in Vietnam, have noted that those who are the most militarily powerful are not always the most politically successful. Military preponderance cannot always be translated into political victory. The United States, for example, was not able to capitalize her virtual nuclear monopoly in the late 1940s and early 1950s by 'winning' the Cold War, and the Vietnam War must be the classic case of a superpower capable of destroying the entire world finding itself unable to defeat a guerrilla movement in what one writer described as a 'rice-based, bicycle-powered, economy'.

However, it is worth pointing out that it is dangerous to deduce from the American experience in Vietnam any general propositions about the utility or otherwise of military power. It may be that the American failure in Vietnam can be attributed to the incompetent way in which military power was used rather than any inherent defect in the military instrument itself. Hanson Baldwin, for example, has suggested that lack of success was a result not of using military power, but of not using enough of it early enough.[6] In other words, so his argument runs, rapid escalation might have induced the enemy to give up by presenting him with intolerable costs. The mistake the Americans made was not fighting the war in the first place, but fighting it at a level which the enemy found tolerable, rather than escalating to a point where the North Vietnamese would find it unbearable.

Nevertheless, the critics of military power undoubtedly have a point. The relationship between military strength and political influence is certainly not the proportional one implied by Mao Tse-tung's famous dictum that 'political power grows out of the barrel of a gun'; but although it is not a straightforward connection, few would dispute that in general terms there is a relationship between military strength and political power. On the whole, those who wield the most military power tend to be the most influential; their wishes the most respected; their diplomacy the most heeded. Of all the great powers, only Japan appears to disprove the connection between military and political strength. As Ian Smart says, 'Japan is allegedly intent upon that alchemist's 'grand experiment', the transmutation of great economic into great political power without the use of any military catalyst.'[7] Whether she will succeed is highly problematic, and the fact that she is trying is not so much because she is confident of success as because she has no real alternative.

The connection between military strength and political power was clearly perceived by R. Chaput, when, commenting on the relative decline of British military strength in the 1930s, he wrote, 'The weight of Great Britain in diplomatic bargaining is, in the last resort, proportionate to the strength of her armaments, and her influence for peace is measurable in terms of the force she can muster to prevent the overthrow of the political equilibrium by armed force.'[8] It is undoubtedly a serious mistake to assume that political influence is proportional to military strength; but it is an even more serious error to deny any connection between the two.

A second arrow in the quiver of those who query the utility of military power in the modern world is the argument that in ideological quarrels military power is an inappropriate weapon because ideas cannot be defeated by force of arms. It is sometimes claimed, for example, that the notion of a 'united Ireland' which gives point to IRA activity in Ulster cannot be defeated by the British military presence, and, therefore, that a political solution must be found to the problems of that troubled province. It is also sometimes claimed that in so far as the West is engaged in an ideological struggle with Communism, its concentration on military confrontation means that it is planning to fight the wrong war. It is, of course, debatable whether the IRA is much interested in a United Ireland or whether the East-West struggle is predominantly ideological, but even if they are, the proposition that ideas cannot be defeated by military force cannot be accepted without serious qualification.

It is perfectly true that ideas cannot be eradicated without destroying all the books where they are written down and killing all the people who have ever heard of them. In that sense the proposition that ideas cannot be destroyed by military force is probably true; but even though it may be impossible to *eliminate* ideas, it is certainly possible to render them politically ineffective by the use of military force. The ideas of Hitler and Mussolini live on in their writings which are accessible to all, but the military defeat of the Axis powers in 1945 went a long way towards relegating Fascism to the periphery of practical politics. Similarly, in Ireland one may speculate that the ruthless use of military power could make the idea of a United Ireland politically irrelevant for the foreseeable future. The word 'ruthless' is important. If the Kremlin had the problem of Ulster to deal with, it is easy to believe that within a period of weeks rather than months, the IRA would have been systematically destroyed, their sympathizers incarcerated and the entire province subjected to military discipline. In other words, criticism about the way in which the British Government has used its military power in Ireland are not criticisms about the effectiveness of the military instrument *per se*; they are only criticisms about the half-hearted, squeamish way in which successive

British Governments, rightly or wrongly, have used it.

The argument that military power cannot defeat political ideas is only part of a more general argument which queries the appropriateness of military power as an instrument of modern statescraft. Today, it is argued, the real stakes of international politics are quite unrelated to such traditional uses of military power as the acquisition of territory and empire. In the modern world, the goals of states are much more intangible, like, for example, improving trade relations, securing markets, gaining political friends, winning the favour of world opinion. And in the pursuit of these objectives, military power is at best irrelevant and at worst counter-productive.

There is a good deal of sense in this view. Certainly there is plenty of evidence that the use of military power for territorial conquest is much less popular than it used to be — at least amongst advanced industrial states. The appetite for conquest has probably become jaded partly because the military, moral and political costs of unprovoked aggression have risen sharply, and partly because the expected value of conquest to advanced industrial states has fallen sharply. It has become increasingly clear that an industrial state bent on improving the material prosperity and standard of living of its citizens would be better advised to use its resources for increasing industrial investment and technological research rather than expending them in wars of conquest. The world contains many examples of states which have become wealthy and prosperous without military power. Japan and West Germany both spring to mind and there are many who see a direct connection between their impressive growth rates and their low military expenditure.

And it is not just outright conquest which has become unfashionable. Enthusiasm for the use of military power to pursue interests in the Third World has also cooled. Over the years, both East and West have invested a great deal of money in attempts to project their influence in uncommitted areas of the world, but it has become clear that the use of the military instrument in this context can easily backfire by provoking the very hostility it was designed to avoid. Anyway, the benefits of access to these uncommitted countries seem much less important and more problematic these days. There is, therefore, a growing tendency to look for 'local' balances of power, and to argue that when it comes to providing stability, intervention is counter-productive. To use Professor Martin's phrase, 'the era of competitive meddling' is over,[9] but it would be dangerous to conclude from this that all military intervention in foreign states is a thing of the past. There are powerful reasons why states may involve themselves, for example, in local wars in spite of the risks and costs involved. First because intervention in local conflicts provides the superpowers with an opportunity to pursue national and ideological goals without running the risks of mutual destruction which are implicit in more direct confrontations. Second, because internal wars cause anxiety even in states not immediately affected. Internal wars constitute a form of social change which is fundamentally unpredictable and 'no situation is more threatening to nations than one whose outcome has become so uncertain as to have moved beyond their control'.[10] In particular, civil violence is a contagious phenomenon, and what is not controlled in one country may, it is feared, spread to others. And the third reason why states may become militarily involved in the internal affairs of others is that few of them are immune from the moral pressure to throw their power behind a just cause even when so doing contravenes the principle of sovereign independence.

And though it is unfashionable to say so, the possibility that powerful states will find it necessary to intervene militarily in order to protect their interests cannot be ruled out. [. . .]

One of the most common — though not the most intelligent — arguments against the continuing usefulness of military power is implied by the assertion that modern weapons, particularly nuclear and thermonuclear weapons, are so destructive of life and property that they cannot reasonably be regarded as a usable instrument of policy. There are, so it is argued, no conceivable political objectives in the pursuit of which these devastating weapons could justifiably be used. In the public mind, at least, there is a widespread belief that any use of nuclear weapons is synonymous with Armageddon. It is claimed, therefore, that we are in the incredible situation of spending vast amounts of money on a kind of armament which cannot be used rationally and which is therefore useless. Walter Millis has put the case very well.

> The great military establishments which exist are not practically usable in the conduct of international relations, and in general are not being so used today; and if it were possible to rid ourselves of the whole apparatus — the military establishments, and the war system they embody — international relations could be conducted far more safely, more efficiently, and more creatively in face of the staggering real problems facing humankind than is now the case.[11]

Though the argument is superficially attractive, it contains several serious flaws. First, and most obvious, it assumes that military power can only be useful if it is used physically, and it ignores the fact that a good deal of modern military power is most useful when it is not being used. Indeed, the most powerful weapons in the arsenals of the superpowers have been specifically acquired in order not to be used. The strategy of deterrence, which has come to dominate East-West relations and which provides the backdrop against which all East-West negotiations take place, is built on the assumption that it is the possession, not the use, of thermonuclear weapons which is sufficient to deter attack. Today, strategic power is designed to promote peace and security by preventing wars rather than by winning them. [. . .]

In this context it may be helpful to make the distinction between military power and military force. Military power may depend to a large extent on the availability of military force, but conceptually it is quite different; it emphasizes a political relationship between potential adversaries rather than a catalogue of military capabilities. In a nutshell, the difference between the exercise of military force and military power is the difference between taking what you want and persuading someone to give it to you. In a sense, therefore, the use of military force represents the breakdown of military power. The physical use of deterrent power shows not how strong a country is but how impotent it has become.

One of the changes which has occurred since the Second World War is the increasing sophistication with which military power is exploited without military force being used. This is the age of 'brinkmanship', 'crisis management', 'deterrence' and 'signalling'. All of these phenomena support the thesis that modern military force tends to be threatened and manipulated in peacetime rather than used in war. An example may reinforce the point. Think, for a moment, of the political attitude of Finland towards the Soviet Union. Though the sovereign independence of their state is not in question, the gross disparity in power between the two countries has forced the Finns into a relationship of reluctant deference towards the Soviet Union which the latter must find very reassuring. Now 'Finlandization' as it is sometimes called, was brought about neither by Soviet threats nor any physical use of Soviet military power against Finland. It was simply an inevitable consequence of Soviet military preponderance in the area; an almost automatic payoff from the possession of powerful military forces. [. . .]

The second major flaw in the Millis thesis is that it is quite illogical to argue from the fact that using the most powerful military weapons is likely to be mutually destructive, that the use of *all* kinds of military force is equally pointless. At the moment of writing only six states have acquired any kind of nuclear capability at all, and although one may reasonably expect nuclear proliferation to continue, it seems clear that in the foreseeable future the vast majority of the world's states will not be able to avail themselves of this peculiarly destructive power, and in their relations with each other are not likely to be much troubled by its terrible potential.

And, of course, it is also worth pointing out that even the nuclear powers have not renounced the physical use of all military power, not even all nuclear military power. Limited wars, that is to say, wars in which the belligerents exercise restraint in their use of military force, still make good political sense to nuclear powers. Indeed it is not always recognized that limited wars are feasible precisely because total wars are not. The major incentive to keep limited wars limited is the fear that they may become total, and it follows, therefore, that the same terrible innovations in weapon technology which have taken total war out of the spectrum of rational options available to nuclear states, have encouraged them to develop strategies of limited and sub-limited war rather than give up the idea of war altogether. In short, though the advent of nuclear and thermo-nuclear weapons may have imposed new restraints upon those who control them, there is no evidence that they have seriously undermined the utility of military power.

What has happened is that states have developed strategies which emphasize the political uses of military power even in war itself. It was never true that diplomacy ended when the shooting started, but in the pre-nuclear age there did seem some sense in the view that war was an *alternative* to diplomacy. But today the distinction is so fudged and blurred as to be almost meaningless. T.C. Schelling's definition of war as a 'bargaining process' or a sort of 'tough negotiation', and his telling phrase 'the diplomacy of violence' all suggest that war, far from signifying the end of diplomacy, has become part of diplomacy itself.

Schelling has invented the terms 'coercive warfare' and 'compellance' to describe the use of military force for goals which are not strictly military at all and where 'the object is to make the enemy behave',[12] rather than to weaken or defeat him. The chief instrument of this 'vicious diplomacy' and 'dirty bargaining' is the power to hurt, to cause pain and suffering. Now all wars involve pain and suffering, and modern wars more than most, but traditionally the anguish caused by war has been no more than an incidental, almost regrettable, by-product of military action. What is being emphasized now is the strategy of using the power to hurt in a deliberate and conscious way to intimidate, demoralize, blackmail and bargain to a position of advantage.

The use of nuclear weapons on Japan at the end of the Second World War is an interesting example of this technique. Though literally dropped on Hiroshima and Nagasaki, there is a sense in which these two atomic bombs were not really aimed at those cities at all. Their target was the decision-makers in Tokyo, and the object of the exercise was not the military one of destroying the war-making capability of Japan, but the political one of inducing her leaders to surrender. In Schelling's words, 'The effect of the bombs and their purpose were not mainly the military destruction they accomplished, but the pain and the shock and the promise of more.'[13] Military power, the power to hurt, was being used physically to intimidate an enemy and make him 'behave'. [. . .]

According to Lasswell and Kaplan, 'an arena is *military* when the expectation of violence is high; *civic* when the expectation is low'.[14] For hundreds of years it has been customary to regard the international system as a military arena in which inter-state war is a more or less normal phenomenon, and the internal structure of states as a civic arena characterized by stability and order and a low expectation of violence. Today, however, there are signs that this situation is being reversed; that is to say, that inter-state violence is becoming comparatively rare, and domestic violence comparatively common. It would, of course, be going too far to describe the modern international system as a civil arena and the modern state as a military arena, but strategic stability at the superpower level combined with political instability in many Afro-Asian states has undoubtedly contributed to the shift of emphasis away from inter-state violence towards intra-state violence.

S. Huntington has pointed out that between 1961 and 1968, 114 of the world's 121 major political units endured some significant form of violent civil conflict.[15] And in 1966 Mr R. McNamara claimed that in the previous eight years, out of 164 internationally significant outbreaks of violence, only fifteen were military conflicts between two states. The statistics may be queried in detail if only because of the ambiguity surrounding the terms, but the overall picture is clear. In many parts of the world, particularly in Southern Asia, Latin America, Africa and the Middle East, intra-state violence in which a non-governmental body attempts to overthrow and replace an established government, has become a common if not normal pattern of political change. Internal wars, described by Eckstein as 'any resort to violence within a political order to change its constitution, government or politics',[16] have become commonplace in the wake of decolonization, modernization, Westernization and rapid economic development. In periods of rapid social, political and economic change many governments were unable to control the tensions which simmered beneath the surface of political life before finally erupting in revolutionary violence. [. . .]

It has been estimated that since the Second World War there have been 84[17] armed conflicts. Without confusing the continued use of military force with its usefulness, it is reasonable to believe that most of the states which engaged in those wars regarded the use of military power as an appropriate and reasoned response to the international situation in which they found themselves. The frequency and persistence of military violence around the world provides *prima facie* evidence that large numbers of people continue to think that military power is a useful, perhaps even indispensable, instrument of policy. The various qualifications which have to be made to the fashionable thesis that military power has lost its utility go a long way towards undermining it completely.

In fact few objective observers dispute the utility of military power in a variety of fields. Anyone who knows anything about Northern Ireland, for example, cannot dispute the useful role which the army performs in keeping an uneasy peace between two hostile communities. Anyone who understands the role and record of the North Atlantic Alliance cannot dispute the defensive role of military power in the European theatre. Anyone familiar with the strategic stalemate between the two superpowers will not need convincing that the 'balance of terror' depends very much on the existence of enormous military power in the arsenals of both the United States and the Soviet Union. Anyone cogniscent of the political and social instability which disrupts so many countries of the world cannot doubt the usefulness of military power both for insurgents and those who seek to counter them. The world around us is full of examples of military power being more or less effectively used. We live in a military age and there are few signs that either our children or grandchildren will experience anything else.

Notes

1. Quoted by C. Hitch, *The Economies of Defence in the Nuclear Age* (Harvard University Press, Cambridge, Mass., 1961), p. 4.
2. See for example, C.W. Mills, *The Power Elite* (Oxford University Press, London, 1956).
3. M. Howard, 'Military Power and International Order', *International Affairs*, vol. XL, no. 3 (July 1964), p. 405.
4. H. Bull, *The Control of the Arms Race* (Weidenfeld and Nicolson, London, 1961), pp. 26-7.
5. L.W. Martin, 'The Utility of Military Force', in 'Force in Modern Societies: Its Place in International Politics', *Adelphi Paper* no. 102 (International Institute for Strategic Studies, London, 1973), p. 14.
6. H. Baldwin, 'The Case for Escalation', *New York Times Magazine* (22 February 1966), pp. 22-82.
7. I. Smart, 'Committee Discussions on the Utility of Military Force in Modern Societies: Report to the Conference', in 'Force in Modern Societies: Its Place in International Politics', *Adelphi Paper* no. 102 (International Institute for Strategic

Studies, London, 1973), p. 22.

8. R. Chaput, *Disarmament in British Foreign Policy* (George Allen and Unwin, London, 1935), p. 372.

9. L.W. Martin, 'The Utility of Military Force', p. 19.

10. J.N. Rosenau, 'International War as an International Event', in J.N. Rosenau (ed.), *International Aspects of Civil Strife* (Princeton, 1964), p. 57.

11. W. Millis, 'The Uselessness of Military Power', in R.A. Goldwin (ed.), *America Armed* (Rand McNally, Chicago, 1961), p. 38.

12. T.C. Schelling, *Arms and Influence* (Yale University Press, New Haven and London, 1966), p. 173.

13. Ibid., p. 18.

14. H.D. Lasswell and M.A. Kaplan, *Power and Society* (Yale University Press, New Haven, 1950), p. 252.

15. S.P. Huntington, 'Civil Violence and the Process of Development', in 'Civil Violence and the International System', *Adelphi Paper* no. 83 (International Institute for Strategic Studies, London, 1971), p. 1.

16. Quoted by R. Falk in *Legal Order in a Violent World* (Princeton University Press, Princeton, NJ, 1968), p. 132 n.

17. Based on a definition of conflict as involving 'The use of regular forces on at least one side and the use of weapons of war with intent to kill or wound over a period of at least one hour'; see A. Wilson, *The Observer Atlas of World Affairs* (George Philip and Son, London, 1971), pp. 24-5.

THE NATURE OF NATIONAL ECONOMIC POWER

Klaus Knorr

Source: *Power and Wealth* (Basic Books, London, 1973), pp. 13-14 and 82-90.

Knorr distinguishes between 'putative' and 'actualized' power, the former representing power as a means that can be possessed and added to, the latter power as an effect that those means can be used to achieve. He goes on to use the distinction to discuss the capabilities which underpin the economic strength of a country and the mechanisms whereby those capabilities can be employed against another country.

The phenomenon of power lends itself to two sharply different conceptions. The inability to grasp this difference leads to inevitable misunderstanding and confusion. Since coercive influence limits the conduct of an actor subjected to it, power can be seen to reside in the capabilities that permit the power-wielder to make effective threats. But it can also be seen as identical with, and limited to, the influence on the actually achieved behavior of the threatened actor. On the first view, power is something that powerful states have and can accumulate; power is a *means*. On the second view, power is an *effect*, that is the influence actually enjoyed. It is generated in an interaction which is an encounter. On the first view, power is something that an actor can hope to bring into play in a range of future situations. On the second, power comes into being, is shaped, and enjoyed only in a specific situation; its measure is the amount of influence actually achieved.

Today, most theorists conceive of power as actually achieved influence, whereas most laymen see it as reposing in the capabilities that permit strong threats to be made. Both concepts catch a part of reality. But it is critically important that we know which one we have in mind when we speak of 'power'. In the following, we will call the one *putative* power and the other *actualized* power.

[Knorr goes on later in the book to examine this distinction in relation to the economic power of a nation. He begins by considering 'economic strength' as a basis of putative power and ends by noting how this putative power can be actualized.]

The sheer magnitude of a state's foreign economic transactions is one element of national economic strength. Obviously, a country accounting for thirty per cent of world exports and imports and of world exports of capital and technical assistance, tends to enjoy far greater leverage than a country accounting for only three per cent. However, it is not advantageous from this point of view that the state's trade and capital exports are also large in relation to GNP. If its trade is large in these terms as well, the country is also susceptible to economic pressure from the outside. In other words, while it provides leverage for application to other states, an important constituent of active economic power, a large volume of trade relative to GNP also tends to reduce passive economic power. Moreover, the larger trade is in relation to GNP, the more difficult will power-induced changes in exports and imports tend to be because of domestic economic disturbances experienced at home. From this point of view then, the United States is superior to the United Kingdom not only because American trade is larger, but also because American trade is much smaller than Britain's in relation to GNP.

Size of foreign trade varies mainly with size of population, degree of economic development, and the degree of international economic specialization. The implications of population size and stage of development are obvious. Even though India is a poor country, it has a larger foreign trade than Switzerland, which is rich; but Switzerland's foreign trade *per capita* is a multiple of India's. Clearly also, a country's foreign trade will tend to vary with the extent to which it is engaged in the international division of labor. This variable, in turn, is principally the consequence of trade policy (e.g. free trade versus protectionism), of breadth of endowment with natural and other resources, and of size of territory (i.e. internal transportation costs, like international transport costs, act like an equivalent import duty). A country's ability to acquire leverage from capital export is also in part a consequence of size (i.e. GNP, which reflects size of population and degree of economic development). If we assume funds for export to come from savings and taxes, or more generally speaking from economic surplus above private and public consumption and capital maintenance, the size of these funds, given the rate of savings and taxation, depends on the size of GNP.

Economic power, however, is a matter of structure as well as magnitude. Economic strength as a basis of national economic power is not the same as economic wealth, although wealth is an ingredient of it. Similarly, economic strength is not simply measured by the volume of a country's trade, even though such trade is another variable condition from which strength is derived. In order to serve the purposes of economic power, a country's economic capabilities and economy must have certain structural characteristics just as such a special (but different) economic structure is needed for the production of military strength. If we concentrate on the ability to alter international merchandise, service, and capital flows, a state would be equipped *structurally* with an ideal base for exercising economic power, if (1) it exported things in urgent demand abroad while importing things regarding which its own demand was highly elastic, and if (2) it held monopoly control over the supply of things demanded by foreign importing countries and monopsony control over the goods foreign countries have to export. Structural conditions also impinge on the ability of states to export capital. Whatever the size of GNP, the propensity to restrain consumption, public or private, is an important factor. In other words, national economic strength will tend to be the greater, the less the outside world can do without its exports and without its domestic market.

There are, of course, no states in the real world fully ideally meeting these structural descriptions. For a few years following World War II, the United States came closer to the ideal base than any other country has ever achieved. But this resulted from evidently exceptional circumstances. The bulk of the world was then impoverished and economically disorganized. To generalize with reference to the real world, the more a state's international economic position approximates the ideal construct, the stronger it will tend to be in terms of economic power. Conversely, the less it approximates the specified characteristics, the weaker a state will tend to be in these terms.

Since presumably no state is interested in exercising economic power *vis-à-vis* the entire outside world all at once, but rather *vis-à-vis* a particular state or group of states, the structural desiderata are not as exacting as the ideal type suggests. Even potential economic power depends then on particular actor relationships of conceivable interest. This is so also in the case of potential military power. There is, however, an important difference between the exercise of economic and military power. In the event of a military conflict between A and B, the number of other states supporting A or B is not usually large. Participation tends to be costly. In the event of a purely economic conflict, however, it is usually in the interest of most other states to provide the opponents with alternative markets and sources of supply. For instance, if A places an embargo on B's exports, B will attempt to shift its exports to other markets. This would impose some difficulties of adjustment but no further ill effects if A, needing the type of goods it had imported from B, switches its purchases to other sources of supply. On the other hand, *B*'s position would be weaker, and *A*'s stronger, if *B* had an important high-cost export industry for which *A* had been the sole or principal outlet. In that case, *A*'s embargo would compel *B* either to export subsidized goods, or to suffer unemployment in its export industry, likewise with an income-depressing effect and with the consequent burden of shifting resources to other fields of production. This example, which can be paralleled by one involving *A*'s resort to an embargo of its own exports to *B*, points up the importance of structural factors and size of market. *A* holds a degree of economic power over *B* only if *A*'s trade is worth something to *B*, in that it is important in scale and irreplaceable, or hard to replace, and if *B* is more dependent economically on *A* than the other way round.

International currency reserves and gold are of some significance to national economic power. Governments require international monies in order to settle any net imbalance in their aggregate payments account with other countries. A country issuing an international key currency has an appreciable advantage from this point of view, as had the United States in the 1960s. Other governments normally maintain official reserves of foreign money to cover regularly or irregularly recurring deficits. Irregular imbalances can occur as a result of shifts in the demand for a state's exports or of sudden changes in capital movements, crop failures, war, or similar exogenous disturbances. (The other way round, similar factors can produce an accumulation of reserves.) Since the International Monetary Fund may help in the event of serious pressure, many governments tend to maintain smaller reserves of their own than caution requires.

In principle, copious foreign-exchange reserves (or gold) clearly can play a part in exerting or resisting economic pressure. *A*'s foreign-exchange hoard is important if it wants to sell *B*'s currency in order to put that currency under speculative pressure, or if it wants to shift imports from *B* to a higher-cost exporting country, or if it wants to cut exports to *B* while unable immediately to find substitute markets. Similarly, *B*'s international currency reserves are an important asset when *A* cuts off its imports from *B*, and *B* does not find satisfactory alternative markets, or if it must pay higher prices in order to replace imports embargoed by *A*. If *B* owns insufficient reserves under such circumstances, its industries depending on exports and imports will suffer with possibly multiplying consequences to employment and income; or *B* may have to borrow foreign currency from third countries on possibly unfavorable terms. Not rarely, a weak reserve position will curtail a government's capacity to engage in warfare at home or abroad. In 1956, when Great Britain and France, in collaboration with Israel, attempted to reoccupy the Suez

Canal, a precipitate flight from sterling was important among the pressures that brought this military intervention to a quick end, especially since the United States government pointedly refused monetary assistance. In 1971, accumulating balance-of-payments deficits in the United States brought about a negotiated realignment of major currency values, depreciating that of the dollar *vis-à-vis* the surplus countries. This experience signaled a diminished international ability of the United States to finance the exercise of military power abroad, even though the currency negotiations also reflected the great economic power of the United States in that the results brought great short-term relief and advantage to it. On the other hand, accumulating large international reserves for various emergency purposes, or for strengthening a state's ability to wage economic warfare — contingent purposes that may not arise — is definitely expensive. Hoarding means foregoing the use of the sequestered funds for purchasing imports, and decreased imports mean either less consumption or less investment.

The foregoing analysis indicates how a state can increase its putative economic power generally and *vis-à-vis* particular countries. It can boost its general economic power by promoting its economic development relative to other states. Japan, which achieved exceptional growth rates throughout the 1960s, clearly had more such power at the end than at the beginning of the decade. However, the degree to which relative economic development enlarges economic power depends crucially on how it affects the structural conditions. Within limits (including costs) imposed by endowment with natural and other productive resources, a state can shift resources so as to lessen its economic dependence on other countries and to increase their economic dependence on itself. Within such limits, it can also cultivate monopolist and monopsonist market power. It can, for instance, develop superior technologies, giving it, at least temporarily, a degree of monopoly over the international supply of certain goods and services.

A state can also attempt to extend its control over resources and markets by forming monopolist or monopsonist arrangements with other states or by becoming the member of a regional bloc or customs union. Thus, states have in the past attempted joint regulation of the international supply of raw materials (e.g. rubber and tin) and are doing so now (e.g. the association of petroleum-exporting countries, sugar, and coffee). Alternatively, groups of private enterprises have set up private international cartels in order to control markets of manufactured products at home and abroad. A currently interesting development of market power is the European Economic Community (EEC) formed by France, Italy, West Germany, and the Benelux countries, which even prior to the entry of Great Britain constituted the world's largest territorial unit in international commerce. Such economic integration between states enlarges the size of international economic transactions, which is one determinant of economic power; and it also tends to extend the limits within which the structural requirements of such power can be promoted.

To the extent that schemes for concerting the economic policies of independent states provide a basis for enhanced economic power, this power is, of course, shared and has, as experience shows, a brittle foundation because the diverging interests of members impede cohesion. Member states frequently differ on the merits of particular policies. Cohesion tends to be especially weak when no one member has superior economic size and decisions are made, formally or informally, on the basis of unanimity, for such a configuration maximizes the veto power of each member. Cohesion will tend to be stronger if one member predominates in economic size *and* enjoys a position of leadership or domination based on political, military, or economic power over the other members. The predominant state may then be able to wield the bloc's economic power for its own or for more or less shared purposes. The leading state's ability to decide on this matter is the greater, the less it needs to bargain with (i.e. make concessions to) member states.

In addition to these measures apt to enhance a state's general economic power, it can do things designed to bolster its putative economic power *vis-à-vis* particular countries. Thus, A can concentrate more of its trade on B, making itself more important to B as an importer and exporter, by giving B preferential access to its market, by offering exports at preferential prices, or on attractive credit conditions, and by offering long-term trade contracts on favourable terms. In doing so, A may pay attention to qualitative factors, as by concentrating on exports for which it has a degree of monopoly power and B's demand is very inelastic, and by concentrating on imports regarding which A enjoys or can build up a degree of monopsony power and for which its demand is elastic. Or A may be able to increase B's dependence by bringing about and exploiting penetration of B's economy by means of fostering direct investment, bribing officials and businessmen in B. Or A may export capital to B on favorable terms and induce a degree of international indebtedness in B that makes it unattractive to other exporters of capital. [. . .] Putative economic power, like putative military power, can become actualized in particular relationships through three mechanisms: (1) A applies economic power purposely for weakening B economically; (2) A applies economic power by threatening B with economic reprisals or by offering economic rewards for compliance with a request by A; (3) B's behavior is influenced by the mere anticipation that, if he pursues actions detrimental to A's interests, A might resort to the exercise of economic power. Clearly, economic domination occurs if A deliberately and regularly resorts to actions identified under (1) and (2). But A's mere ability to take such measures does not involve B's economic domination. The problem is trickier when it comes to the mechanism (3). Clearly, again, once A has had frequent recourse to mechanisms (1) and (2) *vis-à-vis B,* B may henceforth be dominated by the sheer anticipation of such further acts if he should cross A's interests. This is how continued domination will normally operate. But if B has not been subjected to A's economic power via mechanisms (1) and (2), it will be affected through mechanism (3) only if A, by repeated and recent power plays against other states, has displayed a strong predisposition to resort to its economic power. The less A has displayed such a propensity, the less B will be influenced and dominated by A's economic power. Should A have no such propensity, no influence will occur. In any case, economic domination is strong if A deliberately cultivates the actualization of its economic power *vis-à-vis B*. Economic domination will be weaker if A has succeeded frequently in actualizing its economic power against C and D, but not against B. Economic domination does not arise at all if A, despite vastly superior 'economic strength' suitable as a basis of economic power, lacks any reputation for seeking to exploit this capacity, that is to say, for transforming it into economic power.

1.7

THE SPIRAL OF INTERNATIONAL INSECURITY

Robert Jervis

Source: *Perception and Misperception in International Politics* (Princeton University Press, Princeton, 1976), pp. 63-76.

Jervis argues that the attempts of one state to achieve security precipitate a feeling of insecurity in other states. All states tend to assume the worst of others and respond accordingly. Their collective actions unintentionally generate a spiral of insecurity and, in a situation of anarchy, there can be no solution to this security dilemma. The dilemma is further exacerbated, according to Jervis, by the inflexible images that it generates in the minds of decision makers both of their own intentions and of those of their opposite numbers.

The lack of a sovereign in international politics permits wars to occur and makes security expensive. More far-reaching complications are created by the fact that most means of self-protection simultaneously menace others. Rousseau made the basic point well:

> It is quite true that it would be much better for all men to remain always at peace. But so long as there is no security for this, everyone, having no guarantee that he can avoid war, is anxious to begin it at the moment which suits his own interest and so forestall a neighbour, who would not fail to forestall the attack in his turn at any moment favourable to himself, so that many wars, even offensive wars, are rather in the nature of unjust precautions for the protection of the assailant's own possessions than a device for seizing those of others. However salutary it may be in theory to obey the dictates of public spirit, it is certain that, politically and even morally, those dictates are liable to prove fatal to the man who persists in observing them with all the world when no one thinks of observing them towards him.[1]

In extreme cases, states that seek security may believe that the best, if not the only, route to that goal is to attack and expand. Thus the tsars believed that 'that which stops growing begins to rot', the Japanese decision-makers before World War II concluded that the alternative to increasing their dominance in Asia was to sacrifice their 'very existence', and some scholars have argued that German expansionism before World War I was rooted in a desire to cope with the insecurity produced by being surrounded by powerful neighbors.[2] After World War I France held a somewhat milder version of this belief. Although she knew that the war had left her the strongest state on the Continent, she felt that she had to increase her power still further to provide protection against Germany, whose recovery from wartime destruction might some day lead her to try to reverse the verdict of 1918. This view is especially likely to develop if the state believes that others have also concluded that both the desire for protection and the desire for increased values point to the same policy of expansionism.

The drive for security will also produce aggressive actions if the state either requires a very high sense of security or feels menaced by the very presence of other strong states. Thus Leites argues that 'the Politburo ... believes that its very life ... remains acutely threatened as long as major enemies exist. Their utter defeat is a sheer necessity of survival.' This view can be rooted in experience as well as ideology. In May 1944 Kennan wrote: 'Behind Russia's stubborn expansion lies only the age-old sense of insecurity of a sedentary people reared on an exposed plain in the neighborhood of fierce nomadic peoples.'[3]

Even in less extreme situations, arms procured to defend can usually be used to attack. Economic and political preparedness designed to hold what one has is apt to create the potential for taking territory from others. What one state regards as insurance, the adversary will see as encirclement. This is especially true of the great powers. Any state that has interests throughout the world cannot avoid possessing the power to menace others. For example, as Admiral Mahan noted before World War I, if Britain was to have a navy sufficient to safeguard her trading routes, she inevitably would also have the ability to cut Germany off from the sea. Thus even in the absence of any specific conflicts of interest between Britain and Germany, the former's security required that the latter be denied a significant aspect of great power status.

When states seek the ability to defend themselves, they get too much and too little — too much because they gain the ability to carry out aggression; too little because others, being menaced, will increase their own arms and so reduce the first state's security. Unless the requirements for offense and defense differ in kind or amount, a status quo power will desire a military posture that resembles that of an aggressor. For this reason others cannot infer from its military forces and preparations whether the state is aggressive. States therefore tend to assume the worst.

The other's intentions must be considered to be co-extensive with his capabilities. What he can do to harm the state, he will do (or will do if he gets the chance). So to be safe, the state should buy as many weapons as it can afford.

But since both sides obey the same imperatives, attempts to increase one's security by standing firm and accumulating more arms will be self-defeating. [...]

These unintended and undesired consequences of actions meant to be defensive constitute the 'security dilemma' that Herbert Butterfield sees as that 'absolute predicament' that 'lies in the very geometry of human conflict.... [H]ere is the basic pattern for all narratives of human conflict, whatever other patterns may be superimposed upon it later.' From this perspective, the central theme of international relations is not evil but tragedy. States often share a common interest, but the structure of the situation prevents them from bringing about the mutually desired situation. This view contrasts with the school of realism represented by Hans Morgenthau and Reinhold Niebuhr, which sees the drive for power as a product of man's instinctive will to dominate others. As John Herz puts it, 'It is a mistake to draw from the universal phenomenon of competition for power the conclusion that there is actually such a thing as an innate "power instinct". Basically it is the mere instinct of self-preservation which, in the vicious circle [of the security dilemma], leads to competition for ever more power.'[4]

Arms races are only the most obvious manifestation of this spiral. The competition for colonies at the end of the nineteenth century was fueled by the security dilemma. Even if all states preferred the status quo to a division of the unclaimed areas, each also preferred expansion to running the risk of being excluded. The desire for security may also lead states to weaken potential rivals, a move that can create the menace it was designed to ward off. For example, because French statesmen feared what they thought to be the inevitable German attempt to regain the position she lost in World War I, they concluded that Germany had to be kept weak. The effect of such an unyielding policy, however, was to make the Germans less willing to accept their new position and therefore to decrease France's long-run security. Finally, the security dilemma can not only create conflicts and tensions but also provide the dynamics triggering war. If technology and strategy are such that each side believes that the state that strikes first will have a decisive advantage, even a state that is fully satisfied with the status quo may start a war out of fear that the alternative to doing so is not peace, but an attack by its adversary. And, of course, if each side knows that the other side is aware of the advantages of striking first, even mild crises are likely to end in war. This was one of the immediate causes of World War I, and contemporary military experts have devoted much thought and money to avoiding the recurrence of such destabilizing incentives. [. . .]

Psychological Dynamics

The argument sketched so far rests on the implications of anarchy, not on the limitations of rationality imposed by the way people reach decisions in a complex world. Lewis Richardson's path-breaking treatment of arms races describes 'what people would do if they did not stop to think'. Richardson argues that this is not an unrealistic perspective. The common analogy between international politics and chess is misleading because 'the acts of a leader are in part controlled by the great instinctive and traditional tendencies which are formulated in my description. It is somewhat as if the chessmen were connected by horizontal springs to heavy weights beyond the chessboard.'[5]

Contemporary spiral theorists argue that psychological pressures explain why arms and tensions cycles proceed as if people were not thinking. Once a person develops an image of the other – especially a hostile image of the other – ambiguous and even discrepant information will be assimilated to that image. [. . .] If they think that a state is hostile, behavior that others might see as neutral or friendly will be ignored, distorted, or seen as attempted duplicity. This cognitive rigidity reinforces the consequences of international anarchy.

Although we noted earlier that it is usually hard to draw inferences about a state's intentions from its military posture, decision-makers in fact often draw such inferences when they are unwarranted. They frequently assume, partly for reasons to be discussed shortly, that the arms of others indicate aggressive intentions. So an increase in the other's military forces makes the state doubly insecure – first, because the other has an increased capability to do harm, and, second, because this behavior is taken to show that the other is not only a potential threat but is actively contemplating hostile actions.

But the state does not apply this reasoning to its own behavior. A peaceful state knows that it will use its arms only to protect itself, not to harm others. It further assumes that others are not fully aware of this. As John Foster Dulles put it: 'Khrushchev does not need to be convinced of our good intentions. He knows we are not aggressors and do not threaten the security of the Soviet Union.' Similarly, in arguing that "England seeks no quarrels, and will never give Germany cause for legitimate offence", Crowe assumed not only that Britain was benevolent but that this was readily apparent to others.[6] To take an earlier case, skirmishing between France and England in North America developed into the Seven Years' War partly because each side incorrectly thought the other knew that its aims were sharply limited. Because the state believes that its adversary understands that the state is arming because it sees the adversary as aggressive, the state does not think that strengthening its arms can be harmful. If the other is aggressive, it will be disappointed because the state's strengthened position means that it is less vulnerable. Provided that the state is already fairly strong, however, there is no danger that the other will be provoked into attacking. If the other is not aggressive, it will not react to the state's effort to protect itself. This means that the state need not exercise restraint in policies designed to increase its security. To procure weapons in excess of the minimum required for defense may be wasteful, but will not cause unwarranted alarm by convincing the other that the state is planning aggression.

In fact, others are not so easily reassured. As Lord Grey realized — after he was out of power:

> The distinction between preparations made with the intention of going to war and precautions against attack is a true distinction, clear and definite in the minds of those who build up armaments. But it is a distinction that is not obvious or certain to others ... Each Government, therefore, while resenting any suggestion that its own measures are anything more than for defense, regards similar measures of another Government as preparation to attack.

Herbert Butterfield catches the way these beliefs drive the spiral of arms and hostility:

> It is the peculiar characteristic of the ... Hobbesian fear ... that you yourself may vividly feel the terrible fear that you have of the other party, but you cannot enter into the other man's counter-fear, or even understand why he should be particularly nervous. For you know that you yourself mean him no harm, and that you want nothing from him save guarantees for your own safety; and it is never possible for you to realize or remember properly that since he cannot see the inside of your mind, he can never have the same assurance of your intentions that you have. As this operates on both sides the Chinese puzzle is complete in all its interlockings and neither party can see the nature of the predicament

he is in, for each only imagines that the other party is being hostile and unreasonable.[7]

Because statesmen believe that others will interpret their behavior as they intend it and will share their view of their own state's policy, they are led astray in two reinforcing ways. First, their understanding of the impact of their own state's policy is often inadequate − i.e. differs from the views of disinterested observers − and, second, they fail to realize that other states' perceptions are also skewed. Although actors are aware of the difficulty of making their threats and warnings credible, they rarely believe that others will misinterpret behavior that is meant to be more compatible with the other's interests. Because we cannot easily establish an objective analysis of the state's policy, these two effects are difficult to disentangle. But for many purposes this does not matter because both pressures push in the same direction and increase the differences between the way the state views its behavior and the perceptions of others.

The degree to which a state can fail to see that its own policy is harming others is illustrated by the note that the British foreign secretary sent to the Soviet government in March 1918 trying to persuade it to welcome a Japanese army that would fight the Germans: 'The British Government have clearly and constantly repeated that they have no wish to take any part in Russia's domestic affairs, but that the prosecution of the war is the only point with which they are concerned.' When reading Bruce Lockhart's reply that the Bolsheviks did not accept this view, Balfour noted in the margin of the dispatch: 'I have constantly impressed on Mr. Lockhart that it is *not* our desire to interfere in Russian affairs. He appears to be very unsuccessful in conveying this view to the Bolshevik Government.'[8] The start of World War I witnessed a manifestation of the same phenomenon when the tsar ordered mobilization of the Baltic fleet without any consideration of the threat this would pose even to a Germany that wanted to remain at peace. [. . .]

The same inability to see the implications of its specific actions limits the state's appreciation of the degree to which its position and general power make it a potential menace. As Klaus Epstein points out in describing the background to World War I, 'Wilhelmine Germany − because of its size, population, geographical location, economic dynamism, cocky militarism, and autocracy under a neurotic Kaiser − was feared by all other Powers as a threat to the European equilibrium; this was an objective fact which Germans should have recognized.'[9] Indeed even had Germany changed her behavior, she still would have been the object of constant suspicion and apprehension by virtue of being the strongest power in

Europe. And before we attribute this insensitivity to the German national character, we should note that United States statesmen in the postwar era have displayed a similar inability to see that their country's huge power, even if used for others' good, represents a standing threat to much of the rest of the world. Instead the United States, like most other nations, has believed that others will see that the desire for security underlies its actions.

The psychological dynamics do not, however, stop here. If the state believes that others know that it is not a threat, it will conclude that they will arm or pursue hostile policies only if they are aggressive. For if they sought only security they would welcome, or at least not object to, the state's policy. Thus an American senator who advocated intervening in Russia in the summer of 1918 declared that if the Russians resisted this move it would prove that 'Russia is already Germanized'. This inference structure is revealed in an exchange about NATO between Tom Connally, the chairman of the Senate Foreign Relations Committee, and Secretary of State Acheson:

Now, Mr. Secretary, you brought out rather clearly . . . that this treaty is not aimed at any nation particularly. It is aimed only at any nation or any country that contemplates or undertakes armed aggression against the members of the signatory powers. Is that true?

Secretary Acheson. That is correct, Senator Connally. It is not aimed at any country; it is aimed solely at armed aggression.

The Chairman. In other words, unless a nation other than the signatories contemplates, meditates or makes plans looking toward, aggression or armed attack on another nation, it has no cause to fear this treaty.

Secretary Acheson. That is correct, Senator Connally, and it seems to me that any nation which claims that this treaty is directed against it should be reminded of the Biblical admonition that 'The guilty flee when no man pursueth.'

The Chairman. That is a very apt illustration.

What I had in mind was, when a State or Nation passes a criminal act, for instance, against burglary, nobody but those who are burglars or getting ready to be burglars need have any fear of the Burglary Act. Is that not true?

Secretary Acheson. Very true.

The Chairman. And so it is with one who might meditate and get ready and arm himself to commit a murder. If he is not going to indulge in that kind of enterprise, the law on murder would not have any effect on him, would it?

Secretary Acheson. The only effect it would have would be for his protection, perhaps, by deterring someone else. He wouldn't worry about the imposition of the penalties on himself, but he might feel that the statute added to his protection.[10]

[...] When the state believes that the other knows that it is not threatening the other's legitimate interests, disputes are likely to produce antagonism out of all proportion to the intrinsic importance of the issue at stake. Because the state does not think that there is any obvious reason why the other should oppose it, it will draw inferences of unprovoked hostility from even minor conflicts. [...] If, on the other hand, each side recognizes that its policies threaten some of the other's values, it will not interpret the other's reaction as indicating aggressive intent or total hostility and so will be better able to keep their conflict limited.

The perceptions and reactions of the other side are apt to deepen the misunderstanding and the conflict. For the other, like the state, will assume that its adversary knows that it is not a threat. So, like the state, it will do more than increase its arms — it will regard the state's explanation of its behavior as making no sense and will see the state as dangerous and hostile. When the Soviets consolidated their hold over Czechoslovakia in 1948, they knew this harmed Western values and expected some reaction. But the formation of NATO and the explanation given for this move were very alarming. Since the Russians assumed that the United States saw the situation the same way they did, the only conclusion they could draw was that the United States was even more dangerous than they had thought. As George Kennan put the Soviet analysis in a cable to Washington:

It seemed implausible to the Soviet leaders, knowing as they did the nature of their own approach to the military problem, and assuming that the Western powers must have known it too, that defensive considerations alone could have impelled the Western governments to give the relative emphasis they actually gave to a program irrelevant in many respects to the outcome of the political struggle in Western Europe (on which Moscow was staking everything) and only partially justified, as Moscow saw it, as a response to actual Soviet intentions. ... The Kremlin leaders were attempting in every possible way to weaken and destroy the structure of the non-Communist world. In the course of this endeavor they were up to many things which gave plenty of cause for complaint on the part of Western statesmen. They would not have been surprised if these things had been made the touchstone of Western reaction. But why, they might ask, were they being accused precisely of the one thing they had *not* done, which was to plan, as yet, to conduct an overt and unprovoked invasion of Western Europe? Why was the imputation to them of this intention being put forward as the rationale for Western rearmament? Did this not imply some ulterior purpose . . .?[11]

The Russians may have been even more alarmed if, as Nathan Leites has argued, they thought that we behaved according to the sensible proverb of 'whoever says A, says Z' and had knowingly assigned Czechoslovakia to the Russian sphere of influence during the wartime negotiations. 'How could, they must ask themselves, the elevation of an already dominant Czechoslovak Communist Party to full power in 1948 change the policies of Washington which had agreed to the presence of the Soviet Army in Czechoslovakia in 1945? Washington, after all, could hardly imagine that Moscow would indefinitely tolerate the presence of enemies . . . within its domain!' The American protests over the takeover must then be hypocrisy, and the claim that this event was alarming and called for Western rearmament could only be a cover for plans of aggression.[12] [. . .]

The explication of these psychological dynamics adds to our understanding of international conflict, but incurs a cost. The benefit is in seeing how the basic security dilemma becomes overlaid by reinforcing misunderstandings as each side comes to believe that not only is the other a potential menace, as it must be in a setting of anarchy, but that the other's behavior has shown that it is an active enemy. The inability to recognize that one's own actions could be seen as menacing and the concomitant belief that the other's hostility can only be explained by its aggressiveness help explain how conflicts can easily expand beyond that which an analysis of the objective situation would indicate is necessary. But the cost of these insights is the slighting of the role of the system in inducing conflict and a tendency to assume that the desire for security, rather than expansion, is the prime goal of most states. [. . .]

Both the advantages and pitfalls of this elaboration of the security dilemma are revealed in Kenneth Boulding's distinction between

two very different kinds of incompatibility . . . The first might be called 'real' incompatibility, where we have two images of the future in which realization of one would prevent the realization of the other. . . . The other form of incompatibility might be called 'illusory' incompatibility, in which there exists a condition of compatibility which would satisfy the 'real' interests of the two parties but in which the dynamics of the situation or illusions of the parties create a situation of perverse dynamics and misunderstandings, with increasing hostility simply as a result of the reactions of the parties to each other, not as a result of any basic differences of interest.[13]

This distinction can be very useful but it takes attention away from the vital kind of system-induced incompatibility that cannot be easily classified as either real or illusory. If both sides primarily desire security, then the two images of the future do not clash, and any incompatibility must, according to one reading of the definition, be illusory. But the heart of the security dilemma argument is that an increase in one state's security can make others less secure not because of misperception or imagined hostility, but because of the anarchic context of international relations.

Under some circumstances, several states can simultaneously increase their security. But often this is not the case. For a variety of reasons, many of which have been discussed earlier, nations' security requirements can clash. While an understanding of the security dilemma and psychological dynamics will dampen some arms-hostility spirals, it will not change the fact that some policies aimed at security will threaten others. To call the incompatibility that results from such policies 'illusory' is to misunderstand the nature of the problem and to encourage the illusion that if the states only saw themselves and others more objectively they could attain their common interest.

Notes

1. Rousseau, *A Lasting Peace through the Federation of Europe*, translated by C.E. Vaughan (Constable, London, 1917), pp. 78-9.

2. Quoted in Adam Ulam, *Expansion and Coexistence* (Praeger, New York, 1968), p. 5; quoted in Butow, *Tojo and the Coming of the War* (Princeton University Press, NJ, 1961), p. 203; Klaus Epstein, 'Gerhard Ritter and the First World War', in H.W. Koch (ed.), *The Origins of the First World War* (Macmillan and Company, London, 1972), p. 290.

3. Nathan Leites, *A Study of Bolshevism* (Free Press, Glencoe, Illinois, 1953), p. 31; quoted in Arthur Schlesinger Jr, 'The Origins of the Cold War, *Foreign Affairs*, 46 (October 1967), p. 30.

4. Herbert Butterfield, *History and Human Relations* (Collins, London, 1951), pp. 19-20; John Herz, *Political Realism and Political Idealism* (University of Chicago Press, Chicago, 1959), p. 4.

5. Lewis Richardson, *Statistics of Deadly Quarrels* (Boxwood Press, Pittsburgh; Quadrangle, Chicago, 1960), p. xxiv; Lewis Richardson, *Arms and Insecurity* (Boxwood Press, Pittsburgh; Quadrangle, Chicago, 1960), p. 227.

6. Quoted in Richard Nixon, *Six Crises* (Doubleday, Garden City, NY, 1962), p. 62; Eyre Crowe, 'Memorandum on the Present State of Relations with France and Germany, January 1907' in G.P. Gooch and H. Temperley (eds.), *British Documents on the Origins of the War, 1898-1914*, vol. 3 (HMSO, London, 1928).

7. Edward Grey, *Twenty-five Years*, vol. 1 (Hodder and Stoughton, London, 1925), p. 91; Butterfield, *History and Human Relations*, pp. 19-20.

8. Quoted in John Wheeler-Bennett, *Brest-Litovsk* (Norton, New York, 1971), pp. 295-6.

9. Epstein, 'Gerhard Ritter and the First World War', p. 293.

10. Quoted in Peter Filene, *Americans and the Soviet Experiment 1917-1933* (Harvard University Press, Cambridge, Mass., 1967), p. 43; Senate Committee on Foreign Relations, *Hearings, North Atlantic Treaty*, 81st Congress, 1st Session, p. 17.

11. George Kennan, *Memoirs*, vol. 2: *1950-1963* (Little, Brown, Boston, 1972), pp. 335-6.

12. Leites, *A Study of Bolshevism*, pp. 42, 34.

13. Kenneth Boulding, 'National Images and International Systems', *Journal of Conflict Resolution*, 3 (June 1959), p. 130.

1.8

THE BALANCE OF POWER AND INTERNATIONAL ORDER

Hedley Bull

Source: *The Anarchical Society: A Study of Order in World Politics* (Macmillan, London, 1977), pp. 106-17.

In this extract, Hedley Bull is concerned to identify the ways in which a balance of power in the international system might contribute to the maintenance of international order. He examines both the historical and the contemporary relevance of the notion of balance of power, and replies to a number of criticisms which have been levelled at it.

[Bull begins by outlining the characteristics of the balance of power, which he takes as meaning 'a state of affairs such that no one power is in a position where it is preponderant and can lay down the law to others'. Four dimensions of comparison between balances are identified by Bull: simplicity or complexity, general or local scope, subjective or objective manifestations, fortuitous or contrived nature. He then goes on to relate the balance to the problem of international order.]

Functions of the Balance of Power

Preservation of a balance of power may be said to have fulfilled three historic functions in the modern states system:

(i)   the existence of a general balance of power throughout the international system as a whole has served to prevent the system from being transformed by conquest into a universal empire;
(ii)   the existence of local balances of power has served to protect the independence of states in particular areas from absorption or domination by a locally preponderant power;
(iii)   both general and local balances of power, where they have existed, have provided the conditions in which other institutions on which international order depends (diplomacy, war, international law, great power management) have been able to operate.

The idea that balances of power have fulfilled positive functions in relation to international order, and hence that contrivance of them is a valuable or legitimate object of statesmanship, has been subject to a great deal of criticism in this century. At the present time criticism focuses upon the alleged obscurity or meaninglessness of the concept, the untested or untestable nature of the historical generalisations upon which it rests, and the reliance on the theory upon the notion that all international behaviour consists of the pursuit of power. Earlier in the century, especially during and after the First World War, critics of the doctrine of the balance of power asserted not that it was unintelligible or untestable, but that pursuit of the balance of power had effects upon international order which were not positive, but negative. In particular, they asserted that the attempt to preserve a balance of power was a source of war, that it was carried out in the interests of the great powers at the expense of the interests of the small, and that it led to disregard of international law. I shall deal with these latter criticisms first.

Attempts to contrive a balance of power have not always resulted in the preservation of peace. The chief function of the balance of power, however, is not to preserve peace, but to preserve the system of states itself. Preservation of the balance of power requires war, when this is the only means whereby the power of a potentially dominant state can be checked. It can be argued, however, that the preservation of peace is a subordinate objective of the contrivance of balances of power. Balances of power which are stable (that is, which have built-in features making for their persistence) may help remove the motive to resort to preventive war.

The principle of preservation of the balance of power has undoubtedly tended to operate in favour of the great powers and at the expense of the small. Frequently, the balance of power among the great powers has been preserved through partition and absorption of the small: the extraordinary decline in the number of European states between 1648 and 1914 illustrates the attempt of large states to absorb small ones while at the same time following the principle of compensation so as to maintain a balance of power. This has led to frequent denunciation of the principle of the balance of power as nothing more than collective aggrandisement by the great powers, the classic case being the partition of Poland in 1772 by Austria, Russia and Prussia. [. . .]

From the point of view of a weak state sacrificed to it, the balance of power must appear as a brutal principle. But its function in the preservation of international order is not for this reason less central. It is part of the logic of the principle of balance of power that the needs of the dominant balance must take precedence over those of subordinate balances, and that the general balance must be prior in importance to any local or particular balance. If aggrandisement by the strong against the weak must take place, it is better from the standpoint of international order that it should take place without a conflagration among the strong than with one.

It is a paradox of the principle of balance of power that while the existence of a balance of power is an essential condition of the operation of international law, the steps necessary to maintain the balance often involve violation of the injunctions of international law. It is clear that situations in which one state has a position of preponderance are situations in which that state may be tempted to disregard rules of law; preponderant powers are, as Vattel perceives, in a position to 'lay down the law to others'. The most basic of the rules of international law – those dealing with sovereignty, non-intervention, diplomatic immunity and the like – depend for their effectiveness on the principle of 'reciprocity'. Where one state is preponderant, it may have the option of disregarding the rights of other states, without fear that these states will reciprocate by disregarding their rights in turn. [. . .]

But while international law depends for its very existence as an operating system of rules on the balance of power, preservation of the latter often requires the breaking of these rules. Rules of international law where they allow the use or threat of force at all do so only, in Grotius's phrase, 'to remedy an injury received'. Before a state may legitimately resort to force against another state there must first be a violation of legal rights which can then be forcibly defended. Preservation of the balance of power, however, requires the use or threat of force in response to the encroaching power of another state, whether or not that state has violated legal rules. Wars initiated to restore the balance of power, wars threatened to maintain it, military interventions in the internal affairs of another state to combat the encroaching power of a third state, whether or not that state has violated legal rules, bring the imperatives of the balance of power into conflict with the imperatives of international law. The requirements of order are treated as prior to those of law, as they are treated also as prior to the interests of small powers and the keeping of peace.

It is noticeable that while, at the present time, the term 'balance of power' is as widely used as at any time in the past in the everyday discussion of international relations, in scholarly analyses of the subject it has been slipping into the background. This reflects impatience with the vagueness and shifting meaning of what is undoubtedly a current cant word; doubts about the historical generalisations that underlie the proposition that preservation of a balance of power is essential to international order; and doubts about its reliance on the discredited notion that the pursuit of power is the common denominator to which all foreign policy can be reduced.

The term 'balance of power' is notorious for the numerous meanings that may be attached to it, the tendency of those who use it to shift from one to another and the uncritical reverence which statements about it are liable to command. It is a mistake, however, to dismiss the notion as a meaningless one, as von Justi did in the eighteenth century and Cobden in the nineteenth, and some political scientists are inclined to do now.[1] The term is not unique in suffering abuses of this kind, and as with such other overworked terms as 'democracy', 'imperialism' and 'peace', its very currency is an indication of the importance of the ideas it is intended to convey. We cannot do without the term 'balance of power' and the need is to define it carefully and use it consistently.

But if we can make clear what we mean by the proposition that preservation of the balance of power functions to preserve international order, is it true? Is it the case that a state which finds itself in a position of preponderant power will always use it to 'lay down the law to others'? Will a locally preponderant state always be a menace to the independence of its neighbours, and a generally preponderant state to the survival of the system of states?

The proposition is implicitly denied by the leaders of powerful states, who see sufficient safeguard of the rights of others in their own virtue and good intentions. Franklin Roosevelt saw the safeguard of Latin America's rights in US adherence to the 'good-neighbour policy'. The United States and the Soviet Union now each recognise a need to limit the power of the other, and assert that this is a need not simply of theirs but of international society at large. But they do not admit the need for any comparable check on their own power.

One form of this view is Kant's idea that the constitutional state or *Rechtsstaat*, which has its own internal checks on the power of rulers, is capable of international virtue in a way in which the absolutist state is not. Thus he is able to recommend the formation of a coalition of *Rechtsstaaten*, which through accretion may come eventually to dominate international politics, without any sense that this coalition will abuse its power.[2] In the early 1960s doctrines of an Atlantic Community, built upon the coalition of North American and West European power, followed the Kantian pattern: they were put forward without any sense that such a coalition would seem or would be menacing to other states, or that these latter would have a legitimate interest in developing a counterpoise to it.

Against this we have to set Acton's view that power itself corrupts, that no matter what the ideology or the institution or the virtue or good intentions of a state in a position of preponderance, that position itself contains a menace to other states which cannot be contained by agreements or laws but only by countervailing power.[3] States are not prevented from falling foul of this by constitutional systems of checks and balances; the corrupting effects of power are felt not merely by the rulers but by the political system as a whole. [. . .]

Criticism of the doctrine that the balance of power functions to maintain international order sometimes derives from the idea that this is part of a theory of 'power politics', which presents the pursuit of power as the common and overriding concern of all states in pursuing foreign policy. On this view the doctrine we have been discussing involves the same fallacies as the 'power-political' theory of which it is part.

Doctrines which contend that there is, in any international system, an automatic tendency for a balance of power to arise do derive from a 'power-political' theory of this kind. The idea that if one state challenges the balance of power, other states are bound to seek to prevent it, assumes that all states seek to maximise their relative power position. This is not the case. States are constantly in the position of having to choose between devoting their resources and energies to maintaining or extending their international power position, and devoting these resources and energies to other ends. The size of defence expenditure, the foreign-aid vote, the diplomatic establishment, whether or not to play a role in particular international issues by taking part in a war, joining an alliance or an international organisation, or pronouncing about an international dispute – these are the matters of which the discussion of any country's foreign policy consists, and proposals that have the effect of augmenting the country's power position can be, and frequently are, rejected. Some states which have the potential for playing a major role – one thinks of the United States in the interwar period and Japan since her economic recovery after the Second World War – prefer to play a relatively minor one. But the doctrine I have been expounding does not assert any inevitable tendency for a balance of power to arise in the international system, only a need to maintain one if international order is to be preserved. States may and often do behave in such a way as to disregard the requirements of a balance of power.

The Present Relevance of the Balance of Power

[. . .] There clearly does now exist a general balance of power in the sense that no one state is preponderant in power in the international system as a whole. The chief characteristic of this general balance is that whereas in the 1950s it took the form of a simple balance (though not a perfectly simple one), and in the 1960s was in a state of transition, in the 1970s it takes the form of a complex balance. At least in the Asian and Pacific region China has to be counted as a great power alongside the United States and the Soviet Union; while Japan figures as a potential fourth great power and a united Western Europe may in time become a fifth. However, the statement that there is now a complex or multilateral balance of power has given rise to a number of misunderstandings, and it is necessary to clear these away.

To speak of a complex or multiple balance among these three or four powers is not to imply that they are equal in strength. Whereas in a system dominated by two powers a situation of balance or absence of preponderance can be achieved only if there is some rough parity of strength between the powers concerned, in a system of three or more powers balance can be achieved without a relationship of equality among the powers concerned because of the possibility of combination of the lesser against the greater.

Moreover, to speak of such a complex balance of power is not to imply that all four great states command the same kind of power or influence. Clearly, in international politics moves are made on 'many chess-boards'. On the chess-board of strategic nuclear deterrence the United States and the Soviet Union are supreme players, China is a novice and Japan does not figure at all. On the chess-board of conventional military strength the United States and the Soviet Union, again, are leading players because of their ability to deploy non-nuclear armed force in many parts of the world, China is a less important player because the armed force it has can be deployed only in its own immediate vicinity, and Japan is only a minor player. On the chess-boards of international monetary affairs and international trade and investment the United States and Japan are leading players, the Soviet Union much less important and China relatively unimportant. On the chess-board of influence derived from ideological appeal it is arguable that China is the pre-eminent player.

However, the play on each of these chess-boards is related to the play on each of the others. An advantageous position in the international politics of trade or investment may be used to procure advantages in the international politics of military security; a weak position on the politics of strategic nuclear deterrence may limit and circumscribe the options available in other fields. It is from this interrelatedness of the various chess-boards that we derive the conception of over-all power and influence in international politics, the common denominator in respect of which we say that there is balance rather than preponderance. Over-all power in this sense cannot be precisely quantified: the relative importance of strategic, economic and politico-psychological ingredients in national power (and of different kinds of each of these) is both uncertain and changing. But the relative position of states in terms of over-all power nevertheless makes itself apparent in bargaining among states, and the conception of over-all power is one we cannot do without.

Furthermore, to speak of the present relations of the great powers as a complex balance is not to imply that they are politically equidistant from one another, or that there is complete diplomatic mobility among them. At the time of writing a *détente* exists between the United States and the Soviet Union, and between the United States and China, but not between the Soviet Union and China. Japan, while it has asserted a measure of independence of the United States and improved its relations with both the Soviet Union and China, is still more closely linked both strategically and economically to the United States than to any of the others. While, therefore, the four major powers have more diplomatic mobility than they had in the period of the simple balance of power, their mobility is still limited, especially by the persistence of tension between the two communist great powers so considerable as to preclude effective collaboration between them.

We have also to note that the complex balance of power that now exists does not rest on any system of general collaboration or concert among the great powers concerned. There is not any general agreement among the United States, the Soviet Union, China and Japan on the proposition that the maintenance of a general balance of power is a common objective as in the proposition proclaimed by the European great powers in the Treaty of Utrecht. Nor is there any general agreement about a system of rules for avoiding or controlling crises, or for limiting wars.

The present balance of power is not wholly fortuitous in the sense defined above, for there is an element of contrivance present in the 'rational' pursuit by the United States, the Soviet Union and China of policies aimed at preventing the preponderance of any of the others. It may be argued also that there is a further element of contrivance in the agreement between the United States and the Soviet Union on the common objective of maintaining a balance between themselves, at least in the limited sphere of strategic nuclear weapons. There is not, however, a contrived balance of power in the sense that all three or four great powers accept it as a common objective – indeed, it is only the United States that explicitly avows the balance of power as a goal. Nor is there any evidence that such a balance of power is generally thought to imply self-restraint on the part of the great powers themselves, as distinct from the attempt to restrain or constrain one another.

The United States and the Soviet Union have developed some agreed rules in relation to the avoidance and control of crises and the limitation of war. There is not, however, any general system of rules among the great powers as a whole in these areas. Neither in the field of Sino-Soviet relations nor in that of Sino-American relations does there exist any equivalent of the nascent system of rules evolving between the two global great powers. In the absence of any such general system of rules, we cannot speak of there being, in addition to a balance among the great powers, a concert of great powers concerned with the management of this balance.

Finally, the present complex balance of power does not rest on a common culture shared by the major states participating in it, comparable with that shared by the European great powers that made up the complex balances of the eighteenth and nineteenth centuries. In the European international system of those centuries one factor that facilitated both the maintenance of the balance itself and co-operation among the powers that contributed to it was their sharing of a common culture, both in the sense of a common intellectual tradition and stock of ideas that facilitated communication, and in the sense of common values, in relation to which conflicts of interest could be moderated. Among the United States, the Soviet Union, China and Japan there does exist some common stock of ideas, but there is no equivalent of the bonds of common culture among European powers in earlier centuries.

All five of the misunderstandings that have been mentioned arise from the fact that in present-day thinking the idea of a balance of power tends to be confused with the European balance-of-power system, particularly that of the nineteenth century. The latter system is commonly said to have been characterised by rough equality among the five principal powers (Britain, France, Austria-Hungary, Russia and Prussia-Germany); by comparability in the kind of power available to each, which could be measured in terms of numbers of troops; by political equidistance among the powers and maximum diplomatic mobility; by general agreements as to the rules of the game; and by an underlying common culture.

Whether or not the European system of the last century in fact possessed all these qualities might be disputed. Thus there were substantial inequalities between the five powers at different times. It was never possible to reduce British sea power and financial power, and continental land power, to a common denominator. There were ideological inhibitions to diplomatic mobility arising from associations such as the Holy Alliance, the *Dreikaiserbund* and the 'Liberal Alliance' of Britain and France. We do have to recognise, however, that the European balance of the nineteenth century was only one historical manifestation of a phenomenon that has occurred in many periods and continents, and that in asserting that there exists a complex balance of power at the present time we are not contending that this embodies every feature of the European model of the last century.

This presently existing balance of power appears to fulfil the same three functions in relation to international order that it has performed in earlier periods, and that were mentioned in the last section. First, the general balance of power serves to prevent the system of states from being transformed by conquest into a universal empire. While the balance continues to be maintained, no one of the great powers has the option of establishing a world government by force.

Second, local balances of power — where they exist — serve to protect the independence of states in particular areas from absorption or domination by a locally preponderant power. [. . .] It would be going too far to assert that the existence of a local balance of power is a necessary condition of the independence of states in any area. To assert this would be to ignore the existence of the factor of a sense of political community in the relations between two states, the consequence of which may be that a locally preponderant state is able, up to a point, to respect the independence of a weaker neighbour, as the United States respects the independence of Canada, or Britain respects the independence of Eire. We have also to recognise that the independence of states in a particular area may owe less to the existence or non-existence of a balance among the local powers than to the part played in the local equilibrium by powers external to the region: if a balance exists at present between Israel and her Arab neighbours, for example, this balance owes its existence to the role played in the area by great powers external to it.

Third, both the general balance of power, and such local balances as exist at present, help to provide the conditions in which other institutions on which international order depends are able to operate. International law, the diplomatic system, war and the management of the international system by the great powers assume a situation in which no one power is preponderant in strength. All are institutions which depend heavily on the possibility that if one state violates the rules, others can take reciprocal action. But a state which is in a position of preponderant power, either in the system as a whole or in a particular area, may be in a position to ignore international law, to disregard the rules and procedures of diplomatic intercourse, to deprive its adversaries of the possibility of resort to war in defence of their interests and rights, or to ignore the conventions of the comity of great powers, all with impunity.

Notes

1. J.H. von Justi, *Die Chimare des Gleichgewichts in Europa* (Altona, 1758); and Richard Cobden, 'Russia', in *Political Writings* (Ridgeway, London, 1867, and Cassell, London, 1886).

2. Kant, *Perpetual Peace*, translated by H. O'Brien (Liberal Arts Press, 1957).

3. Lord Acton, *Lectures on Modern History*, edited by J.N. Figgis and R.V. Laurence (Macmillan, London, 1910).

STATE POWER AND THE STRUCTURE OF INTERNATIONAL TRADE

Stephen D. Krasner

Source: *World Politics*, vol. XXVIII, no. 3 (Princeton University Press, 1976), pp. 317-47.

Krasner sets out to reassert the power of states to determine the character of the international system. He takes the structure of international trade in the nineteenth and twentieth centuries as an example and demonstrates that the degree of 'openness' in that structure can be partially explained by the distribution of economic power among states. In particular, he argues that the existence of a hegemonic state leads to a higher level of free trade than that found when the distribution of power is more equal.

Introduction

In recent years, students of international relations have multinationalized, transnationalized, bureaucratized, and transgovernmentalized the state until it has virtually ceased to exist as an analytic construct. Nowhere is that trend more apparent than in the study of the politics of international economic relations. The basic conventional assumptions have been undermined by assertions that the state is trapped by a transnational society created not by sovereigns, but by nonstate actors. Interdependence is not seen as a reflection of state policies and state choices (the perspective of balance-of-power theory), but as the result of elements beyond the control of any state or a system created by states.

This perspective is at best profoundly misleading. It may explain developments within a particular international economic structure, but it cannot explain the structure itself. That structure has many institutional and behavioral manifestations. The central continuum along which it can be described is openness. International economic structures may range from complete autarky (if all states prevent movements across their borders), to complete openness (if no restrictions exist). In this paper I will present an analysis of one aspect of the international economy — the structure of international trade: that is, the degree of openness for the movement of goods as opposed to capital, labor, technology, or other factors of production.

Since the beginning of the nineteenth century, this structure has gone through several changes. These can be explained, albeit imperfectly, by a state-power theory: an approach that begins with the assumption that the structure of international trade is determined by the interests and power of states acting to maximize national goals. [. . .]

The Causal Argument: State Interests, State Power, and International Trading Structures

Neoclassical trade theory is based upon the assumption that states act to maximize their aggregate economic utility. This leads to the conclusion that maximum global welfare and Pareto optimality are achieved under free trade. While particular countries might better their situations through protectionism, economic theory has generally looked askance at such policies. [. . .]

State Preferences

Historical experience suggests that policy makers are dense, or that the assumptions of the conventional argument are wrong. Free trade has hardly been the norm. Stupidity is not a very interesting analytic category. An alternative approach to explaining international trading structures is to assume that states seek a broad range of goals. At least four major state interests affected by the structure of international trade can be identified. They are: political power, aggregate national income, economic growth, and social stability. The way in which each of these goals is affected by the degree of openness depends upon the potential economic power of the state as defined by its relative size and level of development.

Let us begin with aggregate national income because it is most straightforward. Given the exceptions noted above, conventional neoclassical theory demonstrates that the greater the degree of openness in the international trading system, the greater the level of aggregate economic income. This conclusion applies to all states regardless of their size or relative level of development. The static economic benefits of openness are, however, generally inversely related to size. Trade gives small states relatively more welfare benefits than it gives large ones. Empirically, small states have higher ratios of trade to national product. They do not have the generous factor endowments or potential for national economies of scale that are enjoyed by larger — particularly continental — states.

The impact of openness on social stability runs in the opposite direction. Greater openness exposes the domestic economy to the exigencies of the world market. That implies a higher level of factor movements than in a closed economy, because domestic production patterns must adjust to changes in international prices. Social instability is thereby increased, since there is friction in moving factors, particularly labor, from one sector to another. The impact will be stronger in small states than in large, and in relatively less developed than in more developed ones. Large states are less involved in the international economy: a smaller percentage of their total factor endowment is affected by the international market at any given level of openness. More developed states are better able to adjust factors: skilled workers can more easily be moved from one kind of production to another than can unskilled laborers or peasants. Hence social stability is, *ceteris paribus*, inversely related to openness, but the deleterious consequences of exposure to the international trading system are mitigated by larger size and greater economic development.

The relationship between political power and the international trading structure can be analyzed in terms of the relative opportunity costs of closure for trading partners. The higher the relative cost of closure, the weaker the political position of the state. Hirschman has argued that this cost can be measured in terms of direct income losses and the adjustment costs of reallocating factors.[1] These will be smaller for large states and for relatively more developed states. Other things being equal, utility costs will be less for large states because they generally have a smaller proportion of their economy engaged in the international economic system. Reallocation costs will be less for more advanced states because their factors are more mobile. Hence a state that is relatively large and more developed will find its political power enhanced by an open system because its opportunity costs of closure are less. The large state can use the threat to alter the system to secure economic or noneconomic objectives. Historically, there is one important exception to this generalization — the oil-exporting states. The level of reserves for some of these states, particularly Saudi Arabia, has reduced the economic opportunity costs of closure to a very low level despite their lack of development.

The relationship between international economic structure and economic growth is elusive. For small states, economic growth has generally been empirically associated with openness.[2] Exposure to the international system makes possible a much more efficient allocation of resources. Openness also probably furthers the rate of growth of large countries with relatively advanced technologies because they do not need to protect infant industries and can take advantage of expanded world markets. In the long term, however, openness for capital and technology, as well as goods, may hamper the growth of large, developed countries by diverting resources from the domestic economy, and by providing potential competitors with the knowledge needed to develop their own industries. Only by maintaining its technological lead and continually developing new industries can even a very large state escape the undesired consequences of an entirely open economic system. [. . .]

From State Preferences to International Trading Structures

The next step in this argument is to relate particular distributions of potential economic power, defined by the size and level of development of individual states, to the structure of the international trading system, defined in terms of openness.

Let us consider a system composed of a large number of small, highly developed states. Such a system is likely to lead to an open international trading structure. The aggregate income and economic growth of each state are increased by an open system. The social instability produced by exposure to international competition is mitigated by the factor mobility made possible by higher levels of development. There is no loss of political power from openness because the costs of closure are symmetrical for all members of the system.

Now let us consider a system composed of a few very large, but unequally developed states. Such a distribution of potential economic power is likely to lead to a closed structure. Each state could increase its income through a more open system, but the gains would be modest. Openness would create more social instability in the less developed countries. The rate of growth for more backward areas might be frustrated, while that of the more advanced ones would be enhanced. A more open structure would leave the less developed states in a politically more vulnerable position, because their greater factor rigidity would mean a higher relative cost of closure. Because of these disadvantages, large but relatively less developed states are unlikely to accept an open trading structure. More advanced states cannot, unless they are militarily much more powerful, force large backward countries to accept openness.

Finally, let us consider a hegemonic system – one in which there is a single state that is much larger and relatively more advanced than its trading partners. The costs and benefits of openness are not symmetrical for all members of the system. The hegemonic state will have a preference for an open structure. Such a structure increases its aggregate national income. It also increases its rate of growth during its ascendency – that is, when its relative size and technological lead are increasing. Further, an open structure increases its political power, since the opportunity costs of closure are least for a large and developed state. The social instability resulting from exposure to the international system is mitigated by the hegemonic power's relatively low level of involvement in the international economy, and the mobility of its factors.

What of the other members of a hegemonic system? Small states are likely to opt for openness because the advantages in terms of aggregate income and growth are so great, and their political power is bound to be restricted regardless of what they do. [...] The potentially dominant state has symbolic, economic, and military capabilities that can be used to entice or compel others to accept an open trading structure.

At the symbolic level, the hegemonic state stands as an example of how economic development can be achieved. Its policies may be emulated, even if they are inappropriate for other states. Where there are very dramatic asymmetries, military power can be used to coerce weaker states into an open structure. [...]

Most importantly, the hegemonic state can use its economic resources to create an open structure. In terms of positive incentives, it can offer access to its large domestic market and to its relatively cheap exports. In terms of negative ones, it can withhold foreign grants and engage in competition, potentially ruinous for the weaker state, in third-country markets. The size and economic robustness of the hegemonic state also enable it to provide the confidence necessary for a stable international monetary system, and its currency can offer the liquidity needed for an increasingly open system.

In sum, openness is most likely to occur during periods when a hegemonic state is in its ascendancy. Such a state has the interest and the resources to create a structure characterized by lower tariffs, rising trade proportions, and less regionalism. There are other distributions of potential power where openness is likely, such as a system composed of many small, highly developed states. But even here, that potential might not be realized because of the problems of creating confidence in a monetary system where adequate liquidity would have to be provided by a negotiated international reserve asset or a group of national currencies. Finally, it is unlikely that very large states, particularly at unequal levels of development, would accept open trading relations.

These arguments, and the implications of other ideal typical configurations of potential economic power for the openness of trading structures, are summarized in the following figure.

Figure 1: Probability of an Open Trading Structure with Different Distributions of Potential Economic Power

		SIZE OF STATES		
		RELATIVELY EQUAL		VERY UNEQUAL
		Small	Large	
Level of Development of States	Equal	Moderate-High	Low-Moderate	High
	Unequal	Moderate	Low	Moderate-High

The Dependent Variable: Describing the Structure of the International Trading System

The structure of international trade has both behavioral and institutional attributes. The degree of openness can be described both by the *flow* of goods and by the *policies* that are followed by states with respect to trade barriers and international payments. The two are not unrelated, but they do not coincide pefectly.

In common usage, the focus of attention has been upon institutions. Openness is associated with those historical periods in which tariffs were substantially lowered: the third quarter of the nineteenth century and the period since the Second World War.

Tariffs alone, however, are not an adequate indicator of structure. They are hard to operationalize quantitatively. Tariffs do not have to be high to be effective. If cost functions are nearly identical, even low tariffs can prevent trade. Effective tariff rates may be much higher than nominal ones. Non-tariff barriers to trade, which are not easily compared across states, can substitute for duties. An undervalued exchange rate can protect domestic markets from foreign competition. Tariff levels alone cannot describe the structure of international trade.

A second indicator, and one which is behavioral rather than institutional, is trade proportions − the ratios of trade to national income for different states. Like tariff levels, these involve describing the system in terms of an agglomeration of national tendencies. A period in which these ratios are increasing across time for most states can be described as one of increasing openness.

A third indicator is the concentration of trade within regions composed of states at different levels of development. The degree of such regional encapsulation is determined not so much by comparative advantage (because relative factor endowments would allow almost any backward area to trade with almost any developed one), but by political choices or dictates. Large states, attempting to protect themselves from the vagaries of a global system, seek to maximize their interests by creating regional blocs. Openness in the global economic system has in effect meant greater trade among the leading industrial states. Periods of closure are associated with the encapsulation of certain advanced states within regional systems shared with certain less developed areas.

A description of the international trading system involves, then, an exercise that is comparative rather than absolute. A period when tariffs are falling, trade proportions are rising, and regional trading patterns are becoming less extreme will be defined as one in which the structure is becoming more open.

[Krasner goes on to investigate the evidence available for the period 1820-1970, using these three indicators, and comes to the following conclusions.]

If we put all three indicators — tariff levels, trade proportions, and trade patterns — together, they suggest the following periodization:

Period I (1820-1879): Increasing openness — tariffs are generally lowered; trade proportions increase. Data are not available for trade patterns. However, it is important to note that this is not a universal pattern. The United States is largely unaffected: its tariff levels remain high (and are in fact increased during the early 1860s) and American trade proportions remain almost constant.

Period II (1879-1900): Modest closure — tariffs are increased; trade proportions decline modestly for most states. Data are not available for trade patterns.

Period III (1900-1913): Greater openness — tariff levels remain generally unchanged; trade proportions increase for all major trading states except the United States. Trading patterns become less regional in three out of the four cases for which data are available.

Period IV (1918-1939): Closure — tariff levels are increased in the 1920s and again in the 1930s; trade proportions decline. Trade becomes more regionally encapsulated.

Period V (1945-c.1970): Great openness — tariffs are lowered; trade proportions increase, particularly after 1960. Regional concentration decreases after 1960. However, these developments are limited to non-

Communist areas of the world.

The Independent Variable: Describing the Distribution of Potential Economic Power Among States

Analysts of international relations have an almost *pro forma* set of variables designed to show the distribution of potential power in the international *political* system. It includes such factors as gross national product, *per capita* income, geographical position, and size of armed forces. A similar set of indicators can be presented for the international *economic* system.

Statistics are available over a long period of time for *per capita* income, aggregate size, share of world trade, and share of world investment. They demonstrate that, since the beginning of the nineteenth century, there have been two first-rank economic powers in the world economy — Britain and the United States. The United States passed Britain in aggregate size sometime in the middle of the nineteenth century and, in the 1880s, became the largest producer of manufactures. America's lead was particularly marked in technologically advanced industries turning out sewing machines, harvesters, cash registers, locomotives, steam pumps, telephones, and petroleum. Until the First World War, however, Great Britain had a higher *per capita* income, a greater share of world trade, and a greater share of world investment than any other state. The peak of British ascendance occurred around 1880, when Britain's relative *per capita* income, share of world trade, and share of investment flows reached their highest levels. Britain's potential dominance in 1880 and 1900 was particularly striking in the international economic system, where her share of trade and foreign investment was about twice as large as that of any other state.

It was only after the First World War that the United States became relatively larger and more developed in terms of all four indicators. This potential dominance reached new and dramatic heights between 1945 and 1960. Since then, the relative position of the United States has declined, bringing it quite close to West Germany, its nearest rival, in terms of *per capita* income and share of world trade. The devaluations of the dollar that have taken place since 1972 are reflected in a continuation of this downward trend for income and aggregate size.

The relative potential economic power of Britain and the United States is shown in the following two tables.

Table 1: Indicators of British Potential Power (Ratio of British value to next highest)

	Per Capita Income	Aggregate Size	Share of World Trade	Share of World Investment[a]
1860	.91(US)	.74(US)	2.01(FR)	n.a.
1880	1.30(US)	.79(1874-83 US)	2.22(FR)	1.93(FR)
1900	1.05(1899 US)	.58(1899 US)	2.17(1890 GERM)	2.08(FR)
1913	.92(US)	.43(US)	1.20(US)	2.18(1914 FR)
1928	.66(US)	.25(1929 US)	.79(US)	.64(1921-29 US)
1937	.79(US)	.29(US)	.88(US)	.18(1930-38 US)
1950	.56(US)	.19(US)	.69(US)	.13(1951-55 US)
1960	.49(US)	.14(US)	.46(1958 US)	.15(1956-61 US)
1972	.46(US)	.13(US)	.47(1973 US)	n.a.

[a]. Stock 1870-1913; Flow 1928-1950.
Years are in parentheses when different from those in first column.
Countries in parentheses are those with the largest values for the particular indicator other than Great Britain.

Table 2: Indicators of US Potential Power (Ratio of US value to next highest)

	Per Capita Income	Aggregate Size	Share of World Trade	Share of World Investment Flows
1860	1.10(GB)	1.41(GB)	.36(GB)	Net debtor
1880	.77(GB)	1.23(1883 GB)	.37(GB)	Net debtor
1900	.95(1899 GB)	1.73(1899 GB)	.43(1890 GB)	n.a.
1913	1.09(GB)	2.15(RUS)	.83(GB)	Net debtor
1928	1.51(GB)	3.22(USSR)	1.26(GB)	1.55(1921-30 UK)
1937	1.26(GB)	2.67(USSR)	1.13(GB)	5.53(1930-38 UK)
1950	1.78(GB)	3.15(USSR)	1.44(GB)	7.42(1951-55 UK)
1960	2.05(GB)	2.81(USSR)	2.15(1958 GB)	6.60(1956-61 UK)
1972	1.31(GERM)	n.a.	1.18(1973 GERM)	n.a.

Years are in parentheses when different from those in first column.
Countries in parentheses are those with the largest values for the particular indicator other than the United States.

In sum, Britain was the world's most important trading state from the period after the Napoleonic Wars until 1913. Her relative position rose until about 1880 and fell thereafter. The United States became the largest and most advanced state in economic terms after the First World War, but did not equal the relative share of world trade and investment achieved by Britain in the 1880s until after the Second World War.

Testing the Argument

The contention that hegemony leads to a more open trading structure is fairly well, but not perfectly, confirmed by the empirical evidence presented in the preceding sections. The argument explains the periods 1820 to 1879, 1880 to 1900, and 1945 to 1960. It does not fully explain those from 1900 to 1913, 1919 to 1939, or 1960 to the present.

[Krasner goes on to examine evidence for the fluctuations in British and American influence, and especially for the fact that there appear to be 'time-lags' in adaptations to a changed power distribution. He concludes thus:]

In sum, although the general pattern of the structure of international trade conforms with the predictions of a state-power argument — two periods of openness separated by one of closure — corresponding to periods of rising British and American hegemony and an interregnum, the whole pattern is out of phase. British commitment to openness continued long after Britain's position had declined. American commitment to openness did not begin until well after the United States had become the world's leading economic power and has continued during a period of relative American decline. The state-power argument needs to be amended to take these delayed reactions into account.

Amending the Argument

The structure of the international trading system does not move in lockstep with changes in the distribution of potential power among states. Systems are initiated and ended, not as a state-power theory would predict, by close assessments of the interests of the state at every given moment, but by external events — usually cataclysmic ones. The closure that began in 1879 coincided with the Great Depression of the last part of the nineteenth century. The final dismantling of the nineteenth-century international economic system was not precipitated by a change in British trade or monetary policy, but by the First World War and the Depression. The potato famine of the 1840s prompted abolition of the Corn Laws; and the United States did not assume the mantle of world leadership until the world had been laid bare by six years of total war. Some catalytic external event seems necessary to move states to dramatic policy initiatives in line with state interests.

Once policies have been adopted, they are pursued until a new crisis demonstrates that they are no longer feasible. States become locked in by the impact of prior choices on their domestic political structures. The British decision to opt for openness in 1846 corresponded with state interests. It also strengthened the position of industrial and financial groups over time, because they had the opportunity to operate in an international system that furthered their objectives. That system eventually undermined the position of British farmers, a group that would have supported protectionism if it had survived. Once entrenched, Britain's export industries, and more importantly the City of London, resisted policies of closure. In the interwar years, the British rentier class insisted on restoring the prewar parity of the pound – a decision that placed enormous deflationary pressures on the domestic economy – because they wanted to protect the value of their investments.

Institutions created during periods of rising ascendancy remained in operation when they were no longer appropriate. For instance, the organization of British banking in the nineteenth century separated domestic and foreign operations. The Court of Directors of the Bank of England was dominated by international banking houses. Their decisions about British monetary policy were geared toward the international economy. Under a different institutional arrangement more attention might have been given after 1900 to the need to revitalize the domestic economy. The British state was unable to free itself from the domestic structures that its earlier policy decisions had created, and continued to follow policies appropriate for a rising hegemony long after Britain's star had begun to fall.

Similarly, earlier policies in the United States begat social structures and institutional arrangements that trammeled state policy. After protecting import-competing industries for a century, the United States was unable in the 1920s to opt for more open policies, even though state interests would have been furthered thereby. Institutionally, decisions about tariff reductions were taken primarily in congressional committees, giving virtually any group seeking protection easy access to the decision-making process. When there were conflicts among groups, they were resolved by raising the levels of protection for everyone. It was only after the cataclysm of the depression that the decision-making processes for trade policy were changed. The Presidency, far more insulated from the entreaties of particular societal groups than congressional committees, was then given more power. Furthermore, the American commercial banking system was unable to assume the burden of regulating the international economy during the 1920s. American institutions were geared toward the domestic economy. Only after the Second World War, and in fact not until the late 1950s, did American banks fully develop the complex institutional structures commensurate with the dollar's role in the international monetary system.

Having taken the critical decisions that created an open system after 1945, the American Government is unlikely to change its policy until it confronts some external event that it cannot control, such as a worldwide deflation, drought in the great plains, or the malicious use of petrodollars. In America perhaps more than in any other country 'new policies', as E.E. Schattschneider wrote in his brilliant study of the Smoot-Hawley Tariff in 1935, 'create new politics',[3] for in America the state is weak and the society strong. State decisions taken because of state interests reinforce private societal groups that the state is unable to resist in later periods. Multinational corporations have grown and prospered since 1950. International economic policy making has passed from the Congress to the Executive. Groups favoring closure, such as organized labor, are unlikely to carry the day until some external event demonstrates that existing policies can no longer be implemented.

The structure of international trade changes in fits and starts; it does not flow smoothly with the redistribution of potential state power. Nevertheless, it is the power and the policies of states that create order where there would otherwise be chaos or at best a Lockian state of nature. The existence of various transnational, multinational, transgovernmental, and other nonstate actors that have riveted scholarly attention in recent years can only be understood within the context of a broader structure that ultimately rests upon the power and interests of states, shackled though they may be by the societal consequences of their own past decisions.

Notes

1. Albert O. Hirschman, *National Power and the Structure of Foreign Trade* (University of California Press, Berkeley, 1945), pp. 13-34.

2. Simon Kuznets, *Modern Economic Growth: Rate, Structure and Spread* (Yale University Press, New Haven, 1966), p. 302.

3. E.E. Schattschneider, *Politics, Pressure and the Tariff: A Study of Free Enterprise in Pressure Politics as Shown in the 1929-1930 Revision of the Tariff* (Prentice-Hall, New York, 1935).

THE POLITICS OF INTERDEPENDENCE AND TRANSNATIONAL RELATIONS

INTRODUCTION

The following twelve articles derive their inspiration from the dissatisfaction of the 1970s with the kind of assumptions underlying the material in the previous section. The character of these assumptions is outlined and challenged in the first article by Keohane and Nye whose work has been of major importance in the development of this perspective. They contest three particular claims: that states are unitary actors and dominant in world politics; that force is a 'usable and effective instrument' in the relations between states; and that there is a clear 'hierarchy of issues' dominated by the need of states for security. The articles that follow can all be seen as pursuing this challenge by seeking to assert a more differentiated set of assumptions about the way in which world politics operate. The end-product might be described as a kind of pluralism at the international level, where actors, processes and outcomes are perceived in much less clear, much less stark, terms than those implicit in the 'Realist' vision.

The position of the state as an actor is contested here in two ways. In the first place, can the state be conceived of as a rational, unitary actor? Both Destler (2.4) and Alger (2.5) deny this. The former draws attention to the way in which the complex procedures of governmental bureaucracy and the competition that rages between its members make it difficult to uphold rational calculation as the mainspring of foreign policy; the latter points to the importance of recognizing the fragmented character of the state and the critical role that interest groups, in particular, play in the formulation of foreign policy as much as of domestic policy. The second question that is directed at the state-centric view asks: is the state the most important actor in world politics? A further three articles suggest that, at the very least, such a position is not self-evident. Huntington (2.7) discusses the transnational organization – in particular, the multinational corporation – and argues that it is very far from being simply the creature of the nation-state: on the contrary, it can play an independent role on the world stage. Reynolds (2.6) looks at the transnational actors from a rather

117

different point of view but he too does not dismiss their role out of hand. Rather, he suggests that it is necessary to identify the conditions which render such organizations more or less powerful. Pentland (2.9) takes the international organization and suggests that it too cannot be dismissed as just an instrument of state policy and that it can indeed have its own particular impact on outcomes in world politics.

What, though, of the processes that are generated by the interaction of the actors involved, be they states or not? Here again the articles suggest that the Realists maintain a view which no longer offers an adequate 'fit' with the phenomena to be explained. Thus Morse (2.3) stresses the importance of modernization within industrial societies as a force which has altered dramatically the character of foreign policy and the way in which it is formulated. Hanrieder (2.2) maintains that the product of the twin forces of nationalism and interdependence has been the 'domestication of international politics', where relations between states no longer are so different from those within them. Keohane and Nye in their second article (2.8) enlarge upon Pentland's argument by drawing attention to the distinctive ways in which international organizations operate and the opportunities that are thus provided for domestic bureaucracies to fashion outcomes that more traditional foreign policies would not have engendered.

The kind of system that emerges from these processes is a very different one from the 'anarchical society' of the first section. Puchala (2.10) uses the phrase 'concordance system' to describe the character of the integration of states in Europe, a system where the use of force is unthinkable and where the efforts of policy makers are directed towards mutually satisfying results. The Sprouts (2.11), for their part, adopt a clearly normative stand in claiming that the interdependence of states has reached such a marked level that the symbols of sovereignty and statehood are a positive barrier to the discovery of solutions to the new problems that face the world community. Brown and Fabian (2.12) also accept the existence of new kinds of problems on the world agenda which underline the basic interdependence of states. They argue for the need to establish 'regimes' or adequate systems of management to cope with these problems, where states are not the sole managers.

Three general points about the articles in this section are worth emphasizing. Firstly, it should not be supposed that the perspective is a unitary one. Two examples illustrate this clearly: Huntington and Keohane and Nye (2.8) adopt very different attitudes towards the importance of international organizations. Indeed, the latters' article was a direct counterattack to the former's claim that 'internationalism is a dead end'. Similarly, the role of the state is far from agreed by all the authors. At different ends of the spectrum are Hanrieder and the Sprouts. Thus, while the former argues for the continuing vitality of the state at the international level, the latter adopt a far more critical view of its viability: for them the state is just about through as an effective actor in world politics. The second point that should be made is that, though much of the material is directed against more traditional analyses of international relations, the arguments are not necessarily in conflict with the Realist view. Keohane and Nye, for example, in their first article suggest that the assumptions that they ascribe to the Realist view represent an 'ideal type' which may indeed correspond to what occurs in world politics under certain conditions. Thus they do not argue that their own competing assumptions provide a better guide for analysis in all situations. It may, for example, not be so easy to dismiss the use of force as an effective instrument of foreign policy once attention is turned away from the industrialized world. This leads to the final point, namely that the geographical origins of the perspective are far less heterogeneous than the view of the world it seeks to project. All the articles with one exception are written by Americans, scholars who have dominated the literature that has emerged within this perspective. Moreover, they concentrate upon and adopt the standpoint of the industrialized world. The orientation is generally reformist but it remains essentially a view of the world 'from the top down'. In this sense it shares many of the assumptions of the first perspective, assumptions that the reader will find vigorously challenged in the final perspective with its view of world politics 'from the bottom up'.

REALISM AND COMPLEX INTERDEPENDENCE

Robert O. Keohane and Joseph S. Nye

Source: *Power and Interdependence* (Little, Brown, Boston, 1977), pp. 23-37.

Keohane and Nye challenge three assumptions of the 'Realist' model of world politics: first, that states are unitary and the dominant actors; second, that force is a usable and effective policy instrument; and third, that there is a hierarchy of issues headed by questions of military security. They offer a competing characterization which they call complex interdependence. This assumes multiple channels of contact between societies, an absence of hierarchy among issues and a minor role for the use of force and generates distinctive political processes including linkage strategies, agenda control and coalition building.

[...] For political realists, international politics, like all other politics, is a struggle for power but, unlike domestic politics, a struggle dominated by organized violence. In the words of the most influential postwar textbook, 'All history shows that nations active in international politics are continuously preparing for, actively involved in, or recovering from organized violence in the form of war.'[1] Three assumptions are integral to the realist vision. First, states as coherent units are the dominant actors in world politics. This is a double assumption: states are predominant; and they act as coherent units. Second, realists assume that force is a usable and effective instrument of policy. Other instruments may also be employed, but using or threatening force is the most effective means of wielding power. Third, partly because of their second assumption, realists assume a hierarchy of issues in world politics, headed by questions of military security: the 'high politics' of military security dominates the 'low politics' of economic and social affairs.

These realist assumptions define an ideal type of world politics. They allow us to imagine a world in which politics is continually characterized by active or potential conflict among states, with the use of force possible at any time. Each state attempts to defend its territory and interests from real or perceived threats. Political integration among states is slight and lasts only as long as it serves the national interests of the most powerful states. Transnational actors either do not exist or are politically unimportant. Only the adept exercise of force or the threat of force permits states to survive, and only while statesmen succeed in adjusting their interests, as in a well-functioning balance of power, is the system stable.

Each of the realist assumptions can be challenged. If we challenge them all simultaneously, we can imagine a world in which actors other than states participate directly in world politics, in which a clear hierarchy of issues does not exist, and in which force is an ineffective instrument of policy. Under these conditions — which we call the characteristics of complex interdependence — one would expect world politics to be very different than under realist conditions.

We will explore these differences in the next section of this chapter. We do not argue, however, that complex interdependence faithfully reflects world political reality. Quite the contrary: both it and the realist portrait are ideal types. Most situations will fall somewhere between these two extremes. Sometimes, realist assumptions will be accurate, or largely accurate, but frequently complex interdependence will provide a better portrayal of reality. Before one decides what explanatory model to apply to a situation or problem, one will need to understand the degree to which realist or complex interdependence assumptions correspond to the situation.

The Characteristics of Complex Interdependence

Complex interdependence has three main characteristics:

1. *Multiple channels* connect societies, including: informal ties between governmental elites as well as formal foreign office arrangements; informal ties among nongovernmental elites (face-to-face and through telecommunications); and transnational organizations (such as multinational banks or corporations). These channels can be summarized as interstate, transgovernmental, and transnational relations. *Interstate* relations are the normal channels assumed by realists. *Transgovernmental* applies when we relax the realist assumption that states act coherently as units; *transnational* applies when we relax the assumption that states are the only units.

2. The agenda of interstate relationships consists of multiple issues that are not arranged in a clear or consistent hierarchy. This *absence of hierarchy among issues* means, among other things, that military security does not consistently dominate the agenda. Many issues arise from what used to be considered domestic policy, and the distinction between domestic and

foreign issues becomes blurred. These issues are considered in several government departments (not just foreign offices), and at several levels. Inadequate policy coordination on these issues involves significant costs. Different issues generate different coalitions, both within governments and across them, and involve different degrees of conflict. Politics does not stop at the waters' edge.

3. Military force is not used by governments toward other governments within the region, or on the issues, when complex interdependence prevails. It may, however, be important in these governments' relations with governments outside that region, or on other issues. Military force could, for instance, be irrelevant to resolving disagreements on economic issues among members of an alliance, yet at the same time be very important for that alliance's political and military relations with a rival bloc. For the former relationships this condition of complex interdependence would be met; for the latter, it would not.

Traditional theories of international politics implicitly or explicitly deny the accuracy of these three assumptions. Traditionalists are therefore tempted also to deny the relevance of criticisms based on the complex interdependence ideal type. We believe, however, that our three conditions are fairly well approximated on some global issues of economic and ecological interdependence and that they come close to characterizing the entire relationship between some countries. One of our purposes here is to prove that contention. [. . .]

Multiple Channels

A visit to any major airport is a dramatic way to confirm the existence of multiple channels of contact among advanced industrial countries; there is a voluminous literature to prove it.[2] Bureaucrats from different countries deal directly with one another at meetings and on the telephone as well as in writing. Similarly, nongovernmental elites frequently get together in the normal course of business, in organizations such as the Trilateral Commission, and in conferences sponsored by private foundations.

In addition, multinational firms and banks affect both domestic and interstate relations. The limits on private firms, or the closeness of ties between government and business, vary considerably from one society to another; but the participation of large and dynamic organizations, not controlled entirely by governments, has become a normal part of foreign as well as domestic relations.

These actors are important not only because of their activities in pursuit of their own interests, but also because they act as transmission belts, making government policies in various countries more sensitive to one another. As the scope of governments' domestic activities has broadened, and as corporations, banks, and (to a lesser extent) trade unions have made decisions that transcend national boundaries, the domestic policies of different countries impinge on one another more and more. Transnational communications reinforce these effects. Thus, foreign economic policies touch more domestic and foreign policy and increasing the number of issues relevant to economic activity than in the past, blurring the lines between domestic foreign policy. Parallel developments in issues of environmental regulation and control over technology reinforce this trend.

Absence of Hierarchy among Issues

Foreign affairs agendas — that is, sets of issues relevant to foreign policy with which governments are concerned — have become larger and more diverse. No longer can all issues be subordinated to military security. As Secretary of State Kissinger described the situation in 1975:

> progress in dealing with the traditional agenda is no longer enough. A new and unprecedented kind of issue has emerged. The problems of energy, resources, environment, population, the uses of space and the seas now rank with questions of military security, ideology and territorial rivalry which have traditionally made up the diplomatic agenda.[3]

Kissinger's list, which could be expanded, illustrates how governments' policies, even those previously considered merely domestic, impinge on one another. The extensive consultative arrangements developed by the OECD, as well as the GATT, IMF, and the European Community, indicate how characteristic the overlap of domestic and foreign policy is among developed pluralist countries. The organization within nine major departments of the United States government (Agriculture, Commerce, Defense, Health, Education and Welfare, Interior, Justice, Labor, State, and Treasury) and many other agencies reflects their extensive international commitments. The multiple, overlapping issues that result make a nightmare of governmental organization.

When there are multiple issues on the agenda, many of which threaten the interests of domestic groups but do not clearly threaten the nation as a whole, the problems of formulating a coherent and consistent foreign policy increase. In 1975 energy was a foreign policy problem, but specific remedies, such as a tax on gasoline and automobiles, involved domestic legislation opposed by auto workers and companies alike. As one commentator observed, 'virtually every time Congress has set a national policy that changed the way people live . . . the action came after a consensus had developed, bit by bit, over the years, that a problem existed and that there was one best way to solve it'.[4] Opportunities for delay, for special protection, for inconsistency and incoherence abound when international politics requires aligning the domestic policies of pluralist democratic countries.

Minor Role of Military Force

Political scientists have traditionally emphasized the role of military force in international politics. [. . .] Survival is the primary goal of all states, and in the worst situations, force is ultimately necessary to guarantee survival. Thus military force is always a central component of national power.

Yet particularly among industrialized, pluralist countries, the perceived margin of safety has widened: fears of attack in general have declined, and fears of attack *by one another* are virtually nonexistent. France has abandoned the *tous azimuts* (defense in all directions) strategy that President de Gaulle advocated (it was not taken entirely seriously even at the time). Canada's last war plans for fighting the United States were abandoned half a century ago. Britain and Germany no longer feel threatened by each other. Intense relationships of mutual influence exist between these countries, but in most of them force is irrelevant or unimportant as an instrument of policy.

Moreover, force is often not an appropriate way of achieving other goals (such as economic and ecological welfare) that are becoming more important. It is not impossible to imagine dramatic conflict or revolutionary change in which the use or threat of military force over an economic issue or among advanced industrial countries might become plausible. Then realist assumptions would again be a reliable guide to events. But in most situations, the effects of military force are both costly and uncertain.

Even when the direct use of force is barred among a group of countries, however, military power can still be used politically. Each superpower continues to use the threat of force to deter attacks by other superpowers on itself or its allies; its deterrence ability thus serves an indirect, protective role, which it can use in bargaining on other issues with its allies. [. . .]

Thus, even for countries whose relations approximate complex interdependence, two serious qualifications remain: (1) drastic social and political change could cause force again to become an important direct instrument of policy; and (2) even when elites' interests are complementary, a country that uses military force to protect another may have significant political influence over the other country.

In North-South relations, or relations among Third World countries, as well as in East-West relations, force is often important. Military power helps the Soviet Union to dominate Eastern Europe economically as well as politically. The threat of open or covert American military intervention has helped to limit revolutionary changes in the Caribbean, especially in Guatemala in 1954 and in the Dominican Republic in 1965. Secretary of State Kissinger, in January 1975, issued a veiled warning to members of the Organization of Petroleum Exporting Countries (OPEC) that the United States might use force against them 'where there is some actual strangulation of the industrialized world'.[5]

Even in these rather conflictual situations, however, the recourse to force seems less likely now than at most times during the century before 1945. The destructiveness of nuclear weapons makes any attack against a nuclear power dangerous. Nuclear weapons are mostly used as a deterrent. Threats of nuclear action against much weaker countries may occasionally be efficacious, but they are equally or more likely to solidify relations between one's adversaries. The limited usefulness of conventional force to control socially mobilized populations has been shown by the United States' failure in Vietnam as well as by the rapid decline of colonialism in Africa. Furthermore, employing force on one issue against an independent state with which one has a variety of relationships is likely to rupture mutually profitable relations on other issues. In other words, the use of force often has costly effects on nonsecurity goals. And finally, in Western democracies, popular opposition to prolonged military conflicts is very high. [...]

The Political Processes of Complex Interdependence

The three main characteristics of complex interdependence give rise to distinctive political processes, which translate power resources into power as control of outcomes. As we argued earlier, something is usually lost or added in the translation. Under conditions of complex interdependence the translation will be different than under realist conditions, and our predictions about outcomes will need to be adjusted accordingly.

In the realist world, military security will be the dominant goal of states. It will even affect issues that are not directly involved with military power or territorial defense. Nonmilitary problems will not only be subordinated to military ones; they will be studied for their politico-military implications. Balance of payments issues, for instance, will be considered at least as much in the light of their implications for world power generally as for their purely financial ramifications. McGeorge Bundy conformed to realist expectations when he argued in 1964 that devaluation of the dollar should be seriously considered if necessary to fight the war in Vietnam. To some extent, so did former Treasury Secretary Henry Fowler when he contended in 1971 that the United States needed a trade surplus of $4 billion to $6 billion in order to lead in Western defense.

In a world of complex interdependence, however, one expects some officials, particularly at lower levels, to emphasize the *variety* of state goals that must be pursued. In the absence of a clear hierarchy of issues, goals will vary by issue, and may not be closely related. Each bureaucracy will pursue its own concerns; and although several agencies may reach compromises on issues that affect them all, they will find that a consistent pattern of policy is difficult to maintain. Moreover, transnational actors will introduce different goals into various groups of issues.

Linkage Strategies

Goals will therefore vary by issue area under complex interdependence, but so will the distribution of power and the typical political processes. Traditional analysis focuses on *the* international system, and leads us to anticipate similar political processes on a variety of issues. Militarily and economically strong states will dominate a variety of organizations and a variety of issues, by linking their own policies on some issues to other states' policies on other issues. By using their overall dominance to prevail on their weak issues, the strongest states will, in the traditional model, ensure a congruence between the overall structure of military and economic power and the pattern of outcomes on any one issue area. Thus world politics can be treated as a seamless web.

Under complex interdependence, such congruence is less likely to occur. As military force is devalued, militarily strong states will find it more difficult to use their overall dominance to control outcomes on issues in which they are weak. And since the distribution of power resources in trade, shipping, or oil, for example, may be quite different, patterns of outcomes and distinctive political processes are likely to vary from one set of issues to another. If force were readily applicable, and military security were the highest foreign policy goal, these variations in the issue structures of power would not matter very much. The linkages drawn from them to military issues would ensure consistent dominance by the overall strongest states. But when military force is largely immobilized, strong states will find that linkage is less effective. They may still attempt such links, but in the absence of a hierarchy of issues, their success will be problematic.

Dominant states may try to secure much the same result by using overall economic power to affect results on other issues. If only economic objectives are at stake, they may succeed: money, after all, is fungible. But economic objectives have political implications, and economic linkage by the strong is limited by domestic, transnational, and transgovernmental actors who resist having their interests traded off. Furthermore, the international actors may be different on different issues, and the international organizations in which negotiations take place are often quite separate. Thus it is difficult, for example, to imagine a militarily or economically strong state linking concessions on monetary policy to reciprocal concessions in oceans policy. On the other hand, poor weak states are not similarly inhibited from linking unrelated issues, partly because their domestic interests are less complex. Linkage of unrelated issues is often a means of extracting concessions or side payments from rich and powerful states. And unlike powerful states whose instrument for linkage (military force) is often too costly to use, the linkage instrument used by poor, weak states – international organization – is available and inexpensive.

Thus as the utility of force declines, and as issues become more equal in importance, the distribution of power within each issue will become more important. If linkages become less effective on the whole, outcomes of political bargaining will increasingly vary by issue area. [. . .]

Agenda Setting

Our second assumption of complex interdependence, the lack of clear hierarchy among multiple issues, leads us to expect that the politics of agenda formation and control will become more important. Traditional analyses lead statesmen to focus on politico-military issues and to pay little attention to the broader politics of agenda formation. Statesmen assume that the agenda will be set by shifts in the balance of power, actual or anticipated, and by perceived threats to the security of states. Other issues will only be very important when they seem to affect security and military power. In these cases, agendas will be influenced strongly by considerations of the overall balance of power.

Yet, today, some nonmilitary issues are emphasized in interstate relations at one time, whereas others of seemingly equal importance are neglected or quietly handled at a technical level. International monetary politics, problems of commodity terms of trade, oil, food, and multinational corporations have all been important during the last decade; but not all have been high on interstate agendas throughout that period.

Traditional analysts of international politics have paid little attention to agenda formation: to how issues come to receive sustained attention by high officals. The traditional orientation toward military and security affairs implies that the crucial problems of foreign policy are imposed on states by the actions or threats of other states. These are high politics as opposed to the low politics of economic affairs. Yet, as the complexity of actors and issues in world politics increases, the utility of force declines and the line between domestic policy and foreign policy becomes blurred: as the conditions of complex interdependence are more closely approximated, the politics of agenda formation becomes more subtle and differentiated.

Under complex interdependence we can expect the agenda to be affected by the international and domestic problems created by economic growth and increasing sensitivity interdependence. Discontented domestic groups will politicize issues and force more issues once considered domestic onto the interstate agenda. Shifts in the distribution of power resources within sets of issues will also affect agendas. During the early 1970s the increased power of oil-producing governments over the transnational corporations and the consumer countries dramatically altered the policy agenda. Moreover, agendas for one group of issues may change as a result of linkages from other groups in which power resources are changing; for example, the broader agenda of North-South trade issues changed after the OPEC price rises and the oil embargo of 1973-74. Even if capabilities among states do not change, agendas may be affected by shifts in the importance of transnational actors. The publicity surrounding multi-national corporations in the early 1970s, coupled with their rapid growth over the past twenty years, put the regulation of such corporations higher on both the United Nations agenda and national agendas.

Politicization — agitation and controversy over an issue that tend to raise it to the top of the agenda — can have many sources, as we have seen. Governments whose strength is increasing may politicize issues, by linking them to other issues. An international regime that is becoming ineffective or is not serving important issues may cause increasing politicization, as dissatisfied governments press for change. Politicization, however, can also come from below. Domestic groups may become upset enough to raise a dormant issue, or to interfere with interstate bargaining at high levels. In 1974 the American secretary of state's tacit linkage of a Soviet-American trade pact with progress in detente was upset by the success of domestic American groups working through Congress to link a trade agreement with Soviet policies on emigration.

The technical characteristics and institutional setting in which issues are raised will strongly affect politicization patterns. In the United States, congressional attention is an effective instrument of politicization. Generally, we expect transnational economic organizations and transgovernmental networks of bureaucrats to seek to avoid politicization. Domestically based groups (such as trade unions) and domestically oriented bureaucracies will tend to use politicization (particularly congressional attention) against their transnationally mobile competitors. At the international level, we expect states and actors to 'shop among forums' and struggle to get issues raised in international organizations that will maximize their advantage by broadening or narrowing the agenda.

Transnational and Transgovernmental Relations

Our third condition of complex interdependence, multiple channels of contact among societies, further blurs the distinction between domestic and international politics. The availability of partners in political coalitions is not necessarily limited by national boundaries as traditional analysis assumes. The nearer a situation is to complex interdependence, the more we expect the outcomes of political bargaining to be affected by transnational relations. Multinational corporations may be significant both as independent actors and as instruments manipulated by governments. The attitudes and policy stands of domestic groups are likely to be affected by communications, organized or not, between them and their counterparts abroad.

Thus the existence of multiple channels of contact leads us to expect limits, beyond those normally found in domestic politics, on the ability of statesmen to calculate the manipulation of interdependence or follow a consistent strategy of linkage. Statesmen must consider differential as well as aggregate effects of interdependence strategies and their likely implications for politicization and agenda control. Transactions among societies – economic and social transactions more than security ones – affect groups differently. Opportunities and costs from increased transnational ties may be greater for certain groups – for instance, American workers in the textile or shoe industries – than for others. Some organizations or groups may interact directly with actors in other societies or with other governments to increase their benefits from a network of interaction. Some actors may therefore be less vulnerable as well as less sensitive to changes elsewhere in the network than are others, and this will affect patterns of political action.

The multiple channels of contact found in complex interdependence are not limited to nongovernmental actors. Contacts between governmental bureaucracies charged with similar tasks may not only alter their perspectives but lead to transgovernmental coalitions on particular policy questions. To improve their chances of success, government agencies attempt to bring actors from other governments into their own decision-making processes as allies. Agencies of powerful states such as the United States have used such coalitions to penetrate weaker governments in such countries as Turkey and Chile. They have also been used to help agencies of other governments penetrate the United States bureaucracy. [...]

The existence of transgovernmental policy networks leads to a different interpretation of one of the standard propositions about international politics — that states act in their own interest. Under complex inter-dependence, this conventional wisdom begs two important questions: which self and which interest? A government agency may pursue its own interests under the guise of the national interest; and recurrent inter-actions can change official perceptions of their interests. As a careful study of the politics of United States trade policy has documented, concentrating only on pressures of various interests for decisions leads to an overly mechanistic view of a continuous process and neglects the important role of communications in slowly changing perceptions of self-interest.[6]

The ambiguity of the national interest raises serious problems for the top political leaders of governments. As bureaucracies contact each other directly across national borders (without going through foreign offices), centralized control becomes more difficult. There is less assurance that the state will be united when dealing with foreign governments or that its components will interpret national interests similarly when negotiating with foreigners. The state may prove to be multifaceted, even schizo-phrenic. National interests will be defined differently on different issues, at different times, and by different governmental units. States that are better placed to maintain their coherence (because of a centralized political tradition such as France's) will be better able to manipulate uneven inter-dependence than fragmented states that at first glance seem to have more resources in an issue area.

[Keohane and Nye go on to discuss the implications of complex inter-dependence for the roles of international organizations in agenda setting and coalition building. (See Selection 2.8 in this volume for fuller dis-cussion.) They offer the table printed below as a summary of their discussion and the distinctions that they offer between realism and complex inter-dependence as ideal types.]

Notes
   1. Hans J. Morgenthau, *Politics Among Nations: The Struggle for Power and Peace*, 4th edn (Knopf, New York, 1967), p. 36.
   2. See Edward L. Morse, 'Transnational Economic Processes', in Robert O. Keohane and Joseph S. Nye, Jr (eds), *Transnational Relations and World Politics* (Harvard University Press, Cambridge, Mass., 1972).
   3. Henry A. Kissinger, 'A New National Partnership', *Department of State Bulletin* (17 February 1975), p. 199.
   4. *New York Times*, 22 May 1975.
   5. *Business Week*, 13 January 1975.
   6. Raymond Bauer, Ithiel de Sola Pool and Lewis Dexter, *American Business and Foreign Policy* (Atherton, New York, 1963), Ch. 35, especially pp. 472-5.

Table 1: Political Processes under Conditions of Realism and Complex Interdependence

	Realism	Complex Interdependence
Goals of actors	Military security will be the dominant goal.	Goals of states will vary by issue area. Transgovernmental politics will make goals difficult to define. Transnational actors will pursue their own goals.
Instruments of state policy	Military force will be most effective, although economic and other instruments will also be used.	Power resources specific to issue areas will be most relevant. Manipulation of interdependence, international organizations, and transnational actors will be major instruments.
Agenda formation	Potential shifts in the balance of power and security threats will set the agenda in high politics and will strongly influence other agendas.	Agenda will be affected by changes in the distribution of power resources within issue areas; the status of international regimes; changes in the importance of transnational actors; linkages from other issues and politicization as a result of rising sensitivity interdependence.
Linkages of issues	Linkages will reduce differences in outcomes among issue areas and reinforce international hierarchy.	Linkages by strong states will be more difficult to make since force will be ineffective. Linkages by weak states through international organizations will erode rather than reinforce hierarchy.
Roles of international organizations	Roles are minor, limited by state power and the importance of military force.	Organizations will set agendas, induce coalition-formation, and act as arenas for political action by weak states. Ability to choose the organizational forum for an issue and to mobilize votes will be an important political resource.

DISSOLVING INTERNATIONAL POLITICS: REFLECTIONS ON THE NATION-STATE

Wolfram F. Hanrieder

Source: *The American Political Science Review*, vol. 72, no. 4 (American Political Science Association, 1978) pp. 1276-87.

Hanrieder contrasts the dramatic increase in the role and power of the state in the domestic arena with the growth in restraints imposed upon state activity in the international arena. He suggests that the result has been a domestication of international politics, in which security issues have diminished in salience and economic issues have increased in frequency and intensity. This has not, however, undermined the nation-state but served to underline its continuing vitality.

Two distinctive forces act on the modern nation-state, and through it, on contemporary international politics. On the one hand, the welfare demands of its citizens have pushed the modern nation-state toward a peak of power and activity unprecedented in its 300-year history. Whatever a country's institutional arrangements, stages of economic growth, or ideological preferences may be, remedies for the economic and social problems of the individual are sought in public policy and collective action. Politics has become the primary arena for the redistribution of income, status and other public satisfactions. Politics everywhere extends into wider areas, touching upon aspects of public and private life that in the past have escaped governmental scrutiny as well as governmental solicitude. The modern state is pervasive in its activities; assertive of its prerogatives; and powerful in what it can give, take or withhold.

On the other hand, the power of the state, although obtrusive and dominant in its domestic context, appears compromised in rather novel ways in its international context — in part because of the restraints imposed by the nuclear balance of terror, and in part because the domestic power of the state can be sustained only through international economic cooperation and political accommodation. In order to meet its responsibilities for mass social and economic welfare, the modern state is compelled to interact with other states in ways which, although not lacking in conflict and competition, demand cooperation, acceptance of the logic of interdependence and a willingness to condone restraints on state behavior and sovereign prerogatives. Internal state power is sustained by external cooperation.

These two forces acting on the nation-state carry with them conflicting as well as complementary implications about the nature of the contemporary international system; and they lead to questions about the balance between independent and interdependent state activities, between security concerns and welfare concerns, between conflict and cooperation, and between domestic and international politics.

Nationalism and the Contemporary International System

The assertive character of the nation-state is reflected in a 'new nationalism', a phenomenon that has a deep impact on global politics. The forces of nationalism, aside from the inhibitions created by the nuclear balance, have proved to be the major restraint placed upon the conduct of the superpowers in the period after World War II. In their attempt to create a world order congenial to their ideological preferences or to their national interests, both the United States and the Soviet Union have had to contend with the stubborn appeal of nationalism, inside as well as outside of their respective alliances. The fissures appearing in both the North Atlantic Treaty Organization and the Warsaw Treaty Organization during the last two decades are in large part attributable to the resistance of secondary alliance members to making their policies conform to the guidelines set forth by their alliance superpower. In many instances, this resistance is based not so much on ideological grounds — nationalism as a counter-ideology to international ideologies — but on pragmatic considerations which suggest that differences among national socioeconomic, cultural and political circumstances warrant different definitions of the public good and require divergent paths toward its realization. The 'new nationalism', although not lacking in emotional overtones, is supported by rational calculations on how to further the national interest within global and regional configurations of power in which the superpowers still exert an overwhelming measure of influence. Nor are these calculations directed solely toward the superpowers. Secondary powers engage in competitive nationalism among themselves, especially in regional ventures such as the European Economic Community where conflicting interests rub against one another abrasively precisely because they are packed together closely.

National divergencies continue to resist attempts to streamline and coordinate policies within alliances. Both the United States and the Soviet

Union have responded to 'deviationists' within their alliances with a good deal of exasperation; and both have sought to contain the centrifugal forces within their spheres of influence as much as possible, although in practical terms they have dealt differently with challenges to their hegemony. [. . .]

The Domestication of International Politics

Nationalism, then, is alive and well. Far from being secondary or obsolete, the nation-state, nationalism, and the idea of the national interest are central elements in contemporary world politics. The international system has remained an interstate system in many of its essential features. At the same time equally powerful forces are at work which have modified the role of the nation-state, broadening its capacity to shape events in some respects, narrowing it in others. These forces are in part the result of the changing nature of the nation-state itself and in part the result of new ways in which nation-states interact. They are developments which go to the roots of the perennial preoccupations of the state: welfare and security.

The meaning of national welfare and the approaches toward its achievement are profoundly affected by the major change in the nation-state that I mentioned at the beginning: its growing responsiveness to the revolution of rising expectations or, as Daniel Bell calls it in a somewhat sharper term, the 'revolution of rising entitlement'.[1] Modern governments have become increasingly sensitive to demands for a wide variety of welfare services and have taken on responsibility for mass social and economic welfare. The improvement through state intervention of the material (and perhaps even psychological) well-being of its citizens has become one of the central functions of state activity. The satisfaction of rising claims by citizens has become a major source of the state's legitimation and of a government's continuance in office.

This has led to an intensive flow of interactions, of social demand-and-supply communications between the state and society, through which politics and the bureaucracy rather than the market have become the major agents for social change and the redistribution of wealth and power. But the demands which are generated and processed through these 'vertical' interactions on the domestic level can be satisfied only by extensive commercial, monetary and technological interactions on the international level. Three types of processes are available for this purpose. There are the 'horizontal' interactions among the units of world politics, on the government-to-government level, which take place in bilateral as well as multilateral settings. This is the stuff of traditional international politics. There are 'lateral' interactions, also called 'transnational', which are the society-to-society dealings across national boundaries among subnational groups and organizations, such as multinational corporations, international banks, export-import firms, professional organizations, coordinating and consultative arrangements among national political parties, labor unions, guerrilla organizations, and so forth. (Although the participants in this type of transaction are 'private' or 'semi-public', their juridical and political status differs from country to country — a point to which I shall return later.) Another type of interaction is 'integrative', involving supranational processes (such as those of the European Economic Community) which are institutionalized and have to some extent diminished national prerogatives. [. . .]

These processes of interaction are interdependent — that is to say they are a system — and they perform a variety of functions, most prominently those of welfare and security. They are the structures through which governments perform a variety of functions; they are the ways in which state and society seek to arrange their domestic and foreign environment. But even in a highly interdependent global system national governments have ample discretion as to what structures, what types of interactions, they wish to employ for performing certain functions. To put it more precisely: the choice of one structure over another is determined as much by internal ideological, institutional, and political orthodoxies as it is by external necessities. Most trading relationships in the industrialized non-communist parts of the world are handled in transnational processes, with national governments deciding how 'private' the enterprise system is allowed to be; in communist countries international trade is a state activity. Security issues everywhere are traditionally processed on the international, government-to-government level; as are such important economic issues as formal currency devaluations and tariff policies. Supranational processes, as exemplified in the European Economic Community, tend to be limited to essentially economic interactions.

In what follows, I shall try to demonstrate that the bulk of today's global political processes are of a kind that are typical of and approximate domestic political processes, leading to the 'domestication' of international politics; and that, contrary to the expectations of functionalists and other theorists, it is not a new type of international politics which is 'dissolving' the traditional nation-state but a new nation-state which is 'dissolving' traditional international politics.

Five aspects of the contemporary global political system have a bearing on my argument. First, interdependence requires a permissive context; it is possible only in a type of international system that allows it. 'Liberalization' of trade and money flows, minimal interference with transnational investment activities, absence of protectionism, and other 'liberal' economic preferences — as well as the political purposes and ideological justifications connected with them — are prerequisites for a highly interdependent political and economic system. Although it is technology that has shrunk the world, politics has kept it that way. International economic systems, as much as military-strategic and political systems, reflect the influence and interests of their predominant members. [. . .]

Second, although domestic demands can be satisfied only by intense participation in international or transnational activities — providing governments with powerful incentives to cooperate with one another — nationalism nonetheless can thrive in a context of interdependence just as interdependence can survive competing nationalisms. Richard Rosecrance and Arthur Stein suggest that

> under the stimulus of economic nationalism . . . nations may occasionally act against the multilateral framework . . . Nationalism might have been expected to reduce interdependence. It might be argued that, if nations seek only to achieve their own goals without reference to the rest of the system, the linkage between units must decline. If nationalistic goals depend on supportive actions by other members of the international community, however, nationalism cannot be achieved in isolation. Not only does interdependence not decline in such circumstances, aggressive nationalism may lead to higher negative interdependence. The greater nationalism of the twentieth century therefore need not entail a reduction of interdependence.[2]

A third point is that in an interdependent system, whether global or regional, domestic political conflicts over the redistribution of wealth and power may extend into the transnational, supranational, or international context. This affects the disposition of issues. Schattschneider says: 'The outcome of all conflict is determined by the *scope* of its contagion. The number of people involved in any conflict determines what happens; every change in the number of participants, every increase or reduction in the number of participants affects the result.'[3] Whether the constituency for conflict resolution is enlarged in an interdependent system depends on the extent to which national governments permit transnational and supranational processes to take place. If these processes are curtailed by governmental restrictions, the scope of conflict remains localized, with the government acting as the gatekeeper between internal and external demand flows.

The same process can work in reverse. Political conflict may be projected not only from the domestic onto the international scene but international conflicts over redistribution of income may be projected onto domestic political scenes. National governments have always been at the fulcrum where foreign and domestic politics meet, where conflicting pressures have to be weighed and adjusted, where the perennial scarcity of resources requires hard choices and rank-ordering of priorities. Governments have to manage two interlocking processes of redistribution of power, influence, and wealth. In most contemporary societies, the government engages in a continuing process of redistributing domestic power and wealth. It does so whether it is an 'activist' government or whether it is content to let 'market forces' make the redistribution. A redistribution takes place in either case. By not acting, the government also acts. At the same time a national government is confronted with a continuous redistributive process in the international system, a constantly shifting configuration of power. In states where the national government allows or encourages a wide range of transnational 'private' interactions — where the government partially forswears the role of gatekeeper between internal and external environment — international redistributive processes reach into national redistributive processes more easily because they are not checked by governmental interposition.

As a result, and this is my fourth point, a new convergence of international and domestic political processes is under way in the industrialized noncommunist parts of the world, with consequences that are most likely irreversible but are neither fully understood nor perhaps fully acceptable. In some major respects, governments find it increasingly difficult, or meaningless, to distinguish between foreign policy and domestic policy. Nowhere is this more clearly visible and institutionalized than in the operations of regional international organizations that are endowed with some measure of supranational authority, however limited. It is difficult to distinguish between domestic and foreign policy in an institution whose policies have consequences that cannot be assessed in terms of either purely external or purely internal consequences. But the fusion of domestic and foreign policy takes place even in the absence of supranational processes; it reflects a process in which the traditional boundaries separating the nation-state from the environing international system are becoming increasingly obscured and permeable.

The fifth point, which is of central importance, is that security issues have diminished in salience relative to economic issues. Although security can become a question of national survival in the nuclear age — and in that sense is unsurpassed in importance — a noticeable shift of emphasis has taken place in world politics, away from the primacy of military-strategic elements of power toward the primacy of economic elements. For one, the likelihood of invasions and direct military aggression has receded, especially in areas which are basically unattractive objects of physical aggression and territorial occupation. Except in parts of the non-industrialized world and in the Middle East, territorial revisions are not a pressing issue in modern international politics. A number of years ago, John Herz argued that for centuries the major attribute of the nation-state was its 'territoriality': its identification with an area that was surrounded by a 'wall of defensibility' and hence relatively impermeable to outside penetration. This territoriality was bound to vanish, so Herz argued, largely because of developments in the means of destruction, such as nuclear weapons, which made even the most powerful nation-state subject to being permeated.[4] Although Herz later modified his views on the future of the nation-state,[5] his argument on the changed meaning and importance of territoriality was clearly valid.

The diminishing salience of territorial issues, the restraints imposed by the nuclear balance, and the day-to-day realities of economic interdependence have changed the meaning of power in global politics. Access rather than acquisition, presence rather than rule, penetration rather than possession have become the important issues. Often one gains the impression that negotiations over such technical questions as arms control, trade agreements, technology transfers, and monetary reform are not only attempts at problem-solving but also re-examinations of the meaning and sources of power in the last third of this century. Many military-strategic and economic issues are at bottom political issues couched in technical terms.

This has led a number of analysts to argue that 'low politics' has replaced 'high politics' as the stuff of international politics. There is a good deal of truth in this; and the distinction is a useful one although it should be sharpened. For one, the dichotomy between 'high' and 'low' politics, between the pursuit of security and power (the dramatic-political-intangible) and the pursuit of welfare and affluence (the economic-incremental-tangible) can be overdrawn. Karl Kaiser was correct when he suggested a number of years ago that what political actors view as either high or low politics depends on specific circumstances, changes over time, and in any case may be different from country to country.[6] Also, there is a difference between high and low politics that has not been sufficiently stressed and that is pertinent to my argument: power, security and defense commodities are indivisible, and hence less subject to the redistributive aspects of political processes, whereas welfare issues are divisible and at the very core of redistribution politics. Goals such as power and security are public goods and subject to the calculus of relative gain. Goals pertaining to welfare, economics and 'profit' are private goods and can be assessed with respect to absolute gain. To put it another way: high politics pertains to indivisible collective goods whereas low politics pertains to divisible private goods.

In combination, the five features of global politics that I have enumerated suggest that international politics is subject to a process of 'domestication'. In particular, the more international political processes concentrate on activities that are distributive the more they resemble traditional domestic political processes. This development is fed from two sources, as I have tried to demonstrate. On the one hand, the diminishing salience of security issues relative to economic issues narrows the area of 'high' nondistributive politics and enlarges the area of 'low' distributive politics. At the same time, distributive processes have increased in frequency as well as in intensity — nationally as well as internationally and transnationally. It isn't so much that welfare issues have emerged as high politics, as some authors would suggest, but rather that distributive political processes have gained in relative importance, and that the mounting demands generated within a society cannot be satisfied without recourse to international and transnational processes. As governments rely on external transactions to meet domestic demands, distributive politics on the international and national levels have become intermingled, leading to a fusion of domestic and foreign policy in the area of distributive politics. In order for this to happen, both international and domestic circumstances must be appropriate. The international system must be sufficiently stable, predictable, and permissive for extensive transnational processes to take place; and national political systems must feature political, institutional, and ideological attitudes that accept these processes.

It is precisely the domestication of international politics which sustains (and demonstrates) the vitality of the nation-state. By extending domestic political processes and their corresponding attitudes into the international environment, the nation-state has eroded traditional aspects of international politics. Many analysts in the postwar period perceived the major change in international political, economic, and strategic processes to come from a gradual weakening of the nation-state. Transnational and international processes were expected to modify the nation-state. Modern international politics was to dissolve the nation-state. What has happened, however, is that the modern nation-state has 'dissolved' a certain type of international politics as the importance of nondistributive processes diminished relative to distributive processes.

This is not to deny the continuing importance of security issues and the extensive residual of traditional international politics that is still visible in global processes. The contemporary international system is a mix of traditional and novel processes, and its essence lies in the dialectic relationship between the old and the new. This dialectic is reflected in what has happened to the idea of the 'national interest'. The concept of the national interest is, practically by definition, an idea based on nondistributive, indivisible values, enjoyed by society as a whole: security, prestige, territoriality, political advantages sought in manipulating the balance of power, and so forth. In short: the idea of the national interest is synonymous with 'high' politics. As international politics becomes more 'domesticated', the policy areas covered by the concept of the national interest become more narrow and ambiguous. Distributive values, unlike nondistributive values, are not shared equally by all segments of society. Since the idea of the nation-state and the national interest have been used in an almost symbiotic sense, at least in traditional parlance, it seems ironic that while the salience of the nation-state has been enhanced, for the reasons enumerated, the analytical usefulness of the term 'national interest' has been seriously diminished.

[Hanrieder suggests that the 'domesticated' international system does not correspond to either the Chinese or the Soviet view of the state, nor to the type of domestic politics found in the Third World. Rather, it matches the kind of politics that operate within the Western industrialized societies. To illustrate this point, he considers the case of European integration and the relation between the United States and her partners in Western Europe.]

Coordination of Politics and the Nation-State

From the beginning of European integration and of the coordinating features of the Atlantic alliance, two contradictory processes (at times of unequal intensity) have been visible: a process of divergence and a process of integration. These contradictory trends have been analyzed in a long series of academic publications, and a review of this literature, as well as of the public debate about the issues themselves, need not detain us here. One might suggest, however, that the processes of 'coordination' of policies among nation-states in the European and Atlantic communities occupy a middle ground between the tendencies toward divergence and the tendencies toward integration. A spectrum of policies and attitudes emerges that goes from divergence to 'parallelism' to coordination to integration, ranging from minimal cooperation to maximal institutional collaboration.

All members of the European and Atlantic communities have at different times, for different reasons, and on different issues, pursued all four categories of policies. There are a number of well-known examples of policy divergencies as well as of integrative processes: de Gaulle's decision to remove France from the unified command structure of NATO (as well as other Gaullist foreign policy projects) is an example of policy divergence, whereas the establishment of the European Community is an example of an integrative type of policy.

Located as they are at the two extremes of the divergence-parallelism-coordination-integration spectrum, such examples tend to be the most dramatic. It seems to me, however, that the more pressing issues in transatlantic and intra-European processes are located in the middle ground of the spectrum, in the areas of parallelism and coordination.

There is no question that in many important respects the political systems of Western Europe have become more and more alike. But parallelism has not impelled them toward more integrative structures but, at best, toward more coordination of national policies. This is so not only because of internal domestic obstacles but also because each member of the European Community has a distinctly different relationship with the United States.

But at the same time governments must employ horizontal and encourage lateral transactions in order to satisfy the vertical demands pressed upon them by their electorates, which can be ignored only at the risk of being removed from office. It is primarily for this reason that the coordination of policies has become a central issue in intra-European as well as transatlantic relationships. Parallel developments, the similarity of domestic problems and of public demands, require some measure of international and transnational cooperation. But since the intensification of integration is unacceptable to many members of the European Community for a variety of reasons, coordination appears to be the only alternative. Policy coordination has become a substitute for integration.

Should the Community be enlarged in the next few years, the prospects for deeper integration become even more remote. But there is a question right now whether there exist compelling economic and monetary reasons for giving community institutions more power, or whether it is sufficient to solidify and streamline them. As Leon Lindberg and Stuart Scheingold have pointed out several years ago[7], important industrial and commercial interests in the Community are interested primarily in sustaining the present level of integration, seeing their interests adequately served by the status quo and shying away from the uncertainties and readjustments which attend changes in the scope and intensity of supranational arrangements.

Solidification and rationalization rather than intensification is the key phrase here — and the trend is as pronounced now as it was years ago. The 'expansive logic of sector integration', as Ernst Haas called it, seems to have turned into the 'status quo logic of sector integration', a logic which welcomes the existing measure of integration but turns to coordination for solving new problems rather than go beyond it. [. . .]

The possibilities for coordination are uneven in the area of indivisible goods, such as security issues and 'high politics' foreign policy issues. The Western stance at the European Security Conference was fairly well coordinated, but this was so in large part because West Germany's *Ostpolitik* and the resulting treaty arrangements had already resolved issues that were vital to the Soviet Union and Eastern Europe. A coordinated European foreign policy is as remote now as it has ever been; and it is difficult to imagine events that would push the Community in that direction, especially in a decade in which governments are less inclined to pursue grandiose schemes for global and regional power rearrangements than in the 1960s.

Coordination on security issues is a particularly instructive example, for here one must distinguish between security as an end — which may be an 'indivisible' product for an alliance as well as for a nation-state — and the means with which that end is achieved (say, weapons procurement) which can be a highly divisible commodity. Whether security is indivisible in the Western alliance, and in its regional European NATO component, is an uncertainty that has plagued NATO for almost two decades. With the institutionalization of strategic nuclear 'parity' and 'equivalence' in the SALT accords, Washington's European NATO partners (and especially the Federal Republic) can hardly feel reassured about the willingness of the United States to meet a conventional attack with a nuclear response. It is still the central paradox of NATO strategy that in dealing with the Soviet Union the United States must implicitly recognize strategic parity whereas a convincing extension of American nuclear protection to Europe implies American superiority. Were it not for the fact that direct military aggression is highly unlikely, the fissures within NATO would be wider and deeper than they are. As it is, the issue has been swept under the rug, and when it tends to reappear — which happens whenever the Europeans see or imagine reasons to question American resolve — the rug is simply moved to cover it up again. [. . .]

Highly divisible aspects of security policy — weapons procurement, weapons standardization, cost-sharing arrangements, and so forth — make coordination much more difficult. The same is true in energy policy and raw materials policy, because high politics tends to mingle with low politics along the lines I have redefined these terms earlier.

Aside from conflicting interests, the obstacles to policy coordination stem from differences among national styles of problem solving and decision making. Even if the problems and their apparent solutions were the same in different countries (which they are not), there would be different ways of approaching them. In each country there are entrenched administrative practices that are unique and that resist international or transnational coordination. While the bureaucratic instinct may be universal and timeless, it cannot be stripped totally of its local historical and institutional context. Equally important, in each country powerful juridical, political and ideological traditions have developed which circumscribe the proper role of government in the economy and society — to use a simple phrase for a highly complex reality. These traditions, and their structural manifestations, are different in different countries. The differences are especially pertinent in policy processes that are distributive rather than nondistributive; they appear in their starkest form in welfare concerns rather than in security concerns. Although governments everywhere are pressured to direct the solution of economic and social problems, their impulses and capacities to act are energized and inhibited in different ways. [. . .]

Nationalism and Interdependence

The processes I have described reflect a dialectic of independence and interdependence. In advancing their interests, governments and subgovernmental groups, society as well as the state, have brought about interdependence. Interdependence is sustained because these interest calculations do not allow the disintegration of interdependence toward a more fragmented and contentious international system but neither propel it toward more integration and supranationality. Interdependence, and the coordination required for its operation, is a halfway house between disintegration and integration of political and economic processes. Interdependence is the prototypical phenomenon of an international system that derives its dynamics from the pursuit of the national interest as well as of interests that are narrower and larger than the national interest.

It must be stressed again that the term 'national interest' in this context is ambiguous and can be misleading. Distributive goods, which are the bulk of interdependence processes, are not shared equally by all segments of society as is the case with nondistributive goods, such as security. If we cannot even properly apply the term 'national interest', with its rationalistic overtones, it would appear to be even more misleading to use the term 'nationalism', with its emotive, irrational and atavistic implications — implications that correspond much more to the nation-state concept that we see as being eroded by various permeative processes. The concept of nationalism is analytically outdated, focusing as it does on an irrelevant view of territoriality and carrying with it the assumption that the nation, incorporated by its people, represents an organic whole. In short, the terminology of nationalism is inappropriate precisely because it rests on the notion of indivisible values and the corresponding idea of 'high politics', at a time when most day-to-day political and economic processes are of the divisible kind.

I am aware of the paradox of having stated earlier that 'nationalism is alive and well', and suggesting now the inapplicability of the term itself. But there is a difference between a concept and a sentiment. The idea of the 'nation' as a communal organization still elicits feelings of commitment and hence enriches public life. This 'psychological' nationalism should perhaps be viewed as a quest for continuity when traditional values are changing and the possibilities for identification with a larger purpose are diminishing. The secularization of both theological and political ideologies brings with it an agnostic pragmatism which provides little more than a utilitarian view of public life. The theme of the 'end of ideology', tattered as it is, still explains a good deal.

Interdependence also narrows the opportunities for national self-identification. The contours of a national identity become nebulous precisely because the interests and values advanced in processes of interdependence cannot be unequivocally defined and experienced in national terms. In part they continue to be national, but they are at the same time larger and smaller — global as well as municipal, cosmopolitan as well as provincial. The nation-state, the social and cultural environment within which most citizens continue to define their spiritual and material well-being, has become deficient in providing that well-being — at the very least in its material sense, but most likely in a spiritual sense as well. Governments, in seeking to meet the demands pressed upon them by their electorates, are compelled to turn to external sources in order to meet these demands. But their reluctance to opt either for divergence or for integration places them in an area of ambiguity where coordination appears as the reasonable as well as the necessary course of action. And yet the obstacles to coordination arise from the differences among industrialized societies and their governmental structures, although the needs that coordination is intended to meet are common and widely shared.

Notes

1. Daniel Bell, 'The Future World Disorder: The Structural Context of Crises', *Foreign Policy*, 27 (1977), pp. 109-35.

2. R. Rosecrance and A. Stein, 'Interdependence: myth or reality?', *World Politics*, XXVI (1973), pp. 1-27.

3. E.E. Schattschneider, *The Semi-Sovereign People* (Holt, Rinehart and Winston, New York, 1964), p. 2.

4. John H. Herz, 'The Rise and Demise of the Territorial State', *World Politics*, IX (1957), pp. 473-93.

5. John H. Herz, 'The Territorial State Revisited — Reflections on the Future of the Nation-State', *Polity*, 1 (1968), pp. 11-34.

6. Karl Kaiser, 'The U.S. and the EEC in the Atlantic System: The Problem of Theory', *Journal of Common Market Studies*, 5 (1967), pp. 338-425.

7. Leon N. Lindberg and Stuart A. Scheingold, *Europe's Would-Be Polity* (Prentice-Hall, Englewood Cliffs, NJ, 1970).

THE TRANSFORMATION OF FOREIGN POLICIES: MODERNIZATION, INTERDEPENDENCE AND EXTERNALIZATION

Edward L. Morse

Source: *World Politics*, vol. XXII, no. 3 (Princeton University Press, 1970), pp. 371-92.

Morse argues that the process of modernization has altered the character of foreign policy in three ways. It has effectively broken down the classical distinction between foreign and domestic policy; it has changed the balance between 'high' and 'low' policies in favour of the latter; and it has significantly reduced the level of control that any state can exercise in the domestic or the international arena.

Foreign policy has been radically transformed by the revolutionary processes of modernization not only in the societies composing the Atlantic region, but wherever high levels of modernization exist. There is a quality about modernization that dissolves the effects of what have generally been considered the major determinants of foreign policy, whether these determinants are based on ideology and type of political system (democratic versus totalitarian foreign policies, for example), or power and capability (great-power versus small-power policies). Wherever modernized societies exist, their foreign policies are more similar to each other than they are to the foreign policies of nonmodernized societies, regardless of the scale of the society or its type of government.

Both the international and the domestic settings in which foreign policies are formulated and conducted are subjected to continual and revolutionary transformation once high levels of modernization exist. Internationally, modernization is accompanied by increased levels and types of interdependencies among national societies. Domestically, it is associated with increased centralization of governmental institutions and governmental decision-making as well as with increased priorities for domestic rather than for external needs.

As a result of these transformations, three general sets of conditions have developed. First, the ideal and classical distinctions between foreign and domestic affairs have broken down, even though the myths associated with sovereignty and the state have not. Second, the distinction between 'high policies' (those associated with security and the continued existence of the state) and 'low policies' (those pertaining to the wealth and welfare of the citizens) has become less important as low policies have assumed an increasingly large role in any society. Third, although there have been significant developments in the instrumentalities of political control, the actual ability to control events either internal or external to modernized societies — even those that are Great Powers — has decreased with the growth of interdependence, and is likely to decrease further.

Modernization and Foreign Policy

[. . .] The general characteristics of modernized societies include the growth of knowledge about and control over the physical environment; increased political centralization, accompanied by the growth of specialized bureaucratic organizations and by the politicization of the masses; the production of economic surpluses and wealth generalized over an entire population; urbanization; and the psychological adjustment to change and the fleeting, rather than acceptance of the static and permanent.

The achievement of high levels of modernization has also been associated with the growth of nationalism and the idealization of the nation-state as the basic political unit. The consolidation of the nation-state, however, is the central political enigma of contemporary international affairs, for modernization has also been accompanied by transnational structures that cannot be subjected to the control of isolated national political bodies. These structures exist in the military field, where security in the nuclear age has everywhere become increasingly a function of activities pursued outside the state's borders. They also exist in the economic field, where the welfare not only of the members of various societies, but of the societies themselves, increasingly relies upon the maintenance of stable commercial and monetary arrangements that are independent of any single national government.

The confrontation of the political structures that have developed along the lines of the nation-state with these transnational activities is one of the most significant features of contemporary international politics. Modernization has resulted in the integration of individual national societies, which face problems that can be solved in isolation with decreasing reliability. In other words, modernization has transformed not only the domestic setting in which foreign policy is formulated; by creating higher levels of interdependence among the diverse national societies, it has also transformed the general structures of international society.

Foreign and Domestic Politics

The fundamental distinction that breaks down under modernization is between foreign and domestic policies, at least in ideal terms. This distinction is much more characteristic of the foreign policies of nonmodernized societies in both ideal and actual terms than it is of modernized states. In modernized societies, it is difficult to maintain because both predominantly political and predominantly nonpolitical interactions take place across societies at high levels, and because transnational phenomena are so significant that either territorial and political or the jurisdictional boundaries are extremely difficult to define. The whole constellation of activities associated with modernization blurs the distinction so that an observer must analyze carefully any interaction in order to ascertain in what ways it pertains to foreign and domestic affairs.

[. . .] Foreign policy has been thought to differ from domestic policy in its ends (the national interest as opposed to particular interests), its means (any means that can be invoked to achieve the ends, as opposed to domestically 'legitimate' means), and its target of operation (a decentralized, anarchic milieu over which the state in question maintains little control, as opposed to a centralized domestic order in which the state has a monopoly of the instruments of social order). Whether the substance of the distinction stresses domestic or foreign affairs, the separation of the two has a strong empirical foundation. Levels of interdependence among all nonmodernized societies were generally so low that governments could take independent actions either domestically or abroad with fairly little likelihood that much spillover between them would take place. The instruments used to implement either domestic or foreign policies had effects on either that were in normal terms negligible. The 'externalities' generated by either domestic or foreign policies did not significantly alter policies in other fields.

This is not to say that domestic factors did not affect foreign policy at all, nor that the general international setting did not affect the substance of policies. What it does suggest is that the normative distinction between foreign and domestic activities was quite well matched by actual conditions. The degrees to which they did not coincide led to debates about ways to improve the efficacy of foreign or domestic policies, or about their goals. But the degree of divergence was not so great as to call the distinction into question.

Regardless of how the distinction is made, it breaks down once societies become fairly modernized. This does not mean, as Friedrich has argued, that 'foreign and domestic policy in developed Western systems constitutes today a seamless web'.[1] Distinctions along the analytic lines I have suggested above still obtain, and governments still formulate policies with a predominant external or internal orientation. But foreign and other policies formulated under modern conditions affect each other in ways that are not salient in nonmodernized or premodernized societies and that derive from both the domestic and international interdependencies associated with modernization. They also derive from the increased scope of governmental activites under modern conditions. Before the Western societies became highly modernized, for example, the major part of government expenditures was devoted to foreign affairs, which was the central concern of government. As the role of the government in the economy and in domestic social life increases, concern for foreign affairs must decrease relative to concern for domestic affairs. In addition, as a result of growing international interdependencies, the external and internal consequences of domestic and foreign policies become more significant, and consequences that are not intended and that may or may not be recognized tend also to increase. Therefore, undesirable policy-consequences also increase. [. . .]

The linkages between domestic and foreign policies constitute the basic characteristic of the breakdown in the distinction between foreign and domestic affairs in the modernized, interdependent international system. This statement does not imply that foreign and domestic policies are indistinguishable; for with regard to articulated goals and problems of implementation, they remain separate. Rather, it is suggestive of the ways in which foreign policies are transformed by the processes of modernization and the development of high levels of interdependence. These processes have put an end to the normative distinctions asserting the primacy of the one or the other. They also overshadow the empirical distinction according to which foreign policies vary in type with the political institutions in which they are formulated.

The Dynamics of Foreign Policies in Modernized Societies

[. . .]

A. The Transformation of Policy Objectives. Preoccupation with high policies and traditional foreign policy objectives and instrumentalities has drawn the attention of scholars away from the changes in policy goals that have accompanied modernization, and specifically from the increased salience of low policies and the merging of goals of power and goals of plenty.

Two general transformations associated with high levels of modernization are responsible for this change. One pertains to the classical instruments of policy, armaments and weapons, and the changes brought about in external goals by the development of nuclear weapons and their delivery systems. The other is related to more general transformations of domestic society.

The effects of nuclear weapons on national external goals have received far greater attention than have the effects of the transformation of domestic society. This one-sided attention is a result of the preoccupation with high policies and serves to obscure more radical changes in policy objectives. It is also related to the assumption that even with the development of nuclear weapons systems *plus ça change, plus c'est la même chose*, or that neither military nor economic interdependence has grown in recent years, but that they may even have diminished considerably. The development of nuclear weapons has had a cross-cutting effect. On the one hand, it makes the territorial state incapable of providing defense and security, by creating the first truly global international system unified by the possibility of generating unacceptable levels of human destruction. On the other hand, nuclear weapons are also said to reaffirm the viability of the nation-state as a political unit, by providing its absolute defense by deterrence.[2]

In any case, the key to the obsolescence of territorial goals that accompanied the development of nuclear weapons is the increased cost of territorial accretion. No modernized state can afford it. It is therefore no accident that major territorial disputes have disappeared from relations among the highly modernized states and now can occur where there is no danger that nuclear weapons will be used and, therefore, accompany nation-building efforts only in the nonmodernized societies. Modernized societies are involved in major territorial disputes only when these disputes also involve a nonmodernized society as well, as in the case of the Sino-Soviet border. Territoriality decreases in importance even further as alliances become less useful. Requisites for American security, once consisting of territorial bases encircling the Soviet bloc, have changed tremendously with the hardening of missiles and the development of Polaris and Poseidon submarines. [. . .]

Rapid domestic economic growth, one of the prime indices of modernization, has a profound effect on both the relative priority of domestic and foreign goals and on the substance of each. Once economic growth sets in as a continuous, dynamic process, the value of accretion of territory and population dwindles and the 'domestic savings and investment and advancement of education, science, and technology are [seen as] the most profitable means and the most secure avenues to the attainment of wealth and welfare'.[3] The logic of economic growth, in other words, turns men's minds away from the external goals associated with the ruling groups of early modern Europe and toward the further development of domestic wealth by domestic means and under conditions of peace.

Domestic economic growth, like the creation of nuclear weapons, offers only a partial explanation of the transformation of foreign policy goals. In addition, the salience of low policies and the expansion of conflictual, zero-sum relations to cooperative strategies result also from transnational structures associated with the modernization and the interdependencies that have developed among the modernized states. Low policies, in this sense, derive from the interactions of citizens in various states and from the actions of governments in the interests of their citizens or their responses to private group behavior in order to assure general stability and the achievement of other goals. These goals are themselves undermined by the scope of nongovernmental transnational and international interchanges and may also be predominantly domestic and pertain to welfare and social services.

Another aspect of the increased salience of low policies pertains to the interests of governments in building new transnational structures in order to achieve both international and domestic goals. For example, one of the motivations for creating a common market in Europe has been the increased wealth it would bring to the citizens of each member-state as a result of increased levels of trade. It is for this reason that one principal characteristic of foreign policies under modernized conditions is that they approach the pole of cooperation rather than the pole of conflict. Conflictual or political activities, therefore, take place within the context of predominantly cooperative arrangements. Plays for power or position among these modernized states occur in the non-zero-sum worlds of the IMF and NATO rather than in predominantly conflictual arenas.

The low policies, in short, have become central to international politics among the modernized states and involve the building up of international collective goods in defense and NATO, and in international wealth-and-welfare organizations such as GATT and the EEC. It is within the parameters set by the need for cooperation that interplays of power and position can occur. [. . .]

Two of the chief characteristics of foreign policies conducted under modernized conditions are, then, (1) their predominantly cooperative rather than conflictual nature; and (2) the change in goals from power and position to wealth and welfare — or, at least, the addition of these new goals to the more classical ones. Both factors are accompanied by the loss of autonomy of any society in international affairs.

B. Increased Domestic Demands and the Allocation of Resources. It is a paradox at the heart of foreign policies in all modernized societies that increased demands on their governments result in a short-term problem of resource allocation, with the result that predominantly external goals decrease in priority relative to predominantly domestic goals. At the same time, however, increased 'inward-looking' has been offset by the increased sensitivity of domestic conditions to international events as a result of international interdependence, and by absolute increases in international activities taken on by the citizens of all modernized societies.

One of the distinctive features of all modernized governments, democratic and authoritarian alike, is that they have assumed great multifunctionality. Both ideally and actually, they are not merely regulative agencies in a 'night-watchman' state, but are and are seen as creators and redistributors of wealth. Increasing demands on governments have helped to create the modern social-service state and themselves result from the increased politicization of citizens in modernized societies. A government is impaled upon the 'dilemma of rising demands and insufficient resources'[4] when its domestic demands are greater than its resources and when at the same time it must maintain even existing levels of commitments abroad. The demands may arise from the politicized poor who want a greater share in economic prosperity, the military for new weapons systems, the need for maintenance of public order in societies increasingly sensitive to labor and minority group disruption, etc. These are added to the 'rising cost and widening scope of activities required to keep mature urban societies viable'.[5] One inexorable result of these increased demands on governments is the curtailment of external commitments, or the decreased relative priority of external goals. Such curtailments add a dimension to the costs of independence. [. . .]

C. Changes in the Processes of Foreign Policy-Making. Like other processes of policy-making, those associated with foreign policy change under modernization. Cabinet-style decision-making gives way to administrative politics as the information that must be gathered for policy-making increases, as the number of states and functional areas that must be dealt with increases, and as personnel standards become professionalized. Despite the predictions made at the turn of the century by the ideologues of democracy, policy-making has not been 'democratized' so much as it has been 'bureaucratized'. At the same time, great losses of control from the top have occurred and have been well documented.

The major transformation brought about by changes in the policy-making process has been the decreased relevance of rationality models for understanding policy and the increased importance of the bureaucratic model. Policy-making in modern bureaucracies undermines the ability of a political leader to pursue rationally any explicit external goals. Rather, interest-group politics assume greater importance and foreign policy becomes more and more a reflection of what occurs in the bureaucracies upon which leadership depends for information and position papers.

Policy-making in modern bureaucracies, with regard to foreign as well as domestic affairs, involves both lateral bargaining among the members of various administrative units and vertical or hierarchical bargaining among members of various strata in a single organization. The single spokesman in foreign affairs, long prescribed as a necessity for security, is made impossible by the characteristics of modern bureaucracies. Plurality in the number of foreign policy voices accompanies the increased significance of routine, daily decision-making in low-policy areas that contrasts with the more unified and consistent nature of decision-making in crises and in high politics. With such increases in routine, control at the top becomes more difficult. The several aspects of control of routine can be summarized under two headings, the organizational problem and the problem of size.

Modern governments are organized predominantly along functional domestic lines into such departments as agriculture, labor, and education. The domestic-foreign distinction that seemed to fit the nineteenth-century model of governmental organization conflicts dramatically with the needs of even the predominantly domestic organizational structures of modernized governments. Here, the distinctive feature is that each domestic function has external dimensions: most of the predominantly domestic departments and ministries of modern governments have some kind of international bureau. The proliferation of these international bureaus severely undercuts the ability of one foreign ministry or department to control the external policies of its government, thus severely restricting the coordination of foreign policies. The problem is all the more serious in so far as the distinction between high policies and low policies in foreign affairs has become increasingly blurred.

One way this problem is dealt with is by the formation of committees that cross-cut several cabinet organizations, serving to coordinate both information and decision-making at several levels. Each American administration since World War II has tried to reorganize foreign policy decision-making to counter the disability, but no permanent decision-making structures have been devised. Other governments tackle the problem by forming *ad hoc* interministerial committees to meet specific problems.

In addition to decreased control as a result of 'domestic orientation' in modern governments, there is the added difficulty of coordinating a large bureaucracy dealing predominantly with foreign affairs. At the turn of the last century, one of the problems of control stemmed from the lack of coordination between foreign ministries and ministries of the armed forces.

Thus, for example, French armed forces often freely occupied under-developed areas in Africa and Southeast Asia without the knowledge of the foreign minister. Today the problem of size presents no less formidable an information gap at the top of large bureaucracies. With more information available than ever, its channeling to the right person has become an organizational problem no foreign ministry has mastered.

Modernization, then — usually associated with the rationalization of political structures that foster increased control over the events in a society as well as over the environment in which men live — also creates certain disabilities that impede rational and efficient foreign policies. But modernization has also exacerbated another problem of control that has always been central to international politics — the control of events external to a state. This problem, which originates in the political organization of international society, is the one to which I now turn.

D. Modern Foreign Policies and Problems of Control. The problem of control in international affairs arises from the condition of international society, which, conceived as a collection of nominally sovereign political units, has no overarching structure of political authority. The difficulty of coordination and control of events external to a society, always the major problem of international stability, is compounded by the development of interdependencies among modernized societies, for interdependence erodes the autonomy of a government to act *both* externally and internally, though the juridical status of sovereign states has not been significantly altered.

With the development of high levels of interdependence, all kinds of catastrophes, from nuclear holocaust to inflation or depression, can also become worldwide once a chain of events is begun. These disasters could be logical consequences of benefits derived from international collective goods.

One reason why modern governments have lost control over their foreign relations is that there has been an increasing number of international interactions, especially among the populations of pluralistic societies, in nongovernmental contexts. This increase was one of the first changes modernization brought in the foreign policies of states. It first became noticeable at the turn of the century with the rise of the 'new imperialism' characterized by the rapidly increased mobility of people, of money, and of military equipment. It is associated today with the multinational corporation and with other new units of international activity that have varying degress of autonomy abroad and whose external operations frequently act at cross-purposes with the foreign policy goals of their governments. They also contribute a large portion of any state's balance-of-payments accounts and therefore affect the monetary stability not only of a single state, but of the system of states in general. [. . .]

A second aspect of the problem of control stems from the decreasing number of instrumentalities relative to the number of goals associated with any government. An optimum policy situation is one where the number of instruments available for use exceeds the number of goals. In principle, an infinite number of policy mixes exist, in that one instrument can substitute for another and 'it will always be possible to find one among the infinity of solutions . . . for which welfare, however defined, is a maximum'.[6] This is not only the most efficient situation, but it is also the fairest, for it allows any pressure to be 'distributed more evenly over the various social groups'.[7] When, however, the number of instruments is smaller than the number of goals, there is no clear solution on grounds of efficiency or fairness.

It is precisely this situation that occurs with the breakdown of the domestic-foreign distinction and with increases in international inter-dependence. As long as the two spheres remain more or less distinct, policies in either area can be implemented with different sets of instru-mentalities. As soon as the separation is eroded, the spillover of effects from one sphere to the other results in the reduction of the number of usable instrumentalities.

This is true for two reasons. First, since policy instruments have recog-nizable effects both internally and externally, it is more and more frequently the case that any one instrument can be used for either domestic or external purposes. However, domestic wage increases can be used for the purpose of establishing higher general levels of living. At the same time, the propensity to consume imported goods increases directly with wage increases and depresses any balance-of-payments surplus – a situation that is worsened by the positive effect of wage increases on prices and the subsequent negative effect on exports.

Second, what is optimally desired is that objectives be consistent. 'If they are not consistent, no number of policy instruments will suffice to reach the objectives.'[8] As long as domestic and foreign affairs were separated, consistency was a problem only within each sphere. With interdependence, not only must domestic and foreign goals be compatible with each other, but so must the goals of a set of societies if welfare effects are to be spread optimally. Consistency then becomes more difficult because of the economic nature of the objectives and the diversity of political units in international society.

Together with increased international transactions associated with

growing interdependence, there have also developed rising levels of transactions internal to modernized states as well as higher levels of national
integration. It is often concluded that the increases in national cohesiveness
that accompany modernization counteract international interdependence.[9]
Actually the reverse is true.

There is a fairly simple relation between rising levels of transactions
internal to one state and increased interdependence among states. As
internal interdependencies increase and as governmental organizations are
institutionalized, even if international transactions remain constant (and
they do not) *international* interdependencies also increase. This is true
because sensitivity to transnational activities increases the domestic
implications of international transactions. For example, as the levels of
interdependence within a state rise, the same order of trade has increased
implications for domestic employment, fiscal, monetary, and welfare
policies. It is precisely this element of interdependence that is fundamental
and that Deutsch and other theorists have overlooked. [: . .]

Conclusions

The transformations in all three aspects of foreign policies – in their
contents, the processes associated with policy formation, and the control
of policy effects – offer the citizens of any modernized society opportunities for increased wealth and welfare that were unthinkable in any
system with much lower levels of interdependence. They also increase the
chances of instability for international society as a whole; for interdependence has increased far in advance of either the instruments capable of
controlling it or of available knowledge of its effects. There are, however,
two aspects of modernization and foreign policy that, in conclusion, must
be highlighted.

First, the various changes discussed above pertain to all modernized
societies and are affected very little by ideology or by particular sets of
political institutions. To be sure, it may make some difference whether
institutions are democratic or nondemocratic in particular instances. In
the long run, however, the general influences that have transformed
foreign policies are ubiquitous.

Second, these changes are likely to be dispersed throughout the international system far ahead of other aspects of modernity. They are, therefore,
likely to characterize the foreign policies of some less modernized societies
before these societies become relatively modernized – or even if they do
not become modernized. The speed with which modernity spreads will,

therefore, only increase the problems of control and will make more urgent the need for establishing new mechanisms of international order.

Notes

1. Carl J. Friedrich, 'Intranational Politics and Foreign Policy in Developed (Western) Societies', in R. Barry Farrell (ed.), *Approaches to Comparative and International Politics* (Evanston, 1966), p. 97.

2. A balanced analysis of both schools of thought can be found in Pierre Hassner, 'The Nation State in the Nuclear Age', *Survey*, LXVII (April 1968), pp. 3-27.

3. K. Knorr, *On the Uses of Military Power in the Nuclear Age* (Princeton, 1966), p. 22.

4. Harold and Margaret Sprout, 'The Dilemma of Rising Demands and Insufficient Resources', *World Politics*, XX (July 1968), pp. 660-93.

5. Ibid., p. 685.

6. Jan Tinbergen, *On the Theory of Economic Policy*, 2nd edn (Amsterdam, 1963), pp. 37-8.

7. Ibid., p. 41.

8. Richard N. Cooper, *The Economics of Interdependence: Economic Policy in the Atlantic Community* (New York, 1968), p. 155.

9. See the works of Karl W. Deutsch, including Deutsch *et al.*, *France, Germany and the Western Alliance: A Study of Elite Attitudes on European Integration and World Politics* (New York, 1967).

ORGANIZATION AND BUREAUCRATIC POLITICS

I.M. Destler

Source: *Presidents, Bureaucrats and Foreign Policy* (Princeton University Press, Princeton, 1974), pp. 52-81.

Destler begins by identifying the main characteristics of the 'bureaucratic politics' school of analysis. He proceeds to a discussion of the possible pitfalls and developments in the approach and ends by considering the troubling implications for the content of foreign policy and the reform of the policy process implicit in the nature of bureaucratic politics.

Bureaucratic politics is the process by which people inside government bargain with one another on complex public policy questions. Its existence does not connote impropriety, though such may be present. Nor is it caused by political parties and elections, though both influence the process in important ways. Rather, bureaucratic politics arises from two inescapable conditions. One is that no single official possesses either the power, or the wisdom, or the time to decide all important executive branch policy issues himself. The second is that officials who have influence inevitably differ in how they would like these issues to be resolved. [. . .]

What specific insights does the bureaucratic politics view of government have to offer? How does it depict the actual workings of the foreign affairs bureaucracy? The basic concepts can be grouped under four general headings:

1. Power and Perspective
2. Issues as a Flow
3. Constraints, Channels, and Maneuvers
4. Foreign Policy as Bureaucratic Political Outcome

1. Power and Perspective

Power is spread unevenly among many individuals in different governmental positions.

a. The 'Diversity of Values and Goals and of Alternative Means and

Policies'.[1] Rational policy-making may be salutary as an ideal, and reasoned analysis may be able to improve policy-making at many points. But there is no way for reason alone to overcome the diversity of goals and means that are inevitable among participants in foreign policy-making. Goals are based on value preferences as well as rational analysis. And even differences as to means of achieving common goals cannot be resolved by reason. Our understanding of the likely consequences of particular policies is very poor, since they involve complex chains of human interaction with each step very hard to predict. [...]

b. Perspective: Men in Positions. More than one sage has been credited with the maxim, 'Where you stand depends on where you sit.' While officials' views and actions are not predetermined by the positions they hold, they are greatly influenced by them. For each official has a separate job to do, whether it be President or Air Force Chief of Staff or Turkey desk officer in State. Each receives a different mix of information. Each is subject to a different mix of pressures. Each must maintain the loyalty of a different group of subordinates, the respect of a different group of peers, the confidence of a different boss. Thus each views a problem from his own particular 'perspective'.

Men's perspectives grow narrower the further down in the hierarchy they sit. Even on a matter as critical as the Cuban missile crisis, the Chief of Naval Operations' determination to run what he judged a militarily sound blockade and protect his ships against possible encounters with Russian submarines conflicted with the President's broader need to avoid provoking the Soviets and give them 'time to see, think, and blink'. And not only do men in positions tend to see issues in terms of their positions. They also tend to press for their resolution in the direction that will most strengthen their ability to do their particular jobs. [...]

c. Bargaining Advantages: Who Influences What How Much. Differences among men sharing power can only be resolved by bargaining. Thus officials strive to be *effective* in influencing their colleagues. But they are not equally successful, and they do not come to the battle equally armed. Nor does the fight necessarily go to the swiftest of tongue, the man with the best rational arguments. For persuasion requires not just logic but a hearing, and some are more listened to than others.

To influence particular issues bureaucrats need 'bargaining advantages', sources of influence which make others take them seriously. Allison lists these as 'drawn from formal authority and obligations, institutional backing, constituents, expertise, and status'. Hilsman cites as 'sources of power' within the executive branch 'the confidence of the President', 'position and title', 'representing a particular constituency', 'institutional backing', and 'statutory or designated authority and responsibility'.[2]

2. Issues as a Flow

The discussion thus far treats 'issues' as if each arose separately, and as though bargaining took place over the issue in its entirety. But officials usually consider issues not as whole but one piece at a time, with decisions on many 'pieces' adding up to 'policy' over time. Also, each piece must compete for their attention with pieces of many other issues. And issues tend to be broader than particular individuals' jurisdictions, so that lateral bargaining becomes a critical element.

a. Issues as Bits and Pieces. Issues generally arise not all at once or once and for all, but bit by bit. So while bureaucrats *may* be thinking in terms of the larger question, battles tend to be fought over how to handle today's problem. [. . .]

b. Issues as Simultaneous Games. 'Players' involved in foreign policy-making, particularly top officials, have 'a full plate', a diet of diverse problems in the form of memos, orders for their signature, Presidential recommendations requested. This diet is so rich and varied that it is difficult for them even to taste all the problems set before them, let alone digest them. They are fighting on a number of issues simultaneously, so they must weigh in on one and quickly move on to the next. They must also consider each policy game not entirely on its own terms, but also for its relationship to other games. [. . .]

c. Issues as Overflowing Jurisdictions. In testifying before the Jackson Subcommittee, Robert Lovett complained that 'the idea seems to have got around that just because some decision may affect your activities, you automatically have a right to take part in making it'.[3] But looked at from the official's vantage point, this 'idea' is inescapable. [. . .]

The concept of foreign policy-making as bureaucratic politics does not *depend* on issues being interdepartmental. If they were not, bargaining would still take place, both up-and-down and laterally between offices within particular departments. But the interdepartmental character of practically all important issues complicates the game considerably by increasing the number of players and the range of perspectives involved. It reduces the number of issues where a decision can be worked out under the general authority of any one official short of the President. Conversely it increases the number which must be resolved by lateral bureaucratic compromises, or by 'escalation' to higher levels.

3. Constraints, Channels, and Maneuvers

Like any political system, the foreign affairs policy-making process is characterized by shared beliefs and allegiances, 'rules of the game' affecting who has a chance to influence what issue when, and a set of relatively standard maneuvers for influence.

a. Common Commitments and Perceptions. There is a widely shared conviction in the government that the United States should have a strong and effective foreign policy, and that positive actions should be taken to further this aim. Thus, as Halperin notes, 'Senior participants in the process ... by and large believe that they should, and do, favor support of policies which are in the national interest.'[4] Partly because of this belief, even those with narrower aims generally feel they can win only by framing their cases as plausible arguments for the broader national interest.

A related factor encouraging agreement is what Halperin calls 'widely shared values and images of the world'. These tend to determine which proposals will be taken seriously and which considered unreasonable. They may at times diverge rather far from reality. For example, a player suggesting the existence of anything but a solid Russia-China alliance at the time of the 1958 Quemoy crisis would have undercut his credibility and his ability to influence that issue, since he would be contradicting the conventional bureaucratic wisdom of the time.

b. Rules of the Game Structuring Bureaucratic Politics. There will always be, at any given time, a set of 'rules' about the channels through which particular types of issues move, the people entitled to be consulted or to 'clear' proposed documents, the individual or office having 'the action' or primary responsibility, etc. Some of these are informal understandings relying heavily on personal relationships. Some are more formal and result from the need for standard operating procedures to handle regular phenomena — rules for routing and answering cables, channeling budget and planning documents, signing off on foreign aid agreements, moving issues up for Presidential or Secretarial action. The influence of such formal procedures is both real and limited. The most critical issues tend to jump the bounds of regular channels, above all because of the involvement of top officials, who seek to handle things their own ways. But their ability to influence these issues effectively can be strongly affected by the involvement and leverage such procedures provide them and their underlings.

c. Maneuvers for Influence. Officials seeking approval or disapproval of particular policy courses or actions will engage in maneuvers designed to make their viewpoints prevail. Not only will they seek to structure their proposals for maximum appeal to others whose agreement is needed or desired. They will also seek on occasion to change the composition of the relevant group of people, shutting some out because 'security' requires it, bringing others in by placing the issue in a broader context or raising it before a broader forum, redefining the issue in order to transfer the action to someone else, eliminate the need for certain concurrences, etc. [. . .]

4. Foreign Policy as Bureaucratic Political Outcome

What results from this bureaucratic political system is, of course, foreign policy. But it is not necessarily 'policy' in the rational sense of embodying the decisions made and actions ordered by a controlling intelligence focusing primarily on our foreign policy problems. Instead it is the 'outcome' of the political process, the government actions resulting from all the arguments, the building of coalitions and countercoalitions, and the decisions by high officials and compromises among them. Often it may be a 'policy' that no participant fully favors, when 'different groups pulling in different directions yield a resultant distinct from what anyone intended'.[5] Any year's defense budget offers innumerable good examples. Often it is difficult to determine where and when in the system a particular policy direction was decided upon.

Moreover, policy is not usually the outcome of any particular battle, but the cumulation of outcomes of a number of battles fought over time. 'Rather than through grand decisions on grand alternatives', Hilsman has written, 'policy changes seem to come through a series of slight modifications of existing policy, with the new policy emerging slowly and haltingly by small and usually tentative steps, a process of trial and error in which policy zigs and zags, reverses itself, and then moves forward in a series of incremental steps.' 'Incrementalism', or step-by-step, trial-and-error policy-making, can be the most rational strategy when the impact of policy changes is hard to assess in advance. Lindblom has made this point with particular persuasiveness. But as it occurs in bureaucratic politics, incremental policy-making reflects more the internal dynamics of decision-making than any conscious design to maximize our ability to cope with an unruly world.[6]

Two Possible Pitfalls of the Bureaucratic Politics View

Any generalizing set of concepts tends to bring certain phenomena to prominence, risking an exaggeration of their importance and a neglect of other factors. Thus, even if one accepts the foregoing description as a generally valid picture of 'the way things are' in foreign policy decision-making, one must guard against its possible pitfalls. Two are of particular importance to those concerned with foreign affairs organization. The first is the danger that concentrating on what happens within the executive branch may lead to neglect of the broader national politics of foreign policy-making. The second is the emphasis which analysts of bureaucratic politics have tended to give to certain types of bureaucratic motivation, and the danger that this might blind one to other types of behavior of considerable importance to organizational reformers. [. . .]

But concentrating on the bureaucracy can be misleading. For though career bureaucrats may deal largely with others within the government, Presidents and Cabinet members must operate in a wider arena. In particular, if our foreign policy goals and means cease to have broad general support in the larger society, the opportunities and channels for outside influence multiply. The President and his top officials must then become effective persuaders in this broader public arena or see important elements of policy slip from their grasp. Thus President Nixon, relatively successful in taming the foreign affairs bureaucracy on the major issues, has suffered far stronger Congressional challenges on national security matters than any predecessor since the pre-war Roosevelt.

Hilsman offers a useful compromise, one that allows concentration on the executive branch while taking broader influences into account. He describes the policy-making arena as a number of 'concentric rings', with the 'innermost circles' being entirely within the executive branch. It makes sense for a study of foreign affairs organization to concentrate on these 'innermost circles', analyzing organizational reforms and strategies heavily in terms of their impact on intra-executive branch decision-making. But it is important not to forget that the politics of the federal bureaucracy is, in the words of one authority, a 'subsystem of the American political system' as a whole.[7]

Problems of Interest and Motivation

A more complicated problem for those applying the bureaucratic politics approach, however, is the question of the interests and motivations of individuals and their organizations.

Politics is often characterized as the interplay of individual and group interests. Yet it is not by accident that nowhere in our description of the fundamentals of bureaucratic politics is the question of individual interest directly discussed, except as it relates to players' perspectives and their needs for effectiveness. Due to the limits of rational analysis and the impact of particular perspectives, bureaucratic politics is a logical outgrowth of the nature of government and foreign policy even if the only interest of each official is to do his own job effectively. The bureaucratic politics view need not assume that officials are inordinately self-seeking, or committed only to the interests of their organizations. In fact, as noted by Schilling, Allison, and Hilsman, one considerable reason why battles are often so heated is that men have strong convictions about what the 'right policy' is.

> When in the late 1950's, for example, intelligence officials leaked secret information foreshadowing an upcoming 'missile gap' to Democratic senators and sympathetic members of the press, it was not because they were disloyal, but because they were deeply convinced that the nation was in peril. They had tried and failed to convince the top levels of the Eisenhower administration of the validity of their projections, and they felt completely justified in taking matters into their own hands by going over the President's head to Congress, the press, and the public.[8]

But men do of course have more selfish interests as well. They may seek power for its own sake, or financial reward, or prestige, or personal advancement, or a larger role for their agency programs. Sometimes they puruse these goals unabashedly, recognizing them as self-interest. More often, probably, they grow to equate the importance of their function and the strength of their organization with the broader national interest and welfare. Admirals are generally sincere when they urge a stronger navy as vital to America's security. Foreign Service officers genuinely believe that the nation benefits when the great majority of Ambassadorships are filled from their ranks.

However, because analysts of bureaucratic politics are concerned primarily with explaining what influences foreign policy, they tend to portray officials who actively seek to affect that policy and strive to build up their bargaining advantages in order to accomplish this aim. Such officials are aggressive about getting involved in issues which relate to their responsibilities. They tend to see this relationship broadly, jumping into matters well beyond those where they have primary action responsibility.

But often men seek not to plunge aggressively into what others see as none of their business, but rather to draw lines separating their jurisdictions so as to minimize conflict. After all, classical economic theorists usually placed more value on competition than business practitioners. The latter often sought protection and security from the buffeting of market forces. Similarly, many officials seek not to expand the range of their jobs but to cut them down to manageable size. Secretary Rusk put the problem succinctly in 1963: 'There are those who think that the heart of a bureaucracy is a struggle for power. This is not the case at all. The heart of the bureaucratic problem is the inclination to avoid responsibility.'[9]

And in contrast to the 'serious bureaucrat' which bureaucratic politics descriptions tend to emphasize, there is that opposite stereotype — of the man who takes refuge in nit-picking rules, refuses to give a straight answer or make a clear decision, lives in a world rather narrowly bounded by his own particular agency and program, and reserves his greatest interest for the annual unveiling of the new government pay scale. His behavior might be described as a flight from bureaucratic politics.

There is, of course, no reason why the foreign affairs government cannot be thought of as a political system without assuming that all participants are equally power-oriented or politically motivated. We certainly think this way about our larger national political system, and our citizens show a wide variance in political interest and effectiveness. But to balance and deepen the basic picture developed so far, it is useful to highlight two important ways in which men tend to be more concerned with protecting the inner life and existence of their organizations than with building broader policy influence. One is the tendency of organizations to develop their own subcultures. The second is the tendency to give priority to a parochial piece of policy 'territory'.

Organizational Subcultures

Many men spend the major part of their working lives in one large government organization or career service. How they relate to those inside the organization may well become more important to both their psychic well-being and their personal advancement than how they relate to those outside. It is not surprising, then, that organizations develop their own informal subcultures, which — like the broader national culture within which they develop — both prescribe certain patterns of belief and behavior and penalize those who do not conform to them.

Probably the most important example of this phenomenon in the international affairs bureaucracy is the State Department's Foreign Service. In a notable effort to describe this subculture, Andrew Scott argues that most Foreign Service officers share an 'ideology' composed of various 'prevalent beliefs' which are 'perfectly plausible' but, like those in most ideologies, contain 'a mix of truths, half-truths, and errors'. A typical belief is that 'the really important aspects of the foreign affairs of the United States are the political ones – the traditional ones of negotiation, representation, and reporting'. One critically important aspect of this ideology, Scott holds, is the 'extent to which it encourages officers to become inward-looking and absorbed in the affairs of the Service'.[10] [. . .]

Parochialism and Jurisdictions

Organizations, like individuals, have parochial perspectives and priorities. Anthony Downs has developed the concept of 'territoriality', suggesting that bureaucracies – like animals and nations – tend to 'stake out and defend territories surrounding their nests or "home bases"'. Certain parts of 'policy space' comprise a bureau's *heartland*, where it is sole determinant of policy; surrounding this will be the *interior fringe*, where the bureau's interest is primary but where other agencies have some influence. Outside of this is *no-man's land*, where no bureau dominates but many have influence.

Territorial boundaries are never absolutely clear; 'the inherent dynamism of human life' prevents jurisdictional lines from ever reaching an equilibrium. Because policy issues often cut across any possible allocation of jurisdictions, 'Every large organization is in partial conflict with every other social agent with which it deals.' But 'the basic nature of all such struggles is the same – each combatant needs to establish a large enough territory to guarantee his own survival'.[11]

The last quotation hints at a broader phenomenon. For, contrary to what certain elements of the bureaucratic politics view might lead one to assume, organizations tend to choose clear primary responsibility for a narrow policy area over the opportunities and dangers inherent in contesting for influence across a broader policy range. They will give primacy to fortifying the heartland. Members of the Joint Chiefs of Staff do not go out of their way to challenge the pet proposals of other services – rather, they trade support of these for reciprocal support of their own services' priorities. Foreign Service officers seldom make hard-nosed challenges of military tactics. They prefer to confine their involvement to the 'political' aspects, and hope the military will reciprocate by staying out of 'diplomacy'. [. . .]

Implications for Foreign Policy-Making

The nature of the bureaucratic political process seems to contradict almost the very notion of our government even pretending to make coherent, purposive foreign policy. And further investigation does nothing to brighten the picture. In fact, when one draws on other analyses of organizational behavior, the problems become even more complex, and even less susceptible to clear-cut reform.

'Pluralists' describing the politics of domestic policy-making have sometimes gone beyond *description* to *prescription*, to asserting 'confidence in the capability of the political process to produce the right results'.[12] Such faith in political competition finds its parallel in Adam Smith's notion of the 'invisible hand', a guiding principle whereby the sum of economic actions taken by individuals for their own selfish purposes would lead to the best possible outcome for society as a whole. But is the outcome of the *internal* competition of bureaucratic politics the kind of policy that will be successful in dealing with a troubled *outside* world?

Huntington feels he can answer this question with 'qualified optimism'. He sees one major virtue as stability: 'the forces of pluralism correct and counterbalance the instabilities, enthusiasms, and irrationalities of the prevailing mood'. Hilsman carries such optimism a step further. 'In spite of the untidiness and turmoil of the politics of policy-making in Washington', he writes,

> such an open process of conflict and consensus-building, debate, assessment, and mutual adjustment and accommodation can be solidly effective in the assessment of broad policy alternatives if the conditions are right. The conditions are, first, that the subject is one on which the competing groups are knowledgeable. Second, both the participating constituencies within the government and the 'attentive publics' outside must be well informed. Third, all levels of government, those who will carry out the policy as well as those who decide it, must be responsive to the decision and persuaded by it. Under these conditions, the chances are good that the policy will be wise, that the effort and sacrifice required will be forthcoming, and that the work of carrying out the policy will go forward intelligently and energetically.[13]

But without denying that wise policy may emerge 'if the conditions are right', it seems doubtful that the results will always, or even usually, be so reassuring. The central danger is inherent in the notion of policy emerging from bureaucratic competition, responsive more to the internal dynamics of our decision-making process than to the external problems on which it is supposed to center. As Schilling has noted, the bureaucratic political process can produce 'no policy at all', stalemate; 'compromised policy', with the direction hardly evident; or 'unstable policy', where 'changes in the *ad hoc* groupings of elites point policy first in one and then in another direction'. It can result in 'contradictory policy', where different government organizations pursue conflicting courses; 'paper policy', officially promulgated without the support needed for effective implementation; or 'slow' policy, since competition and consensus-building take time.[14]

Moreover, just to influence policy, officials need to apply inordinate attention to internal conflict, thereby limiting the time they can focus on the overseas situation toward which policy is ostensibly directed. As Stanley Hoffmann has noted, 'There inevitably occurs a subtle (or not so subtle) shift from the specific foreign-policy issues to be resolved, to the positions, claims, and perspectives of the participants in the policy machine. The demands of the issue and the merits of alternative choices are subordinated to the demands of the machine and the needs to keep it going. Administrative politics replaces foreign policy.'[15]

The troubling logic of policy-making by bureaucratic politics is taken one step further by Halperin. He depicts bureaucrats who are so deeply engrossed in intra-governmental maneuvering that the actions which result are seldom clear signals to other countries. Foreign bureaucrats in turn receive and interpret these signals selectively since they are looking for evidence to support them in their own internal bureaucratic battles. Thus 'communications' between nations tend to become dialogues between the largely deaf and dumb. Similarly, Neustadt's analysis of the Suez and Skybolt crises in *Alliance Politics* emphasizes how American and British officials concentrating on their own intra-governmental games regularly misinterpreted the motives and constraints of their allied counterparts.

Furthermore, if bureaucratic politics causes officials to shift their focus from substantive policy issues to 'the positions, claims, and perspectives of the participants in the policy machine', organizational subcultures can cause a further shift, turning men away from the inter-agency bureaucratic competition and toward concern primarily with relationships within their own organizations. This can lead to strikingly inappropriate, unresponsive behavior in relation to those outside the organization.

Resistance to Change

If the inward-looking nature of the bureaucratic political process seems its most dangerous fault, it is hardly its only one. A closely related problem is the bias against change. Superficially one might expect the opposite. Classical economists thought that competition would cause a steady surge of new ideas, from men seeking the rewards that would come from 'building a better mousetrap'. More recently economists have had doubts, noting that industries which most closely approximated the free enterprise model of many competitive firms (like housing construction) tend to be particularly backward in developing new techniques.

Bureaucratic politics seems to bias policy outcomes against change for not dissimilar reasons. A small businessman cannot afford to innovate because the rewards are uncertain and delayed and because he must survive in today's market. Similarly the bureaucrat seeks effectiveness in today's government, and this generally means moving with prevailing policy tides rather than challenging them. As Roger Fisher writes, a Washington official seeking a quick response to an overseas problem knows that 'if the cable can be worded so that it is simply an application of a prior decision or a prior statement by the President or another high official, the cable will be more difficult for others to object to, it can be cleared at a low level, and it can be dispatched more quickly'.[16]

More generally, the problem is what Schilling has called the 'gyroscopic' effect. Policies once adopted tend to become self-perpetuating because, in Henry Kissinger's words, 'An attempt to change course involves the prospect that the whole searing process of arriving at a decision will have to be repeated.' [. . .]

Resistance to change also arises from certain inherent problems of large organizations. One is the need for routines to structure an organization's response to particular events. To make possible coordinated and effective action by large numbers of people, organizations devise standard operating procedures or programs prescribing the roles of individuals and units in dealing with recurring events or predictable threats. Such 'routines' can range from the standard procedures for processing and funding of technical assistance requests to contingency plans to cope with a Soviet ground invasion of Western Europe. An organization can have only a limited number of such routines in its repertoire; these constitute the organization's coordinated action capabilities at any one time. They are also difficult and time-consuming to change. Those for dealing with crises are necessarily 'precooked', plans devised in advance for contingencies as defined by the organization. When an actual event comes, the organization can only respond to it by doing what it has already established procedures for doing. [. . .]

Resistance to Control

In the end, all of these problems are part of the largest one of all. Running through both our criticism of traditional approaches and our discussion of bureaucratic politics is a common theme – the limits of high officials' control over what the foreign affairs government is doing. Some writers have suggested the problem is insoluble. Gordon Tullock, for example, argues that distortions in the flow of communications, information, and orders up and down the hierarchy lead after a certain point to 'bureaucratic free enterprise', with activities by bureaucrats on the firing line essentially unrelated to what bosses want. Others, like Downs, are more moderate, but still argue that 'no one can fully control the behavior of a large organization', and that 'the larger any organization becomes, the weaker is the control over its actions exercised by those at the top'.[17]

Implications for Organizational Reform

The implications of all this for those who seek to organize for purposive and coherent foreign policy are obvious and unfavorable. The system as it seems to operate directs men's attention more to intra-governmental matters than to the overseas situations policy must influence; clings to old policies because of the difficulty of changing them; and resists efforts to control it from the top. Though competition may sometimes have positive effects, there is no reason to believe that these will be the rule rather than the exception. And if bureaucratic politics turns men's energies inward from the substantive policy problem to the bureaucratic political one, organizational subcultures can narrow attention still further, encouraging a flight from inter-agency bureaucratic politics to an emphasis on intra-agency relationships.

The danger which the existing system poses for coherent and purposive foreign policy may explain the allure of the sorts of reform proposals which have been recurrent in the post-war period. One is tempted to urge that policy-making be 'rationalized', or authority be joined to responsibility. Yet politics and large organizations are not evils to be exorcized by the proper mix of admonition and formal restructuring, but basic, persistent 'facts of life'. The reformer faces a world, to borrow two of Neustadt's characterizations, of 'intractable substantive problems and immovable bureaucratic structures', of 'emergencies in policy with politics as usual'.[18] And he must extend to the entire government Neustadt's depiction of a President who feels the urgent need for wise policy but recognizes that our arrival at such policy is anything but automatic.

For if there is no reason to deny the perils of bureaucratic politics, no more can one ignore its pervasiveness. So the organizational reformer must begin by dealing with the government as it is, not as he would like it to be. The bureaucratic political view is particularly valuable because it forces attention to leverage. If, for example, one proposes to increase policy coherence by establishing a new central official, it makes sense to ask first whether he can achieve the leverage, the 'bargaining advantages' to make his role effective. But one must ask also whether the person being placed in such a position will be one with, in Rusk's words, 'the inclination to avoid responsibility'. For giving a man all of the bargaining advantages in the world is of little use if he will not use them. Interestingly, then, part of organizational reform inevitably involves not the banishment of 'politics' from decision-making, but rather an effort to ensure that officials upon whom one's strategy depends can play the game effectively.

Notes

1. Roger Hilsman, 'The Foreign-Policy Consensus: An Interim Research Report', *Journal of Conflict Resolution* (December 1959), p. 365.

2. Graham T. Allison, 'Conceptual Models and the Cuban Missile Crisis', *American Political Science Review* (September 1969), p. 706; R. Hilsman, *To Move a Nation* (Doubleday, 1967), p. 7.

3. US Senate Committee on Government Operations, Subcommittee on National Policy Machinery, *Organizing for National Security*, vol. 1 (1961), p. 15.

4. Morton H. Halperin, 'The Decision to Deploy the ABM: Bureaucratic Politics in the Pentagon and White House in the Johnson Administration' (prepared for delivery at the 66th Annual Meeting of the American Political Science Association, Los Angeles, California, 8-12 September 1970), p. 8.

5. Allison, 'Conceptual Models', p. 707.

6. Hilsman, *To Move a Nation*, p. 5; C.E. Lindblom, *The Intelligence of Democracy* (Free Press, 1965), Ch. 9.

7. Hilsman, *To Move a Nation*, pp. 541-3; Alan A. Altschuler, *The Politics of the Federal Bureaucracy* (Dodd, Mead and Company, 1968), p. v.

8. Hilsman, *To Move a Nation*, p. 10.

9. US Senate Committee on Government Operations, Subcommittee on National Security Staffing and Operations, *Administration of National Security*, Staff Reports and Hearings (1965), p. 403.

10. Andrew M. Scott, 'The Department of State: Formal Organization and Informal Culture', *International Studies Quarterly* (March 1969), pp. 2-5; 'Environmental Change and Organizational Adaptation: The Problem of the State Department', *International Studies Quarterly* (March 1970), p. 87.

11. Anthony Downs, *Inside Bureaucracy* (Little Brown and Company, 1967), pp. 212-16.

12. Allen Schick, 'Systems Politics and Systems Budgeting', *Public Administration Review* (March/April 1969), p. 142.

13. Samuel P. Huntington, *The Common Defense* (Columbia University Press,

1961), p. 446; Hilsman, *To Move a Nation*, p. 549.

14. Warner R. Schilling, 'The Politics of National Defense: Fiscal 1950', in Warner R. Schilling, Paul F. Hammond and Glenn H. Snyder, *Strategy, Politics and Defense Budgets* (Columbia University Press, 1962), pp. 25, 26, 218-22.

15. Stanley Hoffmann, *Gulliver's Troubles, or the Setting of American Foreign Policy* (McGraw-Hill, for the Council on Foreign Relations, 1968), p. 177.

16. Roger Fisher, *International Conflict for Beginners* (Harper and Row, 1969), p. 180.

17. Gordon Tullock, *The Politics of Bureaucracy* (Public Affairs Press, 1965), pp. 167-70; Downs, *Inside Bureaucracy*, p. 262.

18. Richard E. Nuestadt, 'Staffing the Presidency', in Altschuler, *Politics of the Bureaucracy*, p. 120; *Presidential Power* (Signet, 1960), p. 17.

2.5

'FOREIGN' POLICIES OF US PUBLICS

Chadwick F. Alger

Source: *International Studies Quarterly*, vol. 21, no. 2 (International Studies Association/Sage, 1977), pp. 277-93.

To help American citizens to understand the link between their lives and events and processes in the world outside, Alger suggests that it is necessary to break down the view of states as interacting billiard balls that has dominated scholarly writings and everyday thinking. He offers six stages for differentiating the nation-state which serve to extend the image of a plurality of interests from the arena of domestic policy into that of foreign policy. He ends by suggesting that this breaking up of the state opens up the path for international participation by the individual.

An Undifferentiated Nation-State View

A useful starting point for our consideration of successive stages of analytic differentiation of foreign policy processes is Figure 1. It portrays nations as a set of interacting 'billiard balls'. It presumes that relations between nation-states are largely determined by basic characteristics, such as resources, technology, and population. This image of the world implies that a nation-state has a hard shell that separates it from the rest of the world. This view is reinforced by political maps, and it facilitates the expectation that foreign policy is a single thing that ought to be controlled by one person or one group. But if people involved in a diversity of national and international activities are to be able to develop an efficacious participatory relationship with international processes, they require images of international processes that link them to these processes.

Figure 1: Undifferentiated Nation-State View of International Relations

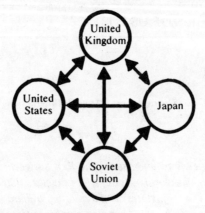

Stages of Nation-State Differentiation

The Internal Society

Gabriel Almond, writing in 1950, provided a classic differentiation of the internal domain. His seminal work, *The American People and Foreign Policy*, did for foreign policy what Wilson's *Congressional Government* had done for the legislative process. Almond laid bare the difference between expectations based on democratic norms and the ways in which foreign policy is formulated in the United States:

> There are inherent limitations in modern society on the capacity of the public to understand the issues and grasp the significance of the most important problems of public policy. This is particularly the case with foreign policy where the issues are especially *complex* and *remote*. The function of the public in a democratic policy-making process is to set certain policy criteria in the form of widely held values and expectations. It evaluates the results of policies from the point of view of their conformity to these basic values and expectations. The policies themselves, however, are the products of leadership groups ('elites') who carry on the specific work of policy formulation and policy advocacy.[1] (emphasis added)

Almond observed that the 'general public' was only occasionally concerned about foreign affairs. More sustained interest comes from the 'attentive public' which 'is informed and interested in foreign policy problems, and which constitutes the audience for the foreign policy discussions among the "elites"'.[2] These elites consist of both governmental officials (divided into administrative elites and political elites) and non-governmental elites (divided into communications elites and interest elites). Importantly, Almond recognizes that the foreign policy interest elites are drawn from elites from a variety of sectors of society – labor, business, agriculture, veterans, women, religion, and ethnic. Figure 2 attempts to portray a few critical aspects of Almond's differentiation of participants in foreign policy-making in the United States. [. . .]

Figure 2: Almond's View of Public Role in Foreign Policy

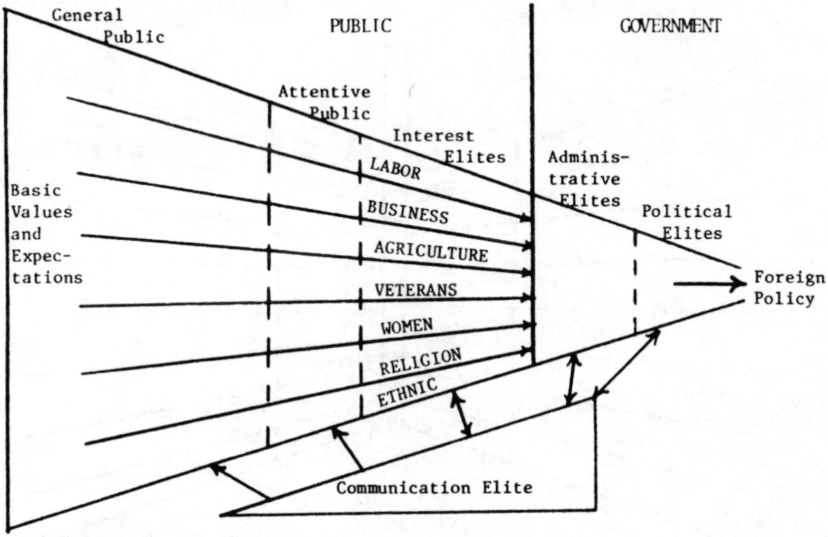

Note: This figure, based on Almond's discussion, was drawn by the author of this paper.

The National Government

A second development in foreign policy analysis has been differentiation of the national governmental participants in international relations. Writing in 1959, Wolfers provided a graphic dissent from the custom of treating national governments as single actors:

> Some democratic states have exhibited such pluralistic tendencies that they offer to the world a picture of near-anarchy. They seem to speak to the world with many and conflicting voices and to act as if one hand – agency or faction – does not know what the other hand is doing . . . [In] some . . . new states . . . integration is so poor that other states must deal with parts, rather than with a fictitious whole, if diplomacy is to be effective.[3]

Evolving tendencies to consider national governments as pluralistic actors are represented by Deutsch's discussion of 'linkage groups',[4] Rosenau's delineation of 'issue areas',[5] and his work on 'linkage politics'.[6] While the analytic perspectives developed under these labels are not limited to governmental actors, it is this aspect of this work that is relevant at this point in our discussion. Figure 3 portrays the differentiation contributed by this perspective.

Figure 3: Linkage Group or Issue Area View of Intergovernmental Relations

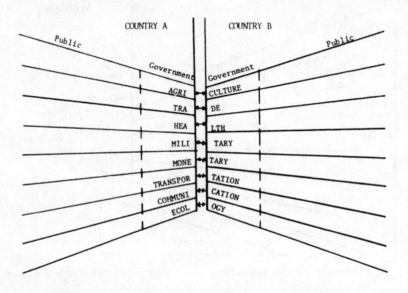

As changes in technology and communication have extended the boundaries of human enterprises, responsible officials in national governments increasingly find that problems like ecology and energy can only be attacked in collaboration with counterparts in other countries. This was dramatized when the Nixon Administration's 'Project Independence' was followed shortly by an effort to set up an International Energy Agency in the context of OECD. Recent UN conferences and other related international collaboration on food, natural resources, population, and environment underline the development of 'linkage groups' in specific 'issue areas'. In many cases the contact among national 'linkage groups' is virtually continuous, such as in the context of the specialized agencies of the UN system. A total of some 200 permanent organizations link national governments in collaboration on fisheries, wheat, coffee, oil, tin, and the like.

A diversity of 'linkage groups' in the US government are simultaneously pursuing the interest of their group and that of their public clientele in the United States. These groups sometimes act at cross-purposes; the diversity of interests pursued by such groups belies the myth of *a* national interest. More correctly, a diversity of interests to be found within the boundaries of the United States are increasingly finding that they cannot effectively pursue their interests in isolation from similar interests in other countries. Wolfers' reference to 'near-anarchy'[7] in describing these 'pluralistic tendencies' is ironic in that international collaboration within these 'issue areas' is vital in order to substitute orderly problem-solving for anarchy.

This differentiation of the foreign relations of the federal government has not yet extensively permeated public thinking. The press still reports in a way that suggests that a single foreign policy is being carried out as represented by the issue the Secretary of State is dramatizing in a specific day or week. But the Secretary of State, particularly in a nation-state with a vast number of 'linkage groups', only perceives some of these groups and actually controls even fewer. His definitions of 'national interest' (plural because they, too, differ from week to week) are only a few among many being implemented by these 'linkage groups'.

The perspective of 'linkage groups', combined with differentiation of nongovernmental interest groups, can provide the citizen with a different orientation. The notion of a national interest that can only be discerned by a few with esoteric training and experience vanishes. Taking the mysticism out of foreign policy through the differentiation of 'issue areas' does not mean that the problems to be faced are simple. However, people who feel competent enough to become involved in domestic issues become more aware of ways to participate in their international dimension. This perspective also suggests that those who attempt to affect governmental policy on a significant domestic issue are likely not to be effective unless they are attentive to the international dimensions of these issues.

Impact of Nongovernmental International Relations on Government Foreign Policies

The analytic differentiation of nongovernmental international relations provides an extended public with a critical analytic tool to facilitate their perception and interpretation of their own actual and potential links to international social and economic processes. 'Transnational relations' is a term which has come into use to refer to the international relations of nongovernmental organizations. Angell analyzes the role of migration, visiting of relatives and friends abroad, service in the Peace Corps, studying and research abroad, technical assistance missions, religious missions, business missions, and participation in international nongovernmental organizations.[8] Keohane and Nye include many of these and add foundations, revolutionary organizations, airlines, labor, space, and nuclear energy.[9]

Angell as well as Keohane and Nye are primarily concerned with the ways in which transnational relations have an impact on the policies of national governments, the third analytic distinction to be treated in this paper. Several mechanisms for this impact are discerned: changed attitudes of those who participate in transnational relations,[10] the development of transnational interest groups, and dependence of governments on services provided by transnational activities (e.g., travel and communications). Figure 4 illustrates the impact of transnational activity on national governments.

The transnational perspective challenges the widespread assumption that all roads to influence on international affairs lead directly to Washington! The domestic or foreign national government may be more effectively reached through an international nongovernmental organization. Furthermore, participation in these activities provides experience and socialization that would be very difficult to replicate through courses in schools or domestic activity alone.

Figure 4: Impact of Transnational Relations on Government Foreign Policy

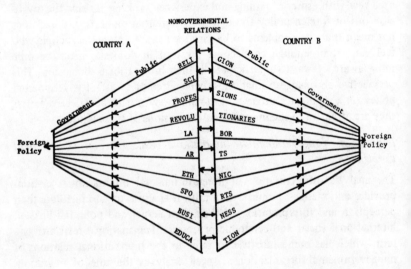

Impact of Governments on Nongovernmental International Relations

Keohane and Nye offer a fourth perspective that is the reverse of the third. National governments sometimes use transnational relations in order to increase their influence on other national governments and other societies. For example, in the mid-1960s the United States attempted to retard the development of France's nuclear capability by forbidding IBM-France to sell certain types of computers to the French government.[11] The CIA has infiltrated a variety of transnational activities (press, business). Because governmental funds are often provided for overseas private philanthropic activity (e.g., surplus food and equipment), the US government often has considerable influence on the distribution of these materials. A figure similar to Figure 4 could be drawn to illustrate the influence which flows from government A through transnational relations to affect the foreign policy of government B.

It is quite customary for private citizens involved in international activity to accede to the request of their national government for assistance and support – in the 'national interest'. Yet governmental collaboration has often engendered suspicion of nongovernmental international activity and diverted it from its own goals. As citizens involved in these activities become increasingly sensitized to the diversity of interests that are served by the foreign activities of governments, they may examine specific governmental activities more carefully before they participate.

Foreign Policies of Nongovernmental Sectors

The fifth perspective does not view nongovernmental international activity as something that is either intended to affect governmental policy or to be used by it for its interests, but as activity that has its own goals. This kind of transnational activity has been most widely recognized in the activities of multinational corporations. Otherwise, it is given only slight attention in the transnational literature, and it is very difficult to enable most people to see this as a distinct foreign policy option. Keohane and Nye recognize the presence of 'autonomous or quasiautonomous *actors* in world politics',[12] with chapters on revolutionary movements, trade unions, multinational business enterprises, and the Roman Catholic Church. But their interest is primarily focused on the interplay between governmental and nongovernmental forces, although their volume includes descriptive material on how nongovernmental interests achieve goals through transnational activity without governmental involvement.

Figure 5 portrays the foreign policies of diverse sectors of the publics of two countries. Interest elites are largely responsible for defining these policies and implementing them in relations with counterparts from other countries. Governments are left out of this figure to signify that interest elites do develop and carry out foreign policies that are intended neither to fulfill governmental policy nor to influence it. For example, much humanitarian activity of churches fulfills policy that is based on humanitarian aspects of church doctrine. The figure is not intended to suggest that governments cannot affect the foreign policies of interest groups; these groups often act independently of governments, although they often defer to national governments in foreign policy questions because of their belief that 'this is how things are done'. This belief is partly caused by the failure of scholars to specify clearly models of international relations that facilitate perception of exceptions to the supremacy of national governments over foreign policy (as in Figure 5).

Figure 5: Foreign Policies of Nongovernmental Sectors

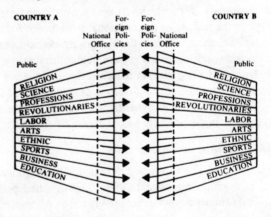

Despite the fact that many people involved in philanthropic, scientific, religious, and professional activity frequently cross national boundaries, most are customarily active only within their national boundaries. For example, most academic and scientific associations in the United States are dependent on information from a global network if they are to make their work relevant to the world in which it will be used. Nevertheless, they organize on a national basis, thereby socializing their members into a relatively provincial fraternity. It becomes necessary to establish special programs of international exchange to resocialize a few members into transnational academic and scientific communities.

Implementation of Foreign Policies Through International Organizations

The sixth step in analytic differentiation of foreign policy analysis has been stimulated by increasing attention to the 200 international governmental organizations (IGOs) and 2,700 international nongovernmental organizations (INGOs), reflecting virtually all the pursuits of humankind, from athletics to zoology. The public at large is only cognizant of a very few of the IGOs, such as the UN and NATO, and only a small number of INGOs, such as the Red Cross and the Olympics. Most members of national organizations have little knowledge, if any, about the international extensions of these associations, because relationships with international bodies are usually carried out by officials in the national office of these associations. Thus, the nation-state model tends to be replicated in nongovernmental international relations. Nongovernmental organizations (NGOs) within nations tend to have a 'national capital' with a 'foreign office' of specialists in the international relations of the association. Local, state, and regional leaders tend to defer to the national office on international issues. One reason that INGOs tend to mirror the nation-state system and thereby reinforce it is that strong national organizations are required if nongovernmental interests are to influence national governments. But it is also because of rote repetition of the nation-state model displayed by national governments.

As national governments have created an increasing number of IGOs to handle common problems, national nongovernmental organizations have followed suit. An increasing number of important issues are being debated in IGOs, such as recent UN conferences on food, population, environment, and the law of the sea, and national organizations in different countries are drawn into collaborative relationships to counter the influence of coalitions of national governments. Certain sectors of labor and of consumers are recognizing that transnational organizations may be required to compete with the transnational activities of business firms and banks.

Figure 6 portrays (for country A) the implementation of foreign policies by nongovernmental groups in one sector, education. Educational nongovernmental organizations from a number of countries come together (left side of figure) in INGOs, such as the International Association of Universities, the Council on International Educational Exchange, and the Association of Arab Universities, to achieve common goals. Educational sectors of national governments do likewise (right side of figure), in organizations such as UNESCO, the Southeast Asian Ministers of Education Organization, and the Central American Office of Education Planning. Efforts are made to influence the educational policies of IGOs in the direction of common policies developed in educational INGOs. Both INGOs and IGOs may also attempt to affect the educational policies of national governments and national nongovernmenatal organizations directly.

Figure 6: Implementation of Foreign Policies of Nongovernmental Sectors through International Organizations

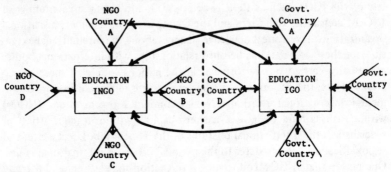

A critical value of analytic differentiation in foreign relations is the diversified strategy it suggests to the citizen interested in understanding and perhaps eventually having some control over the international social and economic processes that impinge on his everyday life. Explication of the various sectors of governmental foreign affairs helps him to pinpoint his efforts to affect governmental policies. But he may also think about participating directly in bilateral and multilateral foreign relations – both as a means for affecting the policies of his national government and other national governments and as a way to achieve international goals directly.

[Alger goes on to differentiate the state still further by looking at the link between cities in different countries and the role of individuals, organizations and sectors of the community within them. He urges an end to the myth of the division between local and international issues and offers a roadmap for the individual to participate in international affairs.]

As the citizen searches for the relevant unit for a specific problem, she might have a mental picture of options something like Figure 7. She can participate through international organizations, national organizations, state (or regional) organizations, and city organizations, or she may choose direct individual activity. With respect to any of the four territorial units, she may choose to (1) influence government directly, (2) work through a nongovernmental organization to influence government, or (3) work through a nongovernmental organization to have direct international impact. This roadmap offers the citizen 13 avenues for international participation.

Figure 7: Routes to International Participation

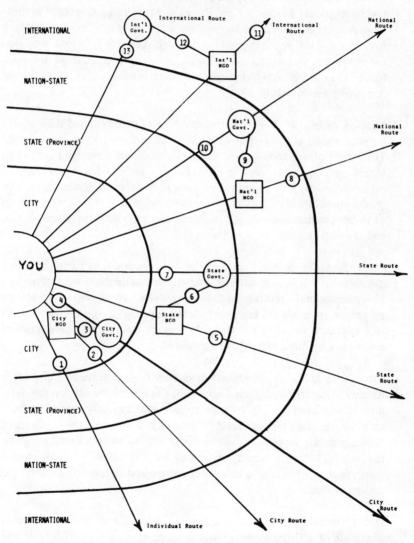

International (11, 12, 13). Those people who tax themselves 1 per cent of their annual income and send it directly to the UN Secretary General use route 13. They do this because of dissatisfaction that their country contributes less a percentage of GNP to the UN than 45 per cent of the member nations. Since they have not been able to change this policy through routes 9 or 10, they have shifted to route 13. Those who support the International League for the Rights of Man in its lobbying efforts for human rights at the United Nations are using route 12. People who work for the rights of political prisoners through Amnesty International often use route 11, attempting to influence policies of national governments (other than their own) through the direct action of an international nongovernmental organization.

National (8, 9, 10). These are the routes most perceived and used by US citizens. Public activity against the Vietnam war used all of these routes. There were efforts to affect the national government directly (10) through letters and personal pleas to officials. A number of nongovernmental organizations, as well as individuals, joined together in demonstrations in Washington, intended to affect governmental policy (9). Representatives of some organizations engaged in direct international activity intended to end the war, including trips to Hanoi (8).

State (5, 6, 7). Route 7 is used by businessmen who try to get state assistance in stimulating exports. Sometimes businessmen work through a nongovernmental organization (6). Some states have responded by setting up permanent trade missions abroad. Occasionally, business organizations will endeavor to stimulate trade directly by sponsoring trade missions abroad and by direct advertising abroad (7).

City (2, 3, 4). Those who profit financially from tourism in a city often directly (4) and through their Chamber of Commerce and other nongovernmental organizations (3) attempt to influence city government to help them to stimulate foreign travel to their city. Sometimes the Chamber of Commerce may engage in direct activity abroad to stimulate tourism to the city (2). Direct activity may also be undertaken by local church congregations who send missionaries abroad and engage in philanthropic activity abroad.

Direct Individual (1). Direct individual international activity covers a multitude of activity, such as letter writing, financial support for relatives and friends abroad, ham radio operators, direct mail purchases, volunteering for service in foreign armies, subscription to foreign magazines and direct purchase of books abroad, depositing funds in foreign banks, and direct participation in revolutionary movements.

Notes

1. G. Almond, *The American People and Foreign Policy* (Praeger, New York, 1950), p. 5.

2. Ibid., p. 138.

3. A. Wolfers, 'The Actors in International Politics', in W.T. Fox (ed.), *Theoretical Aspects of International Relations* (University of Notre Dame Press, Notre Dame, In., 1959), p. 102.

4. K. Deutsch, 'External Influences on the International Behaviour of States', in R.B. Farrell (ed.), *Approaches to Comparative and International Politics* (Northwestern University Press, Evanston, Ill., 1966), pp. 5-26.

5. J.N. Rosenau, 'Pre-theories and Theories of Foreign Policy', in R.B. Farrell (ed.), *Approaches to Comparative and International Politics* (Northwestern University Press, Evanston, Ill., 1966), pp. 167-208.

6. J.N. Rosenau (ed.), *Linkage Politics* (Free Press, New York, 1969).

7. Wolfers, 'The Actors in International Politics'.

8. R. Angell, *Peace on the March* (Van Nostrand, New York, 1969).

9. R.O. Keohane and J.S. Nye (eds.), 'Transnational Relations and World Politics', *International Organization*, 25 (Summer 1971), entire issue.

10. Angell, *Peace on the March*.

11. Keohane and Nye, 'Transnational Relations', p. 341.

12. Ibid.

2.6

NON-STATE ACTORS AND INTERNATIONAL OUTCOMES

Philip A. Reynolds

Source: *British Journal of International Studies*, vol. 5, no. 2 (British International Studies Association/Longman, 1979), pp. 99-110.

Reynolds argues that in order to understand the impact of non-state actors on international relations it is necessary to analyze, firstly, the relationship between non-state actors and state decision-makers and, secondly, at the level of the international system, the effect of technological change, political relationships and systemic structures on this relationship.

From the time when the modern state system came into existence in Western Europe in the sixteenth and seventeenth centuries until the end of the second world war, it was in large measure true to say that the use or threat of force was a common component of international relationships, that the control of the means of violence was effectively monopolized by states, and that governments accordingly regarded the maintenance of armed forces sufficient for defence against attack or for optimum exploitation of opportunities for advancing purposes (frequently in the form of territorial gains) as being of paramount importance. Since the second world war territorial gains have lost some of their significance (since the strategic importance of frontiers has declined, economic advantages may be gained without controlling territory, and political control within the area bounded by frontiers is less total than it was); control of the means of violence is no longer monopolized by states; and some restraints on the use of force are imposed by the nature of modern weapons systems and the risk that armed conflict once started may escalate out of control. At the same time non-military transactions have increased in range and quantity, so the dominant influence on international outcomes exercised by states as a result of their monopolistic military position is now no longer so decisive. This is not to say that states may not be dominant in these other sets of transactions — that point will be considered below — merely that that part of their dominance that derived from their military position is now less decisive because force is itself less determinant of international outcomes.

Within the realm of security however the central question is the extent to which non-state actors now play a role. Three aspects of this question may be identified, of which the last is much the most important. In the first place control of information of strategic significance may not be wholly in the hands of governments. Many multi-national corporations are involved both with research and development and with the production of critical components of weapons systems (computers for instance), and it is very difficult for governments of parent countries to be aware in sufficient detail of the operations of corporation subsidiaries in other countries to be able to ensure that information of strategic importance does not pass out of the country. Both the extent to which this happens and its significance are exceedingly difficult to assess, but the point ought not to be wholly ignored.

A much more obvious incursion of non-state actors in the security field is to be seen in the activity of guerrilla groups and terrorists, some of which at least may be viewed as international non-governmental organizations. Whatever the reason for their rise (such as the decline of governments' competence, the reduced level of satisfaction with or acceptance of value systems, the development of new loyalties across as well as within state frontiers, the availability or ease of manufacture of means of destruction, the swift global passage of information promoting emulative behaviour) the influence of such groups on international outcomes is evident. Their influence may be felt at three levels — on the domestic environment of decision-makers causing diversion of resources to internal security and reduction of capabilities for external purposes (as in the case of the United Kingdom and Northern Ireland); on the pattern of negotiations in relation to a particular problem (illustrated by the role of the Palestine Liberation Organization in the Arab-Israeli conflict), and in some small degree on the development of international institutionalization (as in the slow steps being taken towards a common response to hijacking).

This loss by states of the monopoly control of force that they formerly possessed is strikingly confirmed by the scale and scope of the security function as it is now perceived, at least by the two major powers. In their perspective, security is necessarily conceived in global terms, not merely because of the range of their interests, but because of the range and nature of weapons systems. The mounting costs of these weapons systems increasingly require transnational participation in research and development, and even more insistently an international market in which they may be sold. Thus the global nature of security, the nature of weapons systems which demand maximum geographical limits for defence, and the intolerable economic burden of defence even for states with the resources of the United States and the Soviet Union, have been major reasons why each of the two powers has thought it necessary to create and to maintain alliance systems, of which the most important are NATO and the Warsaw Pact. Whether alliances such as these develop an autonomous decision-making capacity and therefore may be seen as non-state actors, is affected by the various considerations about the political structure of non-state actors already discussed, but also by the command structure, whether forces of different state members are integrated or separately maintained, whether weapons systems are standardized, whether their procurement is rationalized among various states-members, whether infrastructure and logistics support is integrated or maintained under separate state control, whether there are political as well as military decision-making bodies, whether or not there is an independent secretariat and how it is recruited. The more deeply-rooted the habit of political discussion and consultation, the stronger and more independent the secretariat, and the more integrated the command, the forces, the weapons procurement and the infrastructure, the more the alliance as a whole performs the security function for its members, and the less any one member on its own is able to determine security outcomes.

It is however to the economic function — promotion of efficiency, growth, full employment, optimal distribution, price stability, quality of life — that most of the recent literature on non-state actors refers. Merely to list the components of the economic function does of course highlight its political complexion, for these components are by no means all mutually consistent, and choice among them involves value judgments which are political in nature. Moreover the literature tends to assume that the processes, institutions and actors now seen to be involved in performance of the economic function in the international arena represent a new development, whereas a structuralist view would maintain that there is nothing new about them. This view is perhaps best represented by Immanuel Wallerstein, who argues that the only real social systems are those defined by the nature and size of their economic activity (whether subsistence or global), that the capitalist world economy has been able to work because a world-wide division of labour (with free high-wage labour producing high-ranking goods in the core, and coerced low-wage labour producing low-ranking goods in the periphery) was not matched by similarly-ranging political control (which has been exercised under conflicting pressures within separated political units), with the result that the capitalists have had the requisite leeway to orient economic decisions to the world economy, while political decisions have been limited to states within the frontiers where they exercise legal control.[1] On this view the economic function has been performed since the emergence of the capitalist system primarily by non-state actors, and the 'crisis of world capitalism' might be seen to consist in the gradual closing of the gap between economic and political decisions which in the past made the working of the system possible. Interconnectedness, then, to the extent that it is increasing, is likely to make the capitalist system unworkable: this would conform, from a different perspective, with the previously advanced proposition that political entities have declining ability to determine outcomes.

Whether this hypothesis is thought to be persuasive or not, it is worth bearing in mind in an exploration of the linkages, economic-political, domestic-international, governmental-non-governmental which are observable in the determination of economic outcomes. In general terms the growth of economic transactions has had the consequences first (as already noted) that internal interconnectedness has grown so that any disturbance from inside or outside has wide-ranging effects; secondly, that the international dispersal of capital and technology has led to some price equalization in the factors of production thus increasing sensitivities of economies to disturbances; and thirdly, that systemic measures such as increased liquidity and flexible exchange rates are for many modernized states (though for some more than others) inadequate to cope with balance of payment problems without the addition of internal measures such as taxation changes, reductions in public expenditure, interest rate increases, monetary supply controls, exchange controls, capital flow restrictions or import quotas. Thus a variety of actors will be involved: governments of many states; central bankers; trade unions seeking to minimize the unemployment effects of deflationary policies; international monetary authorities; speculators exploiting the uncontrolled wash of international liquidity, of which the Eurodollar market is much the most important component; multinational corporations with their control of large capital and investment resources, and their ability to use such devices as differential pricing and tax havens, and to evade anti-trust laws in parent states by dispersed operations in other countries. Not merely therefore is the control of economic activity widely dispersed, but as mentioned above governments have decreasing ability to determine what the consequences of their actions will be. Even in the case of such an extensively analyzed and widely used tool as currency devaluation, for instance, there is no clear understanding of what the effect will be, because there is no certainty about the accumulated results of the different responses of the various actors that can play roles in the situation.

In these circumstances it is a matter of extreme difficulty to determine ways of assessing the interplay of non-state actors with states in their search after economic goals. The relationship that has been most extensively explored is that between states and multi-national corporations. The central capability possessed by the state is control of territorial access — whether that access is desired for markets, for raw material resources, or for the exploitation of investment opportunities. The central capabilities possessed by MNCs are capital, technology, and access to world markets. Agreements allowing MNC access will reflect the relative capabilities of the two parties in economic, coercive, leadership, and organizational coherence terms, the benefits each party perceives itself as being likely to achieve, and the existence or otherwise of alternative MNCs able to offer equivalent or bigger advantages, or alternative states able to offer equivalent or bigger opportunities.

One of the factors affecting substitutability, as it may be called, is whether the MNC is engaged in extractive, manufacturing or servicing operations. Other things being equal the extractive corporation has less bargaining power in relation to states than the other two because it can engage in its extractive operations only in those countries where the materials or resources in which it is interested can be found, whereas the manufacturer of motor-cars for example can with some loss switch operations to another country or, more probably, concentrate investment expansion plans elsewhere. But substitutability may operate also in the other direction. A state's bargaining position will be improved if there are alternative corporations able and willing to provide similar or improved capital, technological assistance, and marketing opportunities: it is for this reason that Fiat posed a threat to Chrysler (Britain)'s operation in Iran. A third consideration relates to the degree to which divestment by the corporation is possible. Some access agreements include provisions for ownership of part of the equity by the government or by local entrepreneurs, or for increasing participation over time, but this is less possible where the activity is one, like computers, where the level of technological innovation and progress is high and large new investment is constantly required. Corporation resistance to gradual loss of ownership of subsidiaries may lead to state attempts to impose divestment, and this will enter as a new component of the bargaining relationship; but a less hazardous response by a corporation when divestment is not hindered by high technological innovation is to develop product diversification, thus creating a new set of capital, technological and marketing offerings. A still further factor affecting the ability of governments, particularly in less developed countries, to maintain or develop a measure of economic autonomy in relation to MNCs operating in their territory is the amount of vertical integration in the corporation, the extent to which the service package is decomposable, and the type of patent protection. If the level of decomposability is low, the ability of a less developed country to exert effective influence on its economic environment may be reduced to quite small dimensions. Finally the difference should be noted between the components of the interplay when an initial agreement is being negotiated, and the changed context when the operation is in being: should a state for whatever reason feel it necessary to reassert its sovereignty it is likely to incur costs in the form of lost economies of scale, of reliance on a probably lower level of indigenous technology, and in a probably less efficient native entrepreneurship. Any resulting economic deterioration is likely to have undesirable political consequences.

The Systemic Context

International outcomes are in part the result of action in the form of outputs from entities with varying degrees of autonomous decision-making capability, and in the previous pages analysis has been attempted of some of the factors which affect the autonomy respectively of states and of international governmental and non-governmental organizations. But outcomes are also affected by the systemic context within which these actions occur. This context may be seen to vary with the level of technology, with political relationships, and with the system's structure. Technological change creates requirements that either cannot be met by autonomous state action, or are perceived as being unable to be met in this way. The requirements may arise in different forms, may have impact at different levels, and may operate on different time-scales. Some impinge upon the relations among states and affect their freedom of manoeuvre in relation to each other without leading on to the emergence of non-state actors (this effect is outside the scope of this paper and will not be discussed); some have effects of a kind which cannot be contained within state boundaries, and may or may not stimulate the formation or emergence of non-state actors; some create new hazards and opportunities in the international arena, from which new mechanisms for regulation and control may develop; some cannot progress at all without inter-state co-operation, and in these cases non-state actors with influence are most likely to appear.

Some of the effects of technology on the systemic context are illustrated by the global problems associated with economic growth, such as pollution and resource depletion, and by weather and climate modification. On the former there is now so extensive a literature that little needs to be said. The side effects of fertilizers or of pesticides like DDT entering the food chain, the disposal of wastes industrial, nuclear and human and the destruction of life in lakes and seas, the effects of radiation-filtering ozone of aerosol sprays or high-flying jet-aircraft, the increase of carbon dioxide in the atmosphere with possible consequences on the temperature of the earth and on the polar ice-caps – all of these are increasingly discussed and all are developments global in their implications, but non-state actors have not yet emerged for their regulation or control. The main reasons for this are similar to some already discussed in an earlier paragraph – that the experts are deeply divided about the extent of the dangers and the appropriate methods of controlling them, and most of the dangers, and the degree to which they exist, are remote in the sense that they are difficult to understand, require wide vision to appreciate, and seem likely to become acute if at all only in the relatively long term. Conditions of this kind are not those which stimulate the emergence of new actors able to rival the jurisdiction of states. The conditions of resource depletion are similar, with the additional complication that the states with the highest capabilities and so those most able to influence international outcomes are those whose interests would be most affected by controls on resource use (witness President Carter's difficulties in Congress with his energy proposals – which in the global perspective are modest enough in all conscience).

The case of weather and climate modification is a little different. Dealing with the pollution and resource depletion problems is particularly difficult since it involves interfering with long-established activities seen by states as being important to their power and wealth: weather modification by contrast is a new and emerging capability, and establishing institutional structures (and so new actors) for its control would mean not taking away from states something that they already have, but merely preventing them from acquiring something which is only just becoming available to them. In these circumstances the emergence of new actors with power may be seen as being a little less unlikely: but perhaps not very much so, because experts disagree on this subject also, because the advantage one state might gain, for example, from being able to increase its rainfall is not known to mean a disadvantage to another in terms of lost rainfall, because the gains (as for instance for the Soviet Union by damming the Bering Straits and raising the temperature of Siberia) might be very large, and because all of these possibilities have military and strategic implications. Once again the calculation is of the individual gains for one state as against the possible losses for others, the global implications for all, and the increased dangers of international conflict if the issue-area remains a free-for-all.

The technological creation of new hazards and opportunities is perhaps best illustrated by the question of the oceans. Until this century, with the exception of a three-mile strip along the coast, the oceans were regarded as common to mankind, with no state possessing special rights of ownership or control (although denying the use of the oceans to an enemy was of course an important part of warfare). The technology of the second half of the century, however, has made possible long-range machine fishing (thus threatening resources vital to a state's existence, as in the case of Iceland), has raised the question of food supplies on a massive scale from plankton, and has permitted a start to be made on the exploitation of the resources of the sea-bed (such as natural gas and oil, and soon the manganese nodules). In this case, although the interests of states are again fundamentally involved, it is perhaps more difficult to anticipate the handling of the issue without the emergence of new structures of rules and procedures which will require institutions to control them. Since the question is a new one, in which legal and political boundaries have not been set, in which the interests involved are very large, and the technological capacities for exploiting them are unevenly distributed and do not equate with variations in the degree of necessity for a particular resource (like Iceland's fish), the probability of prolonged and dangerous international conflict is very high if an international regime is not created. Whether it can be done successfully however is likely much to depend on whether the issue-area can be decomposed into its different components since — as mentioned above — nonstate actors are more likely to be able to operate effectively if their remit is limited and specific, than if it is general and wide-ranging.

Some small support for this last point is perhaps to be found in the history of the International Atomic Energy Authority, when states' interest in sovereign control of activities in their territory clashed with the general interest in establishing an effective system of control over a technological resource that carried a catastrophic potential for the whole of mankind. Technical and diplomatic skills have joined to find ways of overcoming the political problems created by widespread on-site inspection, and it has thus been possible to arrive at the elements of a safeguard system for control over the production, use and final disposition of fissionable materials within the Authority. The intermingling of security, economic, commercial and industrial concerns enabled some recent negotiations to be focused not on the incursions on sovereignty that are involved, but rather on ensuring that there should be for all parties equity in the inescapable incursions. But however equitable the system it will over time constrain some states more than others as they develop varying nuclear energy requirements, and the significance of the IAEA as an actor will then depend on how far the states in question feel able to weaken the safeguard system in their endeavour to ease some of the constraints on their own behaviour, and on what success they achieve.

The last case of the effect of technology on actors in the international arena is that in which the function cannot be performed without co-operation. Intelsat is perhaps the simplest example. The systems of the International Telecommunications Satellite Organization can work only for and among those states that choose to join the organization and establish links on their territory. The advantages of doing this are considerable, the economic costs not large, and the loss of ability for the states concerned to affect outcomes limited to the extent to which the facility acquires importance and its control is effectively if not formally in the hands of any states-members that retain a monopoly of the technology involved. The critical importance of this last point was recognized in the early negotiations for the establishment of Intelsat, when the European states refused to use the facilities under a lease system but agreed to participate only on the basis of a share in the government of the organization and access to the technology involved. Thus even in an organization causing relatively small loss and bringing relatively large gains, the individual interests of the states were maintained, and Intelsat therefore illustrates very well the variables that affect the probability that technological imperatives will lead to the emergence of new actors or the conferring on them of effective powers under their own autonomous control.

My second component of the systemic context was political relationships. Their significance is obvious. The ability which the United Nations Charter assigned to the Security Council to affect the behaviour of states in different degrees according to whether they were permanent members or not has been nullified by Soviet and United States conflict, by the resulting failure to constitute the forces that were to be the means by which the Council could take military enforcement action, and by the perceived involvement by the United States and the Soviet Union on opposite sides in almost all issues that have come before the Security Council, thus ensuring that action was consistently frustrated. The dispute between the major powers has likewise stultified the Secretary-General's initiatory role, since in order to function he must remain acceptable to both the major powers, and in a polarized world raising any question carried the implication of alignment with one of the powers against the other. Similarly the power of initiation of the European Commission in the Economic Community has been steadily whittled away by the growing predominance of the confederalists, at first led by de Gaulle, but in recent years by the French and British in parallel if not in tandem.

As far as the interplay between multi-national corporations and states are concerned the outcome will again be much affected by the political context. Thus the striking successes of the OPEC countries could be achieved only when the political rivalries among them were subordinated to the enormous economic gains that co-ordinated action could bring; while the contrast is marked between the ability of the unified actor Japan to negotiate tightly-controlled access agreements with United States MNCs, and the inability of the fragmented actor Europe (with its most important economic member, West Germany, being dependent in a strategic sense on the United States) to make agreements of a similar kind.

A strengthening of the ability of states to influence outcomes would result from the emergence of countervailing institutions to MNCs at the international level. It might have been expected, for instance, that a response to the growing role of multi-nationals would be increased international trade unionism, but apart from a few International Trade Secretariats in Europe little co-ordination has developed. This would seem to be due partly to the generally parochial attitude of Trades Unions (the 1971 British Trade Union Congress resolved that it would rely on its own abilities and strength, not on co-operation), and partly to the non-congruence of interest of unions in high- and low-wage economies.

The last factor to which I wish to refer in exploring the relative influences of state and non-state actors in determining international outcomes is the structure of the international system within which both types of actor operate. I select three structural characteristics: the degree of polarization, the nature and extent of stratification, and the presence or absence of systemic norms and values.

It is a commonplace that the international state system has been moving from a relatively high degree of polarization between the late 1940s and early 60s towards greater polycentrism. One component of this move, part cause, part consequence, has been a decline in the level of threat perception between the two major powers, and so among their allies and associates also. One aspect of the reduction in the degree of polarization is that the major power relationship is less sharply seen as zero-sum, so that the two powers do not so strongly feel that they can tolerate no change in any part of the world that is perceived to be disadvantageous. Moreover, in terms of the Deutsch-Singer argument,[2] the more significant centres of power there are in a system the less attention can be devoted by any one centre to any other, and the less therefore any one is inclined towards violent conflict because of the concentration of resources on one centre that conflict demands. These are among the reasons for the view suggested earlier in this paper, that the security function and the role of force have lost some of their salience for states, and in these conditions states may feel it less necessary, as well as actually being less able, to resist the increase of influence of *some* non-state actors. The 'some' is important, because reductions in threat perception and in the paramountcy of the security function mean that non-state actors that are primarily concerned with security are *less* able significantly to constrain states within them: thus the last decade has seen France in NATO and Romania in the Warsaw Pact demonstrating their ability to act with a greater measure of independence from their alliance framework. The observation sharply illustrates the general proposition that increased influence of non-state actors will vary in relation to one state as compared with another, and varies also from issue-area to issue-area: the very systemic factor that tends to increase the influence of non-state actors in the economic or ecological issue-areas may decrease the influence of non-state actors in the security issue-area.

The nature and extent of stratification in the international system refers to the similarity or otherwise of the capabilities of the states-members of the system, and the extent to which states which are high on one component of capabilities are also high on some or all others. In the states system of Western Europe in the eighteenth century the members were roughly similar in capabilities, whereas in the global system of the late twentieth century there is a marked hierarchy, from the two main powers, to between six and twelve middle powers (depending on definition, with China aspiring to join the top two), to sixty or so minor powers and another sixty or so micro-powers. Moreover in the contemporary system there are striking disequilibria, with Japan third on economic capabilities but middle on status-prestige and low on military, the OPEC countries high on one particular commodity capability, but low otherwise, and Iran, until recently, rising fairly rapidly on military and to some extent economic capability, but still relatively low on status-prestige.

The importance of stratification for the role of non-state actors — in the sense of the degree both of hierarchy and of disequilibrium — is difficult to assess. If in a highly hierarchical system part of the predominance of the leading state or states derives from a special role they play in the government of non-state actors, then, other things being equal, hierarchy in the system will tend to decrease the autonomy of non-state actors and increase the extent to which they serve as tools of the major states. It is easy to imagine, for instance, a situation in which the relationship between the United States government and IBM was critically important to a whole range of international outcomes, if IBM's predominance in the computer field became even greater, and when computer technological innovation has made possible the creation of large systems and international networks with huge storage capacity and with controlled access to the information contained within them. In systems displaying a high degree of disequilibrium, non-state actors might be seen as allies by states desiring to attain a status commensurate with their other capabilities, or alternatively the thrust of nationalism might lead to possibly counter-productive efforts to assert sovereignty. There is here a whole range of questions upon which little research has been done.

As far as systemic norms and values are concerned the basic proposition is that the more there is consensus on purposes and values the greater the probability that IGOs and INGOs will reflect them and will be able to impose greater costs on states that defy them. Support for this proposition may perhaps be found in the economic field, where IGOs have been able to develop or maintain little autonomy, and where there is basic disagreement on purposes. One view is that the primary economic goal should be to maximize order and efficiency in order to maximize growth and welfare for the benefit of all. An alternative view is that the primary goal should be to minimize or correct the political injustice of the gross maldistribution of wealth on a global scale: just as international peace and security is the ideology of satisfied powers so liberal market mechanisms for efficiency is the ideology of the rich and the technologically-advanced. Thus there re-appears at the international level a classical problem of political theory: how far should there be limitations by political inter-vention of the inequities produced by the free operation of socio-economic processes? To the extent that consensus is lacking (illustrated by conflicts and disagreement both within and between IMF and IBRD on the one hand and UNCTAD and the group of 77 on the other) institutions of a global character can be less effective in influencing both states and non-state actors such as MNCs. The disagreement on how much intervention for what purposes should there be is reflected in a lack of machinery with a capability to intervene. [. . .]

Notes

1. I. Wallerstein, *The Modern World System* (New York, 1974).
2. K.W. Deutsch and J.D. Singer, 'Multipolar Systems and International Stabili-ty' *World Politics*, XVI (1964), pp. 390-407.

TRANSNATIONAL ORGANIZATIONS IN WORLD POLITICS

Samuel P. Huntington

Source: *World Politics*, vol XXV (Princeton University Press, April 1973), pp. 333-68.

Huntington's aim is to analyze the roots and extent of the 'transnational organizational revolution' in world politics. He begins by assessing the political and other origins of transnational organizations — especially in terms of their links to American political dominance. He goes on to analyze the connections between transnational bodies and national societies, and particularly their requirements for access to those societies. Here, he poses a contrast with intergovernmental bodies, which typically require accord between states as a basis for their operations.

The Transnational Organizational Revolution

Anaconda	J. Walter Thompson	Ford Foundation
Intelsat	Air France	Catholic Church
Chase Manhattan	Strategic Air Command	CIA
AID	Unilever	World Bank

These twelve organizations appear to have little in common. They are public and private, national and international, profit-making and charitable, religious and secular, civil and military, and, depending on one's perspective, benign and nefarious. Yet they do share three characteristics. First, each is a relatively large, hierarchically organized, centrally directed bureaucracy. Second, each performs a set of relatively limited, specialized, and, in some sense, technical functions: gathering intelligence, investing money, transmitting messages, promoting sales, producing copper, delivering bombs, saving souls. Third, each organization performs its functions across one or more international boundaries and, insofar as is possible, in relative disregard of those boundaries. They are, in short, *transnational organizations*, and the activities in which they engage are *transnational operations*. Such organizations have existed before in history. Armies and navies, churches and joint stock companies, as well as other types of organizations have been involved in transnational operations in the past. During the twenty-five years after World War II, however, transnational organizations: (a) proliferated in number far beyond anything remotely existing in the past; (b) individually grew in size far beyond anything existing in the past; (c) performed functions which they never performed in the past; and (d) operated on a truly global scale such as was never possible in the past. The increase in the number, size, scope, and variety of transnational organizations after World War II makes it possible, useful, and sensible to speak of a *transnational organizational revolution* in world politics. The purpose of this essay is to analyze, in a preliminary way, the sources, nature, and dynamics of this revolution, and to speculate on its implications for politics at the national and international levels. [. . .]

The terms 'international', 'multinational', and 'transnational' have been variously used to refer to the control of an organization, the composition of its staff, and the scope of its operations. Terminological confusion is further compounded because one word, 'national', serves as the opposite of each of these three terms. To minimize ambiguity, at least on these pages, and to maintain some critical distinctions, each of these terms will in this essay be used to refer to only one of these organizational dimensions. An organization is 'transnational' rather than 'national' if it carries on significantly centrally-directed operations in the territory of two or more nation-states. Similarly, an organization will be called 'international' rather than 'national' only if the control of the organization is explicitly shared among representatives of two or more nationalities. And an organization is 'multinational' rather than 'national' only if people from two or more nationalities participate significantly in its operations. [. . .]

The Significance of Transnationalism

Nationalism, internationalism, and transnationalism have all been major factors on the contemporary world scene. At the end of World War II, observers of world politics expected nationalism to be a major force, and their expectations were not disappointed. The decline of Europe encouraged the blossoming forth of nationalist movements in Asia and Africa, and by the early 1960s colonialism in the classic familiar forms was virtually finished and scores of new nation-states had been formally recognized. The end of colonialism, however, did not mean the end of nationalism, in the sense of the behavioral and attitudinal manifestations by a people of their presumed ethnic or racial identity, nor the end of the political disruption of the newly independent nation-states. Colonialism led peoples of various ethnic or racial identities to suppress their antagonisms in order to win independence. The achivement of independence raised the question of *whose* independence had been achieved, and led to a re-awakening and, in some cases, a totally new awakening of communal antagonisms. Nationalism increasingly has meant 'subnationalism', and has thus become identified with political fragmentation. Nationalism has remained a force in world politics, but a force which promises almost as much disruption in a world of independent states as it did in a world of colonial empires.

At the close of World War II, internationalism was also expected to be a wave of the future, and the United Nations was created to embody that hope and to make it reality. While nationalism has remained strong but its impact has changed, internationalism, in contrast, has failed to gain the role and significance which it was expected to achieve. The great hopes for international organizations − that is, organizations whose activities involve the active cooperation of distinct national (private or public) delegations − have not been realized. In one form or another, internationalism involves agreement among nation-states. Interests have to be shared or to be traded for an international organization to work. This requirement puts an inherent limit on internationalism. The United Nations and other international organizations have remained relatively weak because they are inherently the arenas for national actors; the extent to which they can become independent actors themselves is dependent on agreement among national actors.

An international organization requires the identification and creation of a common interest among national groups. This common interest may be easy to identify, such as the exchange of mail. Or it may be the product of extensive and time-consuming negotiation among national units. A transnational organization, on the other hand, has its own interest which inheres in the organization and its functions, which may or may not be closely related to the interests of national groups. Nations participate in international organizations; transnational organizations operate within nations. International organizations are designed to facilitate the achievement of a common interest among many national units. Transnational organizations are designed to facilitate the pursuit of a single interest within many national units. The international organization requires *accord* among nations; the transnational organization requires *access* to nations. These two needs, accord and access, neatly summarize the differences between the two phenomena. The restraints on an international organization are largely internal, stemming from the need to produce consensus among its members. The restraints on a transnational organization are largely external, stemming from its need to gain operating authority in different sovereign states. International organizations embody the principle of nationality; transnational organizations try to ignore it. In this sense the emergence of transnational organizations on the world scene involves a pattern of cross-cutting cleavages and associations overlaying those associated with the nation-state.

The emergence of transnational organizations on such a large scale was, in large part, unanticipated. Internationalism was supposed to furnish the threads tying the world together. In actuality, however, every international organization at some point finds itself limited by the very principle which gives it being. Much of the disappointment with the UN and its various agencies stems precisely from the failure to recognize this fact. While national representatives and delegations engage in endless debate at UN conferences and councils, however, the agents of the transnational organizations are busily deployed across the continents spinning the webs that link the world together. The contrast between the two forms of organization can be seen in the difference between the great bulk of UN bodies which are basically international in character and thus dependent for action on agreement among national delegations, and one organization that is formally international in control and related to the UN but in practice quite autonomous, which operates successfully in a transnational manner. Perhaps significantly, that organization, the World Bank, is headquartered in Washington, not in New York.

A similar contrast exists between private transnational organizations and international non-governmental organizations (or INGOs). Like transnational organizations, INGOs multiplied rapidly in numbers and functions in the decades after World War II. Of the INGOs in existence in 1966, 50 per cent were founded after 1950 and 25 per cent were founded in 1960 or later. During these same years, however, the average size of the INGOs did not increase and, if anything, decreased. In 1964 the mean INGO budget was $629,000 and the mean INGO staff encompassed nine people. INGOs simply did not have the resources, scope, or influence of nationally controlled, transnational, non-governmental organizations such as the Ford Foundation, IBM, or Exxon.

Transnational organizations thus may, in theory, be nationally or internationally, privately or governmentally controlled. The need to reach agreement among national units, however, restricts the purposes and activities of international bodies. Free of this internal constraint, nationally controlled organizations are much better able to formulate purposes, to mobilize resources, and to pursue their objectives across international boundaries. [. . .]

A distinctive characteristic of the transnational organization is its broader-than-national perspective with respect to the pursuit of highly specialized objectives through a central optimizing strategy across national boundaries. The 'essence' of a transnational corporation, as Behrman has argued, 'is that it is attempting to treat the various national markets as though they were one — to the extent permitted by governments'.[1] In similar fashion, a transnational military organization treats the problems of defense of different national territories as if they were part of a single whole. For its specialized purpose, its arena assumes continental or global proportions and it thinks in continental or global terms. [. . .]

The American Sources of Transnationalism

The principal sources of the transnational organizational revolution are to be found in American society and in the global expansion of the United States during the two decades after World War II. This does not mean that transnational organizations and operations are only created by Americans. It does mean that the proliferation of transnational operations in recent years was initially and predominantly an American phenomenon. Transnational organizations in large part developed out of American national organizations (governmental or non-governmental) or out of international organizations in which Americans played the leading roles. Transnationalism is one of the more important legacies for world politics of two decades of American expansion into world politics.

Two preconditions, technological and political, exist for the development of transnationalism. For an organization to operate on a global or semi-global basis, it must have means of communication and transportation. Otherwise it will be only a crossnational organization, a federation of local satrapies each of which is more responsive to its local leadership than to centralized direction. There has to be the technological and organizational capability to operate across vast distances and in differing cultures. The transnational corporation rests on the fact that 'technology and corporate organization in all of the advanced countries have now reached levels of capability that permit focus on markets and production across, and indeed without reference to, national boundaries'.[2] Jet aircraft and communications satellites are to the transnational organizations of today what the iron horse and telephone were to the 'trans-state' organizations of the United States in the 1880s. These technological capabilities to make 'illusions of distance', in Albert Wohlstetter's phrase, were in large part developed within the United States and have been pre-eminently employed by the United States.

An organization can normally (there are notable exceptions) employ its technological capability to operate in a society only if it has the permission of the government of that society. Political access, consequently, has to go hand in hand with technical capability to make transnationalism a reality. Throughout the two decades after World War II, the power of the United States Government in world politics, and its interests in developing a system of alliances with other governments against the Soviet Union, China, and communism, produced the underlying political condition which made the rise of transnationalism possible. Western Europe, Latin America, East Asia, and much of South Asia, the Middle East, and Africa fell within what was euphemistically referred to as 'the Free World', and what was in fact a security zone. The governments of countries within this zone found it in their interest: (a) to accept an explicit or implicit guarantee by Washington of the independence of their country and, in some cases, of the authority of the government; and (b) to permit access to their territory by a variety of US governmental and non-governmental organizations pursuing goals which those organizations considered important. Communist governments, of course, by and large did not permit such access, although at times they were incapable of stopping it (for instance, U-2 flights over the Soviet Union in the 1950s). Other governments (Burma, the UAR, Syria) terminated such access or permitted it only on a very restricted basis. The great bulk of the countries of Europe and the Third World, however, found the advantages of transnational access to outweigh the costs of attempting to stop it. [...]

Transnationalism is the American mode of expansion. It has meant 'freedom to operate' rather than 'power to control'. US expansion has been pluralistic expansion in which a variety of organizations, governmental and non-governmental, have attempted to pursue the objectives important to them within the territory of other societies. In some respects, the US surge outward was almost as pluralistic as the outward surge of Western Europe in the sixteenth and seventeenth centuries. One could then speak of Western expansion but not of *the* Western empire because there were Spanish, Dutch, Portuguese, French, and English empires. Similarly, one can properly speak now of American expansion but not of *the* American empire, because there are so many of them. 'The *Pax Americana*', as I.F. Stone put it, 'is the "internationalism" of Standard Oil, Chase Manhattan, and the Pentagon'.[3] And, one must add, of much else besides. [...]

American expansion has thus involved the generation and spread of transnational organizations pursuing a variety of specific goals in a multiplicity of territories. Economic aid missions, military bases, and corporate investments are only the most obvious and tangible symbols of US-based transnationalism. This type of pluralistic, segmented expansion also led groups in other societies to create parallel and often competing transnational structures. The principal legacy of American expansion about the world is a network of transnational institutions knitting the world together in ways that never existed in the past. The question for the future is whether and how the contraction of the world brought about by the expansion of the American role will survive the contraction of that role. Once the political conditions which gave it birth disappear, how much transnationalism will remain?

[Huntington goes on to discuss transnational organizations in terms of the patterns of authority they demonstrate. The first element in such patterns is the source of control; the second is the degree of centralization or decentralization in the organizational structure; and the third is the variation in nationality of the personnel in transnational organizations. At this point, Huntington turns to the links between transnational organizations and national politics.]

Transnational Organizations in National Politics

In most instances, a transnational organization can conduct its operations only with the approval of the government claiming sovereignty over the territory in which it wishes to operate. Consequently, the transnational organization and the national government have to reach an *access agreement* defining the conditions under which the operations of the former will be permitted on the territory of the latter. The contents of this agreement will reflect the relative bargaining strengths of the two parties. In some instances, the transnational organization may have a clear upper hand and be able to secure access on very favorable terms. It may, for instance, in classic imperial form, be able to threaten sanctions by the national government of its home territory if it is not given access on the terms which it desires. More generally, the terms of the access agreement will reflect: (a) the benefits which each side perceives for itself in the conclusion of an arrangement; (b) the inherent strength of each side in terms of economic resources, coercive power, leadership skill, and organizational coherence; and (c) the alternatives open to each side to secure what it wishes through arrangements with another organization or another government.

Apart from the instances where the transnational organization can bring coercive pressure to bear on the national government, the latter will presumably agree to the operations taking place on its territory only if those operations themselves serve the purposes of the national government or are compatible with those purposes, or if the transnational organization has paid a price to the government to make those operations acceptable. In either case, the local national government receives benefits by trading upon its control of access to the national territory. As transnational organizations become larger and more numerous, the demands for access to the territory of nation-states will also multiply. The value of that access, consequently, will also go up. The national governments who control access will thus be strengthened. In this sense, the growth of transnational operations does not challenge the nation-state but reinforces it. It increases the demands for the resource which the nation-state alone controls: territorial access. Within the nation-state, those groups which dominate the national government are similarly able to use the increased value of their control over access to the national territory to strengthen their own position *vis-à-vis* other groups in their society.

The price that a transnational organization has to pay for access to national territory will thus, in part, depend on the extent to which the government controlling that territory perceives those operations as contributing to its purposes. If the operations clearly serve the government's purposes, it may offer considerable inducements to the transnational organization to locate its operations there. This might be the case, for instance, with a factory which not only provided local jobs but also either met an urgent local need for its product or earned needed foreign exchange by the export of its product. It would also be the case with military installations which contributed to local defense. In other instances, however, the installations of the transnational organization may contribute very little to the purposes of the local government. This is presumably more likely to be the case the more global the scope of the overall operations of the transnational organization and the more tightly integrated the conduct of those operations. In these cases, the transnational organization may have to pay a heavy price to conduct its operations on a particular piece of territory. [. . .]

One of the curious phenomena of post-World War II international politics was, indeed, the striking contrast which often existed between the awesome and overwhelming military, logistical, material, technological, and economic presence of US-based transnational organizations in a society, which at times seemed likely to suffocate the local society, and the degree of political influence which the US Government exercised on the government of that society. The former often seemed out of all proportion to the latter. American organizations easily penetrated the local society; the local government easily, blandly, and, to Americans, infuriatingly, resisted the advice and demands of the US Government. The American presence may have been overwhelming; American influence almost always fell far short of that.

The reasons for this gap lie, of course, in the motives for the presence of the US-based transnational organizations and in the nature of their operations. The American organizations were often present in the country not to serve the needs of that country as defined by its rulers and elite, but to serve their own interests which, however, might well be rationalized in terms of the interests of the local country. The Americans were there in the way in which they were there because they were convinced that it was important *for them* for them to be there, not because the local government thought that it was important *for it* for them to be there. [. . .]

The political costs of maintaining a presence thus often exceeded the local benefits generated by that presence. In addition, however, to the extent that the goals of the US-based transnational organizations reflected only the general interests of the organizations and were not specific to the society in which the operation occurred, the transnational organizations themselves had no interest in the local political system so long as it did not obstruct their ability to operate. US-based transnational organizations indeed often went to extreme lengths to deny that their local operations had any effect on local politics. Far from wishing to exercise political influence in the local society, their goal was to be as far removed from local politics as possible. The transnational religious activities of the Catholic Church, it has been argued, are facilitated by the separation of state and church in a country.[4] The transnational economic and military activities of US-based transnational organizations are similiarly facilitated if these operations can be separated from local politics. From the viewpoint of the transnational organization, the ideal situation would be one in which the local political system and the transnational operation had nothing to do with each other. The typical American attitude would be: 'Let us operate our air base; mine copper; provide technical advice to the engineering school — all without involvement with local politics.' The aim of the Americans would not be to control the local government, but to avoid it.

The operations of transnational organizations thus usually do not have political motivations in the sense of being designed to affect the balance of power within the local society. They do, however, often have political consequences that actually affect that balance. Insofar as the transnational organizations have to come to terms with the dominant groups in the local political system in order to secure access to a country, their operations will tend to reinforce, or at least not injure, the position of those groups. The immediate general impact of transnational operations on a society is thus likely to be a conservative one. The longer-run general impact, however, may be quite different. The transnational organization typically brings into the local society new activities which could not be performed as well by local organizations. Insofar as the transnational organization is itself based in an economically more developed society than the one in which it is conducting its operations, it tends to be a major transmission belt for new styles of life, new ideas, new technology, and new social and cultural values that challenge the traditional culture of the local society. In addition, of course, while the immediate impact of transnational operations generally reinforces the powers that be, it may also redistribute power among those powers. The transnational organization brings new resources – equipment, technology, capital, personnel – into the society. Quite apart from whatever purposes it may have, the way in which those resources enter the society, and their location in that society, will benefit some specific groups at the expense of others. Investments by transnational corporations stimulate growth in some industries and regions but not in others. Economic and military assistance programs strengthen economic planning agencies and military services as against other bureaucratic and political groups.

Access agreements between governmentally controlled transnational organizations and national governments obviously appear in the traditional form of intergovernmental agreements. In substance, however, they often differ little from the agreements negotiated between a privately controlled transnational organization and a national government. The weight of the controlling government presumably plays a significantly greater role, however, in the negotiation of the former than of the latter. Officials on both sides may see the intergovernmental access agreement as an integral part of their overall political and diplomatic relations. With respect to private organizations, however, pressure from the home government generally does not, except in unusual cases such as the Middle East in the 1920s, play a significant role in securing initial access. The home government is much more likely to enter the picture if the host government attempts to terminate access or to change the conditions of access. In the past, this could and, at times, did produce US military or paramilitary intervention (as in Guatemala in 1954) to maintain the access of US-controlled transnational corporations and agencies. More frequently, actions by governments denying or curtailing transnational operations are met by diplomatic protests and economic sanctions by the home government. With some exceptions (of which Vietnam is the most notable), the bulk of US Government interventions – military, economic, and political — in the domestic politics of Third-World states after World War II have been relatively discrete, *ad hoc* efforts to maintain or to restore previously existing access conditions for US-based transnational organizations rather than efforts to achieve more comprehensive purposes. [. . .]

Transnational Organization vs. the Nation-State?

The rise of transnational organizations after World War II was a product of American expansion on the one hand and technological development on the other. For a quarter of a century these two trends reinforced each other. Now, however, the American impetus to involvement in the world is waning. The American will to lead, to promote economic and cultural interaction and integration, to maintain militarily the outer boundaries of a world-wide system and to foster politically free access within that system has declined markedly. In the immediate future, US Government-based transnational organizations are likely to decline in importance compared to privately controlled organizations; US-controlled transnational organizations will decline in relative significance compared to those controlled by other nations and by international bodies. The question remains, however, how these changes in the relationships among nation-states will affect the overall role of transnational organizations. The pre-eminence of one nation-state in large portions of the world favors the emergence of transnational organizations under the sponsorship and control of that nation-state. This is peculiarly the case when that state has a highly pluralistic and open political and institutional tradition that is conducive to the generation of transnational bodies. World politics is now moving in the direction of a bipolar military balance between the superpowers, a multi-polar diplomatic and economic balance among the great powers, and increasing discrepancies in power tending toward regional hegemonies among the less developed states. This structure of world politics could be far less conducive to the emergence and operation of transnational organizations than one in which one center predominated. Clearly it favors a dispersion of control over transnational organizations. It may also favor a slowdown in their numerical growth and some restriction in the geographical scope of their activities.

While the political preconditions for transnationalism have changed significantly, the technological dynamic has continued without slowdown. The extraordinary improvements in international communication and transportation seem destined to continue, accompanied by more Intelsats, Concordes, IBM 370s, and all the other modern instruments for shrinking time and space. The relative decline in the costs of communication and transportation is likely to increase the advantages of large-scale producing units and to increase the size of manageable enterprises.'[5] Business corporations, aid agencies, military services, foundations, churches, public service organizations, all will have an increasing capacity to operate on a global scale and, presumably, increasing incentives to capitalize on the opportunities which this capacity gives them. Functional bureaucracies will feel ever more cramped by national boundaries and will devise means to escape beyond the boundaries within which they were born and to penetrate the boundaries within which they can prosper. Existing transnational organizations will find it in their interest to continue to integrate their activities and to tighten the organizational bonds which cut across national borders.

Politics and technology thus seem to be at odds. On the one hand, in an atmosphere of American political withdrawal and balance-of-power diplomacy, national governments may feel increasingly confident in confronting transnational organizations. A nationalist backlash could be in the making, producing new restrictions on the autonomy and scope of transnational organizations, and in some cases ousting transnational organizations from the national territory and bringing their local assets under full national control. Given this scenario, the transnational organization could be seen as a transient phenomenon unable to outlast the political conditions responsible for its emergence. Transnational operations could fragment and disappear in the face of a rise in nationalist autarky.

Some observers, on the other hand, have seen the rise of the transnational organization, particularly the 'multinational' business corporation, as challenging the future of the nation-state. As one leading American banker put it, 'the political boundaries of nation-states are too narrow and constricted to define the scope and sweep of modern business'. We have, consequently, seen the rise of 'the new globalists', the 'advance men' of 'economic one-worldism' who see 'the entire world as a market', and we may be evolving into a period in which 'businessmen often wear the robes of diplomats' and 'are more influential than statesmen in many quarters of the globe'.[6] The transnational corporation, George Ball has said, 'is a modern concept evolved to meet the requirements of the modern age' while the nation-state 'is still rooted in archaic concepts unsympathetic to the needs of our complex world'.[7] In similar terms, Arthur Barber has argued that the transnational corporation 'is acting and planning in terms that are far in advance of the political concepts of the nation-state'. Just as the Renaissance ended feudalism and the dominant role of the Church, so this twentieth-century renaissance is 'bringing an end to middle-class society and the dominance of the nation-state'.[8]

These predictions of the death of the nation-state are premature. They overlook the ability of human beings and human institutions to respond to challenges and to adapt themselves to changed environments. They seem to be based on a zero-sum assumption about power and sovereignty: that a growth in the power of transnational organizations must be accompanied by a decrease in the power of nation-states. This, however, need not be the case. Indeed, as we have argued, an increase in the number, functions, and scope of transnational organizations will increase the demand for access to national territories and hence also increase the value of the one resource almost exclusively under the control of national governments. The current situation is, in this respect, quite different from that which prevailed with respect to state governments and national corporations within the United States in the nineteenth century. There, the Supreme Court held that except in rare circumstances, state governments could not deny or restrict access to their territory by businesses based in other states. The interstate commerce clause left such regulatory power to Congress. In the absence of any comparable global political authority able to limit the exclusionary powers of national governments, transnational organizations must come to terms with those governments.

By and large, private transnational corporations have recognized this fact and have attempted to deal with national governments in a conciliatory manner. The proponents of the transnational corporation also recognize this fact when they argue that the imposition of local restrictions and controls on the operation of the transnational corporation will 'necessarily impede the fulfillment of the world corporation's full potential as the best means yet devised for using world resources according to the criterion of profit, which is an objective standard of efficiency'. To avoid this situation, they advocate creating by treaty an International Companies Law which could 'place limitations . . . on the restrictions that a nation-state might be permitted to impose on companies established under its sanction'.[9] The probability of national governments arriving at an international agreement to limit their own authority, however, would appear to be fairly remote at the present time. In the absence of any such mutual voluntary abnegation of power, the national governments will retain their control over access.

National governments capitalize on that control by granting access on conditions satisfactory to them. A government may, of course, use its control over access foolishly or corruptly. If, however, it uses it wisely, granting access to private, governmental, and international transnational organizations in such a way as to further its own objectives, it is far from surrendering its sovereignty. It is, instead, capitalizing on its control over one resource in order to strengthen itself through the addition of other resources. The widespread penetration of its society by transnational organizations will, obviously, have significant effects on that society. But that does not necessarily mean an impairment of the sovereignty of the national government. [. . .]

The end of the European colonial empires was followed by the creation of a large number of new nation-states often lacking established institutions, consensus on the bases of legitimacy, and sizeable, technically well-trained, and politically skilled elites, as well as any inherited sense of national unity and identity. Many such countries in Africa and some in Latin America and Asia have been labeled 'non-viable'. Yet at the same time, many such countries are also in the grip of fissiparous tendencies that threaten to break up the existing fragile nation-state into even smaller units. While functional imperatives seem to be making transnational organizations bigger and bigger, cultural and communal imperatives seem to be encouraging political units to become smaller and smaller. 'Tribalism' in politics contrasts with 'transnationalism' in economics. Yet these contrasting patterns of development are also, in some measure, reinforcing. The nation-states of today which are labled 'unviable' and those still smaller entities which may emerge in the future could well be made viable by the operations of transnational organizations that link activities within one state to those in other states. The sovereignty of the government may, in this sense, be limited, but the sovereignty of the people may be made more real by the fact that the 'sovereign' unit of government is smaller, closer, easier to participate in, and much easier to identify with.

With respect to the coexistence of the nation-state and the transnational organization, the case can, indeed, be made that at the present time the existence of one not only implies but requires the existence of the other. These two entities serve different purposes and meet different needs. They are often in conflict, but the conflict is rooted in differences rather than similarities in function. Two states may conflict because they wish to exercise sovereignty over the same piece of territory; two corporations may conflict because they sell similar goods in the same market; two parties may conflict because they attempt to win the same votes. In all these cases the competitive entities are similar in function, structure, and purpose. The competing entities are essentially duplicates of each other. Such *duplicative conflict* is often zero sum in character and involves, potentially at least, the survivial of one or both parties to the conflict. *Complementary conflict*, in contrast, involves entities performing essentially different functions; the competition stems from this dissimilarity of function. In these instances, the existence of the parties is not usually at stake. Each has some interest in the survival of the other as an inherent component of a system of which they are both part. Within that system, each also has a role to play which inevitably brings it into conflict with the other type of institution, playing a different role. This conflict is incidental to each institution's performance of its respective functions, and the conflict between the institutions is limited by their difference in functions. In a sense, the conflicts are almost jurisdictional in nature, an inevitable friction in the working of the system. [...]

The conflict between national governments and transnational organizations is clearly complementary rather than duplicative. It is conflict not between likes but between unlikes, each of which has its own primary set of functions to perform. It is, consequently, conflict which, like labor-management conflict, involves the structuring of relations and the distribution of benefits to entities which need each other even as they conflict with each other. The balance of influence may shift back and forth from one to the other, but neither can displace the other.

In fact, the balance between a transnational organization and a national government often does appear to move through three phases. In the first phase, the initiative lies with the transnational organization which often secures access to the territory controlled by the government on very favorable terms. In the second phase, the government asserts control over the local operations, perhaps even displacing the transnational authority completely. In the third phase, the transnational organization returns to the scene and a new equilibrium is worked out between the two entities. [...]

The novelty and, indeed, the revolutionary character of the transnational organization stem in large part from the fact that it has emerged apart from the existing structure of international relations. It is an outgrowth of the nation-state, but it is founded on a principle entirely different from nationality. In economic history, the impetus for change came from neither feudal lord not feudal peasant but rather from a new urban class of merchants and entrepreneurs who developed alongside but outside the feudal social structure. And, as Marx recognized, this was the revolutionary class. Similarly, today the revolutionary organizations in world politics are not the national or international organizations which have been part of the nation-state system, but rather the transnational organizations which have developed alongside but outside that system. Just as the bourgeoisie represented a principle of production foreign to the feudal system, so does the transnational organization represent a principle of organization foreign to the nation-state system. In Marx's terms, the capitalist forces of production outran the feudal relations of production.

Today, man's capacities for organization are outrunning the nation-state system. Internationalism is a dead end. Only organizations that are disinterested in sovereignty can transcend it. For the immediate future a central focus of world politics will be on the coexistence of and interaction between transnational organizations and the nation-state.

Notes

1. Jack N. Behrman, *Some Patterns in the Rise of the Multinational Enterprise*, Research Paper no. 18 (Graduate School of Business Administration, University of North Carolina, Chapel Hill, NC, 1969), p. 61.

2. Sidney E. Rolfe, 'The International Corporation in Perspective', in Sidney E. Rolfe and Walter E. Damm (eds), *The Multinational Corporation in the World Economy* (New York, 1970), p. 12.

3. *I.F. Stone's Bi-Weekly*, XVIII (13 July 1970), p. 1.

4. Ivan Vallier, 'The Roman Catholic Church: A Transnational Actor', in Robert O. Keohane and Joseph S. Nye, Jr (eds), *Transnational Relations in World Politics* (Cambridge, Mass., 1972), pp. 137-8.

5. Raymond Vernon, *Sovereignty at Bay* (New York, 1971), pp. 251-2.

6. William I. Spencer (President, First National City Corporation), 'The New Globalists' (Address before American Chamber of Commerce, Frankfurt, Germany, 6 September 1972).

7. George W. Ball, 'Cosmocorp: The Importance of Being Stateless', *Atlantic Community Quarterly*, VI (Summer 1968), p. 165.

8. Arthur Barber, 'Emerging New Power: The World Corporation', *War/Peace Report*, VIII (October 1968), p. 7.

9. George W. Ball, 'Making World Corporation Into World Citizens', *War/Peace Report*, VIII (October 1968), p. 10.

TRANSGOVERNMENTAL RELATIONS AND INTERNATIONAL ORGANIZATIONS

Robert O. Keohane and Joseph S. Nye

Source: *World Politics*, vol. XXVII, no. 1 (Princeton University Press, 1974), pp. 39-62.

Keohane and Nye set out to contest the 'Realist' claim that international organizations are no more than instruments of state policy. They suggest that such institutions can influence the activities of civil servants, who try to co-ordinate policy with their counterparts in other countries or seek their support for domestic policy initiatives.

'Realist' analyses of world politics have generally assumed that states are the only significant actors; that they act as units; and that their military security objectives dominate their other goals. On the basis of these assumptions it is easy to conclude that international organizations — defined as intergovernmental organizations — are merely instruments of governments, and therefore unimportant in their own right. Compared with the hopes and dreams of world federalists, the Realist position reflects reality: international organizations in the contemporary world are not powerful independent actors, and relatively universal organizations such as the United Nations find it extraordinarily difficult to reach agreement on significant issues. It is therefore not surprising that students of world politics have paid relatively slight attention to these entities, particularly after hopes for a major United Nations peacekeeping role were dashed in the early 1960s.

The Realist model on which the above conclusions about international organizations are based is now being called into question. Faced with a growing complexity of actors and issues, a number of analysts have begun to pay more attention to transnational relations. In this article we will contend that if critiques of Realist models of world politics are taken seriously, they not only call into question state-centric conceptions of 'the international system', but also throw doubt upon prevailing notions about international organizations. If one relaxes the Realist assumptions, one can visualize more significant roles for international organizations in world politics.

In an important recent contribution to the literature on transnational relations, Samuel P. Huntington argues explicitly that international organizations are relatively insignificant in contemporary world politics:

> . . . internationalism involves agreement among nation-states.

> . . . every international organization at some point finds itself limited by the very principle which gives it being.

> The international organization requires *accord* among nations; the transnational organization requires *access* to nations . . . International organizations embody the principle of nationality; transnational organizations try to ignore it.

> While national representatives and delegations engage in endless debate at UN conferences and councils, however, the agents of the transnational organizations are busily deployed across the continents, spinning the webs that link the world together.

> Internationalism is a dead end.[1]

Like Huntington, we begin with the proposition that transnational relations are increasingly significant in world politics. But we reach very different conclusions about the roles of international organizations.

Before making this argument systematically in the remainder of this paper, we must briefly deal with the issue of how transnational relations should be defined. Huntington defines 'transnational organizations' as organizations sharing three characteristics: they are large bureaucracies; they perform specialized functions; and they do so across international boundaries. He explicitly includes governmental entities, such as the United States Agency for International Development (AID) or the Central Intelligence Agency (CIA) and intergovernmental organizations such as the World Bank, along with nongovernmental entities such as multinational enterprises, the Ford Foundation, and the Roman Catholic Church. Although this definition has the virtue of pointing out similarities between governmental and nongovernmental bureaucracies operating across national boundaries, it obscures the differences. Some of Huntington's observations are clearly meant to apply only to nongovernmental organizations. He argues, for instance, that 'The operations of transnational organizations . . . usually do not have political motivations in the sense of being designed to affect the balance of power within the local society.'[2]

But this hardly applies to the Agency for International Development or the Central Intelligence Agency, both of which he designates as 'transnational'. He contends, on the basis of literature about multinational enterprises, that personnel arrangements of transnational organizations move toward dispersed nationality patterns, in which country subdivisions are primarily managed by local personnel; yet no evidence is presented that this is true for AID or the CIA, much less for the Strategic Air Command – another 'transnational' organization by Huntington's definition. Furthermore, the trends over time seem to diverge, and when Huntington discusses these trends, he finds himself distinguishing between 'US Government-controlled transnational organizations' and private groups.[3]

The anomalies into which Huntington is led convince us that for most purposes it it useful to retain the governmental-nongovernmental distinction, thus facilitating the task of examining both the differences between patterns of governmental and nongovernmental activity and the effects of each on the other. Only if one were to use organization theory in a sustained way to explain behavior of large bureaucracies that operate across international boundaries would it seem wise to adopt Huntington's definition.

The argument leads us also to reconsider some of our own past usage. In this article we will restrict the term 'transnational' to nongovernmental actors, and the term 'transgovernmental' to refer to sub-units of governments on those occasions when they act relatively autonomously from higher authority in international politics. In other words, 'transnational' applies when we relax the assumption that states are the only actors, and 'transgovernmental' applies when we relax the assumption that states act as units.

Our choice of definition is not a matter of semantics but is related directly to the argument of this paper. Transnational activity makes societies more sensitive to one another, which may lead governments to increase their efforts to control this nongovernmental behavior. Such efforts, if pursued by more than one government, make governmental policies sensitive to one another: since one government may deliberately or inadvertently thwart the other's purposes, governments must design their own policies with the policies of others in mind. The result of this may well be attempts at policy coordination, which will increase direct bureaucratic contacts among governmental sub-units, and which may, particularly in a multilateral context, create opportunities for international organizations to play significant roles in world politics. [. . .]

Transgovernmental Relations

During the last century, governments have become increasingly involved in attempting to regulate the economic and social lives of the societies they govern. As a result, they have become more sensitive to external disturbances that may affect developments within their own societies. For instance, integration of money markets internationally, in the context of governmental responsibility for national economies, has made government policy sensitive both to changes in interest rates by other governments and central banks, and to movements of funds by nongovernmental speculators. These sensitivities are heightened further by the expanding decision domains of transnational organizations such as multinational business firms and banks, reinforced by decreases in the cost of transnational communications.

As the agenda broadens, bureaucracies find that to cope effectively at acceptable cost with many of the problems that arise, they must deal with each other directly rather than indirectly through foreign offices. [...] There have always been such contacts. What seems to be new is the order of magnitude of transgovernmental relations, as bureaucracies become more complex and communications and travel costs decrease.

We define transgovernmental relations as sets of direct interactions among sub-units of different governments that are not controlled or closely guided by the policies of the cabinets or chief executives of those governments. Thus we take the policies of top leaders as our benchmarks of 'official government policy'. Lack of control of sub-unit behavior by top leadership is obviously a matter of degree, and in practice by no means free of ambiguity. The policy of the central executive is often unclear, particularly on details, and policy means different things at different organizational levels. 'One man's policy is another man's tactics.'[4] As one observer has put it, 'Central policy is always waffled; actors latch on to the waffled parts and form coalitions to shift policy at their level.'[5] Nonetheless, to treat all actors as equal and to ignore the existence of a political hierarchy charged with 'course-setting' and maintaining some hierarchy of goals is to misrepresent both constitutional and political reality. It is precisely because this central policy task has become more difficult in the face of greater complexity that both the opportunities and the importance of transgovernmental interactions may be expected to have increased.

It is quite conceivable that executives entrusted with responsibility for central foreign policy, such as presidents and prime ministers, will themselves attempt to collaborate with one another in ways that conflict with the behavior of their respective bureaucracies. Yet we will regard only the relatively autonomous activities of the lower-level bureaucracies, as opposed to those of top leadership, as being transgovernmental. Otherwise, we would find ourselves in the anomalous position of regarding a head-of-state meeting, at which new initiatives that deviate from established policy are taken, as an example of 'transgovernmental politics' when indeed it is almost the paradigm case for the state-centric model whose inadequacies we are criticizing. The point of our terminology is to focus attention on bureaucratic contacts that take place below the apex of the organizational hierarchy — rather than merely to apply a new label to behavior that is easily subsumed by traditional models.

In view of our interest in the opportunities that transgovernmental relations may create for international organizations, we will concentrate in this essay on *cooperative* behavior among governmental sub-units. It should be recognized, however, that conflict is not excluded from transgovernmental relations any more than from other aspects of world politics. [. . .]

We will distinguish two major types of essentially cooperative transgovernmental behavior. Transgovernmental *policy coordination* refers to activity designed to facilitate smooth implementation or adjustment of policy, in the absence of detailed higher policy directives. Another process, *transgovernmental coalition building*, takes place when sub-units build coalitions with like-minded agencies from other governments against elements of their own administrative structures. At that point, the unity of the state as a foreign policy actor breaks down. Although transgovernmental policy coordination and transgovernmental coalition building are analytically distinct processes, they merge into one another at the margin. While bearing in mind that the distinction is in some cases an artificial convenience, we will look at the two processes in turn.

Transgovernmental Policy Coordination

The most basic and diffuse form of transgovernmental policy coordination is simply informal communication among working-level officials of different bureaucracies. Such communication does not necessarily contradict the conventional conceptualization of states as coherent coalitions *vis-à-vis* the outside world, although it may have side effects that influence policy. Face-to-face communications often convey more information (intended or unintended) than indirect communications, and this additional information can affect policy expectations and preferences. It is well known that international organizations frequently provide suitable contexts for such transgovernmental communication. As one official said of INTERPOL, 'What's really important here are the meetings on a social level — the official agenda is only for show.'

Where patterns of policy coordination are regularized, it becomes misleading to think of governments as closed decision-making units. It has been argued, for example, that in the 1960s Canadian officials in Washington were 'often able to inject their views into the decision-making process at various stages, almost as if they were American, and to actually participate, particularly in the economic sector, in the formulation of American policy'.[6] In the Skybolt affair of 1962, British complacency about American planning, before cancellation was announced, was reinforced by 'a steady stream of reassurances [that] flowed back and forth between the Air Forces. The USAF saw a staunch ally in Her Majesty's Government, and *vice versa*.'[7]

From regularized coordination over a period of time, changes in attitudes may result. When the same officials meet recurrently, they sometimes develop a sense of collegiality, which may be reinforced by their membership in a common profession, such as economics, physics, or meteorology. Individual officials may even define their roles partly in relation to their transnational reference group rather than in purely national terms. [...]

Regularized patterns of policy coordination can therefore create attitudes and relationships that will at least marginally change policy or affect its implementation. This has been evident particularly in relations among close allies or associates, for instance between the United States and Canada or among countries of the British Commonwealth. Even in relations among countries that are politically more distant from one another, policy coordination between bureaucracies with similar interests may occasionally take place. According to press reports, at any rate, United States and Soviet space officials who were engaged in technical talks on space cooperation in 1971 went considerably further than the National Security Council had authorized at that time.

Patterns of regularized policy coordination have a significance that is not limited to the examples we have cited. As such practices become widespread, transgovernmental elite networks are created, linking officials in various governments to one another by ties of common interest, professional orientation, and personal friendship. Even where attitudes are not fundamentally affected and no major deviations from central policy positions occur, the existence of a sense of collegiality may permit the development of flexible bargaining behavior in which concessions need not be requited issue by issue or during each period. [...]

Transgovernmental Coalition Building

Transgovernmental policy coordination shades over into transgovernmental coalition building when sub-units of different governments (and/or intergovernmental institutions) jointly use resources to influence governmental decisions. To improve their chances of success, governmental sub-units attempt to bring actors from other governments into their own decision-making processes as allies. When such coalitions are successful, the outcomes are different than they would be if each coalition partner were limited to his own nationality. The politics of such situations are more subtle and the rules less clear than in the classical coalition theorists' cases of electoral coalitions where resources are directly transferable into influence through a set of generally accepted rules, or national bureaucratic coalitions in which players hold formal positions that legitimize their rights to participate.

Transgovernmental coalitions may be employed by sub-units of powerful states such as the United States as means by which to penetrate weaker governments. US aid agencies in the 1950s and 1960s frequently played a large role in writing requests for aid from the US on behalf of potential recipients, and on occasion even served a liaison function among several ministries of a foreign government. [. . .]

Transgovernmental coalitions, however, can also help agencies of other governments penetrate the US bureaucracy. In 1961, when the US Weather Bureau disagreed with the State Department's position at the United Nations on the control of the World Weather Watch, the Director of the US Weather Bureau telephoned his Canadian counterpart and they discussed the common interests of their respective weather bureaus. The position of the two weather bureaus became the official Canadian position, which led in turn to defeat of the State Department's proposals. In the late 1960s, a US Defense Department official, worried that delay in returning Okinawa to Japanese control might harm United States-Japanese relations, worked out with a Japanese counterpart how to phrase Japanese messages to ensure that they would enter the right channels and trigger the desired response in the US bureaucracy. In 1968, an Air Force general, to whom the responsibility for negotiating with Spain about military bases had been delegated, conferred secretly with his Spanish counterparts without informing civilian officials of the progress of his negotiations, and agreed to a negotiating paper that proved to be unacceptable to the Department of State. As this last case indicates, transgovernmental coalitions are not always successful: the agreement reached, which would have been favorable to the Spanish Government, was disowned by the United States, and a negative reaction against Spain took place in the Senate.

It is obviously a necessary condition for explicit transgovernmental coalitions that sub-units of government have broad and intensive contacts with one another. In some sense, a degree of transgovernmental policy coordination is probably a precondition for such explicit transnational coalitions. A second set of necessary conditions has to do with conflict of interest among sub-units and the degree of central control by top executive leaders. For a transgovernmental coalition to take place, a sub-unit of one government must perceive a greater common interest with another government, or sub-units of another government, than with at least one pertinent agency in its own country; and central executive control must be loose enough to permit this perception to be translated into direct contacts with the foreign governments or agencies in question. Figure 1 illustrates four types of political situations based on these two dimensions.

Sub-units in a governmental system of Type 1 are most likely to seek, or be amenable to, transgovernmental coalitions. High conflict of interest among sub-units of the government suggests that there may be sub-units of other governments with which advantageous coalitions can be made; low executive power indicates that the central officials' ability to deter such coalitions is relatively small. In the other three types, by contrast, the conventional assumption of unitary actors is more likely to be valid for external affairs, although for different reasons. In Type 2 conflict is contained by a strong executive; sub-units may perceive potentially advantageous transgovernmental coalitions, but they do not dare attempt to consummate them directly. In Type 3, low conflict of interest among domestic governmental sub-units ensures that the option of national coalition generally seems more attractive than the transgovernmental alternative, even in the absence of strong central control. Type 4, of course, exemplifies the traditional situation: national coalition reinforced by effective hierarchy.

Figure 1: Conflict of Interest and Executive Power in Foreign Policy: Four Types

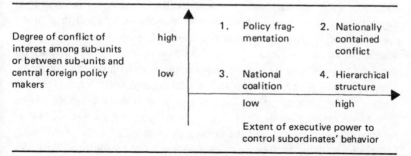

Relatively frequent contacts among governmental sub-units, looseness of governmental hierarchies (low executive control), and relatively high conflict of interest within governments are all necessary conditions for the development of explicit transgovernmental coalitions. But they are not in

themselves sufficient. In the first place, for coalitions to be feasible, actors with common interests must be able to combine their resources effectively. That means that political resources (such as funds, prestige, information, and consent — where required, for instance, by the rules of an international organization) of actors outside a government must be valuable to at least some actors within it. This requires a political context that is relatively open and free of xenophobia, since in a xenophobic society foreign resources are heavily devalued, or regarded negatively, by virtue of their origin. Even in democratic societies, the borderline between legitimate transgovernmental behavior and treason may be unclear.

The need for resources that can be aggregated suggests that transgovernmental behavior may be particularly important in issue areas in which functionally defined international organizations operate. The procedures of the organization itself, for reaching agreement among its members, ensure that the resources of one actor — at least its votes — may be useful to another; insofar as the organization has a specialized, functional orientation, the activities of national representatives may not be closely supervised by top leaders or their agents. More generally, the greater the natural sensitivity of governmental policies and the wider the acceptance of joint decision making on issues that cross national lines, the greater the legitimacy of transgovernmental bargaining is likely to be. An international organization, by symbolizing governments' beliefs in the need for joint decision making, tends to strengthen the legitimacy of this activity.

International Organizations and Potential Coalitions

Recurrent international conferences and other activities of international organizations help to increase transgovernmental contacts and thus create opportunities for the development of transgovernmental coalitions [. . .] The organizations' definitions of which issues cluster together and which should be considered separately may help to determine the nature of interdepartmental committees and other arrangements within governments. In the long run, therefore, international organizations will affect how government officials define 'issue areas'. The existence of the International Monetary Fund and the General Agreement on Tariffs and Trade, for example, helps to focus governmental activity in the monetary and trade fields, in contrast to the area of private direct investment, in which no comparable international organization exists.

The fact that international organizations bring officials together should alert us to their effect in activating *potential* coalitions in world politics.

Many sub-units of governments, which do not as a matter of course come into contact with each other, may have common or complementary interests. Indeed, we may speak of some potential coalitions as *de facto* 'tacit coalitions' if the independent actions of one member seem to serve the interests of others and vice versa. One of the important but seldom-noted roles of international organizations in world politics is to provide the arena for sub-units of governments to turn potential or tacit coalitions into explicit coalitions characterized by direct communication among the partners. In this particular bit of political alchemy, the organization provides physical proximity, an agenda of issues on which interaction is to take place, and an aura of legitimacy. Informal discussions occur naturally in meetings of international organizations, and it is difficult, given the milieu, for other sub-units of one's own government to object to these contacts.

Even without an active secretariat, therefore, international organizations are of considerable relevance in many issue areas of world politics because they help to transform potential or tacit coalitions into explicit ones. When issues are linked or dealt with in institutional arenas with broad mandates, heterogeneous coalitions can be formed. Narrow institutional mandates discriminate against such coalitions. Thus, by defining the issues to be considered together, and by excluding others, international organizations may significantly affect political processes and outcomes in world politics, quite apart from active lobbying by their secretariats.

The second important role for international organizations, however, is the active one. Most intergovernmental organizations have secretariats, and like all bureaucracies they have their own interests and goals that are defined through an interplay of staff and clientele. International secretariats can be viewed both as catalysts and as potential members of coalitions; their distinctive resources tend to be information and an aura of international legitimacy. [...]

Examples of alliances between parts of secretariats and governments are not hard to find. Many organizations have divisions that are regarded as fiefdoms of particular governments. In a number of cases, lower-level officials of a secretariat have lobbied with governments in efforts to thwart the declared policy of their secretaries-general. Representatives of UN specialized agencies in developing countries often strengthen old-line ministries against their rivals in central planning offices. Chilean conservatives have used IMF missions to bolster their political positions. With reference to the World Health Organization (WHO), Harold Jacobson argues that 'many government representatives to WHO almost can be viewed as the director-general's agents or lobbyists within country subsystems'.[8] In some cases, international organizations initiate the formation of transgovernmental coalitions; in others, they or their own sub-units are recruited to the coalitions by sub-units of governments.

It must be recognized, however, that this activist, coalition-building role of international organizations is usually closely circumscribed. By no means is it a sure recipe for success. Yet the alternatives of passivity or of frontally challenging traditional notions of national sovereignty are usually less attractive. Secretariat officials often find the only feasible alternative to be to help governments, or sectors of governments, to perceive problems differently and to use their own resources in innovative ways. [. . .]

Coalition building shades down into transgovernmental policy coordination in this example, as is frequently the case. On a long-term and somewhat diffuse basis, the communications that take place as a result of policy coordination and conferences may be as important as the coalitions that form on particular issues. As we have seen earlier, international organizations facilitate face-to-face meetings among officials in 'domestic' agencies of different governments who would have little to do with each other in traditional interstate politics. Strategically-minded secretariats of international organizations could very well plan meetings with a view toward this transgovernmental communications function. Recurrent interactions can change officials' perceptions of their activities and interests. As Bauer, Pool, and Dexter have pointed out in their discussion of the United States politics of foreign trade, concentrating only on pressures of various interests for decisions leads to an overly mechanistic view of a continuous process and neglects the important role of communications in slowly changing perceptions of 'self-interest'.[9]

Conditions for the Involvement of International Organizations

To the extent that transgovernmental relations are common in a given issue area, under what conditions should we expect international organizations, in the sense of intergovernmental organizations, to be involved in them? One set of cases is obvious: where the international organization itself has created the network of elites. Thus, both the International Labor Organization (ILO) and the World Health Organization (WHO), as described by Cox and Jacobson, are characterized by extensive 'participant subsystems' that link national trade unions, employers, and government officicals to the ILO secretariat, and health-care professionals to WHO's bureaucracy.[10]

More generally, however, we would expect international organizations to become involved in transgovernmental politics on issues requiring some central point or agency for coordination. This implies that international organizations are likely to be most extensively involved on complex, multilateral issues in which major actors perceive a need for information and for communication with other actors, in addition to the traditional functions, as listed by Skolnikoff, of '1) provision of services, 2) norm creation and allocation, 3) rule observance and settlement of disputes, and 4) operation'.[11] Insofar as patterns of politics follow the transgovernmental mode, increasing the number of actors will tend to create greater demands for communication with other actors (often of different types), as well as for information about both technical and political conditions. International secretariats staffed with knowledgeable individuals, even without traditional sources of power, have the opportunity to place themselves at the center of crucial communications networks, and thereby acquire influence as brokers, facilitators, and suggestors of new approaches. They will continue to be dependent on governments for funds and legal powers; but the relevant agencies of governments may be dependent on them for information and for the policy coordination, by a legitimate system-wide actor, which is required to achieve their own objectives.

Notes

1. Samuel P. Huntington, 'Transnational Organizations in World Politics', *World Politics,* XXV (April 1973), pp. 333-68; quotations from pp. 338, 339 and 368 respectively. (See article 2.7 in this section.)

2. Ibid., p. 358.

3. Ibid., pp. 348-9.

4. Raymond Bauer, 'The Study of Policy Formation', in Raymond Bauer and Kenneth Gergen (eds), *The Study of Policy Formation* (New York, 1968), p. 2.

5. M.S. Hochmuth, Comments at Transnational Relations Study Group Seminar, Center for International Affairs, Harvard University, 8 February 1972.

6. Dale Thompson, Testimony before Standing Committee on External Affairs and National Defense, House of Commons (Canada), *Minutes of Proceedings and Evidence,* 28 April 1970.

7. Richard E. Nuestadt, *Alliance Politics* (New York, 1970), p. 37.

8. Harold K. Jacobson, 'WHO: Medicine, Regionalism, and Managed Politics', in Robert W. Cox and Harold K. Jacobson (eds), *The Anatomy of Influence: Decision Making in International Organisation* (New Haven, 1973), p. 214.

9. Raymond Bauer, Ithiel de Sola Pool and Lewis Dexter, *American Business and Foreign Policy* (New York, 1963), Ch. 35, especially pp. 472-5.

10. Jacobson, 'WHO', pp. 194-205 and Robert W. Cox, 'ILO: Limited Monarchy', in Cox and Jacobson (eds), *The Anatomy of Influence,* pp. 114-27.

11. Eugene B. Skolnikoff, 'Science and Technology: The Implications for International Institutions', *International Organization,* XXV (Autumn 1971), p. 772.

INTERNATIONAL ORGANIZATIONS AND THEIR ROLES

Charles Pentland

Source: J. Rosenau, K.W. Thompson and G. Boyd (eds), *World Politics* (Free Press, New York, 1976) pp. 631-56.

Pentland argues that international organizations can play three different, though not mutually exclusive, roles in world politics. Firstly, they can be used by states as instruments of foreign policy in accordance with the traditional state-centric view; secondly, they can serve to modify states' behavior; and thirdly, they can achieve a measure of autonomy and operate as actors in their own right.

International Organizations as Instruments of Policy

As instruments for the collective pursuit of foreign policy goals, international organizations are subject to evaluation by member states in terms of their utility. From national capitals the whole field of international organizations is likely to be perceived as an array of more or less useful pieces of machinery through which to enhance national policy aims. This instrumental outlook means that, as with other modalities of foreign policy, the national policymaker weighs the costs and benefits (insofar as they can be estimated) of participating in an international organization or attempting to mobilize it for specific purposes. Such utilitarian calculations are made both by small states pursuing policy goals through coalitions and by major powers which may by themselves be able decisively to influence the organization's performance.

Clearly states vary greatly in their ability to mobilize and manage international organizations for the pursuit of their foreign policy goals, and organizations in turn vary in the degree to which they can be so used. Major powers can often determine if organizations will be active at all in areas of interest to them. In regional organizations especially, a hegemonic state can usually be assured of sufficient small power backing to permit it to manage the organization toward acceptable decisions. Its calculations will tend to center less on the probability of creating a winning coalition around itself (this being assumed) than on the relative virtues of multilateral and unilateral action. For smaller powers, largely incapable of effective unilateral action and much less sure of their ability to create winning coalitions to control the multilateral setting, the calculations have to be more subtle and complex.

Important for both great and small powers are the power disparities embodied in the organization and the degree to which any working consensus created among the members is likely to be compatible with their particular interests. A good measure of the power relationship is the 'presence' of the state in the organization, reflected in its contribution of finances and personnel, its demands for action, and its level of participation in decision making. The degree of compatibility between the working consensus of the organization and the state's interests can be seen in the responsiveness of the organization's policy decisions and executive actions to the state's original demands.

[Pentland proceeds to discuss this view in the context of global and regional organizations and concludes as follows.]

[. . .] it is comparatively rarely that international organizations serve directly as controlled, effective instruments of one state's foreign policy. In these rare cases the dominant state's support for, and demands on, the organization will far outstrip those of any other member; it will have ready-made majorities of its clientele to determine the outcome of all decisions it considers important; and the actions of the organization will amount to putting a multilateral gloss on a unilateral interest. The cold war alliances, the UN on rare occasions such as the Korean action, and the OAS are about the only international organizations which fit this pattern to any notable extent. It is worth adding that smaller members of a hegemonic organization may find this situation the most rational in terms of their own policy goals. The theory of 'collective goods' suggests that the small can in fact 'exploit' the large, since the marginal cost of producing the good (such as security or wealth) shared by all members of the organization is lowest for the hegemonic state. Collective goods 'may be provided to an almost "optimal" degree in a group in which one member is very much larger than all the other members'.[1] The cost-benefit calculus, then, does not necessarily indicate that collaboration on an egalitarian basis is always the best for a small state seeking to maximize foreign policy goals. Sometimes, to use international organizations as foreign policy instruments may be, in effect, to 'use' the hegemonic state. At other times, it may mean establishing a dominant coalition which controls decisions and allocates the proceeds among its members.

But generally, to speak of international organizations as instruments of state policy is to stress the element of 'free' intergovernmental collaboration toward shared or convergent objectives. In an increasingly interdependent world, unilateralism is impossible because 'more and more goods are becoming collective at the international level'.[2] The calculus of utility for most states, therefore, is concerned neither with the pros and cons of collaboration *per se* nor with the probabilities of successfully manipulating any organization. Rather it is concerned with ongoing judgments about the responsiveness of various organizations in providing the state with an acceptable share of the collective goods produced, and about the optimum amount of resources to commit to their common production. These calculations are rarely all that visible or precise, but the occasional surfacing of debates over the American contribution to the UN budget or over what constitutes a 'just return' from the European Community should remind us of their continuing importance for the functioning of international organizations.

International Organizations as Systemic Modifiers of State Behavior

Since 'instruments' are supposed to be neutral and to lack any life or direction but that imparted by their users, the thrust of the first perspective on international organizations is to minimize their status as independent entities in the international system. Viewed as restraints on the behavior of states, however, international organizations begin to take on a life of their own as part of the landscape of the international system. From this perspective international organizations are not seen as actors in their own right, equivalent to and interacting with states; rather they are institutional channels, obstacles, and aids collectively created by states which modify the traditionally *laissez-faire* character of their relationships.

As such, international organizations become an institutional manifestation of the general set of restraints placed on states by the international system. Their effectiveness as modifiers of state behavior will depend to a great extent on the general structural pattern of this system. Four aspects of this structural pattern are commonly singled out as important in this respect: (1) the degree of polarization, (2) the power and status hierarchies, (3) the linkage of central system and regional subsystems, and (4) the degree of transnational interdependence. The question facing international organizations is the extent to which they must be adapted to these structural patterns in order effectively to influence state behavior.

If they do not adapt at all to structural change, they risk becoming peripheral to states' interests. If, on the other hand, they mirror the structural patterns too accurately, they may be incapable of muting any conflicts which run along those structural lines. The UN's Economic Commission for Europe illustrates this dilemma well. At the height of the cold war, the Commission (concerned with fostering East-West economic cooperation) had little relevance for either side. Had it, however, adapted its decision-making structure and policies to reflect Europe's bipolar structure, it might have forsaken what little integrative influence it had, as well as the opportunity of becoming the economic vehicle for détente.

What mix of structural patterns in the international system is most likely to enhance the restraining role of international organizations? Ideally, first of all, polarization into rigid alliance systems should be at a minimum. Tight bipolarity, in which every state is bound to one bloc or the other, is the least congenial setting for global international organizations, although it may give rise to hegemonic or regional institutions within each bloc as means of control or internal conflict resolution. Between the blocs, however, accommodation and interaction tend to be limited to the leaders, whose bilateral dealings give little role to a global organization. Multipolarity, on the other hand, increases states' freedom of maneuver and the variety of their interactions, while the absence of clientelistic bloc structures means they must pursue collective goods through wider collaboration.

Second, the influence of international organizations is likely to be greater to the extent that power, wealth, and status are distributed evenly among the states. If there are huge disparities between one state and all the rest, international organizations are likely to be instruments of hegemonic control, restraining all states but the superpower. If there are several large states which are in basic agreement about the international order, as in the European Concert, the organization becomes an instrument of oligarchic control. Only a relatively egalitarian system permits a true collective system of restraint to operate, since the capabilities of potential violators are less likely to outweigh those of the rest of the community of states.

Concerning the optimum relationship between global system and regional subsystem, different arguments are defensible. One, which stresses 'islands of peace' and 'division of labor', suggests that discontinuities between the two levels actually aid international organizations. Conflicts can be localized within regional organizations and dealt with by the states most directly concerned. The other argument stresses the 'indivisibility of peace' and points to the superior resources of the global organizations, as well as the dangers of balkanization. In this view the intensification of regional interactions among states is liable to paralyze global organizations.

The development of transnational interdependence, finally, is usually held to be a vital underpinning for international organizations. Steadily growing flows of goods, services, money, people, and ideas between countries represent that fabric which stands to be damaged or destroyed should the states' collective system of self-control fail. We might expect, then, that organizations which follow particularly intense patterns of interdependence would draw the greatest degree of commitment and compliance from their member states. This commitment and compliance would probably be a product not so much of legal or coercive restraints as of a process of socialization occurring among political, economic, and administrative elites as they interacted with each other in a multilateral context. International organizations, in short, can restrain states by means of internalized norms as well as the more evident external pressures.

[Pentland then investigates the relevance of these four factors in the context of empirical examples before coming to the third and final role.]

International Organizations as Actors

Viewed as restraints on the behavior of states, international organizations begin to take on independent life. But it is a limited sort of independence: the organizations are created and sustained by the states in a collective act of self-limitation or self-enhancement, and there is certainly no expectation that they will come to coexist with, or even supersede, their creators as the dominant actors in the international system. In the postwar period, however, it has become apparent that some international organizations promise (or threaten, depending on one's perspective) to do just this. At present their numbers are fewer than some would claim, but their implications are far-reaching for the future of international politics.

Becoming an actor means, essentially, to achieve some degree of autonomy and some capacity to influence other actors. Autonomy is the product of what Schmitter calls 'organizational development', or a 'process whereby an initially dependent system, created by a set of actors representing different and relatively independent nation-states, acquires the capabilities of a self-maintaining and self-steering system, one whose course cannot be predicted solely from knowledge of its environment'.[3] A capacity to influence other actors (or, indeed, to resist influences from other actors) is based on resources — expert information, finances, decision-making capacity, popular support or legitimacy, enforcement capabilities, and diplomatic skills – which accrue independently to the organization. To analyze international organizations in these terms is not necessarily to assume the inevitability or desirability of their challenging the supremacy of the nation-state, or indeed even to assume that such organizational development necessarily occurs at the expense of the national autonomy. It is simply to recognize that some international organizations are more highly developed than others and that their impact on the international system is thus rather more forceful. An important task of the theory of international organization is to determine why this is so.

Focusing on organization development does require one conceptual clarification. Although international organizations are essentially associations of states, it is not the aggregation of states as such which we normally describe as 'developing'. It is, rather, some emergent property which, even in a minimally endowed organization, represents something greater than the sum of the members. That property is best, although by no means exclusively, represented in the institutions of the organization, especially the administrative arm, or secretariat.

[The discussion then considers the varying levels of autonomy enjoyed by the UN Secretariat and the EEC Commission.]

Conclusions

International organizations are of interest to the statesman and the theorist of world politics because of the variety of roles they play in the international system and the widely differing interpretations which can be attached to those roles. First, international organizations are used by states, individually or collectively, as instruments of foreign policy. Second, they act, by their very presence in the system, to modify states' behavior. Third, they sometimes achieve a degree of autonomy and influence as political actors in their own right. The fact that most international organizations are perceived or expected – from a variety of perspectives – to play two or possibly all three of these roles simultaneously underlines that the roles are not mutually exclusive and in fact may at times be mutually reinforcing.

Observers of, or participants in, international organizations may have divergent expectations as to their future development. Accordingly, they may apply different standards in measuring an organization's success or failure. But on such organizations' contribution to the complexity of the international system there is little disagreement. If international organizations alleviate some problems for states, they also create new ones. And if, for the theorist, they do not yet seriously challenge the traditional state-centered model of the international system, they do complicate and compromise it somewhat.

The instrumentalist perspective, being predominantly the view from the national capital, is perhaps easiest reconciled with the classic model. The actions and development of international organizations simply reflect national interest, whether pursued by a hegemonic power or compromised within a more egalitarian multilateral setting. Success is thus judged in terms of utility for the pursuit of national objectives. Viewed as modifiers of state behavior, second, international organizations may still be compatible with the state-centered model, since that model has always acknowledged the constraints placed on states by their existence in the ordered but competitive context of the international system. Minimally, international organizations can be seen simply as the institutional embodiment of this kind of constraint. Clearly, however, they have now developed well beyond that point. The scale of the security problem, as well as that of a wide range of economic, social, and technical problems, has begun to outstrip the capacities of all national governments. Organizations based on the consequent intergovernmental and transnational interdependencies are of a different order entirely from those which represented the constraints of the classic *laissez-faire* state system. Concerning international organizations as actors, finally, expectations are greatest, criteria of success most severe, and the classic state-centered model under the most stress. International organizations are expected to exploit and build upon the interdependence of states to develop their own autonomy and influence in the international system. At the very least, nation-states will have to coexist with new regional and functional actors. And very possibly these actors will gain power and legitimacy at their expense. In such an event, the classic model would begin to look hopelessly outmoded. [. . .]

Notes

1. B.M. Russett and J.D. Sullivan, 'Collective Goods and International Organization', *International Organization*, 25 (Autumn 1971), p. 853.
2. Ibid., p. 849.
3. P.C. Schmitter, 'The "Organizational Development" of International Organizations', *International Organization*, 25 (Autumn 1971), p. 918.

2.10

OF BLIND MEN, ELEPHANTS AND INTERNATIONAL INTEGRATION

Donald J. Puchala

Source: *Journal of Common Market Studies*, vol. 10, no. 3 (Blackwell, 1972), pp. 267-84.

After denying that contemporary international integration is federalism, nationalism at the international level, functionalism or power politics, Puchala suggests it can be best thought of in terms of a Concordance System characterized by a complex set of actors, a distinctive process of institutionalized bargaining and an atmosphere dominated by pragmatism and mutual responsiveness.

[Puchala tells the tale of the blind men who tried to find out what an elephant looked like by touching it. He compares the differing conclusions they reached to the scholarly attempts to theorize about international integration: in both cases concentration on parts of the 'beast' produces erroneous conclusions about what it is like as a whole. He begins his own analysis by claiming that integration is something peculiar to the post-World War II era and then examines and rejects in turn the conventional models used to describe and explain it.]

(1) Contemporary International Integration is not Federalism. At least it is not classical federalism. Thus far, the patterns of political-economic interaction in different regions of the world — Western Europe, Central America, East Africa, Eastern Europe — which have attracted the attentions of students of international integration, have not by and large resembled patterns suggested by the federalist model. For example, no new central governments have been established to assume functions traditionally allotted to federal governments. Not even in Western Europe are new central authorities representing groups of states in international relations. On the occasions when the Commission speaks for the Six internationally, as in the case of the Kennedy Round negotiations or with regard to association agreements, its positions symbolize multi-lateral diplomatic compromises among six governments much more than they represent the

policies of any central or 'federal' government. In addition, even when the Commission intermittently speaks for the 'Six' each member-state continues to speak for itself in world councils and capitals. Then, too, let us not forget that all international integration arrangements currently in existence, including the Western European system, are functionally limited mostly to economic concerns, and therefore poorly approximate the functionally diffuse systems implicit in the federalist model.

In fairness, it is true that analysts using federalist models as guides to inquiry have looked upon contemporary international integration as 'emergent' rather than 'mature' federalism.[1] Nevertheless, the point is that they have been preoccupied (if not obsessed) with questions about the degree of central authority present, the degree of state sovereignty relinquished, and the parcelling of prerogative, power and jurisdiction among national and international authorities. Moreover, these same analysts have tended to equate 'progress' or 'success' in international integration with movement toward central government.

Such analysis is of course legitimate. But it has not been very productive. Most obviously it has not turned up very much federalism in contemporary international integration. But more importantly, conceptualizing and conducting inquiry in terms of the federalist model has tended to blind analysts to a number of interesting questions. Most broadly, is it really true that no progress toward international integration in various parts of the world has been made simply because little movement in the direction of regional central government has been registered? More provocatively perhaps, to what extent does participation in an international integration arrangement actually enhance rather than undermine national sovereignty? Relatedly, to what extent does an international integration arrangement preserve rather than supersede an international state system? Clearly, the analyst in the federalist mode is not prompted to ask these latter sorts of questions. Is he missing something of significance?

(2) Neither is International Integration Actually 'Nationalism' at the Regional Level. So ingrained has the nationalism model become in Western political thinking and analysis, that we find it difficult to conceive of a non-national international actor, or a political system uncomplemented by an underlying community of people or peoples. Naturally, then, when talk of and movement toward regional unity in different parts of the world attracted the attentions of scholars, a good many assumed that movement toward international integration had to be progress toward the social and cultural assimilation of nationalities. [...] But though we were guided by validated and operational theories of nationalism, and despite the fact

that we wielded the most sophisticated methodological tools of modern social science, our researches turned up few 'Europeans', even fewer 'Central Americans' and 'East Africans' and no 'East Europeans', at all.[2] This lacking evidence of progress toward the social and cultural assimilation of nationalities led some analysts to conclude that contemporary international integration was more myth than reality – no nationalism, therefore no integration![3] Others, however, cherished evidence drawn from youth studies and concluded that regional nationalism, at least in Western Europe, was present after all, and that the heyday of European community would arrive as the current younger generation gained maturity and as its members acquired positions of influence and responsibility.[4] Still others, convinced that assimilation simply had to be a component of contemporary international integration, worded and reworded survey questions until 'regional nationality' did at last emerge in poll results, irrespective of whether it existed in respondents' attitudes.

Credit goes to the nationalism analysts for recognizing that contemporary international integration requires a particular kind of attitudinal environment. However, the environment they seek has failed to materialize. Problems in using the nationalism model as a guide to analyzing contemporary international integration are similar to those involved in using the federalism model. First, testing the model against reality in Western Europe, in Central America and elsewhere produces negative results. Regional nationalism, as noted, turns out not to be a component of international integration. Second, as with the federalist case, asking the analytical questions suggested by the nationalism model, deters thinking about a range of interesting alternative questions. For example, the analyst guided by the nationalism model is directed toward asking questions about people-to-people interactions and transactions, about similarities and differences in peoples' life styles, value systems and cultural norms, and especially about their attitudes toward one another and attendant perceptions of 'we-ness'. But are these really the appropriate questions to ask about the attitudinal environments supportive of inter-governmental cooperation and international institutionalization? Does it really matter what peoples think about one another? Or rather, does it perhaps matter more what these people think about international cooperation and about supranational decision-making? The point here is that while the analyst guided by the nationalism model has been primarily concerned with links and bonds among peoples, he has by and large ignored links and bonds between peoples and their governments and between peoples and international organizations and processes. Is he missing something of significance?

(3) Nor is Contemporary International Integration Functionalism in the Mitrany Tradition. Functionalist analysts have achieved greater descriptive accuracy than others grappling with contemporary international integration.[5] Part of this accuracy, of course, must be accounted for by the fact that architects of international integration in Western Europe and elsewhere were directly influenced by functionalist thinking and therefore constructed their systems from functionalist blueprints. Still, let us give credit where credit is due. Functionalist analysts have accurately located the origins of international cooperation in realms of functional interdependence; they have pinpointed the significance of sector approaches; they have grasped the importance of non-governmental transnational actors.

Yet, very little in contemporary international integration has actually 'worked' the way the functionalist design said that it would. Most revealingly, national governments have remained conspicuous and pivotal in internationally integrating systems, quite in contrast to the functionalist model which shunts these to the periphery of action. Leadership, initiative and prerogative have by and large remained with national governments. They have not gravitated to technocrats, bureaucrats and non-governmental actors. Moreover, national governments participating in international integration schemes have proven far more interested in 'welfare' pursuits and far more restrained in 'power' pursuits than functionalist theorizing would have led us to believe. Equally significant, functional task-areas in international economics, communications, science and technology, which the functionalist model stipulates immune from international politics, have in fact turned out to be the central issue-areas in the lively international politics of international integration. There are simply no non-political issues in relations among states!

Most important, the functionalist model misses the essence of the growth and expansion of international regime during international integration. So concerned are functionalist analysts with sector-to-sector task expansion, that many have failed first to recognize that this sectoral 'spillover' is but one possible variety of expansion or growth during international integration. It is also, incidently, the variety of growth that is least in evidence in existing cases. But, at least two other varieties can be monitored. First, there is expansion in the volume of internationally coordinative activities within given functional sectors. In addition, and much more important, there is possible expansion in the *political system* brought into being when functional sectors are integrated internationally. Such systemic expansion is evidenced by the entrance of increasing numbers of actors and interests into international program planning and policy making.

Second, neither have functionalist analysts been fully cognizant of the fact that sector-to-sector task expansion, spillover or its variants index integrative progress only if one assumes that 'functional federation' or multi-sector merger is the end product of international integration. Here again, we are evaluating the present in terms of a hypothetical future which may never come about. If multi-sector merger is not the end product of international integration, if integration does not really go very far beyond the nation-state, then other varieties of systemic growth which reflect activity and complexity rather than extension might be the more telling indicators of healthy and productive international integration.

In sum, the functionalist analyst too has been partially strait-jacketed by his framework for thinking about international integration. He asked how men may achieve international cooperation by circumventing politics among nations. But, he has not asked how international cooperation is in fact achieved during international integration in the very course of international politics. Then, he has asked how functional integration spreads or spills over in the direction of federal government. But, in light of what has actually come to pass in Western Europe, might it not have been more productive to ask how a program of transnational sectoral merger fits into and becomes an integral part of a broader pattern of intra-regional international relations? That is, what if the termination state for international integration in fact resembles Western Europe, *circa* 1970? Why do some sectors get merged and others do not? More significantly, what kind of international politics results in a system where some functional sectors are transnationally merged and others are not? Impressionistically speaking, it would seem that this 'broader pattern of intraregional international relations', this complex of merged and unmerged sectors and the aggregation of associated governing authorities of one type or another begins to approximate what we are really talking about when we speak of contemporary international integration. Does the functionalist analyst really recognize this? Is he missing something if he does not?

(4) Nor, Finally, Is Contemporary International Integration Simply Power Politics. The school of analysts who have looked upon and thought about international integration within the framework of 'Realist' or *Macht Politik* models have fallen short of understanding what the phenomenon is or involves. To these analysts, international integration is a process of mutual exploitation wherein governments attempt to mobilize and accumulate the resources of neighboring states in the interest of enhancing their own power.[6] Power is to be enhanced so that traditional ends of politics among nations may be accomplished – i.e. international autonomy, military

security, diplomatic influence and heightened prestige. In Realist thinking, international organizations created in the course of international integration are but instruments to be used by national governments pursuing self-interests. They are made at the convergent whims of these governments, and flounder or fossilize as their usefulness as instruments of foreign policy comes into question. Over all, the Realist analyst argues that what we are observing 'out there' and calling international integration are really international marriages of convenience, comfortable for all partners as long as self-interests are satisfied, but destined for divorce the moment any partner's interests are seriously frustrated. Hence, international integration drives not toward federalism or nationalism or functionalism, but toward disintegration. It never gets beyond the nation-state.

The wisdom of the Realist model is that it conceives of international integration as a pattern of international relations and not as something above, beyond or aside from politics among nations. But the shortcoming in the model is that it conceives of international integration as *traditional international relations* played by traditional actors, using traditional means in pursuit of traditional ends. So convinced is the political Realist that 'there is nothing new under the sun' in international relations that he never seriously asks whether international actors other than national governments may independently influence the allocation of international rewards. Nor does he ask whether actors committed to international integration may be pursuing any other than the traditional inventory of international goals — autonomy, military security, influence and prestige. Do these really remain important goals in contemporary international relations? Nor, finally, does the Realist ask how actors committed to integration agreements in fact define their self-interests. Could it be that actors engaged in international integration actually come to consider it in their own self-interest to see that their partners accomplish their goals? In sum, by assuming that international politics remains the 'same old game' and that international integration is but a part of it, the Realist analyst is not prompted to ask what is new in contemporary international relations? Is he missing something of significance?

Toward a New Conceptualization

If there has been a central theme running through my review of analytical models, it is that our conventional frameworks have clouded more than they have illumined our understanding of contemporary international integration. No model describes the integration phenomenon with complete accuracy because all the models present images of what integration could be or should be rather than what it is here and now. Furthermore, attempts to juxtapose or combine the conventional frameworks for analytical purposes by and large yield no more than artificial, untidy results. Clearly, to surmount the conceptual confusion we must set aside the old models, and, beginning from the assumption that international integration could very well be something new that we have never before witnessed in international relations, we must create a new, more appropriate, more productive analytical framework. I contend that this new model must reflect and raise questions about what international integration *is* in Western Europe, Central America, East Africa, etc., *at present*. We must, in other words, stop testing the present in terms of progress toward or regression from hypothetical futures since we really have no way of knowing where or how contemporary international integration is going to end up. The remainder of this essay is a very preliminary step in the direction of a new conceptualization of contemporary international integration.

Is It Really An 'Elephant' After All?

Complexity of Structure. I will hypothesize, though I cannot argue the case as convincingly as I would like to at this moment, that *contemporary international integration can best be thought of as a set of processes that produce and sustain a Concordance System at the international level.* 'Concordance', according to dictionaries I have consulted, means 'agreement' or 'harmony', and 'concord', its root, refers to 'peaceful relations among nations'. A 'Concordance System' by my definition is an international system wherein actors find it possible consistently to harmonize their interests, compromise their differences and reap mutual rewards from their interactions. I selected the term 'Concordance System' primarily because I found it necessary to have a name for what I believe I see coming into being 'out there' in the empirical world. But what we call this product of international integration is not very important; how we describe it is centrally important.

What does a Concordance System look like? First, states or nation-states are among the major component units of the system, and national governments remain central actors in it. While it can and will be argued that contemporary international integration does in fact go 'beyond the nation-state' both organizationally and operationally, it nonetheless does not go very far beyond. It certainly does not drive the state into oblivion, economic, political or otherwise. Neither does it relegate the national government to obscurity. Whatever may be the indeterminate future of present-day regional common markets, harmonization agreements and other varieties of integrative ventures here subsumed under the label 'Concordance System' these are presently clusters of cooperatively interacting states. For all we know now, 'international integration' may never be more than this. Therefore, what we are really talking about when we speak of contemporary international integration are neither federations, nor nationalities, nor functional latticeworks, but *international state systems* of a rather interesting kind.

Hopefully having made the point that national governments remain important actors in Concordance Systems, it now must be said that one of the most interesting features of these systems is that national governments are not the only important actors. In fact, the most complex Concordance Systems may include actors in four organizational arenas — the subnational, the national, the transnational and the supranational. In contrast to familiar federal systems, there is no prevailing or established hierarchy or superordination-subordination relationship among the different kinds of actors in the system. Instead, each of the actors remains quasi-autonomous (more or less so depending upon issues in question), all are interdependent, and all interact in pursuit of consensus that yields mutual rewards. [. . .]

Novelty in Process. Aside from complexity of structure, a number of other distinctive features characterize the Concordance System. Some of these have to do with the nature of interaction processes within the system. First, the Concordance System tends to be a highly institutionalized system wherein actors channel the bulk of their transactions in all isssue-areas through organizational networks according to routinized procedures. That is, the process of international interaction within the Concordance System is much more bureaucratic than it is diplomatic. 'Bureaucratic' as I use it here is not meant belittlingly. Quite to the contrary, just as efficient bureaucracy tends to reflect advanced civilization, 'bureaucratic international relations' reflects ordered, standardized, planned, efficient problem-solving in relations among nations. In the Concordance System conflict is effectively regulated and cooperation is facilitated via institutionalized, constitutional, precedential or otherwise standardized, patterned procedures which all actors commit themselves to use and respect. In a way, we can say that the Concordance System characteristic of contemporary international integration is the farthest thing removed from the traditional anarchy of international politics, but which is yet not a state, nation-state or federation. Let it be noted, however, that a Concordance System need not be institutionally centralized. Transactions are channeled through institutions, to be sure, but the Concordance System may include any number of functionally specific organizations and any number of standardized procedures, while it includes nothing even vaguely resembling an overarching central government. In this way, again, the Concordance System remains essentially an international system.

By looking at processes within the Concordance System somewhat more abstractly, we are able to note two further distinctive features of the system. First, political conflict is an integral part of the international interaction pattern. It occurs both within and between all action arenas. But, quite in contrast to the modalities of traditional international relations, and accordingly baffling to analysts of the Realist school, more conflict within the Concordance System follows from divergent views about 'ways to cooperate' rather than from fundamental incompatibilities in the interests of the various actors. That is, common, convergent, or at least compatible ends among actors are prerequisites for the emergence of a Concordance System; if these are not present no Concordance System will develop. What actors within the system tend to disagree about most often are the kinds of procedures they will commit themselves to as they bureaucratize their international relations. Therefore, in observing Concordance Systems we should expect to find conflict, we should expect this to be initiated over questions of establishing new harmonizing procedures, and we should expect it to be terminated in agreements on new procedures acceptable to all actors. In this sense, conflict may well be functional to the Concordance System. But to be sure, incompatibilities in actor's basic interests and questions about ultimate ends and goals do intermittently crop up within Concordance Systems, as they certainly did during Charles de Gaulle's challenges to the EEC system in Western Europe. When such questions do emerge and are openly contested, they become disfunctional to the continuation of the Concordance System and could lead to its deterioration.

Second, *bargaining among actors* toward the achievement of convergent or collective ends is the predominant style of interaction within the Concordance System. This bargaining, with exchanged concessions and ultimate compromises, tends to characterize interactions within and between all action arenas. As such, coercion and confrontation are both alien to the Concordance System, are considered illegitimate by actors and occur infrequently. In the vocabulary of the Theory of Games, primitive confrontation politics and resultant constant-sum gamesmanship are alien to Concordance Systems. Much more typical is the variable-sum game pattern which rewards all actors for their cooperative behavior and penalizes them for competitive behavior. Moreover, the game as played in the Concordance System is a 'full information' game where players readily learn of rewards from cooperation and penalties from competition by communicating openly with one another. In short, there is no premium on secrecy and deception in the politics of the Concordance System as there often tends to be in more traditional diplomacy. Of course, none of this is to say that lapses into confrontation politics, attempts at punishment and retaliation, and zero-sum gamesmanship are completely extinguished in Concordance Systems. Again, however, to the extent that these vestiges of traditional international politics enter into interaction patterns of the Concordance System, the system itself comes into jeopardy.

Some Attributes of Atmosphere. The Concordance System survives and thrives in a distinctive attitudinal environment. Four features of this psychological setting are especially notable.

First, pragmatism is the prevailing political doctrine of the Concordance System. If the term pragmatism sounds overly formal, call it 'down-to-earthism'. What it means is that international social, economic and political problems are looked upon by actors involved first as real, second as soluble and third as approachable by whatever means seem most promising of rapid, efficient solution. Pragmatism does not cherish any cosmic first principles, such as those that found socialism, nationalism, communism or liberalism, nor does it project utopian visions. It rather equips its adherents to pour themselves into problem-solving without anxiety about doctrinal purity. Lerner and Gordon admirably capture the pragmatic atmosphere of the present-day Western European Concordance System: 'The collapse of traditonal ideologies has made the European elites into pragmatists. They have tried to face the new realities of their postwar situation in ways that work. ... They can now work more effectively with each other on problems of common interest even when they do not share a common ideology that tells them how to talk about these problems ... This is what we call, 'the new pragmatism'.[7]

Second, and perhaps relatedly, the Concordance System is supported by perceptions of international interdependence, or, if not this, then at least by perceptions of national inadequacy. Again, after Lerner and Gordon, and with respect to Western European elite thinking: 'Indeed, there has been a convergent consensus in Europe over the last decade (1955-1965) that national options are not viable and that transnational choices are the only realistic alternatives.'[8] One of the first steps toward a Concordance System, perhaps, is the emergence of the realization on the part of governments and peoples that they need one another in vital ways. But, let it be noted that such perceptions of national inadequacy and international interdependence as are found among elites (and masses also) within Concordance Systems are not negations of the nation-state, nor are they reflections of a new cosmopolitanism. They are rather recognitions of modern economic and technological forces that transverse national frontiers, recognitions that states can no longer relieve internal pressures by external imperialism, and indeed affirmations that nation-states can be preserved as distinct entities only through the international pooling of resources to confront problems that challenge their separate existence.

Third, and again probably relatedly, the 'atmosphere' within the Concordance System, especially in councils where common programs are formulated and decided upon, is one of high mutual sensitivity and responsiveness. To begin with, actors within the system tend to possess a good deal more information about one another and about one another's goals, objectives, preferences and needs than is common in more traditional diplomacy where emphasis is upon one's own needs and upon ways to fulfill these regardless of what the other fellow may want. But even more important, actors within the Concordance System feel some compulsion to see to it that their partners' needs as well as their own are fulfilled in decisions made and programs executed. All of this may sound rather strange to the student of traditional international relations. Nevertheless, it is precisely this atmosphere of shared compulsion to find mutually rewarding outcomes, this felt and shared legitimacy in concession-making, and this reciprocal sensitivity to needs that markedly distinguishes between the new international politics of the Concordance System and the traditional politics of the Machiavellian world.

Fourth, and finally, the Concordance System includes people, or, better stated, peoples. These are the mass populations of the nation-states within the system. What is distinctive about these peoples is that they accord legitimacy to the structures and processes of the system. For one thing, they accept the subnational-national-transnational-supranational political environment that surrounds them, and they defer to the outcomes of the bargaining processes in the multi-arena system. Put more simply, the mass populations of the Concordance System see the system itself as legitimate, and its decisional outputs as authoritative. They comply accordingly. Again, this is a far cry from traditional international relations in the age of integral nationalism! In addition, let it be underlined that mass populations within the Concordance System need not be assimilated into a supranationality. In fact, they may not even like one another very much. They do, however, recognize, accept and bow to the necessities of international cooperation in an age of interdependence, and they support international integration accordingly.

Notes

1. William Diebold, 'The Relevance of Federalism to Western European Economic Integration', in Arthur W. Macmahon (ed), *Federalism: Mature and Emergent* (Doubleday, Garden City, NY, 1955), pp. 433-57.

2. K.W. Deutsch *et al., France, Germany and the Western Alliance, A Study of Elite Attitudes on European Integration and World Politics* (Scribner, New York, 1967), pp. 252-64.

3. Ibid., pp. 298-300.

4. Inglehart, 'An End to European Integration?', *American Political Science Review*, 61 (March 1967), pp. 91-105.

5. In this regard see, especially, R. Inglehart and E. Haas, 'International Integration: The European Process and the Universal', *International Organization*, 15:3 (Summer 1961), pp. 366-92.

6. The Realist model is most elegantly set forth in Raymond Aron, *Peace and War: A Theory of International Relations*, translated by Richard Howard and Annette Baker Fox (Doubleday, Garden City, NY, 1966), pp. 21-196.

7. Daniel Lerner and Morton Gordon, *Euratlantica. Changing Perspectives of the European Elites* (MIT Press, Cambridge, Mass., 1969), p. 242.

8. Ibid., p. 241.

2.11

TRIBAL SOVEREIGNTY VS. INTERDEPENDENCE

Harold Sprout and Margaret Sprout

Source: *Towards a Politics of the Planet Earth* (Van Nostrand, New York, 1971), pp. 401-26.

The Sprouts identify five factors which have made nation-states increasingly vulnerable: military penetrability; economic constraints; transnational communication; pollution; and the terms of access to the world's oceans. They recognize the strength of the traditional symbols of sovereignty and independence but suggest that the threats involved are sufficiently strong to question the viability of the state to manage them.

One of the elemental realities is the tendency of thinking and acting to lag far behind events in this era of unprecedentedly rapid change. The human population of the earth may be bound together in a common fate, but parochial tribalism continues to sustain a fragmented international order more relevant to the seventeenth than to the late-twentieth century. Notions of sovereignty, national self-determination and independence still rank high in the scale of political values in every country. Something vaguely thought of as *national* security is still envisaged as the prime objective of *national* statecraft. With rare exceptions, people look to their own rulers, not to some international organization, for protection against real or imagined dangers from abroad. Economic autonomy is a widely proclaimed goal, especially among the former colonial subjects of Western empires. Statesmen try to exclude from their countries foreign persons and ideas deemed to be subversive or otherwise dangerous to the *national* community. Many governments and private entrepreneurs strive for possession or exploitive control of the resources within and beneath the international oceans and seas.

However, it is becoming increasingly evident that interrelatedness, and the interdependencies that interrelatedness entails in the modern world cannot be escaped. All political communities are exposed in some degree, most in very large degree, to adverse intrusions from abroad. None can prevent or evade undesired consequences of events originating outside their jurisdictional boundaries.

245

This vulnerability extends over many fields of activity. We shall concentrate in this chapter on five that are especially salient: (1) military penetrability, (2) economic constraints, (3) transnational communications, (4) pollution of the state's geographic space, and (5) the terms of access to resources outside the sovereign jurisdiction of any state.

Twilight of Military Security

Military technology has evolved from nonexplosive projectiles (stones, clubs, spears) thrown by hand, to rocket-propelled explosive charges capable of reaching any target upon the face of the earth. This enormous increase in the range of military weapons is displayed statistically in Table 2.11.1. The table ends with the year 1954, but by that date the killing area from any point upon the earth was estimated to equal the entire land and water surface of the earth.

Since the introduction of chemical explosives in the fifteenth century, the upward trend of destructive force has been spectacular. There seems to be little ground for doubt that weapons now in existence are far more than sufficient to destroy any country, and perhaps sufficient to make all or most of the earth uninhabitable. Many reputable scientists and engineers doubt that antiballistic missiles or any other technical devices are likely to restore any significant fraction of the security which conventional military forces formerly provided. This is the context within which we consider several further aspects of the interdependence arising from the advance of military technology.

Formation of the modern state system coincided in history with the introduction of chemical explosives into the technology of war. This was the so-called 'gunpowder revolution'. On this issue all students of international politics are indebted to John Herz, Professor of International Relations in the City University of New York.[1] As he and a few others have emphasized, it was chiefly the introduction of explosive fire-power, especially in the form of mobile artillery, that rendered medieval castles and walled towns indefensible in a military sense. Artillery fire could knock down the strongest walls, and did so on many occasions, most notably in the historic siege of Constantinople in 1453.

Development of more destructive cannon and more mobile gun carriages, together with some improvement in roads, made it possible to defend a larger geographic perimeter against military intrusion, as well as to administer and police a larger area from a central capital. Thus the 'gunpowder revolution', together with other innovations, expedited the emergence of larger political entities, larger both in population and in territory. In due course, these 'sovereign states' superseded castles and walled towns as the basic units of public order and personal security in the Europe of the fifteenth century and thereafter.

Table 1: World-record-breaking Ranges of Projectiles, 1,000,000 BC to 1954 AD

Date	Type of Projectile	Maximum range in miles[a]	Killing area in square miles[b]
From before 1,000,000 BC to at least 200,000 BC nothing better than rock missile, thrown club, or simple javelin		0.01	0.0003
Period between javelin and arrow		0.03	0.005
Starting somewhere between 75,000 BC and 10,000 BC bow and arrow		0.10	0.09
From about 500 BC to 1453 AD, catapult and ballista		0.35	0.8
1453	Cannon	1.0	3
1670	Cannon	1.1	4
1807	Rocket	2.0	13
1830	Coast artillery	3.0	28
1859	Breech-loading rifle gun	5.0	78
1900	Coast artillery	6.3	125
1910	Coast artillery	10.2	326
1912	Coast artillery	11.4	408
1915	Zeppelin raid on London	200	126,000
1918	Bombing plane	280	246,000
1938	Av. European bombing formation	750	1,761,000
1943	Bombing plane	1,200	4,480,000
1944	Bombing plane	2,050	12,900,000
1945	Bombing plane	2,500	19,000,000
1948	Bombing plane	3,900	45,000,000
1949	Bombing plane	5,000	69,000,000
1954	Bombing plane refueled in flight	12,500	197,000,000

a. Record-breaking range of projectiles (maximum range in miles) defined as 'longest nonstop distance, from base to target, over which a missile intended to destroy life or demolish structures has been hurled or piloted through the air'.
b. Killing area (in square miles) defined as 'maximum area within which lives and property may be destroyed by such projectiles'.

Source: Data from the late Hornell Hart's 'Acceleration in Social Change', in F.R. Allen *et al.*, *Technology and Social Change* (Appleton-Century-Crofts, Educational Division, Meredith Corporation, New York, 1957), p. 36; reproduced by permission.

[The Sprouts note that attempts to maintain security were not able to keep pace with further technological developments. The spread of roads and railways and the invention of the aircraft proved particularly devastating.]

In the Second World War for the first time in history, crowded cities and their industrial plants located hundreds of miles inside a country's interior were laid waste without blasting a way across fortified land frontiers or storming ashore upon strongly defended beaches. *The effect in the aggregate was reminiscent of the destructive impact of the gunpowder revolution on medieval castles and walled towns.*

However, to the end of World War II, geographic space still counted heavily as a defensive cushion – but only for a large country. No country in Western Europe proved large enough to absorb the shock of modern mobile armies. None possessed sufficient geographic depth for protracted retreat and protective dispersal of vital industries and population. In Russia, on the contrary, defending armies could retreat through hundreds of miles, and factories could be bodily transported to the comparative safety of inner Asia.

Introduction of nuclear explosives in 1945 and the vastly more destructive weapons that followed within a decade, accompanied by increase in the range and capacity of airborne and ballistic carriers, have further depreciated the military value of space, even for countries of continental size. Today, no country, however large, can reasonably expect to escape crippling devastation if attacked with the thermonuclear weapons now deployed. There is literally no place to hide. Historic two-dimensional security has evolved into today's three-dimensional vulnerability. In the historic seesaw between offensive and defensive military innovations, the technology of offense has decisively outstripped the defense, at least for the near future. [. . .]

We are not suggesting that the sovereign territorial state is about to wither away from erosion of its military viability. As we have said before, institutions tend to live on long after they have ceased to perform the essential functions for which they were created. The thrust of the evidence is simply that the goal of national security as traditionally conceived – and as still very much alive – presents problems that are becoming increasingly resistant to military solutions. To the extent that this is perceived to be so, it imposes constraints on the actions of statesmen quite at variance with the historic myths of sovereignty and independence, myths that in many if not in most societies still inform the attitudes of rulers and citizens alike. [. . .]

The Tightening Screw of Economic Interdependence

Legally sovereign political communities have become economically inter-dependent to an extent not generally appreciated. Such interdependence derives from various sources. These include economic specialization, growth of external commerce, transnational flows of capital, industrial enterprises that operate simultaneously in several or many countries more or less beyond effective control by host governments, the international monetary system, and the working of the balance of payments. In general, economic interdependence increases with progress along the road of modernization. All facets of such interdependence present opportunities for political leverage and conversely impose constraints on the effective exercise of the autonomy legally vested in the sovereign state.

Contemporary economic interdependence evolved largely as a by-product of the Industrial Revolution which encouraged specialization and the resultant growth of commerce among nations. Economic interdependence spread and tightened throughout the nineteenth century. Despite all efforts to counteract it, this trend has accelerated in the twentieth century. It is a salient feature of the milieu in which international politics is carried on, and seems likely to attain additional dimensions of constraint in the years ahead.

For reasons beyond the scope of this discussion, the Industrial Revolution began earlier in Britain than elsewhere. For several decades British industries held a strong lead over foreign competitors. British imports of food and raw materials, paid for by coal, manufactures, and essential services, came by the middle of the nineteenth century to constitute by far the largest national component of the total commerce among nations. Most of the profits were reinvested, increasingly overseas. To facilitate this worldwide complex of trade and investment, British bankers evolved an international monetary system. Its essence was unrestricted movement of gold and convertibility of British currency, sterling, into all foreign currencies. London became the world center of banking, insurance, and other financial services – in short, the financial capital of an economic empire that came to embrace not only the British dominions and colonies but also most of the sovereign political communities in every continent.

In consequence, without much evident planning, economies throughout the world became attuned to Britain's. Foreign societies acquired a vested interest in uninterrupted access to British manufactures, markets, capital, and financial services. It was a state of affairs in which British commercial and fiscal policies, as well as the flow of commerce, affected the structure of societies and imposed constraints on the behavior of statesmen throughout the world.

The spread of industrialism to the Continent, to North America, to Japan and elsewhere eventually destroyed the primacy of Britain, but did not diminish the interdependence of nations. On the contrary! The volume of international commerce continued to increase. And the pattern of commerce continued to reflect specialization, including the exchange of manufactures and services from the industrialized societies in return for foodstuffs and raw materials both from the unindustrialized colonies of the European empires and from the nominally sovereign but economically less modernized polities of Asia, Latin America, and elsewhere. [...]

Interdependence can be a source either of political strength or of political weakness. British experience exemplifies both conditions. Vulnerability was dramatically revealed in the British government's ill-fated attempt to repossess the Suez Canal in 1956. Most of the liquid fuels consumed in Britain came from the region around the Persian Gulf. This oil was paid for in British currency (sterling) or in local Middle Eastern currencies with which the British economy was adequately supplied. When (for reasons that need not concern us here) President Nasser of Egypt dispossessed the private corporation that owned and operated the Canal, the British and French governments reacted violently. By this act Nasser had gained presumptive ability to set the terms on which tankers could bring oil to Western Europe. This was an intolerable state of affairs from the French and British perspective. When their forces invaded Egypt to repossess the Canal, Nasser blocked it by sinking ships in the channel. In consequence the British community had to obtain oil elsewhere, chiefly in the Americas. But American oil had to be paid for in dollars, and the British economy was short of dollars. Thus the British government found itself at the mercy of those who controlled the dollars and who demanded that the invader withdraw — which they did!

A century ago such an outcome would have been scarcely conceivable. The British economy in the 1850s was as interdependent with the outside world as in the 1950s. But as previously indicated, interdependence in that era contributed to towering strength — for Britain. Why? In large degree, it would seem, because of Britain's concomitant naval primacy. In those days the British navy wielded a largely undisputed command of the seas. *The combination of fleets and finance* enabled British statesmen to exert an influence abroad which neither ingredient alone could have accomplished. As long as British naval power was widely perceived to be presumptively supreme, no foreign adversary could exploit Britain's heavy dependence upon imported food and raw materials. With advances in technology, accompanied by changes in the geography of international politics, Britain's economic interdependence with the outside world was insidiously transformed into a position of extreme vulnerability.

Put more generally, if the ratio of exports and imports to the total national product is high, it indicates that the nation's economic life (in the words of a British report) 'is linked with the outside world in many different ways', with the consequence, as a rule, that foreign economic events and trends 'can have a profound effect upon it'. Such an economy is inherently more sensitive, often extremely vulnerable, to foreign commercial regulations (tariffs, import quotas, and others), to exchange fluctuations and controls, to foreign dumping (sales of goods abroad at ruinous prices), to changes in world prices of commodities, especially *differential* changes in the prices of primary materials and manufactures, and to other external events.

For various reasons the trend nearly everywhere is toward greater interdependence among national economies. Even the United States, once more nearly self-contained than any other industrial society, has become increasingly sensitive to external conditions and events. The same trend seems certain to overtake the Soviet Union in the near future, and Communist China too in due course. No government today, not even the United States, can buttress interdependence with a global military primacy that was the essence of the mid-nineteenth-century Pax Britannica.

[The Sprouts go on to discuss the role of international organizations, the impact of business across state boundaries and the constraints of the international monetary system as factors serving to underline this basic interdependence.]

Psychological Penetration and Interdependence

Interdependence is also manifest in the growing psychological penetration of national communities. One has to go back no further than the early nineteenth century to appreciate how recently psychological isolation was the normal, nearly universal state of affairs. Today the situation is reversed in many countries, and in process of reversal in the rest. News of the outside world penetrates 'iron curtains', 'bamboo curtains', and every other kind of man-made barrier to transnational communications. Ideologies – systems of ideas and beliefs – circulate without much regard for political geography and censorship. In many countries – and the number is increasing – television brings the outside world into uncounted millions of homes; and in less affluent societies radio broadcasts perform a similar if less dramatic function.

Transnational carriers of information, values, and beliefs are numerous and varied. The more obvious ones include tourists and other travelers, interpersonal letters, telegrams and telephone calls, books, newspapers and magazines, and above all radio and television mentioned above. By these and other means, information is transmitted, social movements are organized and directed, and ideologies are insinuated into the minds of men. [...]

This spread and circulation of news and ideas is widely regarded as a prime source of the discontents which afflict not merely the underdeveloped countries but also the most affluent urban societies as well. The more pervasive the discontents, the more receptive a community seems to become to new prescriptions for reform. Hence the widespread use and fear of ideological intrusion calculated to focus and channel frustrations, demands, and expectations, and otherwise to influence the behavior of whole populations.

An aspect of psychological penetration that deserves more attention than it generally receives has been the disruptive impact of American affluence on the underdeveloped societies. The popular view in America and generally in the West has been that communism is the most disruptive psychological force in those societies. It is doubtless difficult for most Americans to conceive of their own culture as a force inspiring revolt and even fostering the spread of communism. Yet a by-product, perhaps in the long run the most important by-product, of the display of American affluence abroad during and since World War II appears to have been precisely that. American soldiers, civil servants, business men, and a flood of American tourists have carried willy-nilly the message that ordinary citizens can possess and enjoy the material amenities restricted in most Asian, African, and Latin American countries to a tiny privileged elite at the top of the social pyramid. From this perspective Americans appear as the 'terrible instigators of social change and revolution'.[2]

Some writers on international politics appear to believe that pscyhological penetration operates only in one direction — from the strong to the weak. In this view, Great Powers are masters of their own destiny. Only those political communities that are small, poorly organized, economically underdeveloped, or otherwise weak and vulnerable, are likely to be significantly 'penetrated' by external influences. Such is plainly not the case. Even the Superpowers can be penetrated by the weak — and are! One has only to consider such examples as Israeli influence in Washington, the influence of Chang Kai-shek on American attitudes through the 1950s and '60s, or the more recent influence exerted on successive administrations by client regimes in Vietnam and elsewhere. In the words of one percipient observer, 'Informal penetration is a pervasive phenomenon in contemporary international politics which works in both directions: Small states can penetrate large ones as well as vice versa.'[3]

Insidious Intruders

Less attention has been given to another class of intruders into sovereign national communities, intruders that present far greater dangers in many instances than the most pervasive human subverters and ideologies. We refer to the pollutants that degrade the quality of human life, and may severely affect the health of entire populations. [...]

Advances in technology – especially in the technology of economic production and transportation – have enormously increased the quantity of air- and waterborne pollution and the mobility of organisms that attack plants, animals, and humans. In general, air and water pollution is most severe where *per capita* productivity is highest and the consuming population large. It becomes a transnational menace, thus an international problem, where winds and currents carry the pollutants from the air source in one country across political boundaries into others. [...]

Invention and testing of atomic and thermonuclear explosives raised the danger from airborne pollution. Following test explosions by the United States, Soviet Union, Britain, France and China, lethal fallout has invariably appeared quickly, at great distances from the testing site, and over vast areas, emphasizing the global continuity of the earth's atmosphere. Scientists and engineers engaged in weapons research and development have generally minimized the risk to plants, animals, and humans. But nagging uncertainty persists, buttressed by considerable evidence, regarding the longer-range injurious effects of radioactive fallout. This concern is reflected in the 'strenuous efforts' of the Russian and American governments 'to universalize worldwide control of the proliferation of nuclear tests in the atmosphere'.[4]

The migratory habits of pests, parasites and other invasive organisms have been well known for a century or more. Governments have fought against these insidious intruders with embargoes, border quarantines and other inhibitory regulations. Such measures have been only partially effective. Development of antibiotics and other drugs have provided additional defenses. Working in the opposite direction has been the rising speed and volume of intercountry and intercontinental commerce and travel. The 1918 pandemic of virulent influenza was a frightening reminder of the catastrophic worldwide effects of a swiftly migrating deadly new disease. [...] All these insidious intruders dramatize the elemental reality that in many respects vital to human health and survival, we are all parts of a single ecosystem coterminous with the earth.

There is a persistent tendency in affluent societies, especially in the United States, to spurn this elemental reality. Those who favor ending, or drastically reducing, economic and technical assistance to the modernizing countries habitually minimize any risk in doing so. Their prescription: quarantine the plague spots, and forget about them! Apart from the inhumanity of such an attitude, it reflects gross ignorance or reckless disregard of the mobility of migratory pollutants and other insidious intruders. As has been argued on many occasions by some of the most sophisticated and best informed experts: the United States cannot exist indefinitely as an island of health and affluence in an ocean of malnutrition, disease, and destitution.

The Interrelating Ocean

[...] For thousands of years the oceans and larger seas separated and isolated human communities. Transoceanic migrations occurred in prehistorical eras, but infrequently and on a very small scale. Even as late as the 1400s, the oceans presented a formidable barrier to human movement and served more to separate than to integrate the widely scattered aggregates of humanity.

All this changed rather abruptly following the historic voyages of the later fifteenth century. Once it became reasonably safe to venture beyond sight of land and technically possible to make preselected landfalls across any body of water however wide, the oceans and larger seas provided highways that became progressively interrelating. Ships carried goods, colonists, and armed men to land thousands of miles overseas. Until well into the twentieth century, the surface of these waters carried virtually all intercontinental commerce and much of the local traffic between coastal points on the same continent. Command of the sea became a prize of prime political value; the layout of the continents and narrow seas profoundly affected the geopolitical patterns of international politics for several centuries. The prodigious growth of overland transport and of intercontinental airborne traffic, supplemented in the military sphere by long-range ballistic missiles, has reduced the importance historically attributed to 'command' of the ocean's surface. But the global ocean and its connecting seas have acquired other values that stimulate new rivalries, alter conceptions of national interest, and in various ways extend and tighten the interdependence of nations. [...]

According to traditional international law, the ocean and connecting seas (except for a narrow coastal zone) constitute the 'high sea' that lies outside the sovereign jurisdiction of any state. The coastal zone of 'territorial waters' historically extended about three miles from shore. During the past half century, various governments have asserted a 'right' to exercise jurisdiction for various purposes farther from their shores. In 1958 a major breach in the traditional law was made by an international treaty which extended the jurisdiction of maritime states over the resources upon and beneath the seabed of the continental shelf to a depth of 600 feet, 'or beyond that limit to where the depth of the superadjacent waters admits to the exploration of the natural resources of the said areas'.

In short, such sovereignty 'may be exercised over a continuous stretch of seafloor starting with the beach and extending outwards and downwards to whatever depth the nation is able to work its benthic resources [that is, resources upon or beneath the seafloor]'.[5]

There are plenty of indications that this is only the beginning of what may become another phase of ruthless international competition and conflict, or alternatively, the forerunner of a massive experiment in international order. As things stood in the early 1970s, the only effective constraints on exploitation of the seafloor to any depth were those imposed by the transient limitations of a rapidly advancing technology and the availability of huge amounts of capital. Since only a very few political communities commanded both the necessary technology and the capital, the outlook was that those few — USA, USSR, Japan, and perhaps two or three others — would progressively preempt development and control of the resources in the more remote ocean depths. A review of the situation in 1969 concluded that 'the great powers will not accept control by an international body', and that 'the great industrial complexes that have been doing preliminary work will not look favorably on the idea of sharing profits' with other nations which lack the marine frontage, or the requisite technology, or the necessary capital to exploit the ocean depths.[6] [...]

While nationalistic rivals mobilize to contest control of the resources of the seabed, two sets of forces are eroding the ecology of the ocean as a whole. These forces are excessive fishing and progressive pollution of the environment in which fish and other marine organisms subsist.

The fact and potentially disastrous consequences of large-scale industrialization of fishing — especially but not exclusively by the Russians and Japanese — have evoked protests of alarm from ecologists in numerous countries. In the measured rhetoric of a recent United Nations report, it is stated with no qualification that destruction or depletion of marine resources has been a continuing process in the absence of effective control and management. The decline of certain species of whales and seals, of sea turtles, of the Pacific sardine and Atlantic salmon fisheries, as well as the continuing over-exploitation of the eastern Pacific anchoveta fishery are examples. The growing dependence of mankind upon the sea as a source of protein requires that its resources be properly managed.[7]

The UN report asserts further that 'pollution of the sea is a continued threat to its future productivity'. The report cites specifically the ecological damage caused by oil spills from tankers and from underwater oil drilling and pumping rigs. But these are by no means all, or necessarily the most serious, sources of marine pollution. Hundreds of millions of tons of sewage and industrial wastes from scores of countries are being dumped annually into coastal waters and thence out to sea — with the volume rising steadily year by year. Destruction of spawning sites by these pollutants and by the draining of tidal marshes, damming of rivers that discharge into the sea, and other projects and operations go on around the world without regard to their destructive effects on marine ecology.

Recurrent testing of nuclear weapons in marine seas, chiefly in the western Pacific, has released incalculable quantities of lethal radioactive debris, carried around the earth by the currents of the global ocean. Some radioactive contamination as well as a large amount of heat find their way into coastal waters via the spent coolant of atomic power plants, the number of which is steadily increasing. Ecologists view with concern the tendency of radioactivity to accumulate and concentrate in marine organisms through time, to become in the not distant future a menace to human consumers of the products of the sea.

It is further regarded as virtually certain that, in the absence of adequate and rigorously enforced regulations, mining of minerals upon and beneath the ocean floor will produce at least as much environmental damage as comparable operations on land have produced, and are still producing, in scores of countries.

Finally, one notes the grim warnings from ecologists that continued drainage of pesticide residues, industrial effluents, and other pollutants into the ocean will sooner or later slow down, possibly even utterly disrupt, the photosynthesis in marine organisms, starting chain reactions that could eventually so transform the ecology of the ocean as to endanger *all life upon the earth*.

This is admittedly a controversial issue on which many expert opinions are still tentative and even agnostic. As usual, when experts disagree or seem uncertain, politicans and most of their constituents opt for quick gains at least cost and let the future take care of itself. In this instance, as Paul Ehrlich, the Stanford University biologist, reminds us, the risks may be more than minimal:

No one knows how long we can continue to pollute the seas with chlorinated hydrocarbon insecticides, polychlorinated biphenyls, and hundreds of thousands of other pollutants without bringing on a worldwide ecological disaster. Subtle changes may already have started a chain reaction in that direction.[8]

Whether and when a marine catastrophe occurs as predicted from these and other causes depends upon the human response. Much remains to be learned about the short- and longer-range effects of the conditions and trends outlined above. But certain possibilities are no longer in doubt. Sooner or later, what happens within and beneath the water of the global ocean is likely to produce major consequences for the human condition everywhere, even for communities hundreds of thousands of miles from tidewater. Unregulated nationalistic competition for, and exploitation of, marine life and the minerals in seawater and upon and beneath the ocean floor are likely to hasten the worst ecological effects predicted. The ancient British maxim, 'The sea is one', expresses an international reality that picks up new dimensions and salience with every passing year.

Notes

1. J. Herz, 'The Rise and Demise of the Territorial State', *World Politics*, IX (July 1957), pp. 473 ff.

2. I.C. Lundberg, 'World Revolution – American Plan', *Harper's Magazine* (December 1948), p. 39.

3. R.O. Keohane, 'Lilliputians' Dilemmas: Small States in International Politics', *International Organization*, 23 (Spring 1969), p. 306.

4. Abel Wolman, 'Pollution As an International Issue', *Foreign Affairs*, 47 (1968), p. 172.

5. E.W. Seabrook Hull, 'The Political Ocean', *Foreign Affairs*, 45 (April 1967), p. 498. (Copyright 1967 by the Council on Foreign Relations; reprinted by permission.)

6. 'For Planners at the U.N., the Ocean Floor is New Frontier', *New York Times*, 24 November 1969.

7. *Problems of the Human Environment*, Report of the Secretary-General, United Nations, 26 May 1969 (Economic and Social Council, 47th Session, Agenda Item 10, par. 48).

8. P.R. and A.H. Ehrlich, *Population, Resources, Environment: Issues in Human Ecology* (Freeman, San Francisco, 1970), p. 180.

2.12

TOWARDS MUTUAL ACCOUNTABILITY IN THE NONTERRESTRIAL REALMS

Seyom Brown and Larry L. Fabian

Source: *International Organization*, vol. 29, no. 3 (1975), pp. 877-92.

Brown and Fabian argue that the existing rules governing the management of the oceans, outer space and the weather are out of date. They reject the idea of greater authority being exercised by governments or of incremental changes in the functions of existing international organizations and argue instead that only a major commitment to strengthening the processes of international accountability and control will suffice.

The expansion of economically and politically consequential uses of the ocean, outer space, and the weather has pushed fundamental policy questions for each of these nonterrestrial realms (NTRs) high on the international agenda. What criteria and procedures should determine who enjoys access to these realms and how their resources can be exploited? How should conflicts among users be resolved? How can these realms be best protected from ecological damage?

These questions are now inseparable from the dominant international concerns of the post Cold War period: the growing capability of more countries to affect one another for ill or for good; the press of the world's increasing population and industrialization on finite natural resources and fragile global ecosystems; and the widening alienation of the poorer peoples from the more affluent. Such concerns raise major political issues about what institutions, laws, and decision processes should be relied on to manage the NTRs. For unlike the land areas of the planet, the oceans, outer space, and the weather system are still largely 'up for grabs'.

The NTRs have remained mostly unappropriated by states or private parties for two basic reasons: (1) their essential properties — fluid, moving, intangible — have made them less susceptible than land areas to being sliced up into multiple political jurisdictions; and (2) their vastness or presumed abundance of resources encouraged, until recently, general acceptance of regimes allowing open access and free use.

New capabilities for exploring, economically exploiting, and otherwise altering the natural conditions of the NTRs, however, are raising doubts about the practicality and justice of the inherited regimes of open access and free use.

Previously plentiful resources have become 'scarce' and subject to dangerous depletion or degradation in the absence of substantial regulation. Resources which have remained plentiful have become more valuable and thus more prone to generate serious conflict among potential exploiters. Concurrently, changing international political norms have made it increasingly costly for the technologically advanced countries to use the NTRs merely at their whim, without obtaining at least the consent of other countries.

Most efforts, underway or projected, to respond to these developments fall into either of two categories: (1) substantially greater assumption of management authority, and sovereign control where possible, by various nation-states; and (2) marginal increases, on an eclectic basis, of limited management authority at various levels of the international system – national, regional, and global – resulting in a mix of specialized functional institutions, with a residue of open access and free use.

However, for reasons to be articulated below, we find both of these responses to the obsolescence of the open access and free use regimes for the NTRs grossly inadequate on grounds of practicality and legitimacy. We shall outline an alternative response as being more adaptive to the technological and political trends of the last quarter of the twentieth century.

The National Authority Approach

The most prevalent response thus far to the 'opening up' of the ocean, outer space, and the weather to political and economic competition and ecological damage has been to attempt to apply the land-oriented system of national responsibility and authority to the uses of these realms.

National governments, after all, still provide the most readily available institutions with a capacity for assuring that users of the NTRs act in accord with some conception of public interest, either nationally or internationally defined. Without the assertion of national discretion, it can be argued, no one possessing real power and economic weight will be responsible for the performance of the increasingly complicated management tasks.

The most conspicuous extensions of national authority have been occurring in the ocean. Twelve-mile territorial seas are about to be universally recognized. Beyond these, many coastal states now lay claim to the seabed resources out to the farthest widths of their continental margins. Many are also claiming exclusive national fisheries, unilaterally proclaiming wide pollution control zones, and insisting on controlling all scientific research activities off their coasts. Hard mineral mining interests are pressuring their governments to license and underwrite commercial exploitation of the deep seabed.

Practical arguments are advanced for these attempts to supplant the traditional ocean regime of open access and free use (beyond the narrow three-mile territorial sea) with zones clearly under the authority of specific national governments. Developing country coastal states contend this is the only way to protect the economically exploitable resources off their coasts from raiding by more industrially advanced countries or multi-national corporations. Coastal interests cite the need to enforce pollution control, navigational lanes, and traffic separation schemes in congested straits and other crowded international waterways without waiting for the sluggish international negotiating process to standardize rules, which will probably be too lax in any event. Mining interests argue that only national governments can provide the security of license and title arrangements conducive to further progress by venturesome firms now developing the capability to extract hard minerals from the deep sea bed.

The users of outer space are accountable thus far primarily to national space authorities — The International Telecommunications Union and International Telecommunications Satellite Organization (INTELSAT) being the main exceptions. The International Telecommunications Union (ITU), with ostensible responsibilities for frequency spectrum and orbital allocations, in fact operates as little more than a coordinating agency and clearinghouse for arrangements worked out among national telecommunications authorities; it has virtually no power to induce efficient and equitable allocations of these limited resources. INTELSAT has evolved into a true international consortium for transmitting international telephonic and TV communications traffic via satellite. But most other current and planned earth-oriented applications of satellites — in such fields as broadcasting, remote sensing, sea and air traffic control — are being developed and managed at least initially within national frameworks.

To the extent that there is to be any implementation of the vague obligations in the Outer Space Treaty of 1967 to use space for the common benefit, under the current regime it is to be by those who build and put up the hardware and design the software. It is these space-capable actors themselves who are interpreting their obligations to the rest of the international society, and resist any authoritative external direction over their activities.

On efficiency grounds, the space-capable actors have convincing sounding reasons for preferring to keep decisions about the design, deployment, and management of international space services in their own hands. The space applications field involves large capital outlays for research and development, and the day-to-day operation of deployed capabilities requires highly-trained technical personnel. The needed investment capital, it is argued, will not be forthcoming, from either private sources or public treasuries, if there is any lowering of performance standards in order to serve international participation objectives.

Even in the field of collecting and analyzing weather information, where there has been up to now a rather impressive record of international sharing, the rising pattern of unilateralism has given some countries fear that the space-capable powers, increasingly able to obtain all their needed weather information from their own satellites, may turn off their automatic transmission of data to the World Weather Watch. And when it comes to weather modification, there is reluctance on the part of those with the technology to subject their projects to advance international scrutiny, let alone authorization. Here too, the case for national unilateralism rests primarily on grounds of control over investments and efficiency of operations.

The nationalistic response to the increasing use and value of the NTRs, however, must be viewed as basically retrogressive. Most nations of the world are becoming more dependent upon the cooperation of others in these realms in order to protect themselves from harm or to implement constructive projects. More so in the NTRs than perhaps anywhere else, the fact that mankind has irreversibly become an international society, if not yet a community, is clear at least on the level of physical interdependence. To react to this mutual physical sensitivity by attempting to add bricks to the protective walls of national sovereignty is only to prolong and exacerbate the contradictions between the evolving material world and the traditional international political system. To assign national authorities responsibilities beyond their scope of real competence can lead only to an undermining of their legitimacy.

The deficiencies of the national authority approach are the most telling in the ocean. Being a major medium of navigation and commerce for virtually all societies, for the ocean to have a crazy-quilt pattern of overlapping and at times conflicting rules and regulations is to increase the costs of goods and services for most people. The requisite amount of international standardization, both with respect to the substantive content of the rules of the road and their enforcement, simply cannot be attained if rules are mainly established through unilateral promulgation and if the attempt to harmonize national regulations is left exclusively to traditional bilateral and multilateral negotiations.

The inadequacies of the national authority approach are even more glaring when it comes to maintaining the overall ecological health of the sea and its living resources. Marine pollutants are introduced at many points, and are distributed and redistributed so erratically in the ocean's volatile currents as to confound attempts to assign control over them to any particular national political jurisdictions. Fish resources migrate widely, and fishing policies adopted in one part of the sea have repercussions in distant regions. Thus ocean ecological 'commons' problems, such as overfishing or overusing the sea as a waste-disposal sink, cannot be solved as the English solved the problem of overgrazing their pasture commons — i.e., by dividing up the commons among private parties, and fencing off the parcels.

Even for ocean resources of relatively fixed location the national authority approach leaves much to be desired. Many petroleum pools, though imbedded in solid geological formations, have yet to be discovered, so many national seabed jurisdictions drawn today to conform to the locations of known pools would not adequately comprehend those yet to be discovered, and some of the future pools will undoubtedly traverse the already established jurisdiction lines. For efficient exploitation of the hard minerals in the deep seabed, the assignment to national governments of exclusive title to delineated blocks of the seabed might appear rational, but there is no natural basis for assigning deep seabed areas to one country rather than another. If countries with the technical capabilities to mine the deep seabed are accorded title simply on the basis of their readiness to engage in the enterprise, this would negate the prevalent expectation that the deep seabed resources are to be treated as the 'common heritage of mankind' and revenues from their exploitation are to be shared by the entire international community, with special equity considerations for the poorer countries.

The deficiencies of the national authority approach to the use of outer space are becoming evident with the deployment of advanced satellite systems for observing earth resources and for broadcasting television directly into receiving sets all around the globe. Some countries fear that the newly accessible information about their natural resources and crops may be used against them by economic or political rivals. Some countries are concerned that satellite-relayed TV programs may override local cultural sensibilities or be used to politically subvert their populations. If the space-capable powers insist on unilaterally managing their activities in these fields, many potential target populations, rightly or wrongly, will regard themselves as victims of 'technological imperialism' and can be expected to mobilize coalitions in the UN and other international institutions to restrict activities in space that might otherwise be of general benefit, and of substantial particular benefit to many developing countries.

Similarly — assuming a continuation of present unilateralist trends in the experimentation with weather modification capabilities — the growing recognition that major economic harm as well as benefits could befall populations on the basis of man-initiated changes in the weather, and that these consequences may traverse many nations and might have global effects, is likely to generate restrictive rather than promotive reactions to the experiments of the technologically-capable powers.

Functional Eclecticism

A more optimistic picture of the meaning of current trends envisions the emergence of a national-international mix of regulatory arrangements for the NTRs, superimposed on the open access and free use regimes. This prognosis puts its trust in the normal give and take of bilateral and multilateral negotiations to generate technically workable and politically durable resolutions of conflicts among users of the NTRs. The processes of diplomacy would spawn a kind of institutional and policy 'pluralism' for these realms. The expectation is that, for particular activities, economy of scale considerations, immediate conflict avoidance considerations, and current conservation and anti-pollution imperatives will drive various groups of countries into multilateral arrangements to restrain or coordinate their actions, and in some cases to participate in the joint management of projects. International arrangements and institutions — some bilateral, some limited-member multilateral, a few global — would evolve on a case-by-case basis, allowing for a flexible experimentation with varied forms. But it is further assumed that the most influential constituencies can be expected to remain highly resistant to suggestions that control over security, wealth, or welfare matters be transferred to decision-making authorities responsive to demands from wide international constituencies.

This approach takes the existing complex of international arrangements, and ongoing negotiations such as the Law of the Sea Conference, as starting points, but also as guides to what can and should be expected over the next decade or so. If such functional eclecticism does indeed shape the international bargaining, prevailing arrangements for the NTRs in the late 1970s can be expected to exhibit features approximating the following:

Outer space would continue to be governed by practical arms control restraints. The ocean denuclearization agreement of 1971 would remain in force, but would increasingly be strained by the advances of undersea military technology and by the progressive deployment of strategic forces in the ocean. Both the ocean and outer space would continue to serve as major arenas for nonnuclear activities. Weather warfare possibilities would be brought under the control of at least some general principles limiting military application of some weather changing technologies.

With regard to economic uses of the oceans, extant international institutions would remain fragmented, technically-oriented, and relatively powerless to affect the fundamental political order. Some, like the Intergovernmental Maritime Consultative Organization (IMCO), would remain technically effective facilitators for standard setting and implementation in specialized fields such as ship construction and navigation performance. Others, like the Food and Agricultural Organization of the UN (FAO) or the Intergovernmental Oceanographic Commission (IOC), would continue to provide specialized communities with data, and to develop cooperative frameworks for technical endeavors, or to resolve technical problems.

Coastal states would have territorial seas of twelve miles and would have primary economic title over seabed resources, largely oil and gas deposits, out to 200 miles or to the edge of their continental margins, subject to certain minimum, not heavily intrusive international standards for pollution control and the like.

All parties would have a presumed right to navigate and fly over any part of the ocean, subject to the right of coastal states to protect themselves against clear and present dangers to their safety, health, and economic welfare. Conflicts in the ambiguous grey areas between navigational and coastal security rights would be resolved *ad hoc* through political negotiations by the involved parties, or by agreed intermediary or legal mechanisms.

Coastal states would have priority fishing rights off their own coasts, subject to regional conservation and allocation arrangements negotiated with their neighbors and voluntary limitations they have accepted on harvesting migratory species. Long distance fishing fleets operating in national or regional fishing grounds without permission of the local states would generally be regarded as engaging in hostile acts.

Mining operations on the deep seabed beyond the continental margins would be licensed by national governments within national blocs leased, on the basis of some kind of auction system, from an international seabed authority. Leasing revenues and a portion of national licensing revenues and taxes from profits on operations would be used for economic development assistance and technology transfer projects in the poorer countries.

Responsibilities for setting national standards for the care of ecologies would be divided among various multinational functional agencies; some standard setting would devolve upon coastal states; enforcement authority would generally be retained by the nation-states.

Coastal states would have the right to prior consent to scientific activities of other states or corporations within coastal state territorial seas or resource zones, and to insist upon result-sharing, technical assistance, and participation arrangements according to their preferences.

Telecommunications broadcasts relayed internationally by space satellite to community or home receivers would take place on the basis of consent from receiving countries; and bilateral or limited-member multilateral arrangements would facilitate recipient country programming.

Remote sensing via space satellites of earth resources, ecosystems, and environmental conditions would take place on a continuing basis by the space-capable countries – despite persisting unhappiness by many countries that they are being observed without their consent. There would be overlapping and duplicative remote sensing operations conducted unilaterally by the US and the USSR, and possibly also by Japan and by a Western European consortium. Some technical assistance in data interpretation would be provided by the technologically advanced countries to the technologically deficient countries, most of it bilaterally, but some of it, perhaps, through multilateral regional or global institutions such as the World Weather Watch or new sharing arrangements.

Various of the space-capable countries and corporations would be in the business of providing maritime navigational communications and other specialized communication services via satellites, possibly on a regional basis to Europe, with considerable overlapping and duplication of effort, and competition for preferred frequencies and orbital slots, particularly those servicing the communications-congested regions around North America and Western Europe.

The ITU would continue to register, rather than truly allocate, frequencies and orbital space primarily on the basis of agreements worked out among the most powerful communications industries, and, failing such agreements, on the basis of the traditional first-come, first-use pattern.

INTELSAT would remain the principal international body responsible for facilitating transmission of point-to-point satellite transmissions. The recent political controversy over the organization would recede as decision making is shared more widely in INTELSAT policy bodies, as the organization settles into a technical service role (a kind of global common carrier and switchboard), and as members feel fewer restraints on setting up other space application organizations for special purposes.

Weather modification experiments and projects would be conducted unilaterally by the technologically advanced countries, except in particular situations where a fuss by other affected populations compels some degree of multilateral planning and participation.

There are persuasive arguments in favor of endorsing such an evolution of NTR regimes. The *ad hoc* nature of the arrangements, and the trial-and-error attitude, would avoid the paralysis that comes from a failure to implement grand international designs. And the absence of a need to settle on some grand design would reduce the tendency of members of competing ideological camps to support or oppose particular projects apart from their practical merits. Coalitions for and against particular projects would cut across the coalitions on other projects, providing a cushion against intense total nation-vs.-nation or alliance-vs.-alliance hostility that could lead to threats of military force.

But such a complex intersection of interests, bilateral and multilateral agreements, and international institutions portends a highly confused political accountability structure. In each of the nonterrestrial realms this outcome would augur ill for a stable and just international order over the long run, and would risk failure to conserve scarce resources and adequately tend to the health of important ecosystems.

The uncoordinated international pluralism likely to grow out of the eclectic approach would not have built into it means for assuring that functions in the ocean arena, which are highly interdependent, are adequately related to, and consistent with, one another. The global proliferation of space applications authorities and consortia would sometimes duplicate one another functionally, overlap one another geographically, and compete with one another politically. Pressures on preferred communications frequencies and orbits would increase, dispute settlement procedures would tend to be less effective, and, particularly in a field with as much technical complexity as space applications, dominant national corporate entities would preserve their ability to avoid meaningful accountability to national and international public interest authorities. Finally, resources or ecologies that transcend function specific or region specific institutions are unlikely to be efficiently exploited, or adequately cared for, given the fragmented institutional patterns of the uncoordinated pluralistic system — a regime not well equipped for authoritatively allocating so-called 'external' costs. This structural deficiency is particularly glaring in cases of inadvertent large-scale environmental damage or climate modification where users of a resource do not themselves expect to suffer, and are content to pass the costs on to neighboring societies or future generations.

In short, functional eclecticism is superficially attractive in that it implies experimentation and pluralism instead of premature insistence that international society be molded into more structural unity than would be consistent with its natural diversity. It is deficient, however, in its lack of world community vision and constraints on narrow self-interested unilateralism. Only such vision and constraints are likely to generate the institutions and processes required to reduce the role of force in international politics, to adequately care for the earth's resources and ecologies, and to counter the widening alienation of the poorer peoples from the more affluent.

Mutual Accountability

The deficiencies of the eclectic approach could be avoided by retaining its experimental spirit and its resort to functionally-specific institutions for management of the nonterrestrial realms, while embodying these features in a set of wider-community imperatives. The wider-community imperatives would be derived from a concept of mutual accountability.

This approach would be based on the twin assumptions of the essential non-divisibility of the nonterrestrial realms *and* the scarcity or high values of many of their important resources. It would also incorporate the normative judgment that NTRs belong to all human beings in common, and therefore no segment of the human community, be it a corporation or a nation-state, should derive from the realms disproportionate gain at the expense of others. (This would not rule out the need, in advance of legitimate collective arrangements, to vest temporary authority over the commonweal in groups acting only as custodians for the entire human community, and ultimately accountable to it.)

Thus, the recommended approach would attempt to build flexibly and realistically from the currently evolving mix of regimes in the nonterrestrial realms. *But it would accept national and limited-member multinational arrangements only as expedient temporary delegations of authority by the whole international community for managing parts of the common heritage;* and would insist that such management serve the whole international community's interests — to the extent such interests are expressed by recognized bodies of the international community, or to the extent there clearly are presumptive world interests involved. This approach would actively attempt to stimulate the building of political accountability structures capable of reflecting the widest scope of involved interests, and their current and emerging functional interdependencies.

The recommended approach would not attempt to impose structural unity on the inherently diverse plurality of international arrangements; but it would actively promote effective international overview of such arrangements where desirable on ground of functional effectiveness and/or mutual accountability. And it would *actively promote the bringing of highly interdependent functions under umbrella institutions.*

Institutional Targets

The inherited network of international organizations for the most part does not have and is not likely to have the capacity to translate any such concept of mutual accountability into political action regarding the ocean, outer space, and weather — principally because this network reflects preoccupations and solutions that predate the challenge posed to international order by dramatically expanding uses of the nonterrestrial realms. Moreover, the press of science and technology on these realms will have increasingly universal impacts, thereby widening the arena of necessary mutual accountability to include more and more of the human community, and thereby enlarging the necessity for correspondingly inclusive decision structures enjoying the confidence of affected communities.

We are driven then, if we take this concept seriously, to urge that statesmen now give serious consideration to a number of major international institutional innovations. These can be expressed in the form of first-decade institutional targets — that is, institutions that should be in being and functioning by the mid 1980s — and would include the following structures:

1. A Comprehensive Ocean Authority. Whatever the specialized international management tasks — navigation, fishing, seabed resource exploitation, ecological care, scientific research — there would be an overarching global ocean authority to coordinate the various management tasks. It would be desirable for the plenary body of the comprehensive ocean authority to consist of all member states of the international community. This plenary body would be regarded as the source of basic policy in the entire network of ocean institutions, and its decisions would be binding on all member states and specialized ocean regimes. The ocean authority would maintain standby panels for dispute consultation and resolution services. Implementation of the decisions of the plenary body and dispute resolution panels could still be the responsibility of nation-states and regional ocean authorities; so the executive arm of the comprehensive ocean authority might be in the main a secretariat — monitoring and reporting on the activities of subordinate ocean authorities, providing scientific information and commissioning studies.

2. An Outer Space Projects Agency. Concrete international impetus would be given to the UN Outer Space Treaty provision that outer space is the 'province of mankind' and its exploitation and use 'shall be carried out for the benefit and in the interests of all countries'. The agency, to which all countries would belong, would absorb and strengthen the frequency and orbit management functions of the ITU and would serve as a coordinating agency for INTELSAT and other similar international satellite consortia such as those now being considered for maritime navigation systems. The agency would have no control, however, over the content of messages and broadcasts carried by satellites. Any controls on content would be entirely dependent upon arrangements worked out between transmitting and receiving parties. The agency would be empowered to give final approval to all earth observation satellite projects and outer space exploration projects for civilian purposes, under guidelines requiring international participation and the international dissemination of all data and results.

3. A Global Weather and Climate Organization. There would be a global weather and climate organization to coordinate all weather and climate modification activities, ensure that all concerned parties assent to programs which may adversely affect them, and enjoin those projects which could have severe adverse effects on weather and climate and which did not have the assent of those that would be affected.

Concerned parties would have the authority to initiate regulatory action to control the man-made sources of climatic change. For large-scale projects designed to modify weather or climate, parties would have to submit the project to the advisory panel for assessment and agree to abide by their recommendation, obtain approval from all parties that might be affected, and provide means of compensating those adversely affected. This would apply also to industrial, agricultural, and other large-scale projects referred to it by other agencies or brought to its attention by concerned parties as likely to affect the weather or climate even though not designed to do so. For hurricane modification or modification of similarly severe storms, the global organization would have the power to ensure that parties carried out at the regional level processes of assessment, consultation, consent, and compensation, and upon the appeal of a party that this had not been done, to initiate independent assessment of the program and enjoin the project if necessary. If the panel of advisors found that the program would have significant weather or climatic effects outside of the particular state or group of states proposing the program, the organization could delay the program until the concerned parties had worked out arrangements for handling the effects. For problems of inadvertent modification of weather from air pollution, the organization would serve as a forum for consultation and action, if such problems were not being adequately handled on a regional basis.

4. A Scientific Commission on Global Resources and Ecologies. Comprised of international interdisciplinary teams of geologists, biologists, meteorologists, resource economists, and general ecologists, the global resource and ecology commission (either attached to the United Nations Environmental Program or supplementing it) would continually monitor basic biospheric conditions and how they are affected by human activities. It would refer all cases of probable dangerous disruption of existing biospheric balances to the appropriate functional agencies and to public information media. It would also provide technical evaluations of remedial alternatives. Its judgments would be solicited by the more specialized and operational agencies, including their adjudicatory mechanisms. It would have unimpeded access to all areas of the ocean and outer space, and would have priority claim on all oceanographic meteorological data. It also would have presumptive entry rights to all land areas for purposes of determining the effects of land-based activities on internationally shared resources and ecologies.

Transitional Strategies

The first-decade targets envisage global institutions capable of exercising continuing oversight and authoritative guidance on the use of the nonterrestrial realms. But the requisite institutions can not, and perhaps should not, be constructed speedily. Rather, transitional policies need to be implemented that translate the mutual accountability concept into international arrangements that give those communities most directly and substantially affected by particular uses of these realms a commensurate role in authorizing and overseeing such uses.

The mutual accountability concept as stated does not point to an obvious single best means of assuring its practical implementation. Contemporary political and economic trends in specific uses of the ocean, outer space, and the weather make it clear that the means will have to vary and be specifically tailored. Function by function, they will have to take into account not only the technical characteristics of particular uses, but also variations in the number, location, and economic and political power of the relevant actors and affected populations.

Nor does the mutual accountability concept necessarily imply policy departures that are entirely novel. Instruments and habits of mutual accountability have long been part of international politics. The fabric of international laws, the obligations of membership in international organizations, the imperatives of regional and bilateral dealings among nations, the involvement in transnational associations and interactions – all prompt nations to collaborate, to explain and defend their policies, and to become enmeshed with each other in various types of commitments. But we are not content to see the prevailing pattern merely work itself out in the politics of the oceans, outer space and weather. Such a 'business as usual' course would eventually allow the dominant impulses of unilateralism to overpower incentives for cooperation among users of those realms. Moreover, we believe that the practical effect of the inherited structures of international politics and law is, on balance, that nations have been able to manipulate these structures to avoid rather than be responsive to normative precepts of international accountability. The protective shield of asserted sovereign rights has traditionally diminished rather than increased accountability, and the overwhelmingly parochial defenses of national interests have traditionally narrowed rather than widened the scope of accountability. For all these reasons we believe that substantial modifications in the operation of the prevailing patterns, as it applies to the NTRs, are essential.

[Fabian and Brown suggest that the transnational strategies should involve:

(a) greater efforts to acquire information on an international basis;
(b) more international consultation;
(c) efforts to limit extensions of national sovereignty.]

Coda

We recognize that the means chosen to implement the accountability concept will sometimes be shaped by a clash between the values implicit in this concept and other vital international values – such as the reduction of war and coercion, the conservation of depletable natural resources, and the care of essential ecosystems – which may not be adequately served by regimes that function well on accountability criteria alone.

Thus, while mutual accountability should stand as a cardinal policy objective, it ought not to be expected to override other values in all circumstances. One of the growing international demands is that there be an equitable distribution of goods and reduction of risks to meet the needs of the world's disadvantaged peoples. Unless this value is strongly upheld by statesmen interested in mutual accountability in the NTRs, the powerless will reject the new structures for these realms as merely perpetrating social injustices and inequities. Conflict reduction is another persistent consideration. A system of mutual accountability alone may in some circumstances serve to defuse potential conflicts in the NTRs but peaceful order in these realms will demand dispute resolution techniques that take account of the political complexity, legal ambiguities and scientific and technological uncertainties surrounding future developments.

Securing mutual accountability is not, therefore, an objective to be pursued unconditionally and single-mindedly; it must, rather, be coupled with deliberate, sustained efforts to further sound justice and peaceful accommodation of inevitably conflicting interests in the nonterrestrial realms.

We recognize also that the forces making for inertia and ineffectiveness will persist as the international community grapples more intensively with the problem of regime building for the NTRs. While the logical and architectural appeal of unified, hierarchical, and truly supranational solutions will remain theoretical rather than practical, we nevertheless believe that the nonterrestrial realms are ripe for new, more flexible institutional and political patterns, and that the imperatives of interdependence in the realms will increasingly provide an underlying and compelling rationale for such patterns.

Part 3

THE POLITICS OF DOMINANCE AND DEPENDENCE

INTRODUCTION

Whereas the 'politics of power and security' and the 'politics of inter-dependence and transnational relations' represent two strands in the development of 'Western' or 'developed world' thinking about world politics, the 'politics of dominance and dependence' as a perspective arise from rather different roots. Embodying elements of 'classical' Marxist-Leninist writings on the nature and implications of monopoly capitalism and imperialism, they also reflect the more specific experience of new and less developed countries in an international system moulded by 'Western' political and economic activity. The perspective in general stresses the importance of the overall structure of relations within which political action occurs, and the mechanisms by which the structural dominance of some groups is consolidated to the disadvantage of others. As a consequence, it also emphasizes the desirability (or likelihood) of a fundamental trans-formation of the structure so as to create a new world system based on global principles of justice, whilst concerning itself with the ways in which the established structure can accommodate some degree of change and redistribution.

The selections in the Section fall into several broadly defined categories, although all are concerned with the central problem of action and change within all-pervading structural constraints. In the first category, the selections by O'Connor, Frank and Galtung deal with the broad issues raised by the phenomenon of dominance and dependence and also illustrate some of the ways in which thinking about the problem has evolved. O'Connor (3.1) discerns three broad lines of development in the study of economic imperialism: the first treats it as a 'political' phenomenon, the second as an expression of monopoly capitalism through territorial coloni-alism, and the third as an expression of contemporary global capitalism without the symptoms of territorial occupation. Frank (3.2), on the other hand, is concerned primarily with the workings of centre-periphery relationships, in which the interests of capitalist groups within dominant and dependent societies produce a process of 'underdevelopment', with the dependent areas serving the needs of the capitalist centres. This line of argument, which expresses many of the concerns felt by those in the Third World about the difficulties of economic development and political autonomy, is carried further by Galtung (3.3) in his analysis of the possible combinations within a spectrum of centre-periphery relationships.

Galtung also deals in outline with some of the mechanisms by which dependent relationships are consolidated − an area of inquiry which is the central concern of the second group of readings. The selections here embody two approaches to the problem. Firstly, the pieces by Bodenheimer and Weisskopf examine the origins and expressions of dependency as it can be seen to exist between developed and less developed nations. Bodenheimer (3.4) focuses on the relationship between the United States and Latin America, which has been fertile ground for theorists of dependency; her argument, however, is that a full explanation of the phenomenon demands the use both of Marxist-Leninist theory (which stresses the internal dynamics of capitalist societies) and of the later theories of dependency, which stress the structural and systemic constraints on development. Weisskopf (3.5) focuses his attention on the implications of dependence for the less developed countries more generally, and particularly on the ways in which economic and social processes can be seen to contribute to the growing disadvantage of the dependent. The next three selections − by Hymer, Luckham and Stewart − develop in more detail some of the areas mentioned in earlier pieces, by focusing on specific issues and activities. Hymer (3.6) concentrates his attention on the ways in which multinational corporations (MNCs) as representatives of 'big capital' operate to accentuate the unevenness of development between rich and poor countries. Luckham (3.7), in contrast, examines the role of the military in expressing and helping to consolidate the global structure, by providing mechanisms of order and authority without which capital could not achieve many of its objectives. Finally, Stewart (3.8) assesses the various ways in which technological dependence can reduce the possibilities of national economic development and confirm the role of MNCs in encouraging dependence.

It can be seen that, although there are variations in approach and the kinds of evidence used, all of these authors share a focus on the ways in which the structure of global relations, in both political and economic terms, conditions the possibilities for change and development among the less privileged. One reaction to this analysis has been to advocate revolutionary transformation (see Weisskopf, for example); others are more reformist (see Stewart). A rather different approach is taken by Immanuel Wallerstein in the final selection (3.9): he examines the ways in which some mobility is possible within the existing world system − primarily through the 'upward mobility' of a group of 'semi-peripheral' states – but argues that this form of development is far from adequate to the needs of a truly just world order. In so doing, he brings together many of the shared assumptions of ealier selections, which see actors in the world system as constrained by their place within its over-all structure, participating in processes which express large-scale trends in dominance and dependence and fostering a set of outcomes which demand radical transformation.

3.1

THE MEANING OF ECONOMIC IMPERIALISM

James O'Connor

Source: R.I. Rhodes (ed.), *Imperialism and Underdevelopment: a Reader* (Monthly Review Press, New York, 1970), pp. 101-50.

O'Connor identifies three general doctrines of imperialism: the first disassociates capitalism from imperialism and explains the European expansion which began in the 1880s in political terms; the second examines that same expansionism but interprets it in terms of the needs of monopoly capitalism; and the third concentrates on contemporary world capitalism and identifies a neo-imperialism which does not require the territorial control of traditional colonialism.

Imperialism: A Political Phenomenon

The first doctrine disassociates capitalism from imperialism. For Joseph Schumpeter, the leading exponent of this view, imperialism is 'a heritage of the autocratic state ... the outcome of precapitalist forces which the autocratic state has reorganized ... [and] would never have been evolved by the "inner logic" of capitalism itself'.[1] The 'inner logic' of capitalism consists of nothing more or less than free trade and 'where free trade prevails *no* class has an interest in forcible expansion as such ... citizens and goods of every nation can move in foreign countries as freely as though those countries were politically their own'. Only the 'export monopolist interests' — in particular, monopolies in the metropolitan countries which dump surplus commodities abroad behind high tariff walls — profit from imperialism. Schumpeter was confident that these interests would not survive capitalism's 'inner logic'. His confidence was, of course, misplaced; as we will see, the national and regional economic policies of the advanced capitalist countries today rightly merit Joan Robinson's label — the New Mercantilism. The reason is not hard to find: Schumpeter selected one characteristic of capitalism, 'rationality', which he considered central, to the exclusion of other features.

The vast majority of bourgeois economists in the past and present adopt a position similar to Schumpeter's, even though few today would share his optimism in connection with the revival of free trade. The generally accepted 'comparative advantage' theory of Ricardo and Mill holds that all parties in international commodity trade under competitive conditions benefit in accordance with the strength of the demand for their respective commodities. Nationalist economic policy and monopoly restricted free trade and inhibited the growth of income and economic well-being, but these barriers have been lowered by the breakup of the European empires. The trademark of this doctrine is that exploitative economic relations between the advanced and backward capitalist countries cannot survive in a world of politically independent countries. According to this line of thinking, the real problems of world capitalism today spring from the misplaced faith of the ex-colonies that nationalist economic policies which have created new and higher barriers to international investment and trade can put the backward countries on the path of self-sustained economic growth.

Schumpeter and other bourgeois writers uncritically disassociate capitalism from imperialism for three reasons: first, because their criteria for distinguishing and identifying imperial and colonial relationships are ordinarily political and not economic (for example, Hans Kohn has developed the most sophisticated typology of imperialism, which he understands in terms of the distribution of political power[2]); second, because they do not consider capitalism as such to be an exploitative system; third, because imperialism historically has contained certain features identified with the theme of expansionism which have not been uniquely associated with any given economic and social system. Thus bourgeois writers have concluded not only that imperialism predates capitalism, but also that imperialism is essentially an anachronistic system.

[O'Connor then considers how both in pre-capitalist and capitalist societies and in mercantile and industrial capitalist societies economic expansionism has assumed very different forms, before returning to the second general doctrine.]

[In relation to this doctrine] Lenin's ideas have dominated the field. Yet Lenin owed much to John A. Hobson's *Imperialism*, published in 1902, a book which is frequently (and legitimately) read as the precursor of Lenin's study. Thus we will begin by sketching out the main ideas of Hobson and Lenin, later subjecting them to analysis on the basis of theoretical and historical studies published in recent years.

Hobson and Lenin wrote about imperialism during the heyday of colonialism (1885-1914), which naturally enough appeared to be *the* most significant economic-political phenomenon of the time. By making colonialism their focal point, however, both men equated imperialism and colonialism and thus failed to understand the significance of the 'imperialism of free trade' – an expression coined to describe British economic expansion from the 1840s to the 1880s. Moreover, they barely acknowledged United States expansion and could not anticipate future modes of imperialist controls which have proved to be even more effective than formal colonial rule.

The distinctive feature of Hobson's theory is his conception of colonialism as the reflection of the unfulfilled promise of liberal democracy. As Hobson saw it, inequalities in the distribution of wealth and income in Britain dampened the consumption power of the British working classes, which in turn made it unprofitable for capitalists to utilize fully their industrial capacity. Unable to find profitable investment outlets at home, British capitalists subsequently sought them abroad in the economically underexploited continents. Britain therefore acquired colonies as a dumping ground for surplus capital. The end of imperialist conquest and de-colonization would come about only when the British working classes acquired more economic and political power through trade unionism and parliamentary representation, which would set the stage for a thoroughgoing redistribution of income and hence the development of a home economy in which the volume of consumption corresponded more closely to the volume of production.

Hobson supported his thesis not only by his faith in the promise of liberal democracy, but also by reference to changes in Britain's trade and investments. He tried to show that the expansion of empire during the last two decades of the nineteenth century, when most of the world not already independent or under European rule was carved up among the European powers, resulted in a *decline* in British trade with her colonies in relation to trade with noncolonies. He also underlined the obvious fact that the new colonies in Africa and Asia failed to attract British settlers in significant numbers. Through a process of elimination Hobson thus hit on what he considered to be the crucial element in British imperialism – foreign investments. He linked the vast outflow of capital from Britain during this period – British overseas investments rose from 785 million pounds in 1871 to 3,500 million pounds in 1911 and annual net foreign investments were frequently greater than gross domestic fixed investments – with the frantic struggle by the European powers for colonies, and inferred that the former caused the latter. The political struggles between the major European powers were thus dissolved into struggles for profitable investment outlets, and the explorers, missionaries, traders, and soldiers of the period were seen as the puppets of London's financial magnates.

Lenin agreed with Hobson that the prime cause of capital exports was the vast increase in the supply of capital in the metropolitan countries, especially Britain, and played down the role of the demand for capital in the underdeveloped regions. He also, like Hobson, causally linked foreign investments with the acquisition of colonies. The distinctive element in Lenin's theory related to the *cause* of the surplus of capital.

Lenin understood that imperialism is a *stage* of capitalist development, and not merely one possible set of foreign policy options among many. In particular, imperialism is the monopoly capitalist stage, and exhibits five basic features:

(1) The concentration of production and capital, developed so highly that it creates monopolies which play a decisive role in economic life.
(2) The fusion of banking capital with industrial capital and the creation, on the basis of this financial capital, of a financial oligarchy.
(3) The export of capital, which has become extremely important, as distinguished from the export of commodities.
(4) The formation of the international capitalist monopolies which share out the world among themselves.
(5) The territorial division of the whole earth completed by the great capitalist powers.[3]

The key element is the formation of local and international monopolies behind high tariff barriers in the metropolitan countries. Monopolistic organization develops 'precisely out of free competition' in essentially four ways. First, the concentration (growth in absolute size) of capital leads to the centralization (growth in relative size) of capital. Second, monopoly capital extends and strengthens itself by the seizure of key raw materials. Third, financial capital, or the investment banks, 'impose an infinite number of financial ties of dependence upon all the economic and political institutions of contemporary capitalist society', including nonfinancial capital. Fourth, 'monopoly has grown out of colonial policy. To the numerous "old" motives of colonial policy, the capitalist financier has added the struggle for the sources of raw materials, for the exportation of capital, for "spheres of influence", i.e., for spheres of good business, concessions, monopolist profits, and so on; in fine, for economic territory in general.' In short, the new colonialism opposes itself to the older colonial policy of the 'free grabbing' of territories.

The cause of the surplus of capital and capital exportation, and of monopolistic industry, is the tendency of the rate of profit to fall. Two underlying forces drive down the rate of profit in the metropolitan country. First, the rise of trade unions and social democracy, together with the exhaustion of opportunities to recruit labor from the countryside at the going real wage, rule out possibilities for increasing significantly the rate of exploitation. Second, labor saving innovations increase the organic composition of capital. Monopoly is thus in part formed in order to protect profit margins. At the same time, economies of large-scale production (internal expansion) and mergers during periods of economic crises (external expansion) strengthen pre-existing tendencies toward monopolistic organization.

Meanwhile, in the economically underexploited regions of the world, capital yields a substantially higher rate of return. For one thing, the composition of capital is lower; for another, labor is plentiful in supply and cheap; and, finally, colonial rule establishes the preconditions for monopolistic privileges. Rich in minerals and raw materials required by the development of metals, automotive, and other heavy industries in the metropolitan powers, the underexploited regions naturally attract large amounts of capital. Consequently, foreign investment counteracts the tendency for the rate of profit to fall in the metropolitan economy. On the one hand, high profit margins in the colonies pull up the average return on capital; on the other hand, the retardation of capital accumulation in the home economy recreates the reserve army of the unemployed, raises the rate of exploitation, and, finally, increases the rate of profit.

Pushing this thesis one step forward, the precondition for a truly 'favorable' investment climate is indirect or direct control of internal politics in the backward regions. Economic penetration therefore leads to the establishment of spheres of influence, protectorates, and annexation. Strachey suggests that the backward regions assumed a dependency status (the last step before outright control) in relation to the metropolitan powers chiefly because the former were in debt to the latter. What was significant about the shift from consumer goods to capital goods in world trade was that the colony-to-be needed long-term credits or loans to pay for the capital goods, and that, finally, the relationship between the backward country and the metropolitan country became one of debtor and creditor. And from this it was but a small step to dependence and domination.

Whatever the exact sequence of events which led to colonialism, Lenin's economic definition of colonialism (and imperialism) is monopolistically regulated trade and/or investment abroad at higher rates of profit than those obtaining in the metropolitan country. 'As soon as political control arrives as handmaid to investment', Dobb writes, 'the opportunity for monopolistic and preferential practices exists'. The essential ingredient of colonialism therefore is 'privileged investment: namely, investment in projects which carry with them some differential advantage, preference, or actual monopoly, in the form of concession-rights or some grant of privileged status'.[4]

[O'Connor then raises three objections to these theories: that Lenin exaggerated the break in continuity generated by the events of the 1880s; that both Hobson and Lenin were wrong in supposing that vast amounts of capital flowed into the new colonies; and that formal political control was not necessary in order to maintain Britain's economic interests.]

Neo-Imperialism: Control Without Colonialism

A brief sketch cannot even begin to resolve the many theoretical and historical questions which run through the two major contending doctrines of nineteenth-century imperialism. It is clear, however, that two features of imperialism are not in dispute. The first concerns the general description of economic organization and economic policy. As we have seen, Dobb considers the essential ingredient of imperialism to be 'privileged investment ... investment in projects which carry with them some differential advantage'. This feature must be placed in a wider frame of reference, as in Paul Sweezy's description of imperialism as 'severe rivalry [between advanced capitalist countries] in the world market leading alternatively to cutthroat competition and international monopoly combines'.[5] Schumpeter's view of imperialism is very similar. Cutthroat competition and international monopoly combines are seen as 'protective tariffs, cartels, monopoly prices, forced exports (dumping), an aggressive economic policy, and aggressive foreign policy generally'.[6] A second general area of agreement (generally implicit in the writings of both Marxists and non-Marxists) is that modern imperialism, whatever its causes, depends on colonial rule as the main form of economic and political control of the economically backward region and that political independence would significantly reduce, or eliminate entirely, exploitative imperialist relations.

Opposed to these doctrines is what may be called the neo-Leninist, or modern Marxist theory of imperialism. The increasing economic domination exercised by the United States in the world capitalist economy and the failure of the ex-colonies to embark on sustained economic and social development have caused older Marxist economists to rework original doctrines and have given rise to a new theory of neo-colonialism. Many of its outlines are still indistinct, but there is broad agreement that a sharp distinction should be made between colonialism and imperialism, while the original Leninist identity between monopoly capitalism and imperialism should be retained. In this view, monopoly capitalism remains an aggressively expansionist political-economic system, but colonialism is seen as merely one *form* of imperialist domination, and frequently an ineffective one at that.

The phrase 'neo-colonialism' was first used in the early 1950s. Anti-colonial leaders in Asia and Africa focus on the element of control — in the words of Sukarno, 'economic control, intellectual control, and actual physical control by a small but alien community, within a nation'.[7] To cite a specific illustration of economic neo-colonialism, Nkrumah denounced as 'neo-colonialism' the economic association of France's African colonies with the European Common Market. An example in which the political element was in the fore was France's claim to the right to suppress the revolt against the puppet ruler of Gabon in February 1964 in order to defend French economic interests in that country. A comprehensive summary of the chief manifestations of neo-colonialism was made at the Third All-African People's Conference held in Cairo in 1961:

This Conference considers that neo-colonialism, which is the survival of the colonial system in spite of formal recognition of political independence in emerging countries, which become the victims of an indirect and subtle form of domination by political, economic, social, military, or technical [forces], is the greatest threat to African countries that have newly won their independence or those approaching this status . . . This Conference denounces the following manifestations of neo-colonialism in Africa:

(a) Puppet governments represented by stooges, and based on some chiefs, reactionary elements, antipopular politicians, big bourgeois compradors, or corrupted civil or military functionaries.

(b) Regrouping of states, before or after independence, by an imperial power in federation or communities linked to that imperial power.

(c) Balkanization as a deliberate political fragmentation of states by creation of artificial entities, such as, for example, the case of Katanga, Mauritania, Buganda, etc.

(d) The economic entrenchment of the colonial power before independence and the continuity of economic dependence after formal recognition of national sovereignty.

(e) Integration into colonial economic blocs which maintain the under-developed character of African economy.

(f) Economic infiltration by a foreign power after independence, through capital investments, loans, and monetary aids or technical experts, of unequal concessions, particularly those extending for long periods.

(g) Direct monetary dependence, as in those emergent independent states whose finances remain in the hands of and directly controlled by colonial powers.

(h) Military bases sometimes introduced as scientific research stations or training schools, introduced either before independence or as a condition for independence.[8]

This description supports two broad generalizations. First, modern imperialism requires the active participation of the state in international economic relationships; imperialist nations cannot singly or collectively implement a neo-colonialist policy — via agencies such as the European Common Market, for example — without state capitalism. Secondly, neo-colonialist policy is first and foremost designed to prevent the newly independent countries from consolidating their political independence and thus to keep them economically dependent and securely in the world capitalist system. In the pure case of neo-colonialism, the allocation of economic resources, investment effort, legal and ideological structures, and other features of the old society remain unchanged — with the single exception of the substitution of 'internal colonialism' for formal colonialism, that is, the transfer of power to the domestic ruling classes by their former colonial masters. Independence has thus been achieved on conditions which are irrelevant to the basic needs of the society, and represents a part denial of real sovereignty, and a part continuation of disunity within the society. The most important branch of the theory of neo-colonialism is therefore the theory of economic imperialism.

The definition of economic imperialism which we employ is the economic domination of one region or country over another — specifically, the formal or informal control over local economic resources in a manner advantageous to the metropolitan power, and at the expense of the local economy. Economic control assumes different forms and is exercised in a number of ways. The main form of economic domination has always been control by the advanced capitalist countries over the liquid and real economic resources of economically backward areas. The main liquid resources are foreign exchange and public and private savings, and real resources consist of agricultural, mineral, transportation, communication, manufacturing and commercial facilities and other assets. The most characteristic modes of domination today can be illuminated by way of contrast with examples drawn from the colonial period.

Examples of control over foreign exchange assets are numerous. In the colonial era the metropolitan powers established currency boards to issue and redeem local circulating medium against sterling and other metropolitan currencies. In its purest form, the currency board system required 100 per cent backing of sterling for local currency. The East African Currency Board, for example, was established in 1919, staffed by British civil servants appointed by the Colonial Office, and at one time exercised financial domination over Ethiopia, British and Italian Somaliland, and Aden, as well as the East African countries. The Board did not have the authority to expand or contract local credit, and therefore expenditures on local projects which required imported materials or machinery were limited to current export earnings, less outlays for essential consumer goods, debt service, and other fixed expenses. Measures to expand exports were thus necessary preconditions of local initiatives toward economic progress. In this way, British imperialism indirectly controlled the allocation of real resources.

This mode of control still survives in modified form in the Common-wealth Caribbean economies and elsewhere. The Jamaican central bank, for example, has limited power to influence the domestic money supply, but sterling and local currency are automatically convertible in unlimited amounts at fixed rates of exchange. The local government is thus prohibited from financing investment projects by inflation, or forced savings; nor are exchange controls and related financial instruments of national economic policy permitted. The structure and organization of the commercial banking system aggravates the situation. Local banks are branches of foreign-owned banks whose headquarters are located in the overseas financial centers and are more responsive to economic and monetary changes abroad than in the local economy; specifically, local banks have contracted credit at times when foreign exchange assets have been accumulating. This combination of monetary and financial dependence has caused artificial shortages of funds and prevented the Jamaican government from allocating local financial resources in a rational manner.

A more characteristic form of control over foreign exchange today is private direct investment. In the nineteenth and early twentieth centuries, backward countries were often able to attract portfolio investments and local governments and capitalists were thus able to exercise some control over the use of foreign exchange made available by long-term foreign investment. Today direct investment constitutes the great mass of long-term capital exported on private account by the metropolitan countries. Foreign exchange receipts typically take the form of branch plants and other facilities of the multinational corporations — facilities which are difficult or impossible to integrate into the structure of the local economy. What is more, satellite countries which depend on direct investment ordinarily provide free currency convertibility and hence foreign-owned enterprises which produce for local markets have privileged access to foreign exchange earned in other sectors of the economy.

Another feature of economic domination is the control of local savings, which assumes two forms. First, economic rule means that local government revenues, or *public* savings, are mortgaged to loans received from the metropolitan powers. An extreme example is Liberia — a country with an open door policy with regard to foreign capital — which in 1963 expended 94 per cent of its annual revenues to repay foreign loans. In the nineteenth century, persuasion, coercion, and outright conquest often insured that tariffs and other taxes were turned over to foreign bondholders. In the absence of direct colonial rule, however, foreign lending was frequently a precarious undertaking. Latin American countries, for example, had an uneven history of bond payments. Foreign loans today are secured in more peaceful and more effective ways. The international capital market is highly centralized and dominated by the agencies of the main imperialist powers — the International Bank for Reconstruction and Development, the International Monetary Fund, and other financial institutions. No longer is it possible for borrowing countries to play one lending country off against another, or to default on their obligations or unilaterally scale down their debt without shutting the door on future loans.

[. . .] Secondly, *private* savings are mobilized by foreign corporations and governments in order to advance the interests of foreign capital. Foreign companies float local bond issues, raise equity capital, and generally attempt to monopolize available liquid resources in order to extend their field of operations and maximize profits. World Bank affiliates finance local development banks which scour the country for small and medium-size savings to funnel into local and foreign enterprise. The United States government acquires a significant portion of the money supply of India and other countries through its policy of selling surplus foodstuffs for local currencies which it makes available to United States corporations. In these and other ways foreign interests today exercise control of local private savings.

A final feature of economic domination is the control of mineral, agricultural, manufacturing, and other real assets, and the organization and management of trade by foreign corporations. In Africa, for example,

French bulk-buying companies in the ex-colonies monopolize the purchase and sale of coffee, peanuts, palm-oil products, and other commodities produced by small and medium-sized growers. In Mexico, one foreign corporation organizes the great part of cotton production and exportation. Frequently control of commerce necessitates financial domination. The United States, for example, has penetrated Mexico's financial structure with the aim of restricting Mexican-Latin American trade in order to insure control of Latin American markets for itself. Control of iron, copper, tin, oil, bauxite, and other mineral resources is in the hands of a handful of giant corporations. In some countries, foreign interests dominate the commanding heights of the economy – transportation, power, communication, and the leading manufacturing industries. These examples should suffice to show that foreign control of real, as well as of liquid, assets extends into all branches of local economies and penetrates every economically backward region in the world capitalist system.

[Later in the article O'Connor seeks to identify the characteristics of an imperialist foreign policy in the changed circumstances of the modern world.]

Modern Imperialism's Foreign Policy

Whether or not private capital responds to the incentives held out by national governments and international agencies depends on a host of factors, chief among which are the investment 'climate' in the satellite economies and the character of other state political-economic policies. Suffice it for now to note some of the major differences between imperialist foreign policy in the nineteenth century and mid-twentieth centuries.

First, and most obvious, modern imperialism attempts to substitute informal for formal modes of political control of countries in the backwash of world capitalism. The methods of establishing political control are varied. The use of old economic and political ties is practised whenever possible; these include the relationships formed within the British Commonwealth and the French Community, closed currency zones, preferential trading systems, military alliances, and political-military pacts. Economic, political and cultural missions, labor union delegations, joint military training programs, military grants, bribes to local ruling classes in the form of economic 'aid', substitute for direct colonial rule. Only when indirect policies fail are the older instruments of coercion and force brought into play, and the principle of continuity in change applies. An excellent example is the US-instigated and supported counter-revolution in Guatemala in 1954, the accomplishments of which the State Department listed under four headings:

1. The conclusion of an agreement with a United Fruit Company subsidiary providing for the return of property expropriated by the Arbenz Government.
2. The repeal of the law affecting remittances and taxation of earnings from foreign capital.
3. The signing of an Investment Guarantee Agreement with the United States.
4. The promulgation of a new and more favorable petroleum law.

Within Guatemala, the Armas regime in the post-1954 period was maintained in office via contracts with United Fruit, Bond and Share, and other monopolies.

Secondly, contemporary imperialist states enjoy relatively more financial, and hence political, autonomy. In the nineteenth century, imperialist countries regarded themselves as dependent on the private capital market for raising funds for discretionary state expenditures and were compelled to pursue economic and fiscal policies designed to make it possible for their colonies to meet their private debt service. The dominant state capitalist countries today are financially independent and can follow a more flexible policy toward their satellites. The reason is that both the potential and actual economic surplus are comparatively large. The potential surplus is large because the normal tendency of monopoly capitalist economies is stagnation and unemployment of labor and capital, attributable to a deficiency of aggregate demand. State expenditures — including military expenditures and foreign loans and grants — normally increase not only aggregate demand but also real income and output, and hence the tax base. A rise in expenditures thus increases revenues, even if tax rates remain unchanged. State expenditures are partly self-financing and virtually costless in terms of the real resources utilized. The actual economic surplus constitutes a relatively large portion of national product because of technological and productivity advances. For these reasons, taxes (and state expenditures) make up a large share of national product with few serious adverse effects on economic incentives, and thus on total production itself.

The significance of the financial independence of the contemporary imperialist state for foreign policy lies in its ability to export capital — or absorb the surplus overseas — without a *quid pro quo*. The Marshall Plan, the extensive program of military aid and grants, and the low-cost loans extended to backward countries by AID are the main examples of this mode of surplus absorption. The surplus absorption capacity of satellite countries which are closely tied to the United States' political-military bloc is for practical purposes unlimited. Two factors, however, circumscribe state grants without a *quid pro quo*. First, low-cost state loans and grants-in-aid, or capital exports which are not extended on normal commercial principles, compete 'unfairly' with private loans and are resisted by private capitalist interests in the metropolitan economy. Second, metropolitan governments are unable to discipline their satellites effectively unless there are economic strings attached to international loans. Moreover, state bilateral and multilateral loans financed in private capital markets in the advanced countries must earn a return sufficient to cover the cost of borrowing and administration. Opportunities for capital exports extended on commercial principles are limited by the availability of profitable investment projects.

Nineteenth- and mid-twentieth-century imperialism depart in a third important respect. In the nineteenth century there were few important antagonisms between Great Britain's role as the leading national capitalist power on the one hánd, and as the dominant imperialist power on the other. Policies designed to expand Britain's home economy extended capitalist modes of production and organization to the three underexploited continents, directly and indirectly strengthening the growing British imperial system. For this reason, foreign policy ordinarily served private foreign investors and other private interests oriented to overseas activity. Only occasionally — as in the case of Disraeli's decision to purchase Suez Canal shares in 1875 — was foreign investment employed as a 'weapon' of British foreign policy. Even less frequently did Britain promote private foreign investments with the purpose of aiding global foreign policy objectives.

By way of contrast, the national and international ambitions of the United States in the mid-twentieth century are continually in conflict. In the context of the limited absorption capacity of the backward capitalist world and international competition from other advanced capitalist economies and the socialist countries, the United States is compelled to employ a wide range of policies to expand trade and investment. To further national ends, a 'partnership' between 'public lending institutions' and 'private lenders' — with the former 'leading the way' for the latter — has been formed. Underlining the role of the state in the service of the multinational corporations, in 1962 Secretary of State Rusk described the newer government policies which extend beyond state loan programs; investment guarantee programs in forty-six backward capitalist countries which cover currency inconvertibility, expropriation, war, revolution, and insurrection; instructions to local embassies to support business interests by making 'necessary representations to the host governments'; the creation of a new Special Assistant for International Business in the State Department in order to insure that private business interests receive 'prompt representation' in the government. Especially in the case of disguised public loans or special forms of private loans (see above), the commitment of the United States government to national capitalist interests inhibits state policies which seek to strengthen the industrial bourgeoisie and ruling classes in other advanced countries and the national bourgeoisie in the backward nations. Perhaps this is the most important limit on capital exports on public account.

As the leading international power, the United States is under constant and growing pressure to strengthen world capitalism as a system, including each of its specific parts. Policies which aim to recruit new members for local comprador groups, stimulate the development of capitalist agriculture and the middle farmers, reinforce the dominance of local financial and commercial classes, and reinvigorate local manufacturing activities — these general policies pose a potential or real threat to the interests of United States' national capital. Alliance for Progress funds destined for the middle sectors of Latin American agriculture, Export-Import Bank loans to foreign commercialists, loans and grants to foreign governments dominated by the urban bourgeoisie, loans and subsidies to the Indian iron and steel industry, Mexican industry and agriculture, and other branches of production in countries which are slowly industrializing — these and other stopgap and long-range measures help to keep the backward countries in the imperialist camp in the short run, but directly or indirectly create local capitalist interests which may demand their independence from United States' capital in the long run.

United States' private capital increasingly requires the aid of the state, and the state enlists more and more private and public capital in its crusade to maintain world capitalism intact. Specific and general capitalist interests serve each other, finally merging into one phenomenon, a certain oneness emerges between them. This must have, finally, its institutional reflection. The multinational corporation has become the instrument for the creation and consolidation of an international ruling class, the only hope for reconciling the antagonisms between national and international interests.

Notes

1.   Joseph Schumpeter, *Imperialism and Social Classes* (1919; reprinted August-us Kelly, New York, 1951), pp. 98, 128.

2.   Hans Kohn, 'Reflections on Colonialism', in Robert Strausz-Hupé and Harry W. Hazard (eds), *The Idea of Colonialism* (London, 1958).

3.   V.I. Lenin, *Imperialism: The Highest Stage of Capitalism* (New York, 1926), pp. 71-6.

4.   Maurice Dobb, *Political Economy and Capitalism* (London, 1937), pp. 239, 234.

5.   Paul M. Sweezy, *The Theory of Capitalist Development* (1942; reprinted, Monthly Review Press, New York, 1964).

6.   Schumpeter, *Imperialism and Social Classes*, p. 110.

7.   Kenneth J. Twitchett, 'Colonialism: An Attempt at Understanding Imperial, Colonial and Neo-Colonial Relationships', *Political Studies*, vol. 13, no. 3 (October 1965).

8.   'Neo-Colonialism', *Voice of Africa*, vol. 1, no. 4 (April 1961), p. 4.

THE DEVELOPMENT OF UNDERDEVELOPMENT

André Gunder Frank

Source: *Monthly Review* (September 1966), pp. 17-30.

Frank argues that underdevelopment in Latin America needs to be understood in terms of a metropolis-satellite structure which has responded to the historical development of the world capitalist system. To test the claim he puts forward a number of hypotheses which stress that the level of underdevelopment depends upon the closeness of the link between satellite and metropolis.

[. . .] It is generally held that economic development occurs in a succession of capitalist stages and that today's underdeveloped countries are still in a stage, sometimes depicted as an original stage of history, through which the now developed countries passed long ago. Yet even a modest acquaintance with history shows that underdevelopment is not original or traditional and that neither the past nor the present of the underdeveloped countries resembles in any important respect the past of the now developed countries. The now developed countries were never *under*developed, though they may have been *un*developed. It is also widely believed that the contemporary underdevelopment of a country can be understood as the product or reflection solely of its own economic, political, social, and cultural characteristics or structure. Yet historical research demonstrates that contemporary underdevelopment is in large part the historical product of past and continuing economic and other relations between the satellite underdeveloped and the now developed metropolitan countries. Furthermore, these relations are an essential part of the structure and development of the capitalist system on a world scale as a whole. A related and also largely erroneous view is that the development of these underdeveloped countries and, within them of their most underdeveloped domestic areas, must and will be generated or stimulated by diffusing capital, institutions, values, etc., to them from the international and national capitalist metropoles. Historical perspective based on the underdeveloped countries' past experience suggests that on the contrary in the underdeveloped countries economic development can now occur only independently of most of these relations of diffusion.

Evident inequalities of income and differences in culture have led many observers to see 'dual' societies and economies in the underdeveloped countries. Each of the two parts is supposed to have a history of its own, a structure, and a contemporary dynamic largely independent of the other. Supposedly, only one part of the economy and society has been importantly affected by intimate economic relations with the 'outside' capitalist world; and that part, it is held, became modern, capitalist, and relatively developed precisely because of this contact. The other part is widely regarded as variously isolated, subsistence-based, feudal, or precapitalist, and therefore more underdeveloped.

I believe on the contrary that the entire 'dual society' thesis is false and that the policy recommendations to which it leads will, if acted upon, serve only to intensify and perpetuate the very conditions of underdevelopment they are supposedly designed to remedy.

A mounting body of evidence suggests, and I am confident that future historical research will confirm, that the expansion of the capitalist system over the past centuries effectively and entirely penetrated even the apparently most isolated sectors of the underdeveloped world. Therefore, the economic, political, social, and cultural institutions and relations we now observe there are the products of the historical development of the capitalist system no less than are the seemingly more modern or capitalist features of the national metropoles of these underdeveloped countries. Analogously to the relations between development and underdevelopment on the international level, the contemporary underdeveloped institutions of the so-called backward or feudal domestic areas of an underdeveloped country are no less the product of the single historical process of capitalist development than are the so-called capitalist institutions of the supposedly more progressive areas. [...]

II

The Secretary General of the Latin American Center for Research in the Social Sciences writes in that Center's journal:

The privileged position of the city has its origin in the colonial period. It was founded by the Conqueror to serve the same ends that it still serves today; to incorporate the indigenous population into the economy brought and developed by that Conqueror and his descendants. The regional city was an instrument of conquest and is still today an instrument of domination.[1]

The Instituto Nacional Indigenista (National Indian Institute) of Mexico confirms this observation when it notes that 'the mestizo population, in fact, always lies in a city, a center of an intercultural region, which acts as the metropolis of a zone of indigenous population and which maintains with the underdeveloped communities an intimate relation which links the center with the satellite communities'.[2] The Institute goes on to point out that 'between the mestizos who live in the nuclear city of the region and the Indians who live in the peasant hinterland there is in reality a closer economic and social interdependence than might at first glance appear' and that the provincial metropoles 'by being centers of intercourse are also centers of exploitation'.[3]

Thus these metropolis-satellite relations are not limited to the imperial or international level but penetrate and structure the very economic, political, and social life of the Latin American colonies and countries. Just as the colonial and national capital and its export sector become the satellite of the Iberian (and later of other) metropoles of the world economic system, this satellite immediately becomes a colonial and then a national metropolis with respect to the productive sectors and population of the interior. Furthermore, the provincial capitals, which thus are themselves satellites of the national metropolis — and through the latter of the world metropolis— are in turn provincial centers around which their own local satellites orbit. Thus, a whole chain of constellations of metropoles and satellites relates all parts of the whole system from its metropolitan center in Europe or the United States to the farthest outpost in the Latin American countryside.

When we examine this metropolis-satellite structure, we find that each of the satellites, including now-underdeveloped Spain and Portugal, serves as an instrument to suck capital or economic surplus out of its own satellites and to channel part of this surplus to the world metropolis of which all are satellites. Moreover, each national and local metropolis serves to impose and maintain the monopolistic structure and exploitative relationship of this system (as the Instituto Nacional Indigenista of Mexico calls it) as long as it serves the interests of the metropoles which take advantage of this global, national, and local structure to promote their own development and the enrichment of their ruling classes.

These are the principal and still surviving structural characteristics which were implanted in Latin America by the Conquest. Beyond examining the establishment of this colonial structure in its historical context, the proposed approach calls for study of the development — and underdevelopment – of these metropoles and satellites of Latin America through-out the following and still continuing historical process. In this way we can understand why there were and still are tendencies in the Latin American and world capitalist structure which seem to lead to the development of the metropolis and the underdevelopment of the satellite and why, partic-ularly, the satellized national, regional, and local metropoles in Latin America find that their economic development is at best a limited or underdeveloped development.

III

That present underdevelopment of Latin America is the result of its centuries-long participation in the process of world capitalist develop-ment, I believe I have shown in my case studies of the economic and social histories of Chile and Brazil.[4] My study of Chilean history suggests that the Conquest not only incorporated this country fully into the expansion and development of the world mercantile and later industrial capitalist system but that it also introduced the monopolistic metropolis-satellite structure and development of capitalism into the Chilean domestic economy and society itself. This structure then penetrated and permeated all of Chile very quickly. Since that time and in the course of world and Chilean history during the epochs of colonialism, free trade, imperialism, and the present, Chile has become increasingly marked by the economic, social, and political structure of satellite underdevelopment. This develop-ment of underdevelopment continues today, both in Chile's still increasing satellization by the world metropolis and through the ever more acute polarization of Chile's domestic economy.

The history of Brazil is perhaps the clearest case of both national and regional development of underdevelopment. The expansion of the world economy since the beginning of the sixteenth century successively con-verted the Northeast, the Minas Gerais interior, the North, and the Center-South (Rio de Janeiro, São Paulo, and Paraná) into export economies and incorporated them into the structure and development of the world capitalist system. Each of these regions experienced what may have appeared as economic development during the period of its respective golden age. But it was a satellite development which was neither self-generating nor self-perpetuating. As the market or the productivity of the first three regions declined, foreign and domestic economic interest in them waned; and they were left to develop the underdevelopment they live today. In the fourth region, the coffee economy experienced a similar though not yet quite as serious fate (though the development of a synthetic coffee substitute promises to deal it a mortal blow in the not too distant future). All of this historical evidence contradicts the generally accepted theses that Latin America suffers from a dual society or from the survival of feudal institutions and that these are important obstacles to its economic development.

IV

During the First World War, however, and even more during the Great Depression and the Second World War, São Paulo began to build up an industrial establishment which is the largest in Latin America today. The question arises whether this industrial development did or can break Brazil out of the cycle of satellite development and underdevelopment which has characterized its other regions and national history within the capitalist system so far. I believe that the answer is no. Domestically the evidence so far is fairly clear. The development of industry in São Paulo has not brought greater riches to the other regions of Brazil. Instead, it converted them into internal colonial satellites, de-capitalized them further, and consolidated or even deepened their underdevelopment. There is little evidence to suggest that this process is likely to be reversed in the foreseeable future except insofar as the provincial poor migrate and become the poor of the metropolitan cities. Externally, the evidence is that although the initial development of São Paulo's industry was relatively autonomous it is being increasingly satellized by the world capitalist metropolis and its future development possibilities are increasingly restricted. This development, my studies lead me to believe, also appears destined to limited or underdeveloped development as long as it takes place in the present economic, political, and social framework.

We must conclude, in short, that underdevelopment is not due to the survival of archaic institutions and the existence of capital shortage in regions that have remained isolated from the stream of world history. On the contrary, underdevelopment was and still is generated by the same historical process which also generated economic development: the development of capitalism itself. This view, I am glad to say, is gaining adherents among students of Latin America and is proving its worth in shedding new light on the problems of the area and in affording a better perspective for the formulation of theory and policy.

V

The same historical and structural approach can also lead to better development theory and policy by generating *a series of hypotheses* about development and underdevelopment such as those I am testing in my current research. The hypotheses are derived from the empirical observation and theoretical assumption that within this world-embracing metropolis-satellite structure the metropoles tend to develop and the satellites to underdevelop. The first hypothesis has already been mentioned above: that in contrast to the development of the world metropolis which is no one's satellite, the development of the national and other subordinate metropoles is limited by their satellite status. It is perhaps more difficult to test this hypothesis than the following ones because part of its confirmation depends on the test of the other hypotheses. Nonetheless, this hypothesis appears to be generally confirmed by the non-autonomous and unsatisfactory economic and especially industrial development of Latin America's national metropoles, as documented in the studies already cited. The most important and at the same time most confirmatory examples are the metropolitan regions of Buenos Aires and São Paulo whose growth only began in the nineteenth century, was therefore largely untrammelled by any colonial heritage, but was and remains a satellite development largely dependent on the outside metropolis, first of Britain and then of the United States.

A second hypothesis is that the satellites experience their greatest economic development and especially their most classically capitalist industrial development if and when their ties to their metropolis are weakest. This hypothesis is almost diametrically opposed to the generally accepted thesis that development in the underdeveloped countries follows from the greatest degree of contact with and diffusion from the metropolitan developed countries. This hypothesis seems to be confirmed by two kinds of relative isolation that Latin America has experienced in the course of its history. One is the temporary isolation caused by the crises of war or depression in the world metropolis. Apart from minor ones, five periods of such major crises stand out and seem to confirm the hypothesis. These are: the European (and especially Spanish) Depression of the seventeenth century, the Napoleonic Wars, the First World War, the Depression of the 1930s, and the Second World War. It is clearly established and generally recognized that the most important recent industrial development — especially of Argentina, Brazil, and Mexico, but also of other countries such as Chile — has taken place precisely during the periods of the two World Wars and the intervening Depression. Thanks to the consequent loosening of trade and investment ties during these periods, the satellites initiated marked autonomous industrialization and growth. Historical research demonstrates that the same thing happened in Latin America during Europe's seventeenth-century depression. Manufacturing grew in the Latin American countries, and several of them such as Chile became exporters of manufactured goods. The Napoleonic Wars gave rise to independence movements in Latin America, and these should perhaps also be interpreted as confirming the development hypothesis in part.

The other kind of isolation which tends to confirm the second hypothesis is the geographic and economic isolation of regions which at one time were relatively weakly tied to and poorly integrated into the mercantilist and capitalist system. My preliminary research suggests that in Latin America it was these regions which initiated and experienced the most promising self-generating economic development of the classical industrial capitalist type. The most important regional cases probably are Tucumán and Asunción, as well as other cities such as Mendoza and Rosario, in the interior of Argentina and Paraguay during the end of the eighteenth and the beginning of the nineteenth centuries. Seventeenth- and eighteenth-century São Paulo, long before coffee was grown there, is another example. Perhaps Antioquia in Colombia and Puebla and Querétaro in Mexico are other examples. In its own way, Chile was also an example since, before the sea route around the Horn was opened, this country was relatively isolated at the end of the long voyage from Europe via Panama. All of these regions became manufacturing centers and even exporters, usually of textiles, during the periods preceding their effective incorporation as satellites into the colonial, national, and world capitalist system.

Internationally, of course, the classic case of industrialization through non-participation as a satellite in the capitalist world system is obviously that of Japan after the Meiji Restoration. Why, one may ask, was resource-poor but unsatellized Japan able to industrialize so quickly at the end of the century while resource-rich Latin American countries and Russia were not able to do so and the latter was easily beaten by Japan in the War of 1904 after the same forty years of development efforts? The second hypothesis suggests that the fundamental reason is that Japan was not satellized either during the Tokugawa or the Meiji period and therefore did not have its development structurally limited as did the countries which were so satellized.

VI

A corollary of the second hypothesis is that when the metropolis recovers from its crisis and re-establishes the trade and investment ties which fully re-incorporate the satellites into the system, or when the metropolis expands to incorporate previously isolated regions into the world-wide system, the previous development and industrialization of these regions is choked off or channelled into directions which are not self-perpetuating and promising. This happened after each of the five crises cited above. The renewed expansion of trade and the spread of economic liberalism in the eighteenth and nineteenth centuries choked off and reversed the manufacturing development which Latin America had experienced during the seventeenth century, and in some places at the beginning of the nineteenth. After the First World War, the new national industry of Brazil suffered serious consequences from American economic invasion. The increase in the growth rate of Gross National Product and particularly of industrialization throughout Latin America was again reversed and industry became increasingly satellized after the Second World War and especially after the post-Korean War recovery and expansion of the metropolis. Far from having become more developed since then, industrial sectors of Brazil and most conspicuously of Argentina have become structurally more and more underdeveloped and less and less able to generate continued industrialization and/or sustain development of the economy. This process, from which India also suffers, is reflected in a whole gamut of balance-of-payments, inflationary, and other economic and political difficulties, and promises to yield to no solution short of far-reaching structural change.

Our hypothesis suggests that fundamentally the same process occurred even more dramatically with the incorporation into the system of previously unsatellized regions. The expansion of Buenos Aires as a satellite of Great Britain and the introduction of free trade in the interest of the ruling groups of both metropoles destroyed the manufacturing and much of the remainder of the economic base of the previously relatively prosperous interior almost entirely. Manufacturing was destroyed by foreign competition, lands were taken and concentrated into latifundia by the rapaciously growing export economy, intra-regional distribution of income became much more unequal, and the previously developing regions became simple satellites of Buenos Aires and through it of London. The provincial centers did not yield to satellization without a struggle. This metropolis-satellite conflict was much of the cause of the long political and armed struggle between the Unitarists in Buenos Aires and the Federalists in the provinces, and it may be said to have been the sole important cause of the War of the Triple Alliance in which Buenos Aires, Montevideo, and Rio de Janeiro, encouraged and helped by London, destroyed not only the autonomously developing economy of Paraguay but killed off nearly all of its population which was unwilling to give in. Though this is no doubt the most spectacular example which tends to confirm the hypothesis, I believe that historical research on the satellization of previously relatively independent yeoman-farming and incipient manufacturing regions such as the Caribbean islands will confirm it further. These regions did not have a chance against the forces of expanding and developing capitalism, and their own development had to be sacrificed to that of others. The economy and industry of Argentina, Brazil, and other countries which have experienced the effects of metropolitan recovery since the Second World War are today suffering much the same fate, if fortunately still in lesser degree.

VII

A third major hypothesis derived from the metropolis-satellite structure is that the regions which are the most underdeveloped and feudal-seeming today are the ones which had the closest ties to the metropolis in the past. They are the regions which were the greatest exporters of primary products to and the biggest sources of capital for the world metropolis and which were abandoned by the metropolis when for one reason or another business fell off. This hypothesis also contradicts the generally held thesis that the source of a region's underdevelopment is its isolation and its pre-capitalist institutions.

This hypothesis seems to be amply confirmed by the former super-satellite development and present ultra-underdevelopment of the once sugar-exporting West Indies, Northeastern Brazil, the ex-mining districts of Minas Gerais in Brazil, highland Peru, and Bolivia, and the central Mexican states of Guanajuato, Zacatecas, and others whose names were made world famous centuries ago by their silver. There surely are no major regions in Latin America which are today more cursed by underdevelopment and poverty; yet all of these regions, like Bengal in India, once provided the life blood of mercantile and industrial capitalist development — in the metropolis. These regions' participation in the development of the world capitalist system gave them, already in their golden age, the typical structure of underdevelopment of a capitalist export economy. When the market for their sugar or the wealth of their mines disappeared and the metropolis abandoned them to their own devices, the already existing economic, political, and social structure of these regions prohibited autonomous generation of economic development and left them no alternative but to turn in upon themselves and to degenerate into the ultra-underdevelopment we find there today.

[Frank goes on to look in more detail at the function of latifundia (plantations or estates) in agrarian exploitation in Latin America, emphasizing their role as an expression of demand from metropolitan areas. He then concludes as follows:]

All of these hypotheses and studies suggest that the global extension and unity of the capitalist system, its monopoly structure and uneven development throughout its history, and the resulting persistence of commercial rather than industrial capitalism in the underdeveloped world (including its most industrially advanced countries) deserve much more attention in the study of economic development and cultural change than they have hitherto received. Though science and truth know no national boundaries, it is probably new generations of scientists from the underdeveloped countries themselves who most need to, and best can, devote the necessary attention to these problems and clarify the process of underdevelopment and development. It is their people who in the last analysis face the task of changing this no longer acceptable process and eliminating this miserable reality.

They will not be able to accomplish these goals by importing sterile stereotypes from the metropolis which do not correspond to their satellite economic reality and do not respond to their liberating political needs. To change their reality they must understand it. For this reason, I hope that better confirmation of these hypotheses and further pursuit of the proposed historical, holistic, and structural approach may help the peoples of the underdeveloped countries to understand the causes and eliminate the reality of their development of underdevelopment and their underdevelopment of development.

Notes

1. *América Latina*, Año 6, no. 4 (October-December 1963), p. 8.
2. Instituto Nacional Indigenista, *Los centros coordinadores indigenistas* (Mexico, 1962), p. 34.
3. Ibid., pp. 33-4, 88.
4. 'Capitalist Development and Underdevelopment in Chile' and 'Capitalist Development and Underdevelopment in Brazil' in *Capitalism and Underdevelopment in Latin America* (Penguin, Harmondsworth, 1971).

3.3

A STRUCTURAL THEORY OF IMPERIALISM

Johan Galtung

Source: *Journal of Peace Research*, vol. 13, no. 2 (1971), pp. 81-94.

Galtung develops a theory of imperialism to account for inequality within and between nations and the resistance of this inequality to change. He distinguishes between Centre and Periphery countries and argues that those in power in the former have a community of interest with those in power in the latter. The result is a relationship which operates at the expense of the majority of the people in Peripheral countries, but which is largely in the interest of the majority of the people in Centre countries.

Introduction

This theory takes as its point of departure two of the most glaring facts about this world: the tremendous inequality, within and between nations, in almost all aspects of human living conditions, including the power to decide over those living conditions; *and* the resistance of this inequality to change. The world consists of Center and Periphery nations; and each nation, in turn, has its centers and periphery. Hence, our concern is with the mechanism underlying this discrepancy.

[Galtung goes on to discuss this discrepancy in terms of imperialism.]

Briefly stated, imperialism is a system that splits up collectivities and relates some of the parts to each other in relations of *harmony of interest*, and other parts in relations of *disharmony of interest*, or *conflict of interest*.

Defining 'Conflict of Interest'

'Conflict of interest' is a special case of conflict in general, defined as a situation where parties are pursuing incompatible goals. In our special case, these goals are stipulated by an outsider as the 'true' interests of the parties, disregarding wholly or completely what the parties themselves say explicitly are the values they pursue. One reason for this is the rejection of the dogma of unlimited rationality: actors do *not* necessarily know, or they are unable to express, what their interest is. Another, more important, reason is that rationality is unevenly distributed, that some may dominate the minds of others, and that this may lead to 'false consciousness'. Thus, learning to suppress one's own true interests may be a major part of socialization in general and education in particular.

Let us refer to this true interest as LC, *living condition*. It may perhaps be measured by using such indicators as income, standard of living in the usual materialistic sense — but notions of *quality of life* would certainly also enter, not to mention notions of *autonomy*. But the precise content of LC is less important for our purpose than the definition of conflict of interest:

There is *conflict*, or *disharmony of interest*, if the two parties are coupled together in such a way that the LC *gap* between them is *increasing*.

There is *no conflict*, or *harmony of interest*, if the two parties are coupled together in such a way that the LC *gap* between them is *decreasing down to zero*.

[. . .] It is clear that the concept of interest used here is based on an ideology, or a *value premise of equality*. An interaction relation and interaction structure set up such that inequality is the result is seen as a coupling not in the interest of the weaker party. This is a value premise like so many other value premises in social science explorations, such as 'direct violence is bad', 'economic growth is good', 'conflict should be resolved', etc. As in all other types of social science, the goal should not be an 'objective' social science freed from all such value premises, but a more honest social science where the value premises are made explicit.

Defining 'Imperialism'

We shall now define imperialism by using the building blocks presented in the preceding two sections. In out two-nation world, imperialism can be defined as one way in which the Center nation has power over the Periphery nation, so as to bring about a condition of disharmony of interest between them. Concretely, *imperialism* is a relation between a Center and a Periphery nation so that

(1)   there is *harmony of interest* between the *center in the Center* nation and the *center in the Periphery* nation,

(2)   there is more *disharmony of interest* within the Periphery nation than within the Center nations,

(3)   there is *disharmony of interest* between the *periphery in the Center* nation and the *periphery in the Periphery* nation.

Diagrammatically it looks something like Figure 1.This complex definition, borrowing largely from Lenin, needs spelling out. The basic idea is, as mentioned, that the center in the Center nation has a bridgehead in the Periphery nation, and a well-chosen one: the center in the Periphery nation. This is established such that the Periphery center is tied to the Center center with the best possible tie: the tie of harmony of interest. They are linked so that they go up together and down, even under, together.

Figure 1: The Structure of Imperialism

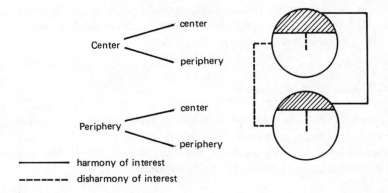

Inside the two nations there is disharmony of interest. They are both in one way or another vertical societies with LC gaps — otherwise there is no possibility of locating a center and a periphery. Moreover, the gap is not decreasing, but is at best constant. But the basic idea, absolutely fundamental for the whole theory to be developed, is that *there is more disharmony in the Periphery nation than in the Center nation*. At the simplest static level of description this means there is more inequality in the Periphery than in the Center. At the more complex level we might talk in terms of the gap opening more quickly in the Periphery than in the Center, where it might even remain constant. Through welfare state activities, redistribution takes place and disharmony is reduced for at least some LC dimensions, including income, but usually excluding power.

If we now would capture in a few sentences what imperialism is about, we might perhaps say something like this:

In the Periphery nation, the center grows more than the periphery, due partly to how interaction between center and periphery is organized. Without necessarily thinking of economic interaction, the center is more enriched than the periphery. However, for part of this enrichment, the center in the Periphery only serves as a transmission belt (e.g. as commercial firms, trading companies) for value (e.g. raw materials) forwarded to the Center nation. This value enters the Center in the center, with some of it drizzling down to the periphery in the Center. Importantly, there is less disharmony of interest in the Center than in the Periphery, so that *the total arrangement is largely in the interest of the periphery in the Center.* Within the Center the two parties may be opposed to each other. But in the total game, the periphery see themselves more as the partners of the center in the Center than as the partners of the periphery in the Periphery — and this is the essential trick of the game. Alliance formation between the two peripheries is avoided, while the Center nation becomes more and the Periphery nation less cohesive — and hence less able to develop long-term strategies. [. . .]

The Mechanisms of Imperialism

The two basic mechanisms of imperialism both concern the *relation* between the parties concerned, particularly between the nations. The first mechanism concerns the *interaction relation* itself, the second how these relations are put together in a larger interaction structure:

(1)   the principle of *vertical interaction relation*
(2)   the principle of *feudal interaction structure.*

The basic point about interaction is, of course, that people and nations have different values that complement each other, and then engage in exchange. Some nations produce oil, other nations produce tractors, and they then carry out an exchange according to the principles of comparative advantages. Imagine that our two-nation system has a prehistory of no interaction at all, and then starts with this type of interaction. Obviously, both will be changed by it, and more particularly: a gap between them is likely to open and widen if the interaction is cumulatively asymmetric in terms of what the two parties get out of it.

To study whether the interaction is symmetric or asymmetric, on equal or unequal terms, *two* factors arising from the interaction have to be examined:

(1)   *the value-exchange between the actors* – *inter*-actor effects
(2)   *the effects inside the actors* – *intra*-actor effects.

In *economic* relations the first is most commonly analyzed, not only by liberal but also by Marxist economists. The inter-actor flow can be observed as flows of goods and services in either direction, and can literally be measured at the main points of entry: the customs houses and the national banks. The flow both ways can then be compared in various ways. Most important is the comparison in terms of *who benefits most*, and for this purpose intra-actor effects also have to be taken into consideration. [. . .]

It is certainly meaningful and important to talk in terms of unequal exchange or asymmetric interaction, but not quite unproblematic what its precise meaning should be. For that reason, it may be helpful to think in terms of three stages or types of exploitation, partly reflecting historical *processes* in chronological order, and partly reflecting types of *thinking* about exploitation.

In the first stage of exploitation, A simply engages in looting and takes away the raw materials without offering anything in return. If he steals out of pure nature there is no human interaction involved, but we assume that he forces 'natives' to work for him and do the extraction work. It is like the slave-owner who lives on the work produced by slaves – which is quantitatively not too different from the landowner who has land-workers working for him five out of seven days a week.

In the second stage, A starts offering something 'in return'. Oil, pitch, land, etc. is 'bought' for a couple of beads – it is no longer simply taken away without asking any questions about ownership. The price paid is ridiculous. However, as power relations in the international systems change, perhaps mainly by bringing the power level of the weaker party up from zero to some low positive value, A has to contribute more: for instance, pay more for the oil. The question is now whether there is a cut-off point after which the exchange becomes equal, and what the criterion for that cut-off point would be. Absence of subjective dissatisfaction – B says that he is now content? Objective market values or the number of man-hours that have gone into the production on either side?

There are difficulties with all these conceptions. But instead of elaborating on this, we shall rather direct our attention to the shared failure of all these attempts to look at *intra*-actor effects. Does the interaction have enriching or impoverishing effects *inside* the actor, or does it just lead to a stand-still? This type of question leads us to the third stage of exploitation, where there may be some balance in the flow between the actors, but great differences in the effect the interaction has within them.

As an example let us use nations exchanging oil for tractors. The basic point is that this involves different levels of processing, where we define 'processing' as an activity imposing Culture on Nature. In the case of crude oil the product is (almost) pure Nature; in the case of tractors it would be wrong to say that it is a case of pure Culture, pure *form* (like mathematics, music). A transistor radio, an integrated circuit, these would be better examples because Nature has been brought down to a minimum. The tractor is still too much iron and rubber to be a pure case.

The major point now is the *gap in processing level* between oil and tractors and the differential effect this gap will have on the two nations. In one nation the oil deposit may be at the water-front, and all that is needed is a derrick and some simple mooring facilities to pump the oil straight into a ship – e.g. a Norwegian tanker – that can bring the oil to the country where it will provide energy to run, among other things, the tractor factories. In the other nation the effects may be extremely far-reaching due to the complexity of the product and the connectedness of the society. [...]

If the first mechanism, the *vertical interaction relation*, is the major factor behind inequality, then the second mechanism, the *feudal interaction structure*, is the factor that maintains and reinforces this inequality by protecting it. There are four rules defining this particular interaction structure:

(1)   interaction between Center and Periphery is *vertical*;
(2)   interaction between Periphery and Periphery is *missing*;
(3)   multilateral interaction involving all three is *missing*;
(4)   interaction with the outside world is *monopolized* by the Center, with two implications:
   (a) Periphery interaction with other Center nations is *missing*
   (b) Center as well as Periphery interaction with Periphery nations belonging to other Center nations is *missing*.

This relation can be depicted as in Figure 2. As indicated in the Figure, the number of Periphery nations attached to any given Center nation can, of course, vary. In this Figure we have also depicted the rule 'if you stay off my satellites, I will stay off yours'.

Figure 2: A Feudal Center-Periphery Structure

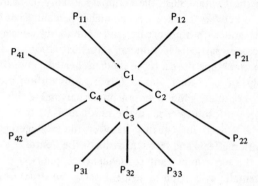

Some important *economic* consequences of this structure should be spelled out.

First and most obvious: the *concentration on trade partners*. A Periphery nation should, as a result of these two mechanisms, have most of its trade with 'its' Center nation. In other words, empirically we would expect high levels of *import concentration* as well as *export concentration* in the Periphery, as opposed to the Center, which is more free to extend its trade relations in almost any direction — except in the pure case, with the Periphery of other Center nations.

Second, and not so obvious, is the *commodity concentration:* the tendency for Periphery nations to have only one or very few primary products to export. This would be a trivial matter if it could be explained entirely in terms of geography, if e.g. oil countries were systematically poor as to ore, ore countries poor as to bananas and coffee, etc. But this can hardly be assumed to be the general case: Nature does not distribute its riches that way. There is a historical rather than a geographical explanation to this. A territory may have been exploited for the raw materials most easily available and/or most needed in the Center, and this, in turn, leads to a certain social structure, to communication lines to the deposits, to trade structures, to the emergence of certain center groups (often based on ownership of that particular raw material), and so on. To start exploiting a new kind of raw material in the same territory might upset carefully designed local balances; hence, it might be easier to have a fresh start for that new raw material in virgin territory with no bridgehead already prepared for imperialist exploits. In order to substantiate this hypothesis we would have to demonstrate that there are particularly underutilized and systematically underexplored deposits precisely in countries where one type of raw materials has already been exploited.

The combined effect of these two consequences is a *dependency* of the Periphery on the Center. Since the Periphery usually has a much smaller GNP, the trade between them is a much higher percentage of the GNP for the Periphery, and with both partner and commodity concentration, the Periphery becomes particularly vulnerable to fluctuations in demands and prices. At the same time the center in the Periphery depends on the Center for its supply of consumer goods. Import substitution industries will usually lead to consumer goods that look homespun and unchic, particularly if there is planned obsolescence in the production of these goods in the Center, plus a demand for equality between the two centers maintained by demonstration effects and frequent visits to the Center.

However, the most important consequence is political and has to do with the systematic utilization of feudal interaction structures as a way of protecting the Center against the Periphery. The feudal interaction structure is in social science language nothing but an expression of the old political maxim *divide et impera*, divide and rule, as a strategy used systematically by the Center relative to the Periphery nations. How could — for example — a small foggy island in the North Sea rule over one quarter of the world? By isolating the Periphery parts from each other, by having them geographically at sufficient distance from each other to impede any real alliance formation, by having separate deals with them so as to tie them to the Center in particularistic ways, by reducing multilateralism to a minimum with all kinds of graded membership, *and* by having the Mother country assume the role of window to the world.

However, this point can be much more clearly seen if we combine the two mechanisms and extend what has been said so far for relations between Center and Periphery *nations* to relations between center and periphery *groups* within nations. Under an imperialist structure the two mechanisms are used not only between nations but also within nations, but less so in the Center nation than in the Periphery nation. In other words, there is vertical division of labor within as well as between nations. And these two levels of organization are intimately linked to each other (as A.G. Frank always has emphasized) in the sense that the center in the Periphery interaction structure is also that group with which the Center nation has its harmony of interest, the group used as a bridgehead.

Thus, the combined operation of the two mechanisms at the two levels builds into the structure a subtle grid of protection measures against the major potential source of 'trouble', the periphery in the Periphery. [. . .]

Obviously, the more perfectly the mechanisms of imperialism within and between nations are put to work, the less overt machinery of oppression is needed and the smaller can the center groups be, relative to the total population involved. *Only imperfect, amateurish imperialism needs weapons; professional imperialism is based on structural rather than direct violence.*

The Types of Imperialism

We shall now make this more concrete by distinguishing between five types of imperialism depending on the *type* of exchange between Center and Periphery nations:

(1)   *economic*
(2)   *political*
(3)   *military*
(4)   *communication*
(5)   *cultural.*

The order of presentation is rather random: we have no theory that one is more basic than the others, or precedes the others. Rather, this is like a Pentagon or a Soviet Star: imperialism can start from any corner. They should all be examined regarding the extent to which they generate interaction patterns that utilize the two *mechanisms* of imperialism so as to fulfill the three *criteria* of imperialism, or at least the first of them.

The most basic of the two mechanisms is *vertical* interaction, which in its modern form is conceived of as interaction across a gap in processing level. In other words, what is exchanged between the two nations is not only not the same things (which would have been stupid) but things of a quite different kind, the difference being in terms of where the most complex and stimulating operations take place. One tentative list, expanding what has been said in the previous section about economic interaction, might look like Table 1. [. . .]

The vertical nature of this type of *economic* interaction has been spelled out in detail above since we have used that type of imperialism to exemplify definition and mechanisms. Let us look more at the other types of vertical interaction.

The *political* one is clear: the concept of a 'mother' country, the Center nation, is also an indication of how the decision-making center is dislocated, away from the nation itself and towards the Center nation. These decisions

Table 1: The Five Types of Imperialism

Type	Center nation provides:	Periphery nation provides:
Economic	processing, means of production	raw materials, markets
Political	decisions, models	obedience, imitators
Military	protection, means of destruction	discipline, traditional hardware
Communication	news, means of communication	events, passengers, goods
Cultural	teaching, means of creation — autonomy	learning, validation — dependence

may then affect economic, military, communication, and cultural patterns. Important here is the division of labor involved: some nations produce decisions, others supply obedience. The decisions may be made upon application, as in 'bilateral technical assistance', or in consultation — or they may simply emerge by virtue of the model-imitator distinction. Nothing serves that distinction quite so well as unilinear concepts of 'development' and 'modernization', according to which Center nations possess some superior kind of structure for others to imitate (as long as the Center's central position is not seriously challenged), and which gives a special aura of legitimacy to any idea emanating from the Center. Thus, structures and decisions developed in the 'motherland of liberalism' or in the 'fatherland of socialism' serve as models by virtue of their place of origin, not by virtue of their substance.

The *military* implications or parallels are also rather obvious. It cannot be emphasized enough that the economic divison of labor is also one which ensures that the Center nations economically speaking also become the Center nations in a military sense: only they have the industrial capacity to develop the technological hardware — and also are often the only ones with the social structure compatible with a modern army. He who produces tractors can easily produce tanks, but he who delivers oil cannot defend himself by throwing it in the face of the aggressors. He has to depend on the tank-producer, either for protection or for acquisition (on terms dictated by the Center). And just as there is a division of labor with the Center nation producing manufactured goods on the basis of raw materials extracted in the Periphery nation, there is also a division of labor with the *Center nations processing the obedience provided by the Periphery nations into decisions that can be implemented.* Moreover, there is also a division of labor with the Center providing the protection (and often also the officers or at least the instructors in 'counter-insurgency') and the

Periphery the discipline and the soldiers needed − not to mention the apprentices of 'military advisors' from the Center.

As to the fourth type, *communication* imperialism, the emphasis in the analysis is usually turned toward the second mechanism of imperialism: the feudal interaction structure. That this largely holds for most world communication and transportation patterns has been amply demonstrated. But perhaps more important is the vertical nature of the division of labor in the field of communication/transportation. It is trivial that a high level of industrial capacity is necessary to develop the latest in transportation and communication technology. The preceding generation of *means of communication/transportation* can always be sold, sometimes second-hand, to the Periphery as part of the general vertical trade/aid structure, alongside the *means of production* (economic sector), the *means of destruction* (military sector), and the *means of creation* (cultural sector). The Center's planes and ships are faster, more direct, look more reliable, attract more passengers, more goods. And when the Periphery finally catches up, the Center will already for a long time have dominated the field of communication satellites.

One special version of this principle is a combination of cultural and communication exchange: *news communication*. We all know that the major agencies are in the hands of the Center countries, relying on Center-dominated, feudal networks of communication. What is not so well analyzed is how Center news takes up a much larger proportion of Periphery news media than vice versa, just as trade with the Center is a larger proportion of Periphery total trade than vice versa. In other words, the pattern of partner concentration as something found more in the Periphery than in the Center is very pronounced. The Periphery nations do not write or read much about each other, especially not across bloc borders, and they read more about 'their' Center than about other Centers − because the press is written and read by the center in the Periphery, who want to know more about that most 'relevant' part of the world − for them.

Another aspect of vertical division of labor in the news business should also be pointed out. Just as the Periphery produces raw material that the Center turns into processed goods, *the Periphery also produces events that the Center turns into news*. This is done by training journalists to see events with Center eyes, and by setting up a chain of communication that filters and processes events so that they fit the general pattern.

The latter concept brings us straight into *cultural* imperialism, a subtype of which is scientific imperialism. The division of labor between teachers and learners is clear: it is not the division of labor as such (found in most situations of transmission of knowledge) that constitutes imperialism, but the location of the teachers, and of the learners, in a broader setting. If the Center always provides the teachers and the definition of that worthy of being taught (from the gospels of Christianity to the gospels of Technology), and the Periphery always provides the learners, then there is a pattern which smacks of imperialism. The satellite nation in the Periphery will also know that nothing flatters the Center quite so much as being encouraged to teach, and being seen as a model, and that the Periphery can get much in return from a humble, culture-seeking strategy (just as it will get little but aggression if it starts teaching the Center anything — like Czechoslovakia, who started lecturing the Soviet Union on socialism). For in accepting cultural transmission the Periphery also, implicitly, validates for the Center the culture developed in the center, whether that center is intra- or international. This serves to reinforce the Center as a center, for it will then continue to develop culture along with transmitting it, thus creating lasting demand for the latest innovations. Theories, like cars and fashions, have their life-cycle, and whether the obsolescence is planned or not there will always be a time-lag in a structure with a pronounced difference between center and periphery. Thus, the tram workers in Rio de Janeiro may carry banners supporting Auguste Comte one hundred years after the center of the Center forgot who he was . . .

In science we find a particular version of vertical division of labor, very similar to economic division of labor: the pattern of scientific teams from the Center who go to Periphery nations to collect data (raw material) in the form of deposits, sediments, flora, fauna, archeological findings, attitudes, behavioral patterns, and so on for data processing, data analysis, and theory formation (processing, in general) in the Center universities (factories), so as to be able to send the finished product, a journal, a book (manufactured goods) back for consumption in the center of the Periphery — after first having created a demand for it through demonstration effect, training in the Center country, and some degree of low level participation in the data collection team. This parallel is not a joke, it is a *structure*. If in addition the precise nature of the research is to provide the Center with information that can be used economically, politically, or militarily to maintain an imperialist structure, the cultural imperialism becomes even more clear. And if to this we add the *brain drain* (and body drain) whereby 'raw' brains (students) and 'raw' bodies (unskilled workers) are moved from the Periphery to the Center and 'processed' (trained) with ample benefits to the Center, the picture becomes complete.

3.4

DEPENDENCY AND IMPERIALISM: THE ROOTS OF LATIN AMERICAN UNDERDEVELOPMENT

Susanne Bodenheimer

Source: *Politics and Society*, vol. 1, no. 3 (1971), pp. 327-57.

Bodenheimer argues that traditional explanations of the failure of United States aid to foster development in Latin America are inadequate. She suggests instead that it is necessary to use a dependency model based upon a recognition of the integral relationship between Latin America and the rest of an international system dominated by the developed states. She first discusses the model in terms of an 'infrastructure of dependency' within the underdeveloped states created and sustained by the international system and then maintains that only a Marxist theory of imperialism provides an adequate complement to the model in terms of explaining the logic behind the expansion of capitalism in the dominant nations.

The Dependency Model

The basic premises of the dependency model, as first elaborated by a group of Latin American social scientists, differ sharply from those of American social science development theories. 'Dependency' is conceived as a 'conditioning situation', i.e. one which 'determines the limits and possibilities for human action and conduct' — in this case, for development in Latin America. We shall accept the definition of dependency as:

 a situation in which the economy of a certain group of countries is conditioned by the development and expansion of another economy, to which their own [economy] is subjected . . . an historical condition which shapes a certain structure of the world economy such that it favors some countries to the detriment of others, and limits the development possibilities of the [subordinate] economies.[1]

What does this mean? That Latin America has fulfilled certain definite functions in the 'world economy' or world market, and the domestic development of Latin America has been limited or conditioned by the needs of the dominant economies within that world market. To be sure, no nation has ever developed entirely outside the context of the world market. The distinguishing feature of dependent (as contrasted with interdependent) development is that growth in the dependent nations occurs as a reflex of the expansion of the dominant nations, and is geared toward the needs of the dominant economies − i.e., foreign rather than national needs. In the dependent countries imported factors of production (e.g., capital and technology) have become the central determinants of economic development and socio-political life. And while the world market served as an instrument of expansion in European and American development, it restricts autonomous development in the dependent nations. Dependency means, then, that the alternatives open to the dependent nation are defined and limited by its integration into and functions within the world market.

At this point, we must clarify the concrete meanings of the 'world market' and the 'international system'. By itself, the world market encompasses all flows of goods and services among nations outside the Communist trade bloc − all capital transfers (including foreign aid and overseas investment) and all commodity exchanges. But the world market is the core of a broader 'international system'. This international system includes not only a network of economic (market) relations, but also the entire complex of political, military, social, and cultural international relations organized by and around that market (e.g., the Monroe Doctrine, the Organization of American States, 'Free World' defense treaties and organizations, and media and communications networks). The international system is the static expression and outcome of a dynamic historical process: the transnational or global expansion of capitalism.

By focusing on the international system, the dependency model proceeds from a basic concrete fact of Latin American history: that since the Spanish conquest − that is, since its existence as Latin American rather than indigenous Indian society − Latin America has played a certain role in the political economy of one or another dominant capitalist nation (Spain and Portugal in the colonial and early post-independence period, England during most of the nineteenth century, and the US since the beginning of the twentieth century). Thus, unlike *un*developed societies (those few which have *no* market relations with the industrialized nations), the *under*developed Latin economies have always been shaped by the global expansion and consolidation of the capitalist system, and by their own incorporation into that system. In this sense, Latin societies 'brought into existence with their birth' their relation to the international system, and hence their relations of dependency.

Although the particular function of Latin America in the international system has varied, the development of that region has been shaped since the Spanish conquest by a general structural characteristic of capitalist expansion: its unevenness. 'Unevenness' means that some nations or regions have developed more rapidly than — often at the expense of — others. For Latin America this has entailed increasing relative poverty, as the gap in income and growth rates between the industrial nations and Latin America is constantly widening. (Since 1957, for example, the growth rate of *per capita* income in Latin America has been less than 1.5 per cent a year, as contrasted with nearly 2.5 per cent in the US and 4 per cent in Europe.) Similar disparities have marked the uneven development of various regions within Latin America.

This unevenness has been manifested through an 'international division of labor'; while Western Europe and the US industrialized, Latin America remained for centuries an exporter of primary raw materials and agricultural products. Even the faltering steps toward industrialization more recently have not altered the fundamentally complementary character of the Latin economies: the industrial sectors remain dependent on imports (of capital goods) and, as a result of the increasing foreign control over these sectors, growth is still governed largely by the needs of foreign economies. The international division of labor has persisted (the 1969 *Rockefeller Report* even calls for making it 'more efficient'); only its form has changed. This complementarity is not incidental but essential to the underdevelopment of the Latin economies. As is widely recognized, the periods of relative growth and development in Latin America (e.g., industrialization in the 1930s) have occurred during the phases of relative contraction in the world market (during periods of international war or depression), when the region's ties to that market and to the dominant nations have been weakest. Politically as well, Latin American development has been limited by the fact that policy decisions about resource allocation and all aspects of national development are conditioned and limited by the interests of the developed societies.

From the foregoing, it becomes clear that underdevelopment in Latin America is structurally linked to development in the dominant nations. European and American development and Latin underdevelopment are not two isolated phenomena, but rather two outcomes of the same historical process: the global expansion of capitalism.

Insofar as Latin American development has been limited since the sixteenth century by fulfilling one or another function in the international system, the *fact* of dependency has been a constant. But the *forms* of dependency, in particular countries at particular historical moments, have varied according to the specific characteristics of the international system at that time and the specific functions of the Latin country within the system.

Characteristics of the international system:
1. the prevalent form of capitalism (mercantile or industrial, corporate or financial);
2. the principal needs of the dominant nation(s) in the international system (agricultural commodities, minerals, cheap labor, commodity markets, capital markets, etc.);
3. the degree of concentration of capital in the dominant nation(s) (competitive or monopolistic capitalism);
4. the degree of concentration internationally (one hegemonic power or rival powers and, if one hegemonic power, which nation [Spain, England, or the US]);
5. the typical form of world trade (mercantilism, 'free trade', or protectionism).

Characteristics of the Latin country within the international system:
1. function primarily as a supplier of raw materials or agricultural products, as a market for manufactured goods, as a supplier of certain manufactured commodities, as an arena for direct foreign investment, or any combination of the preceding;
2. the degree of relative autonomy (periods of international war or depression *vs.* 'normal' periods of capitalist expansion);
3. the degree of foreign control in the principal economic sectors;
4. the nature of political tie to the dominant power(s) (colonial or nominal independence).

The specific forms of dependency in Latin America in any given historical period are shaped by the characteristics of the international system and of Latin America's function within it. Latin America was first integrated into the international system in its mercantile phase, under Spanish dominance, and served primarily as a provider of raw materials and agricultural commodities. Thus dependency during the colonial period and during much of the nineteenth century was manifested primarily through the development of export-import 'enclaves'. The conditions which shape Latin dependency today are quite distinct. The international system today is characterized by: advanced industrial capitalism (corporate integrated with financial capital); the dominant nations' need for raw materials and, more important, for commodity and capital markets; monopolistic concentration of capital; American hegemony (*vis-à-vis* Latin America); and increasing international integration of capital. Trade within the international system is increasingly protectionist (tariffs or quotas imposed by the dominant nations) and is increasingly incorporated within the structure of the multinational corporations. Latin America's function within the system is shifting from a supplier of raw materials and agricultural commodities to an arena where certain phases of industrial production are carried out — but still under the auspices of foreign corporations. The degree of foreign control in the principal economic sectors is increasing, and Latin America's integration into the orbit of the dominant capitalist nations is becoming more complete, despite nominal political independence.

These characteristics of the international system and of Latin America's function within it impose definite limitations on the possibilities for Latin development. Nevertheless, it would be an oversimplification to say that the international system causes underdevelopment directly; it does so *indirectly*, by generating and reinforcing within Latin Amerca an *infra-structure of dependency*. What is the infrastructure (internal structures) of dependency? The international system affects development in Latin America by means of certain institutions, social classes, and processes (industrial structure, socio-economic elites, urbanization, and so on). These aspects of Latin society become part of the infrastructure of dependency when they function or occur in a manner that responds to the interests or needs of the dominant powers in the international system, rather than to national interests or needs. It is through the infrastructure of dependency that the international system becomes operative within Latin America. And it is through the infrastructure of dependency that the legacy of Latin America's integration into the international system is transmitted and perpetuated within Latin America, thereby limiting the possibilities for development.

Let us take two examples of the infrastructure of dependency.

(a) Industrialization in the broadest sense implies far more than the construction of new factories and the production or processing of com-modities. In most Latin nations the industrial sectors lie at the heart of the entire national economy. In addition the quality of industrialization is integrally related to, among other things, political decision-making, social structure, and urbanization. Industrialization is not by nature dependent; it becomes so when the industrial structure is integrated into and complementary to the needs of foreign economies. Some specific characteristics of dependent industrialization are: 1) increasing foreign

control over the most dynamic and strategic industrial sectors through direct ownership and control over production, control of marketing and distribution, or control of patents and licenses (in many sectors foreign corporations have been buying out formerly national industries); 2) increasing competitive advantages for (often monopolistic) foreign enterprises over local firms, particularly in industries of scale; 3) as a result of foreign owernship, outflow of capital (profits) abroad; 4) despite some production for the internal market, adaptation of the entire economic structure to the needs of the buyers of Latin exports in the dominant nations; 5) introduction of advanced, capital-intensive foreign technology, without regard to size or composition of the local labor market, and consequent aggravation of unemployment (which in turn results in restriction of the domestic market): in several countries (e.g. Chile, Colombia, Peru) employment in manufacturing industry actually declined as a percentage of total employment between 1925 and 1960; 6) also as a result of foreign control over technology, its restriction to those sectors in which foreign capital has a direct interest; 7) lack of a domestic capital goods industry in most countries, and consequently an increased rather than reduced dependence on imports and rigidities in the composition of imports. In short, dependent industrialization has aggravated rather than resolved such basic problems as balance of payments deficits, unemployment, income disparities, and an insufficient domestic market.

(b) Intersecting the process of dependent industrialization is another, equally fundamental, dimension of dependency: the creation and/or reinforcement of clientele social classes. Clientele classes are those which have a vested interest in the existing international system. These classes carry out certain functions on behalf of foreign interests; in return they enjoy a privileged and increasingly dominant and hegemonic position within their own societies, based largely on economic, political, or military support from abroad. In this sense the clientele classes come to play in Latin America today the role historically performed by the *comprador* bourgeoisie (export-import mercantile elites, whose strength, interests, and very existence were derived from their function in the world market). Like their behavior, the ideologies of these classes reflect their dual position as junior partners of metropolitan interests, yet dominant elites within their own societies. The clearest example of clientele classes today are those elements of the Latin industrial bourgeoisie which 'expand and thrive within the orbit of foreign capital ... [whether as] wholesalers ... or as suppliers of local materials to foreign enterprises or as caterers to various other needs of foreign firms and their staffs'.[2]

The state bureaucracy and other sectors of the middle class — for example, the technical, managerial, professional or intellectual elites — become clientele when their interests, actions, and privileged positions are derived from their ties to foreign interests. Particularly with the expanded role of the state in the national economy, the state bureaucracy (including the military in many countries) has been viewed by some as the key to national autonomy. Nevertheless, when the primary function of the state is to stimulate private enterprise, when the private sector is largely controlled by foreign interests, and when the state bureaucracy itself relies on material and ideological support from abroad (as in Brazil today), the 'autonomy' of the state bureaucracy must be illusory.

The alliances and conflicts of clientele classes with other domestic classes are shaped to a considerable extent by their previous and present alliances with foreign interests. Thus, for example, no less important than the alliances or conflicts of a São Paulo industrialist with the Brazilian proletariat or coffee-growing interests are his economic and ideological alignments with Wall Street bankers or foreign industrial interests; indeed the former are often shaped by the latter. The existence of these clientele classes in the dependent nation, whose interests correspond to those of the dominant classes in the dominant nations, is the kingpin and the *sine qua non* of dependency.

From the preceding discussion, it may be seen that dependency does not simply mean external domination, unilaterally superimposed from abroad and unilaterally producing 'internal consequences'. The internal dynamics of dependency are as much a function of *penetration* as of domination. It is in this way that dependency in Latin America differs from that of a formal colony: while the chains binding the latter to the mother country are overt and direct (administrative control), those of the former are subtler and are internal to the nation — and for that reason are much more difficult to break. In this sense, the infrastructure of dependency may be seen as the functional equivalent of a formal colonial apparatus — the principal difference being, perhaps, that since all classes and structures in Latin society have to a greater or lesser degree internalized and institutionalized the legacy of dependency, that legacy is much more difficult to overcome.

From this analysis follow certain political implications. Even if the US and every other dominant capitalist nation were to suddenly disappear, Latin American dependency would not be immediately ruptured. And thus, by implication, Latin nations cannot break the chains of dependency merely by severing (or attempting to sever) their ties to the international system. A total rupturing of dependency as an internal condition of underdevelopment requires simultaneously — and indeed as a precondition for lasting autonomy or independence from the international system — a profound transformation, an anticapitalist, socialist transformation, of their own socio-economic order.

Thus, as experience has demonstrated, the various efforts to build 'bourgeois nationalist' or 'national capitalist' or, more recently, 'state capitalist' solutions must fail in the end because the social classes on whom such solutions are based (the bourgeoisie) are themselves limited by their role in the international system. They may advocate a foreign policy 'independent' of the US (as in Brazil during the early 1960s); or they may successfully expropriate foreign holdings in some sectors, as has been done in Peru and as may be increasingly the case in other countries. But so long as they follow the capitalist road of development, they will continue to depend upon foreign investment, and thus will eventually have to make their compromises with and cater to foreign interests. And regardless of their intentions to implement far-reaching domestic reforms, they will be limited in practice by the legacy of dependency as institutionalized within their own class interests and alliances, within the existing industrial base, and so on. To break out of dependency means, then, to break out of the capitalist order whose expression in Latin America is dependency.

[After reviewing predecessors of the dependency model, including the work of Gunder Frank (see article 3.2 in this Reader), she proceeds to seek to integrate the model with an appropriate theory explaining capitalist state behaviour towards the underdeveloped nations. She begins by considering and dismissing conventional international relations theories and non-Marxist theories of imperialism as explanations of United States policy towards Latin America.]

In most conventional international relations theories the international context is depicted as an arena in which independent (though not necessarily equal) players bargain about competing or conflicting national interests, and in which war occasionally erupts when the bargaining process breaks down. In the case of US relations with Latin America this model is inappropriate. It assumes that Latin American nations are separate units, led by autonomous decision-makers. It implicitly or explicitly postulates a clear dichotomy between internal and international structures, thus ignoring the reality of Latin American dependency. In addition, international relations theories tend to deal with 'policy choices', the implication being that Latin governments, acting autonomously, could make alternative decisions. In fact, so long as they remain within the international capitalist system, the range of alternatives open to these governments is limited to changing certain minor aspects of their relation to the dominant nations (for example, gaining trade concessions, more economic or military aid). This restricted range of options is, in fact, a principal feature of Latin American dependency. Moreover, the autonomy of Latin American decision-makers is not to be taken for granted; while they may go through the motions of deciding policy, the substance of their decisions often reflects foreign interests more nearly than national interests.

From the standpoint of the US as well, international relations theories tend to obscure the essentials of US-Latin American relations. They generally treat those relations in terms of policies and policy-choices, which presumably could have been or could be changed by more 'enlightened' policy-makers. (Thus, for example, the Alliance for Progress and, thirty years earlier, the Good Neighbor Policy were seen as real departures from previous US policies.) To be sure, American strategies and policies toward Latin America *do* change; but these changes represent variations of a less flexible underlying relationship between the US and Latin America, rather than alterations in the basic relationship. The exclusive focus on US policy also precludes attention to the institutions and social groups within the US socio-economic system which shape these policies. Given the dichotomy between domestic and international politics, foreign policy is seen as part of the state (public) apparatus, is assumed to reflect the 'public interest', and hence is seldom examined in terms of dominant private interests within the US. By obscuring the essential relationship between public policy and private interests, international relations theories must devise *ad hoc* explanations – or excuses – for the failure of policies such as the Alliance for Progress; their own assumptions preclude a real understanding of its roots, and thus of its consequences.

The basic assumption of most international relations theories, that there exists at least a minimal autonomy and freedom of action for all nations as actors in the international arena, is challenged by all theories of imperialism. The notion of an imperialistic relation between two or more nations implies (regardless of the particular theory of imperialism) a decisive inequality between those nations, an exploitative relationship (that is, one which serves the interests of the dominant nation at the expense of the subordinate nation), and the crippling of the latter's autonomy. The subordinate nation becomes, to one degree or another, the object of the needs and interests of certain groups in the dominant nation. Beyond the very general notion of imperialism as exploitative, however, Marxist theories differ sharply from most non-Marxist theories in analyzing the nature and causes of imperialism.

Given the great diversity of non-Marxist theories of imperialism, these remarks must be limited to those tendencies which have direct bearing on Latin American dependency. First, there is a tendency to associate imperialism with expansionism (territorial expansion or protracted political domination) and/or the military aggression and intervention generally accompanying such expansion. By associating imperialism with a phenomenon that has characterized international political relations since the beginning of time, this conception is so broad as to deprive the term 'imperialism' of any specific meaning. Nor does it contribute toward an explanation of dependency in Latin America: for dependency is not created by occasional military interventions or even gunboat diplomacy (which historically involved prolonged occupation and/or overt political control by the US or other hegemonic powers). Rather, dependency has been a chronic condition of Latin development, maintained by the day-to-day and for the most part peaceful relations between Latin America and the dominant nations. The very identification of imperialism with physical or direct coercion projects an oversimplified image of overt domination, and almost automatically excludes from examination the subtler mechanisms through which dependency has been internalized and perpetuated in Latin America.

Second, non-Marxist theories tend to dissociate imperialism from the economic system (for our purposes, capitalism) in the dominant country. Thus they may resort to ideological-political-military explanations (such as the obsessive anti-Communism of American leaders, the doctrine of the 'American responsibility' held by the 'national security bureaucracy', independent of economic interests, and the needs of the defense establishment). Or they may argue that imperialism is 'unprofitable' or 'irrational' in a capitalist society, basically a 'vestige' or 'atavism' surviving from a pre-capitalist era. By conceptualizing imperialism too narrowly in terms of the actions of the state, or implicitly distinguishing *a priori* the interests of the state ('national security') from those of the dominant socio-economic classes, these theories do not consider imperialism to be systemically related to capitalism. But if imperialism is dissociated from capitalism, then it must be regarded as little more than a policy; in this respect the logical conclusions of many non-Marxist theories of imperialism almost converge with those of international relations theory. And if imperialism is dissociated from the global expansion of capitalism on the international level, the concept loses its potential as an explanation of dependency in Latin America.

In contrast to the above, a Marxist theory of imperialism addresses itself directly to the economic basis (as well as the political-military aspects) of American policies and to the causes of dependency and underdevelopment in Latin America. For our purposes the adoption of a Marxist framework implies an integral relation between the action of the US government abroad and the structure of the American socio-economic system; it analyzes US relations with Latin America as one aspect of American capitalism. In this sense American imperialism is not 'irrational' or 'accidental', but rather is a necessary extension of capitalism. It is not a fleeting policy, but *a stage in the development of capitalism as a world system*. Moreover while recognizing the importance, necessity and inevitability of military or coercive actions abroad, a Marxist analysis understands these not as the essence of imperialism, but rather as the ultimate recourse, when the subtler mechanisms of imperialism are insufficient to contain a threat to the existing international system. This analysis is appropriate to a specific feature of contemporary US relations with Latin America: namely, the attempt to avoid and to obviate the need for overt military intervention or direct political control wherever possible. To accept a theory of economic imperialism as a general hypothesis does not imply the necessary reduction of every *specific* political or military action by the state to pure economic motives; there are occasions (such as the Cuban missile crisis) when 'security' considerations are decisive. This theory insists, however, that isolated military or political actions be understood in their over-all context, which is the preservation of capitalism as an economic order.

To introduce the model of contemporary imperialism, we begin with a skeletal description of the main units of contemporary capitalism and imperialism. This sketch is based on a particular Marxist model which takes *monopoly capital* as the defining feature of the US political economy today:

> Today the typical unit in the capitalist world is not the small firm producing a negligible fraction of a homogeneous output for an anonymous market, but a large-scale enterprise producing a significant share of the output of an industry or even several industries, and able to control its prices, the volume of its production, and the type and amounts of its investments. The typical economic unit, in other words, has the attributes which were once thought to be possessed only by monopolies.[3]

The outstanding features of these economic units are, briefly: 1) increasing concentration of capital and resources under the control of fewer units, through the traditional forms: horizontal integration (increasing concentration of control over the production of a commodity or class of commodities) and vertical integration (increasing concentration of control over all phases of the production process, from the supply of raw materials to the marketing and distribution of the commodity to consumers); 2) a growing tendency toward conglomeration or diversification – that is, the control by a smaller number of corporations over production in various different and often unrelated sectors, thus augmenting the corporation's strength, and simultaneously minimizing the risks of production or marketing, in any one sector; 3) increasing 'internationalization' or 'multinationalization' of the operation (*not* the ownership or control) of capital. Multinational corporations are: 'plants that purchase inputs from one branch of a corporation located in the same or a different country and sell outputs to another branch of the same corporation located elsewhere . . . [They] are able to mobilize, transform, and dispose of capital on a regional or even world-wide scale – in effect constituting themselves as extra-territorial bodies'[4] – in short, the (non-Communist) world has replaced the nation as the arena for their operations in both production and marketing; 4) the progressive shift from rivalry among the capitalist powers (such as prevailed, for example, during the heyday of colonialism, from 1870 to 1914) toward closer integration of the capitalist world, and inability of the secondary capitalist powers thus far to offer a serious challenge to American hegemony. (This is especially the case *vis-à-vis* Latin America.)

These characteristics of contemporary capitalism give rise to certain generally shared interests of the multinational corporations with respect to their overseas operations. First, there arises a need to control all aspects of the production process, including the sources of supply and processing of raw materials, as well as the markets or outlets for commodities. Second, as the scale, monopolistic concentration, conglomeration, and internationalization of private capital increase, the dependence upon immediate profit returns from overseas investments is reduced. The emphasis shifts toward long-range planning, maximum security and avoidance of risk, and preservation of a favorable climate (ideological, political, and social as well as economic) for the *perpetuation* of corporate operations and for long-range profits – a concern frequently expressed by US businessmen themselves. To insure against sudden changes in the 'rules of the game', controls over the political situation in Latin America – generally informal and indirect – must be tightened. And in the international environment there is need of an apparatus to guarantee not only the rationalization of international capital flows and monetary transactions, but also maximum political stability. 'Hemispheric security' comes to mean protection not against interference by non-hemispheric powers or even 'International Communism', but rather against the threat of truly independent regimes of any type in Latin America.

Third, corporate capitalists acquire an interest in a limited measure of 'development' in Latin America. A moderate redistribution of income in Latin America provides a larger market for US exports, as well as a safeguard against potential political instability. A relatively healthy Latin economy improves the climate for investment and trade. In this sense modern imperialism has an element of 'welfare imperialism'. Under these conditions, however, Latin development responds primarily to the needs of the foreign corporations, rather than national needs; it is, in short, fragmented, dependent, and ultimately illusory development. Fourth (and partly as a response to the failure to achieve real income redistribution or expansion of the domestic market in Latin countries), there is an interest in regional integration of markets. As *Fortune* (June 1967) points out, the advantages of integration are that it not only eliminates tariff barriers, but it also provides 'the chance to move to the broader, more competitive, and potentially more profitable task of supplying a market big enough to be economic on its own terms'.

Finally, the nature of private corporate operations overseas is such that they require protection by the (imperialist) state. Thus the multinational corporation has an increasing stake in consolidating its influence over 'public' or (US) government decisions, that is, over the apparatus of the state. This implies not only a strong influence over government foreign policies, but also the active participation of the state in international economic relationships which serve their interests. As the interests of the state come to overlap with those of the multinational corporations, 'the state enlists more and more private capital in its crusade to maintain world capitalism intact', and there arises a 'partnership' between public and private capital.[5] For our purposes, the significance of this partnership is that the state performs certain services which are essential to the overseas operations of the multinational corporations. [. . .]

This analysis is not to imply that the state *never* acts independently of, or even in direct opposition to, private corporate interests in particular situations. Indeed there have been notable instances. Moreover, the state is sometimes faced with conflicting interests among the multinational corporations. In short, the state (and even the corporations themselves) are sometimes forced to sacrifice specific interests in order to serve the 'higher interest' – the preservation of the capitalist system as a whole. In this sense the overriding task of the modern capitalist state is the stabilization and rationalization of world capitalism and imperialism as a socio-economic order.

We may now draw together the two parts of the analysis. By itself the dependency model provides a view 'from below'. It traces Latin American underdevelopment to that region's function in the world market and international system, which is governed by the interests of the dominant nations. The theory of imperialism provides a view 'from above' — an explanation of the specific nature of the international system and its roots in the dominant nations. Through it the principal force which has conditioned Latin development — the global expansion of capitalism, which is the engine of the international system — is personified. For the theory of imperialism specifies *whose* particular needs or interests in the dominant nations — that is, those of the corporate and financial capitalists — are served by the international system. And on the basis of the ties between the state and private interests in the dominant nations, the theory offers an account of US relations with Latin America, thus converging with the dependency model. Dependency and imperialism are, thus, two names for one and the same system.

Notes

1. T. Dos Santos, 'Crisis de la Teoria del Desarollo y las Relaciones de Dependencia en America Latina', reprint from *Boletin de CESO* (October-November 1968), pp. 26, 29.

2. Paul Baran, *The Political Economy of Growth* (Monthly Review Press, New York, 1957), pp. 194-5.

3. Paul Baran and Paul Sweezy, *Monopoly Capital* (Monthly Review Press, New York, 1966), p. 6.

4. James O'Connor, 'The International Corporations and Economic Underdevelopment', *Science and Society* (Spring 1970), pp. 45-6.

5. James O'Connor, 'The Meaning of Economic Imperialism', (p. 289 of this Reader).

3.5

CAPITALISM, UNDERDEVELOPMENT AND THE FUTURE OF THE POOR COUNTRIES

Thomas E. Weisskopf

Source: J.N. Bhagwati (ed.), *Economics and World Order* (Collier-Macmillan, London, 1972), pp. 43-69.

Weisskopf argues that the spread of capitalism is likely to perpetuate rather than reduce underdevelopment in two ways: it will tend to heighten the subordination of the poor countries to the rich and to aggravate rather than diminish inequalities in the distribution of income within poor countries. He concludes by reviewing the possibilities for change and suggests that the most likely outcome is a revolution against capitalism with the less privileged class wresting power from the ruling elites in the poor countries.

[The first section of the article outlines some of the economic and socio-political characteristics of contemporary underdevelopment, including the growing gap between poor and rich countries, the extreme inequality of wealth distribution in poor countries, the economic dependence of the poor countries upon the rich and the concentration of power within the class structure of poor countries. In the next section Weisskopf goes on to argue that these features are likely to become more pronounced.]

Increasing Subordination

There are several factors at work within the world capitalist system to reinforce the subordination of the poor to the rich countries. These can briefly be described as the demonstration effect, the monopoly effect, the brain-drain effect, and the factor-bias effect. Each of these effects serves to intensify the demand of the poor countries for resources and skills available mainly in the rich, thereby contributing directly to economic dependence, and indirectly also to political and cultural subordination.

First of all, the increasingly close ties between the poor and the rich countries that accompany the integration of world capitalism give rise to a *demonstration effect* whereby the consumption patterns of the rich countries are to some extent emulated by those citizens in the poor countries who are in a position to afford it. Of course, the majority of the population of a poor country cannot afford to consume like the majority of the population in a rich country; however, the elite classes in the poor countries (and, to some extent, the middle classes) can orient their consumption patterns towards those of their counterparts in the rich countries. To the extent that they do so, their consumption tends to rise and to be oriented towards characteristically foreign types of goods. This in turn leads to a relatively high demand for foreign exchange, either because the goods must be directly imported from a foreign country, or because their production in the underdeveloped countries requires the import of foreign raw materials, technology or expertise.

The second important factor that tends to perpetuate the economic dependence of the poor on the rich countries arises from the *relationship between domestic and foreign private enterprise*. Foreign enterprise has a distinct advantage *vis-à-vis* domestic enterprise in the poor countries with respect to technology, know-how, markets, finance, etc.; often their monopolistic control of some or all of these factors accounts for their interest in investing in the poor countries. Even when the poor country does not rely directly on foreign enterprise to produce goods and services, it is often the case that it must rely on collaboration with foreign firms, or on some kind of indirect affiliation with foreign private enterprise. While such collaboration and affiliation may serve to increase the productive capacity of the economy, at the same time it carries with it an unavoidable relationship of dependence. Furthermore, it is typically within the interest of foreign private enterprise to maintain the conditions in which its activities or its aid are essential, for considerable monetary rewards accrue to its monopoly of productive techniques and expertise. Thus the incentives are structured in such a way that it is usually not in the interest of a foreign firm to impart to a domestic counterpart the knowledge or the skills or the advantages upon which its commercial success is based. Under such circumstances, domestic enterprise remains in a subordinate position and an important part of the indigenous capitalist class remains dependent upon foreign capitalists. The interest of this part of the indigenous capitalist class becomes associated with that of their foreign collaborators or benefactors, and the impetus as well as the means for them to develop into an autonomous national bourgeoisie is dulled.

The technical and managerial dependence of poor on rich countries is often exacerbated by a substantial *'brain drain'*; the emigration of scientists, engineers, business managers and other highly educated professionals from the poor to the rich countries where they can expect better-paying jobs, and a more stimulating work environment. This outward flow of skilled labor, small in absolute size but very great in potential value because of its scarcity in the poor countries, is both facilitated and promoted by the increasing integration of world capitalism. Where people are encouraged to respond to individual monetary rewards, rather than collective social goals, and where strong forces are operating to attract valuable resources from backward to advanced areas, disparities tend to become cumulatively greater over time.

The last general factor that tends to reinforce the economic dependence of the poor on the rich countries within the world capitalist system results from the *choice of production techniques* adopted in the poor countries. The technology that is used by both foreign and domestic firms in the modern sectors of the economy is typically very much influenced by production techniques that are used in the rich countries. Such techniques, arising as they do from an economic environment in which labor is scarce and capital is relatively abundant, tend to be more capital intensive and labor-saving than would be desirable in poor countries. Since the required capital goods — and often also the patents and other rights associated with the production and marketing of the output — must often be imported from abroad, these techniques tend also to be relatively foreign exchange intensive. This effect is most pronounced when a foreign firm establishes itself directly in a poor country, because that enterprise will have an interest in using equipment and services from its own country. But the same effect comes about indirectly when domestic firms collaborate with foreign firms, or even if they simply borrow technology from a rich country.

Continued economic dependence implies also continued *political subordination*. So long as governments of poor countries must seek short- and long-term economic aid from the advanced capitalist countries and the international organizations that are primarily funded by those same countries (the International Bank for Reconstruction and Development, the International Monetary Fund, etc.), their political autonomy will be severely restricted. Furthermore, it follows from the nature of the links between domestic and foreign capital described above that a significant part of the domestic capitalist class is likely to be relatively uninterested in national autonomy insofar as it conflicts with the interests of its foreign capitalist partners or benefactors. Thus the state is likely to be under considerable domestic pressure to curtail whatever nationalist instincts it might otherwise have.

Finally, the continuation of economic and political dependence is likely to limit the development of *cultural autonomy* as well. The more dependent the country is on foreign help of one kind or another, the greater will be the foreign presence in the country, and the greater the impact on indigenous social and cultural life. International capitalism is especially threatening to the cultural autonomy of poor countries because of the strong interest that capitalist firms have in transmitting the kind of consumerist mentality that stimulates the market for their products. The same kind of demonstration effect that biases demand in the poor countries in favor of foreign goods and services also serves to favor the import of foreign styles and fashions at the expense of domestic cultural autonomy. Just as a concentration of purchasing power in the hands of the elite classes accentuates the demand bias, so the dominance by the foreign-oriented elite — and often foreigners themselves — of educational institutions, communications media, and cultural resources tends to amplify the threat to indigenous cultural development.

Increasing Inequality

Under capitalism, each individual is rewarded according to the price at which he can sell the factors of production which he owns. Among these, it is useful to distinguish the following basic factors of production: unskilled labor, labor skills, land (including natural resources), and physical capital (buildings, plant and equipment). In addition, the intangible factor 'knowledge', or technological know-how, can bring important economic rewards to those who have initial or exclusive control over it. Since unskilled labor is relatively abundant and the other factors relatively scarce in the poor countries, labor alone usually commands a relatively low price.

The vast majority of the population of the poor countries control only their own labor power, supplemented here and there with a few skills and/or a little land. The ownership and control of most skills, land and capital, as well as access to new and better technology, is largely confined to the elite groups that constitute the ruling class. Thus it is hardly surprising that income is so unequally distributed. In order for the distribution of income to improve in the future, there would have to be either (a) a more equitable distribution of claims to the scarce factors of the economy, or (b) an increase in the share of national income representing the returns to the most equally distributed factor: unskilled labor. It will be argued below that the growth of capitalism in the poor countries is likely to preclude both of these alternatives, and therefore that one can only expect increasing inequality of income in the non-socialist poor countries.

A redistribution of existing claims to scarce and valuable factors of production is not likely to get very far. In the first place, the respect for private property that is fundamental to capitalism precludes any large-scale dispossession of the rich in | favor of | the | poor. The requirement of compensation and the political strength of the rich *vis-à-vis* the poor will work to limit the comprehensiveness and the effectiveness of any measures of redistribution. Thus, existing land, existing capital and existing control of technology are unlikely to be redistributed among the population as a whole in a manner that will significantly affect the overall distribution of income. And, of course, the skills and the education acquired by the educated elites cannot, by definition, be redistributed among the population.

For similar reasons the incremental supply of valuable assets is unlikely to be any more equitably distributed. Capitalist development has always been characterized by a tendency towards increased concentration of ownership and control; this results directly from the capitalist principle of building upon the best. The biggest landowners are in the best position to take advantage of new irrigation facilities for expanding acreage and to apply new techniques for expanding productivity. The biggest capitalists are in the best position to accumulate and borrow more capital in order to multiply their physical assets, and they also have the best access to new technology and new markets. Even the distribution of new skills through the expansion of educational institutions tends to provide disproportionately great benefits for those classes already most favored. To expect intervention by the state to counter effectively these tendencies is to attribute to the lower classes a degree of political power and influence that could only result from a fundamental transformation of the social structure of the society.

The prospects for any improvement in the distribution of income thus appear to hinge on the possibility of an increase in the share of national income due to unskilled labor. The amount of income due to unskilled labor is equal to the product of the number of fully employed workers (or their equivalent) and the basic annual wage paid for unskilled labor. In order for this amount to increase as a share of national income, either the level of employment or the basic wage rate (or some combination of the two) would have to rise more rapidly than the total income of the economy.

In most of the poor countries in recent times the rate of growth of population has not been as rapid as the rate of growth of total income and we can infer that the growth of the labor force has also lagged behind the growth of income. Under such circumstances, it would take a continuous and substantial reduction in the rate of unemployment merely to enable the level of employment to keep pace with the growth of income. A long-run increase in the share of total income due to unskilled labor would most likely depend upon a rise in the basic wage rate more rapid than the growth of income. In fact, however, there are several forces which restrain the growth of demand for unskilled labor in a non-socialist poor country and thereby limit reduction of unemployment and increases of the basic wage rate. As a result, the share of total income due to unskilled labor is unlikely to increase over time.

First of all, there is a *bias against unskilled labor* in the composition of goods and services produced in the non-socialist poor countries. The very unequal distribution of income which places disproportionate purchasing power in the hands of the elite classes results in a relatively heavy demand for luxury goods and services (e.g. consumer durables) rather than necessities (e.g. food and clothing). Not only are the luxuries relatively foreign exchange intensive, but they are also generally more capital intensive and less labor intensive than the necessities which are demanded by the majority of the population. Thus inequality in the non-socialist poor countries is self-reinforcing because it tends to accentuate the demand for capital and to limit the demand for labor.

Secondly, several forces are at work to *bias the choice of technique* used to produce any given good or service in favor of physical capital and skilled labor and against unskilled labor. The tendency already noted to adopt techniques that have been developed under conditions in rich countries, where capital is more plentiful and unskilled labor more scarce, results in just such a bias. This is particularly likely when foreign firms invest directly in a poor country; but for reasons suggested earlier, the same bias is likely to hold where domestic firms either collaborate or enter into licensing agreements with foreign concerns.

Another factor influencing the choice of techniques by capitalist enterprise in the poor countries relates to the *problem of labor discipline*. Because of the difficulty of organizing large numbers of unskilled workers, the individual capitalist employer often has an incentive to keep down the size of his work force and to pay a small number of more skilled laborers relatively high wages rather than pay a large number of unskilled laborers low wages. Similarly, the capitalist class as a whole has an interest in cultivating a labor aristocracy whose interests will be tied to those of the ruling elites, rather than to the masses; this serves to fragment the labor force and thus to inhibit the development of a revolutionary working class consciousness. To the extent that such forces operate, the benefits of employment are limited to only a part of the laboring classes and skilled labor substitutes for unskilled labor.

The tendency to under-employ unskilled labor is further reinforced by the *disequilibrium prices* that often characterize markets in the non-socialist countries. It has become a commonplace among development economists to observe that money wage rates in urban areas of poor countries are higher than the rate at which employers would be willing to hire all the available labor. This results *inter alia* from concessions made by the state to organized labor in response to union pressures; it favors the minority of organized workers at the expense of the majority of the unorganized. At the same time, it is also widely recognized that the price of capital to private enterprise is often understated because of the various types of government programs, subsidies and other benefits which aid the investor. The result is that firms tend to use more capital and less labor than would be desirable from the point of view either of greater efficiency or of a more equitable distribution of income.

All of these biases serve to restrain the growth of demand for unskilled labor in the poor non-socialist countries. As a result, the share of unskilled labor in national income is likely to decrease over time, and growing inequalities in the ownership of the other factors will contribute to growing inequality in the overall distribution of income. Corresponding to this increasing economic inequality – and continually reinforcing it – will be an increasing inequality in the distribution of political power as well.

[The next two sections carry the argument further: in the first he argues that capitalist institutions both domestically and internationally limit the possibilities for resource mobilization and utilization and for adequate growth in the poor countries; in the second he presents some recent empirical evidence which, though fragmentary, tends to confirm that there has been little change in the over-all pattern of subordination of the poor countries. He then turns to the likely consequences for the future of his evidence and argument.]

Prospects for the Future

Both the theoretical analysis and the empirical evidence presented above point to the likelihood of increasing subordination, increasing inequality and inadequate growth in poor countries that are integrated into the world capitalist system. This prospect is obviously antithetical to the economic and social development of the poor countries and to the construction of a decent world society. Furthermore, the situation is inherently unstable. In the long run, the masses of people in the poor countries will not tolerate social and economic conditions that serve the interests primarily of an elite minority. For the increasing penetration of capitalism into the poor countries creates greater awareness of deprivation on the part of the deprived, while at the same time it erodes the traditional sources of stability and security afforded by precapitalist institutions.

Under these circumstances it is not surprising that popular unrest has grown in many parts of the underdeveloped world. Although few popular revolutionary movements have yet risen directly to power, an increasing number of governments in the poor countries have had to contend with threats from below. The world capitalist system is obviously not in imminent danger, but the conflicts inherent in the present situation are likely to increase over time and confront the ruling classes in the poor countries as well as in the rich countries with increasingly difficult problems.

The elites in any society naturally seek to preserve their privileged position. They attempt to resist the varying degrees of pressure brought upon them by other classes to change the distribution of income and power. Among a whole spectrum of possible outcomes of this class conflict we may distinguish three broad possibilities. First, the ruling elites may hold on to all of their privileges and hold off the majority of the population by the successful exercise of repressive power – economic, political or military, as the case may demand. Second, the ruling elites may preserve the *relative* position which they enjoy in the society by buying off the discontent of the other classes with selective improvements in their *absolute* – but not relative – economic position. The third possible outcome is a successful revolution in which power is wrested from the ruling elites by some of the less privileged classes.

In the rich capitalist countries, conflicts over the distribution of income and power have tended to result in the second outcome. This has been possible for several reasons. First of all, the rich capitalist economies typically manage to generate a rate of economic growth that is rapid enough to allow the upper classes to keep improving their economic position while at the same time permitting a gradual but steady rise in the material welfare of most of the other classes as well. Furthermore, the upper and middle classes are together numerous enough so that they can share the burden of providing something for the poorest classes (often in fact the middle classes can be made to bear the brunt of the burden). These classes are also diverse enough so that conflicts among them can at times be used by the poorer classes to press their demands.

The conditions which help to bring about the second outcome in the rich capitalist countries are, however, largely absent in the poor countries. In the first place, the rate of growth of *per capita* income tends to be lower, with the result that there is less incremental income to redistribute. Second, the masses of the very poor represent a much greater proportion of the population as compared with the middle and upper classes. These latter are relatively limited in number and much less prepared to assume the major burden of providing for the huge numbers of poor. Finally, the limited membership of the domestic privileged classes also reduces the possibility of conflict among them which could lead to political alliances across the line that divides them from the masses.

While it is thus illusory to expect the more privileged classes of the poor countries to redistribute a significant amount of income to the rest of the population, one might conceive of such a transfer from the more affluent classes of the rich capitalist countries. Yet the politics of the world capitalist system warrant little confidence in such a solution. It is very hard to imagine how the masses in the poor countries could bring sufficient political pressure upon the ruling elites of the rich countries to induce them to undertake a serious effort on their behalf. The masses in the poor countries are geographically and socially so distant from the elites in the rich countries that they are easily ignored and have no power to elicit substantial concessions. Even the established governments of the poor countries have been unable to induce the rich capitalist countries to supply modest levels of foreign aid or to reduce significantly the protective tariffs that exclude so many exports from the poor countries.

Thus the second outcome has not often resulted from class conflict in the poor non-socialist countries and is no more likely to do so in the future. There is little prospect that the hardships experienced by the great majority of the population in the underdeveloped world will be offset by compensatory action on the part of the elite beneficiaries of the world capitalist system. So far the outcome has most often been the first one described above: the concentration of privilege in the hands of a minority that has held down the majority in more or less authoritarian fashion. Where radical threats to the *status quo* have arisen, they have generally been repressed with help where necessary from the major capitalist powers.

As revolutionary consciousness grows, however, a repressive policy becomes increasingly difficult to maintain. The repression itself is likely to breed greater hostility to the *status quo*, and the cost of controlling popular unrest will rise. The elites of the poor countries will have to rely more heavily on external assistance and military support, and the cost to the major powers of maintaining the capitalist system in the poor countries will also rise.

Herein lies one of the major contradictions of contemporary capitalism that offers some hope to the poor countries of escaping the syndrome of capitalist underdevelopment. To pay the human and economic cost of increasing military intervention in favor of repressive regimes in the poor countries will generate increasing and ultimately unmanageable domestic unrest in the rich capitalist countries. The Vietnam war has done more to threaten the fabric of American society than anything else in the last decade; the capitalist system cannot afford many more such ventures.

Yet at the same time the rich capitalist countries will be unable to contain the increasing tension in the poor countries by promoting the second outcome, the one that has served in the past to defuse class conflict within the rich countries. Billions of dollars can be raised to support armed forces in the name of defending the 'free world', but only a fraction of this amount can be raised for redistribution abroad. Even if far-sighted capitalists with a large stake in the expansion of the world capitalist system support vastly increased expenditures on foreign aid, they cannot counter the strength of an ideology that condemns 'unearned' income – not to mention the domestic political forces pressing internal ahead of external claims to government attention.

Thus in time the dependent elites of the poor countries may begin to lose critical support from the major capitalist powers. To the extent that this is the case, they will become more vulnerable to domestic unrest and to political change. Initially this change is most likely to see the power of the foreign-oriented elites captured by more nationalistic groups from among the middle or upper classes who are hostile to the penetration of foreign influence and determined to break the subordinate relationship of the poor with the rich capitalist countries. Such a change has already occurred in several of the poor countries.

In the long run, however, the fundamental problems of underdevelopment – inadequate growth, increasing inequality and increasing subordination – are unlikely to be soluble without a complete break with capitalist institutions both domestically and internationally. Only radical changes in the structure of power within the poor countries are likely to result in significant changes in the pattern of economic and social development. Until such changes do occur, conflicts and tensions will become increasingly serious in many parts of the underdeveloped world. Ultimately, however, revolutionary socialist movements are likely to succeed because of the failure of capitalism to eradicate underdevelopment and the limited capacity of the world capitalist system to defend itself against mounting revolutionary activity in the underdeveloped areas.

3.6

THE MULTINATIONAL CORPORATION AND THE LAW OF UNEVEN DEVELOPMENT

Stephen Hymer

Source: J.N. Bhagwati (ed.), *Economics and World Order* (Collier-Macmillan, London, 1972), pp. 113-40.

Hymer describes the process by which multinational corporations contribute to the development of an international hierarchy and thus restrict the possibilities for national development in peripheral areas. He then examines the possibilities for the continued viability of a global economy based on MNCs, given the problems created by the exclusion of many areas from the benefits of their activities, the need to maintain a modernized 'centre' to the world economy, and the rather ambivalent role of state authorities.

[Hymer begins the article by outlining the historical evolution of the multinational corporation and then turns to the implications for the future of the pattern of industrial organization implicit in that evolution.]

Uneven Development

Suppose giant multinational corporations (say 300 from the US and 200 from Europe and Japan) succeed in establishing themselves as the dominant form of international enterprise and come to control a significant share of industry (especially modern industry) in each country. The world economy will resemble more and more the United States economy, where each of the large corporations tends to spread over the entire continent, and to penetrate almost every nook and cranny. What would be the effect of a world industrial organization of this type on international specialization, exchange and income distribution? The purpose of this section is to analyze the spatial dimension of the corporate hierarchy.

A useful starting point is Chandler and Redlich's scheme for analyzing the evolution of corporate structure. They distinguish 'three levels of business administration, three horizons, three levels of task, and three

337

levels of decision making ... and three levels of policies'.[1] Level III, the lowest level, is concerned with managing the day-to-day operations of the enterprise, that is with keeping it going within the established framework. Level II, which first made its appearance with the separation of head office from field office, is responsible for coordinating the managers at Level III. The functions of Level I — top management — are goal-determination and planning. This level sets the framework in which the lower levels operate. In the Marshallian firm, all three levels are embodied in the single entrepreneur or undertaker. In the national corporation, a partial differentiation is made in which the top two levels are separated from the bottom one. In the multidivisional corporation, the differentiation is far more complete. Level I is completely split off from Level II and concentrated in a general office whose specific function is to plan strategy rather than tactics.

The development of business enterprise can therefore be viewed as a process of centralizing and perfecting the process of capital accumulation. The Marshallian entrepreneur was a jack-of-all-trades. In the modern multidivisional corporation, a powerful general office consciously plans and organizes the growth of corporate capital. It is here that the key men who actually allocate the corporation's available resources (rather than act within the means allocated to them, as is true for the managers at lower levels) are located. Their power comes from their ultimate control over *men* and *money* and although one should not overestimate the ability to control a far-flung empire, neither should one underestimate it. [...]

What is the relationship between the structure of the microcosm and the structure of the macrocosm? The application of location theory to the Chandler-Redlich scheme suggests a *correspondence principle* relating centralization of control within the corporation to centralization of control within the international economy.

Location theory suggests that Level III activities would spread themselves over the globe according to the pull of manpower, markets, and raw materials. The multinational corporation, because of its power to command capital and technology and its ability to rationalize their use on a global scale, will probably spread production more evenly over the world's surface than is now the case. Thus, in the first instance, it may well be a force for diffusing industrialization to the less developed countries and creating new centres of production. (We postpone for a moment a discussion of the fact that location depends upon transportation, which in turn depends upon the government which in turn is influenced by the structure of business enterprise.)

Level II activities, because of their need for white-collar workers, communications systems, and information, tend to concentrate in large cities. Since their demands are similar, corporations from different industries tend to place their coordinating offices in the same city, and Level II activities are consequently far more geographically concentrated than Level III activities.

Level I activities, the general offices, tend to be even more concentrated than Level II activities, for they must be located close to the capital market, the media, and the government. Nearly every major corporation in the United States, for example, must have its general office (or a large proportion of its high-level personnel) in or near the city of New York, because of the need for face-to-face contact at higher levels of decision making.

Applying this scheme to the world economy, one would expect to find the highest offices of the multinational corporations concentrated in the world's major cities – New York, London, Paris, Bonn, Tokyo. These, along with Moscow and perhaps Peking, will be the major centres of high-level strategic planning. Lesser cities throughout the world will deal with the day-to-day operations of specific local problems. These in turn will be arranged in a hierarchical fashion: the larger and more important ones will contain regional corporate headquarters, while the smaller ones will be confined to lower-level activities. Since business is usually the core of the city, geographical specialization will come to reflect the hierarchy of corporate decision making, and the occupational distribution of labour in a city or region will depend upon its function in the international economic system. The 'best' and most highly paid administrators, doctors, lawyers, scientists, educators, government officials, actors, servants and hairdressers, will tend to concentrate in or near the major centres.

The structure of income and consumption will tend to parallel the structure of status and authority. The citizens of capital cities will have the best jobs – allocating men and money at the highest level and planning growth and development – and will receive the highest rates of remuneration. (Executives' salaries tend to be a function of the wage bill of people under them. The larger the empire of the multinational corporation, the greater the earnings of top executives, to a large extent independent of their performance. Thus, growth in the hinterland subsidiaries implies growth in the income of capital cities, but not vice versa.)

The citizens of capital cities will also be the first to innovate new products in the cycle which is known in the marketing literature as trickle-down or two-stage marketing. A new product is usually first introduced to a select group of people who have 'discretionary' income and are willing to experiment in their consumption patterns. Once it is accepted by this group, it spreads, or trickles down to other groups via the demonstration effect. In this process, the rich and the powerful get more votes than everyone else; first, because they have more money to spend, second, because they have more ability to experiment, and third, because they have high status and are likely to be copied. This special group may have something approaching a choice in consumption patterns; the rest have only the choice between conforming or being isolated.

The trickle-down system also has the advantage − from the centre's point of view − of reinforcing patterns of authority and control. According to Fallers[2], it helps keep workers on the treadmill by creating an illusion of upward mobility even though relative status remains unchanged. In each period subordinates achieve (in part) the consumption standards of their superiors in a previous period and are thus torn in two directions: if they look backward and compare their standards of living through time, things seem to be getting better; if they look upward they see that their relative position has not changed. They receive a consolation prize, as it were, which may serve to keep them going by softening the reality that in a competitive system, few succeed and many fail. It is little wonder, then, that those at the top stress growth rather than equality as the welfare criterion for human relations.

In the international economy trickle-down marketing takes the form of an international demonstration effect spreading outward from the metropolis to the hinterland. Multinational corporations help speed up this process, often the key motive for direct investment, through their control of marketing channels and communications media.

The development of a new product is a fixed cost; once the expenditure needed for invention or innovation has been made, it is forever a bygone. The actual cost of production is thus typically well below selling price and the limit on output is not rising costs but falling demand due to saturated markets. The marginal profit on new foreign markets is thus high, and corporations have a strong interest in maintaining a system which spreads their products widely. Thus, the interest of multinational corporations in underdeveloped countries is larger than the size of the market would suggest.

It must be stressed that the dependency relationship between major and minor cities should not be attributed to technology. The new technology, because it increases interaction, implies greater interdependence but not necessarily a hierarchical structure. Communications linkages could be arranged in the form of a grid in which each point was directly connected to many other points, permitting lateral as well as vertical communication. This system would be polycentric since messages from one point to another would go directly rather than through the centre;

each point would become a centre on its own; and the distinction between centre and periphery would disappear.

Such a grid is made *more* feasible by aeronautical and electronic revolutions which greatly reduce costs of communications. It is not technology which creates inequality; rather, it is *organization* that imposes a ritual judicial asymmetry on the use of intrinsically symmetrical means of communications and arbitrarily creates unequal capacities to initiate and terminate exchange, to store and retrieve information, and to determine the extent of the exchange and terms of the discussion. Just as colonial powers in the past linked each point in the hinterland to the metropolis and inhibited lateral communications, preventing the growth of independent centres of decision making and creativity, multinational corporations (backed by state powers) centralize control by imposing a hierarchical system.

This suggests the possibility of an alternative system of organization in the form of national planning. Multinational corporations are private institutions which organize one or a few industries across many countries. Their polar opposite (the antimultinational corporation, perhaps) is a public institution which organizes many industries across one region. This would permit the centralization of capital, i.e. the coordination of many enterprises by one decision-making centre, but would substitute regionalization for internationalization. The span of control would be confined to the boundaries of a single polity and society and not spread over many countries. The advantage of national planning is its ability to remove the wastes of oligopolistic anarchy, i.e. meaningless product differentiation and an imbalance between different industries within a geographical area. It concentrates *all* levels of decision making in one locale and thus provides each region with a full complement of skills and occupations. This opens up new horizons for local development by making possible the social and political control of economic decision making. Multinational corporations, in contrast, weaken political control because they span many countries and can escape national regulation.

A few examples might help to illustrate how multinational corporations reduce options for development. Consider an underdeveloped country wishing to invest heavily in education in order to increase its stock of human capital and raise standards of living. In a market system it would be able to find gainful employment for its citizens within its *national boundaries* by specializing in education-intensive activities and selling its surplus production to foreigners. In the multinational corporate system, however, the demand for high-level education in low-ranking areas is limited, and a country does not become a world centre simply by having a better educational system. An outward shift in the supply of educated people in a country, therefore, will not create its own demand but will create an excess supply and lead to emigration. Even then, the employment opportunities for citizens of low-ranking countries are restricted by discriminatory practices in the centre. It is well known that ethnic homogeneity increases as one goes up the corporate hierarchy; the lower levels contain a wide variety of nationalities, the higher levels become successively purer and purer. In part this stems from the skill differences of different nationalities, but more important is the fact that the higher up one goes in the decision-making process, the more important mutual understanding and ease of communications become; a common background becomes all-important.

A similar type of specialization by nationality can be expected within the multinational corporation hierarchy. Multinational corporations are torn in two directions. On the one hand, they must adapt to local circumstances in each country. This calls for decentralized decision making. On the other hand, they must coordinate their activities in various parts of the world and stimulate the flow of ideas from one part of their empire to another. This calls for centralized control. They must, therefore, develop an organizational structure to balance the need for coordination with the need for adaptation to a patch-work quilt of languages, laws and customs. One solution to this problem is a division of labour based on nationality. Day-to-day management in each country is left to the nationals of that country who, because they are intimately familiar with local conditions and practices, are able to deal with local problems and local government. These nationals remain rooted in one spot, while above them is a layer of people who move around from country to country, as bees among flowers, transmitting information from one subsidiary to another and from the lower levels to the general office at the apex of the corporate structure. In the nature of things, these people (reticulators) for the most part will be citizens of the country of the parent corporation (and will be drawn from a small, culturally homogeneous group within the advanced world), since they will need to have the confidence of their superiors and be able to move easily in the higher management circles. Latin Americans, Asians and Africans will at best be able to aspire to a management position in the intermediate coordinating centres at the continental level. Very few will be able to get much higher than this, for the closer one gets to the top, the more important is 'a common cultural heritage'.

Another way in which the multinational corporations inhibit economic development in the hinterland is through their effect on tax capacity. An important government instrument for promoting growth is expenditure on infrastructure and support services. By providing transportation and communications, education and health, a government can create a productive labour force and increase the growth potential of its economy. The extent to which it can afford to finance these intermediate outlays depends upon its tax revenue.

However, a government's ability to tax multinational corporations is limited by the ability of these corporations to manipulate transfer prices and to move their productive facilities to another country. This means that they will only be attracted to countries where superior infrastructure offsets higher taxes. The government of an underdeveloped country will find it difficult to extract a surplus (revenue from the multinational corporations, less cost of services provided to them) from multinational corporations to use for long-run development programmes and for stimulating growth in other industries. In contrast, governments of the advanced countries, where the home office and financial centre of the multinational corporation are located, can tax the profits of the corporation as a whole as well as the high incomes of its management. Government in the metropolis can, therefore, capture some of the surplus generated by the multinational corporations and use it to further improve their infrastructure and growth.

In other words, the relationship between multinational corporations and underdeveloped countries will be somewhat like the relationship between the national corporations in the United States and state and municipal governments. These lower-level governments tend always to be short of funds compared to the federal government which can tax a corporation as a whole. Their competition to attract corporate investment eats up their surplus, and they find it difficult to finance extensive investments in human and physical capital even where such investment would be productive. This has a crucial effect on the pattern of government expenditure. For example, suppose taxes were first paid to state government and then passed on to the federal government. What chance is there that these lower-level legislatures would approve the phenomenal expenditure on space research that now goes on? A similar discrepancy can be expected in the international economy with overspending and waste by metropolitan governments and a shortage of public funds in the less advanced countries.

The tendency of the multinational corporations to erode the power of the nation state works in a variety of ways, in addition to its effect on taxation powers. In general, most governmental policy instruments (monetary policy, fiscal policy, wage policy, etc.) diminish in effectiveness the more open the economy and the greater the extent of foreign investments. This tendency applies to political instruments as well as economic, for the multinational corporation is a medium by which laws, politics, foreign policy and culture of one country intrude into another. This acts to reduce the sovereignty of all nation states, but again the relationship is asymmetrical, for the flow tends to be from the parent to the subsidiary, not vice versa. The United States can apply its anti-trust laws to foreign subsidiaries to stop them from 'trading with the enemy' even though such trade is not against the laws of the country in which the branch plant is located. However, it would be illegal for an underdeveloped country which disagreed with American foreign policy to hold a US firm hostage for acts of the parent. This is because legal rights are defined in terms of property-ownership, and the various subsidiaries of a multinational corporation are not 'partners in a multinational endeavour' but the property of the general office.

In conclusion, it seems that a regime of multinational corporations would offer underdeveloped countries neither national independence nor equality. It would tend instead to inhibit the attainment of these goals. It would turn the underdeveloped countries into branch-plant countries, not only with reference to their economic functions but throughout the whole gamut of social, political and cultural roles. The subsidiaries of multinational corporations are typically amongst the largest corporations in the country of operations, and their top executives play an influential role in the political, social and cultural life of the host country. Yet these people, whatever their title, occupy at best a medium position in the corporate structure and are restricted in authority and horizons to a lower level of decision making. The governments with whom they deal tend to take on the same middle management outlook, since this is the only range of information and ideas to which they are exposed. In this sense, one can hardly expect such a country to bring forth the creative imagination needed to apply science and technology to the problems of degrading poverty. [. . .]

The Political Economy of the Multinational Corporation

The viability of the multinational corporate system depends upon the degree to which people will tolerate the unevenness it creates. It is well to remember that the 'New Imperialism' which began after 1870 in a spirit of Capitalism Triumphant, soon became seriously troubled and after 1914 was characterized by war, depression, breakdown of the international economic system and war again, rather than Free Trade, Pax Britannica and Material Improvement.

A major, if not the major, reason was Great Britain's inability to cope with the byproducts of its own rapid accumulation of capital; i.e. a class-conscious labour force at home; a middle class in the hinterland; and rival centres of capital on the Continent and in America. Britain's policy tended to be atavistic and defensive rather than progressive, more concerned with warding off new threats than creating new areas of expansion. Ironically, Edwardian England revived the paraphernalia of the landed aristocracy it had just destroyed. Instead of embarking on a 'big push' to develop the vast hinterland of the Empire, colonial administrators often adopted policies to slow down rates of growth and arrest the development of either a native capitalist class or a native proletariat which could overthrow them.

As time went on, the centre had to devote an increasing share of government activity to military and other unproductive expenditures; they had to rely on alliances with an inefficient class of landlords, officials and soldiers in the hinterland to maintain stability at the cost of development. A great part of the surplus extracted from the population was thus wasted locally.

The new Mercantilism (as the Multinational Corporate System of special alliances and privileges, aid and tariff concessions is sometimes called) faces similar problems of internal and external division. The centre is troubled: excluded groups revolt and even some of the affluent are dissatisfied with the roles. (The much talked about 'generation gap' may indicate the failure of the system to reproduce itself.) Nationalistic rivalry between major capitalist countries (especially the challenge of Japan and Germany) remains an important divisive factor, while the economic challenge from the socialist bloc may prove to be of the utmost significance in the next thirty years. Russia has its own form of large-scale economic organizations, also in command of modern technology, and its own conception of how the world should develop. So does China to an increasing degree. Finally, there is the threat presented by the middle classes and the excluded groups of the underdeveloped countries.

The national middle classes in the underdeveloped countries came to power when the centre weakened but could not, through their policy of import substitution manufacturing, establish a viable basis for sustained growth. They now face a foreign exchange crisis and an unemployment (or population) crisis – the first indicating their inability to function in the international economy, and the second indicating their alienation from the people they are supposed to lead. In the immediate future, these national middle classes will gain a new lease on life as they take advantage of the spaces created by the rivalry between American and non-American oligopolists striving to establish global market positions. The native capitalists will again become the champions of national independence as they bargain with multinational corporations. But the conflict at this level is more apparent than real, for in the end the fervent nationalism of the middle class asks only for promotion within the corporate structure and not for a break with that structure. In the last analysis their power derives from the metropolis and they cannot easily afford to challenge the international system. They do not command the loyalty of their own population and cannot really compete with the large, powerful, aggregate capitals from the centre. They are prisoners of the taste patterns and consumption standards set at the centre, and depend on outsiders for technical advice, capital and, when necessary, for military support of their position.

The main threat comes from the excluded groups. It is not unusual in underdeveloped countries for the top 5 per cent to obtain between 30 and 40 per cent of the total national income, and for the top one-third to obtain anywhere from 60 to 70 per cent. At most, one-third of the population can be said to benefit in some sense from the dualistic growth that characterizes development in the hinterland. The remaining two-thirds, who together get only one-third of the income, are outsiders, not because they do not contribute to the economy, but because they do not share in the benefits. They provide a source of cheap labour which helps keep exports to the developed world at a low price and which has financed the urban-biased growth of recent years. Because their wages are low, they spend a moderate amount of time in menial services and are sometimes referred to as underemployed as if to imply they were not needed. In fact, it is difficult to see how the system of most underdeveloped countries could survive without cheap labour since removing it (e.g. diverting it to public works projects as is done in socialist countries) would raise consumption costs to capitalists and professional elites. Economic development under the multinational corporation does not offer much promise for this large segment of society and their antagonism continuously threatens the system.

The survival of the multinational corporate system depends on how fast it can grow and how much trickles down. Plans now being formulated in government offices, corporate headquarters and international organizations sometimes suggest that a growth rate of about 6 per cent per year in national income (3 per cent *per capita*) is needed. (Such a target is, of course, far below what would be possible if a serious effort were made to solve basic problems of health, education and clothing.) To what extent is it possible?

The multinational corporation must solve four critical problems for the underdeveloped countries, if it is to foster the continued growth and survival of a 'modern' sector. First, it must break the foreign-exchange constraint and provide the underdeveloped countries with imported goods for capital formation and modernization. Second, it must finance an expanded programme of government expenditure to train labour and provide support services for urbanization and industrialization. Third, it must solve the urban food problem created by growth. Finally, it must keep the excluded two-thirds of the population under control.

The solution now being suggested for the first is to restructure the world economy allowing the periphery to export certain manufactured goods to the centre. Part of this programme involves regional common markets to rationalize the existing structure of industry. These plans typically do not involve the rationalization and restructuring of the entire economy of the underdeveloped countries but mainly serve the small manufacturing sector which caters to higher-income groups and which, therefore, faces a very limited market in any particular country. The solution suggested for the second problem is an expanded aid programme and a reformed government bureaucracy (perhaps along the lines of the Alliance for Progress). The solution for the third is agribusiness and the green revolution, a programme with only limited benefits to the rural poor. Finally, the solution offered for the fourth problem is population control, either through family planning or counter-insurgency.

It is doubtful whether the centre has sufficient political stability to finance and organize the programme outlined above. It is not clear, for example, that the West has the technology to rationalize manufacturing abroad or modernize agriculture, or the willingness to open up marketing channels for the underdeveloped world. Nor is it evident that the centre has the political power to embark on a large aid programme or to readjust its own structure of production and allow for the importation of manufactured goods from the periphery. It is difficult to imagine labour accepting such a re-allocation (a new repeal of the Corn Laws as it were), and it is equally hard to see how the advanced countries could create a system of planning to make these extra hardships unnecessary.

The present crisis may well be more profound than most of us imagine, and the West may find it impossible to restructure the international economy on a workable basis. One could easily argue that the age of the multinational corporation is at its end rather than at its beginning. For all we know, books on the global partnership may be the epitaph of the American attempt to take over the old international economy, and not the herald of a new era of international cooperation.

Conclusion

The multinational corporation, because of its great power to plan economic activity, represents an important step forward over previous methods of organizing international exchange. It demonstrates the social nature of production on a global scale. As it eliminates the anarchy of international markets and brings about a more extensive and productive international division of labour, it releases great sources of latent energy.

However, as it crosses international boundaries, it pulls and tears at the social and political fabric and erodes the cohesiveness of national states. Whether one likes this or not, it is probably a tendency that cannot be stopped.

Through its propensity to nestle everywhere, settle everywhere, and establish connections everywhere, the multinational corporation destroys the possibility of national seclusion and self-sufficiency and creates a universal interdependence. But the multinational corporation is still a private institution with a partial outlook and represents only an imperfect solution to the problem of international cooperation. It creates hierarchy rather than equality, and it spreads its benefits unequally.

In proportion to its success, it creates tensions and difficulties. It will lead other institutions, particularly labour organizations and government, to take an international outlook and thus unwittingly create an environment less favourable to its own survival. It will demonstrate the possibilities of material progress at a faster rate than it can realize them, and will create a world-wide demand for change that it cannot satisfy.

The next round may be marked by great crises due to the conflict between national planning by governments and international planning by corporations. For example, if each country loses its power over fiscal and monetary policy due to the growth of multinational corporations (as some observers believe Canada has), how will aggregate demand be stabilized? Will it be possible to construct super-states? Or does multinationalism do away with Keynesian problems? Similarly, will it be possible to fulfill a host of other government functions at the supranational level in the near future? During the past twenty-five years many political problems were put aside as the West recovered from the depression and the war. By the late sixties the bloom of this long upswing had begun to fade. In the seventies, power conflicts are likely to come to the fore.

Whether underdeveloped countries will use the opportunities arising from this crisis to build viable local decision-making institutions is difficult to predict. The national middle class failed when it had the opportunity and instead merely reproduced internally the economic dualism of the international economy as it squeezed agriculture to finance urban industry. What is needed is a complete change of direction. The starting point must be the needs of the bottom two-thirds, and not the demands of the top third. The primary goal of such a strategy would be to provide minimum standards of health, education, food and clothing to the entire population, removing the most obvious forms of human suffering. This requires a system which can mobilize the entire population and which can search the local environment for information, resources and needs. It must be able to absorb modern technology, but it cannot be mesmerized by the form it takes in the advanced countries; it must go to the roots. This is not the path the upper one-third chooses when it has control.

The wealth of a nation, wrote Adam Smith two hundred years ago, is determined by 'first, the skill, dexterity and judgement with which labour is generally applied; and, secondly by the proportion between the number of those who are employed in useful labour, and that of those who are not so employed'.[3] Capitalist enterprise has come a long way from this day, but it has never been able to bring more than a small fraction of the world's population into useful or highly productive employment. The latest stage reveals once more the power of social cooperation and division of labour which so fascinated Adam Smith in his description of pin-manufacturing. It also shows the shortcomings of concentrating this power in private hands.

Notes

1. A.D. Chandler and F. Redlich, 'Recent Developments in American Business Administration and their Conceptualization', *Business History Review* (Spring 1961).
2. L.A. Fallers, 'A Note on the Trickle Effect', in P. Bliss (ed.), *Marketing and the Behavioral Sciences* (Allyn and Bacon, 1963).
3. A. Smith, *The Wealth of Nations* (The Modern Library, New York, 1937 edn).

MILITARISM: FORCE, CLASS AND INTERNATIONAL CONFLICT

Robin Luckham

Source: M. Kaldor and A. Eide, *The World Military Order* (Macmillan, London, 1979), pp. 243-55.

Luckham analyzes the role of the military in developing societies in terms of its relationship to the requirements of international capital and dependent capitalist development. He compares the different 'class projects' undertaken by the military in specific circumstances, and assesses their relationship to external intervention and internal contradictions.

There is no more eloquent testimony to the internationalism of the relations of domination than the uniformity of certain characteristics of professional armies: the hierarchy of ranks, the exclusiveness of the military brotherhood, the emphasis on rituals and emblems of rank, the codes of honour, the class distinctions between officers and other ranks. Part of this can be accounted for by the fact that a small number of models — basically British, French, German and American — have been consciously transplanted in the third world. But where other transplants like the ill-fated 'Westminster model' of parliamentary democracy did not take root, military organisations flourished. Organised force is essential for the reproduction of modern nation-states, voting is not.

Nevertheless armies are seldom monolithic institutions on which members of ruling classes can always rely. The use of military force to repress opponents of the regime or to settle struggles for political power often moves the conflict into the armed forces themselves, accentuating their internal contradictions and precipitating coups, mutinies and power struggles.

The majority of the countries of Africa, Asia, the Middle East and Latin America are under military rule. Still more of them have experienced military intervention or periods of military rule at some point or other during the past 30 years. And if one adopts broader criteria there are scarcely any where organised military force has *not* been used to keep in office or to change the regime or ruling class during the past three decades.

Against this background most of the things social scientists have to say seem exceedingly banal. Much of the existing literature takes as its starting point the problem of assuring 'civilian control' over the military establishment: which can be looked at over a whole continuum of military participation in politics, ranging from gentlemanly bargaining over strategy or appropriations, outright blackmail of the regime, participation in the reshuffling of ruling élites right through to direct military control of all the major political institutions of a society.

The absence of civilian control is only a 'problem', however, when contrasted with an idealised view of the relationship between soldiers and governments in the advanced bourgeois democracies. It is not an especially useful way of looking at the political institutions of Africa, Asia, the Middle East and Latin America, where military participation rather than civilian control might be viewed as the 'normal' state of affairs. Nor does the idea of a continuum from civilian to military take us very far. To be sure, the difference between a military establishment which intervenes as a 'moderating power' to resolve conflicts between civilian factions as in Brazil before 1964 and one which attempts permanently to substitute itself for parts of the state superstructure, to become the State as it were, as in the same country after 1967, is important. Yet to view this as just a change from less to more military participation in political life is superficial, for the military's formal participation in politics is less important than the question of how far the state superstructure is or is not held together by organised coercion. To what extent do those who control that superstructure rely on repressive rather than ideological mechanisms to establish their hegemony?

The distinction between civilian and military regimes may well be less important than the similarities in the way they govern. Take a country like the Philippines where, under a civilian regime, civil liberties have been curtailed, the media browbeaten, trade unions deprived of the right to strike, opponents of the regime repressed. There is intensive surveillance by the police and military intelligence networks, internal warfare is waged against dissident Moslem minority groups, the military is frequently consulted about major government decisions, martial law is in operation and political offences are tried before military rather than civilian tribunals.

[. . .] Coups and military regimes are, to be sure, the prevailing trend in the third world, and this is hardly surprising. For when organised coercion is the main basis of state power, coups are to be expected merely because more 'democratic' methods of transferring power between different factions of the ruling classes cease to operate. But struggles to gain or to remain in power can also be waged by assassination, mob violence, surveillance and terror by the secret police, bribery and the skilful dispensation of political patronage. Frequent coups *may* betoken instability in the framework of the state — but not necessarily more so than votes of no confidence, reshufflings of cabinets and frequent elections in bourgeois democracies. Like the latter they speed the circulation of élites and the realignment of factions of the ruling classes more often than they bring about fundamental change in the organisation of state power and its allocation between (rather than within) social classes.

In Karl Marx's classic analysis of Bonapartism it was recognised that in periods of acute crisis or of historical transition between modes of production members of the ruling class would often be prepared to accept authoritarian government by a state machine over which it had relatively little direct control: the bourgeoisie would sometimes sacrifice its own class rule in order to secure the political stability on which the smooth functioning of a capitalist economy and its own class interests depend.[1]

Bonapartism, however, is not a magical category into which the analysis of the military can be hammered. The historical circumstances of the present-day third world bring together a different combination of elements from that which prevailed in nineteenth-century France. The crisis of hegemony suffered by ruling classes is permanent and endemic rather than temporary and exceptional. Uneven development superimposes all the contradictions between centre and periphery, capitalist and pre-capitalist social formations, class and tribe, region, religion and nation: and makes it all the more difficult for any single ruling class or fraction thereof to establish its ideological claims to rule.

Add to this the effects of a colonial situation in which an alien ruling class had to rely on state repression to secure its domination. And a process of decolonisation from which there emerged a disjuncture between the national ruling class on the one hand and the economically dominant class with its commanding heights in the boardrooms of international firms on the other. This gives the crisis of hegemony a peculiar neocolonial twist. For it has retarded the formation of homegrown bourgeoisies and made it more difficult for the latter to function as effective ruling classes able through their policies to exert control over the national economy. But at the same time it creates a problem for the representatives of international capital who have to find ways of influencing policy and the political structure in peripheral countries, despite their inability to act directly as a faction of the ruling class.

On the face of it the military seems to meet the political requirements of international capital under these troubled circumstances almost better than any other institution. A powerful, relatively autonomous state-apparatus — buttressed by military coercion — provides a framework of stability and predictability within which it is relatively easy for multinational capital to operate. Further, the fact that the military usually depends for its weapons purchases on international purchasing power earned in the world market and appropriated through the state tends to cement the alliance with international capital. In the same measure that external penetration weakens the class structure, it increases — through arms supplies, military assistance, and political support — the military establishment's size, claims on productive resources and autonomy relative to other fractions of the ruling class.

Yet to postulate in these general terms that the military appears to fit the political requirements of international capital — stability and a solution to the problems created by international capital's inability to act directly as a ruling class — does not mean that in any given country it will in fact carry out these functions; or do so in a uniform way from one country to another. To begin with, the military and military regimes are hardly ever in a simple sense the political servants of international capital or of great power governments. It would be quite grotesque to label Colonel Gadaffy of Libya, Lt. Colonel Mengistu of Ethiopia, the members of the Peruvian junta or indeed General Idi Amin as the agents of imperialism. Even the most reactionary Latin American regimes have a degree of autonomy: witness for example the edifying spectacle of the governments of Argentina, Brazil, Chile, El Salvador and Uruguay threatening to turn elsewhere for arms and military assistance if President Carter continues to cut back aid to countries with a record of violation of human rights.

Indeed, the military's *own* institutional and material interests lie in the direction of a strong nation-state with control over the surpluses generated in the national economy. This determines the *class project* carried out by the military in two main ways. First, through the compact established between the state and international capital in which the military has a direct interest as a state institution and an indirect interest through its linkages with the international arms economy. Second, through the role of organised force in resolving — or rather in repressing the symptoms of — the crises generated under different conditions of dependent capitalist development.

Accordingly, in Table 1 an attempt is made to show how different patterns of incorporation in the world economy shape the varying class projects of the military establishment. The first two patterns set forth in the table arise in economies which are based on the production of raw materials for the world market, though it makes a considerable difference whether these are produced (like many agricultural commodities) by

Table 1: Variations in Military's Class Projects in Dependent Capitalist Countries

Structure of Economy	Nature of State Project	Nature of Crises	Nature of Military Project
1. *Petty capitalist commodity production* Agricultural and natural resource based commodities produced for export and/or local sale by indigenous producers under petty capitalist or pre-capitalist relations of production. Examples: most countries of sub-Saharan Africa, Bangladesh.	1. Minimum conditions of law and order. 2. Mediation between petty producers and world market, either (i) via foreign merchant capital, or (ii) directly via state marketing monopolies. 3. Extraction of surplus from export-import trade and conversion into (i) increases in size, power and military spending of state apparatus or (ii) industrialisation programmes.	1. Political crises brought on by reinvigoration of pre-capitalist formations and loyalties (tribe, religion, languages, region etc.) in response to competition for state power, jobs, economic resources and benefits. 2. Instability induced by fluctuations in commodity prices in world market, undermining regimes and their long-term economic plans.	1. (a) Holding fragile nation-state together and/or (b) using state machinery to establish hegemony of the particular tribal, religious, linguistic or regional groups who happen to control the military hierarchy. 2. Intervention to secure changes of regime in response to externally induced economic and political crises. 3. Reinforcement (through arms purchases) of pressure to earn foreign exchange in world market or to save it by engaging in import-substituting industrialisation.
2. *Enclave commodity production* Agricultural commodities produced or natural resources extracted on large scale (a) by international capital or (b) by state capital incorporated in circuits of international capital through export of commodities and imports of technology. Examples: most oil-producing	1. Minimum conditions of law and order. 2. Mediation between capital and labour in enclave enterprises, ensuring stability and quiescence of labour, in the last resort by physical repression. 3. Either (a) State is directly coopted by foreign capital and serves its interests (e.g. Gabon, Central American banana republics)	1. Conflicts between central regions/groups/towns sharing the benefits of economic activity and employment created by enclave and peripheral regions/groups/ rural areas. 2. Conflicts between capital and labour in enclave. 3. (a) Instability induced by fluctuations in commodity prices in world market, undermining	1. Establishment of physical control by centre over peripheral regions. 2. Intervention in conflicts between foreign or state capital and labour. 3. (a) Direct physical repression on behalf of foreign capital, particularly in times of economic and political crisis (e.g. Chile) or (b) intervention against foreign

(OPEC) countries and copper-producing (CIPEC) countries.

regimes and their long-term plans, precipitating conflict between states and foreign capitalists *except* (b) when associations of producers (especially OPEC) exercise monopoly control in world market, minimising direct effect of externally induced crises on state machinery.

capital on behalf of nationalist capital to assure state control over natural resources (or support for such interventions by other groups or governments).
4. Reinforcement (through arms purchases) of pressures to maximise natural resource rents and to participate in international arms economy.

3. *Import-substituting industrialisation*
Development of industrial base through either (a) foreign investment or (b) state investment or both, replacing goods previously imported.

Examples: Brazil, Mexico, Argentina, Philippines and (combined with 2, above) Indonesia, Iran, Venezuela, Chile and Nigeria.

1. Maintenance of political stability to assure smooth process of industrialisation and to prevent flight of foreign capital.
2. Mediation between capital and labour; repression of latter to subsidise investment by the former.
3. State promotion of industrialisation, bringing about symbiosis of state, local and international capital. Variations in extent of penetration by international capital, in the mechanisms (e.g. direct investment versus sales of technology) by which it is achieved and in extent of state control over the process.

1. Conflicts between industrial/urban centres and rural/agricultural peripheries, intensified to extent that the latter subsidise process of industrialisation.
2. Conflicts between capital and labour in industrial sector, intensified to extent that profits and investment subsidised by low wages.
3. Marginalisation, creation of 'reserve army of unemployed' by industrialisation/urbanisation processes.
4. Crises created by exhaustion of process of import-substitution.
Cycle of foreign exchange shortages, inflation, unrest, repression, military

1. Establishment of physical control by centre over periphery. Repression of peasant movements, rural guerrillas etc.
2. Intervention in conflict between foreign or state capital and labour, usually to repress the latter on behalf of the former, but not always (e.g. the Peronist alliance between the military and unions in Argentina).
3. Establishment of physical 'security' in restive urban areas. Repression of crime, squatters, demonstrations, urban guerrillas etc.
4. Reinforcement (through arms purchases and sometimes arms

Table 1: Variations in Military's Class Projects in Dependent Capitalist Countries—*continued*

Structure of Economy	Nature of State Project	Nature of Crises	Nature of Military Project
		spending and more shortages, inflation, etc.	manufacture) of import-substitution and of the crises induced by it.
4. *Export-promoting industrialisation* Examples: South Korea, Taiwan, Singapore and (combined with 3, above) Philippines.	As above except foreign capital (a) more footloose because not tied to domestic resources or markets (b) tends to an even greater extent to be vertically integrated production and markets in central countries. For these reasons (a) political stability (and organised physical repression) are even more vital, and (b) the bargaining power of the State is weaker relative to that of international capital.	As above except (a) low wages often essential to attract foreign capital and hence greater repression of labour force (b) vulnerability to crises in international markets for manufactures rather than to constraints of narrowness of domestic market.	As above, except military involved to an even greater extent in establishment of physical security (particularly in urban centres), repression and counter-revolution.

numerous indigenous petty producers; or are extracted (like most minerals) through large investments of foreign capital. The third and fourth patterns are determined by the nature of a country's process of industrialisation — whether by import-substitution or by the export of cheap manufactures produced by low-cost labour.

Armies and military regimes are seldom *directly* subservient to foreign capital. Even in countries whose economies are based on primary products extracted and sold abroad by foreign corporations, they often take up natural resource ideologies, and favour state expropriation of foreign capital to the extent this can be achieved (as by the oil producers) without serious damage to the economy's international earning power. In industrialising countries the same factors incline the military towards state investment and regulation of the economy. Such regulation need not interfere with the compact established with international capital and may indeed create a new, more organic symbiosis between the state and multinational corporations. Even when the major means of production are no longer in foreign hands militarism and state capitalism together may still reinforce the integration of the national economy and its class structure in the circuits of the international economy: because foreign exchange still has to be earned to pay for armaments, technology and the expansion of the state and military bureaucracy.

Few countries fit fair and square into any one of the categories in the table. Indeed, the military often plays a critical role in the transition from one pattern to another. The crisis which led first to the rise to power of the Allende regime in Chile and then to its overthrow by the soldiers in 1973 was, for example, brought on by the exhaustion of the process of import-substitution and the international forces set in motion by the government's expropriation of the foreign copper monopolies. In response to these external forces the military government has adopted economic policies — economic liberalisation, sale of state enterprises, the curtailment of import-substitution, withdrawal from the Andean Pact — which virtually amount to a reassertion of its traditional position in the international division of labour as a raw material producer.

Further, it is not necessary to assume that the class project the military finally takes up is necessarily agreed in advance or even understood by the officer corps, still less their men, nor that it will be stable. Periods of crisis bring major shifts in the way the military interposes itself in class conflict, which are usually accompanied by violent internal struggles. The social origins of the soldiers who win such struggles, their civilian allies and their original intentions will have some influence on the class project the military undertakes, but may be distorted by the circumstances with which they have to cope once they take power. Examples are not difficult to find: the Nigerian army intervened to establish national unity in 1966 but broke up into tribal and regional factions six months later; the Chilean military seized power with the active support of the national bourgeoisie in order to halt what was perceived as a process of national disintegration, and ended up restoring the dominance of foreign monopoly capital; the soldiers who took power in Brazil in 1964 quickly dropped their programme of economic and political liberalisation in favour of state-sponsored industrialisation under an authoritarian regime.

Although the crises of dependent capitalist development provoke military repression, this repression does not necessarily establish political order. Sometimes the military's weapons have simply turned conflict into more bloody conflict: witness, for example, the effects of military violence in Uruguay, in Bangladesh just before its war of liberation from Pakistan or indeed in Northern Ireland. Or the military itself has become deeply divided – as in Nigeria and the Lebanon before and during their respective civil wars – and thus unable to stand above the conflict. Nevertheless the fact that military force settles things in the last resort is critical, particularly in societies in permanent crisis, where the last resort is always close at hand.

Nor can one automatically assume that the military will intervene in these crises as the compliant ally of the dominant classes. Its internal fissures, as we have already seen, may create radical as well as reactionary tendencies both in the officer corps and among ordinary soldiers. On a number of occasions the military establishment has sided with the periphery against the centre – as in some African states where the recruitment base of the army has traditionally been in the less developed parts of the country – or with labour in its struggles with capital – as in the alliance between sections of the army and organised labour in Peronist Argentina in the 1940s.

Yet although particular factions of the military élite may intervene on behalf of peripheral or excluded classes and groups in times of crisis, the military establishment *as a whole* has a vested interest in what military ideologists call 'national security' and what its opponents call state and class domination. The natural response of professional soldiers is to suppress class struggle when it appears because it divides the nation, undermines the international economic standing of the economy – causing flights of foreign capital – and imposes certain real costs – casualties, disruption of routine, threats to its structure and its monopoly of organised force – upon the military establishment itself.

Let us turn, therefore, to the interrelation between the international system and armed force. This can be analysed at a number of levels.

In the first place a world in which conflict is endemic and force governs the relations between nation-states enhances the influence of military organisations. More than 30 years ago Harold Lasswell suggested that growing international conflict would increasingly turn the world powers into 'garrison states' in which the influence of military managers of violence would predominate:[2] though he omitted to say that this conflict can sometimes itself be the consequence of the influence of these military managers in whose interests it is to exaggerate threats to security.

International insecurity contributes equally to military influence at the periphery. The armed forces are large and influential in most countries at the edge of the Cold War, like Greece, Turkey, Iran, Thailand and South Korea; and also in countries at the nodes of regional conflict as in the Middle East and the Horn of Africa. Military coups have frequently swept aside civilian governments which have failed (in the soldiers' view) to provide adequately for their country's security: for example the over-throw of the Egyptian monarchy by the Free Officers after humiliating defeats suffered at the hands of Israel; or the 1969 coup in Somalia which swept aside a civilian government which had pursued the border conflict with Ethiopia with less enthusiasm than the soldiers desired. Soldiers are also quick to react to the international aspects of internal struggles. For example the contagion effects between military coups, such as those which swept through west and central Africa in 1965-6. Or the spread of military garrison states in Latin America in the 1960s and 1970s; responding on the one hand to the establishment of socialism in Cuba and the spread of revolutionary movements across national boundaries; and on the other to the trans-nationalisation of American counter-insurgency training and doctrine.

As with military intervention in the internal politics of a country, so too there is a whole continuum of external intervention: from diplomatic pressure, economic aid and military assistance programmes; various forms of blackmail such as threats to withdraw economic and military assistance; covert subversion and the destabilisation of regimes in the style of the CIA or KGB; reassurance of recognition and support to coup-makers if successful; actual material support for a coup, or alternatively support in putting one down; military assistance and advice in counter-revolutionary operations; taking direct part in such operations (the US in the early stages of the Vietnam conflict); direct participation in a revolutionary war (the Chinese in Korea or the Cubans in Angola); through to actual invasion by troops in the intervening power (the US in the Dominican Republic and in Vietnam, or France and Britain in the Suez crisis).

Yet one cannot measure the effect of external pressures on the military, the class structure or the political system as a whole solely by the level to which overt foreign interference has *actually* been pushed. In some countries, like Chile, intervention may have taken place precisely because the contradictions are sharper than elsewhere and the hegemony of imperialist powers less secure. In others the class structure and internal political forces may be self-sustaining and direct intervention unnecessary. The arms trade and discreet military assistance programmes are often all that is required to keep the professional military establishment in operation and the stability of the political system within tolerable limits. And in others again, like Iran, Indonesia or Zaire, external penetration may be massive but multi-faceted, so that to take one aspect alone such as support for a coup, covert CIA activities, foreign aid and investment, military assistance, or diplomatic pressure, may give an incomplete picture of foreign influence because all are important together.

Conversely, however, direct intervention has sometimes created more contradictions than those it represses. The Suez crisis, the American intervention in Vietnam and the South African invasion of Angola are perhaps the most glaring examples, but there are several others. Failure to examine abortive as well as successful interventions might lead one to underestimate the *limits* imperialism faces, the contradictions it creates for itself and the strength of the forces opposed to it on the periphery. These limits arise at a number of different levels.

First, the strength and disposition of anti-imperialist forces themselves: in Vietnam for example, the military effectiveness of the liberation armies and the presence of the Russian nuclear deterrent to discourage escalation of the conflict by the Americans; in Angola the extremely prompt and effective assistance provided by the Cubans and Russians and the reluctance of the USA to risk a diplomatic showdown in Africa by openly intervening.

Second, differences among the major Western powers, as during the Suez crisis, when the disapproval of the Americans and their refusal to support British borrowing from the IMF to halt the run on the pound caused by the crisis, brought the Anglo-French invasion of Egypt to a grinding halt.

Third, the internal contradictions by which imperialist powers are sometimes weakened: the bitter opposition to the Suez invasion by the Labour party; or the economic burden of arms spending by the US government in Vietnam and the gathering strength of the anti-war movement. There are strong pressures impelling the major capitalist powers to intervene in their interests at the periphery. But it would be a mistake to regard them as monolithic and to underestimate the constraints according to which they operate.

Intervention, furthermore, is not exclusive to capitalist powers but has also been an integral part of the struggle against them. External support has been a crucial element in most contemporary revolutions: Russian support (however grudging) for the Chinese revolution; Russian and Chinese assistance in Vietnam; Arab and communist bloc help to the Algerians in their war of national liberation from France; the assistance of the Russians and Chinese and of neighbouring African countries to the armed struggle in Guinea-Bissau, Angola and Mozambique.

Nevertheless such assistance is not without its own contradictions. External aid cannot overcome unfavourable objective conditions; witness, for example, the failure of Che Guevara to bring revolution to Bolivia. It all too easily triggers off nationalist responses and accusations of 'social imperialism' against the donor: visible already, for instance, in the ambivalence of the Angolans about the continued presence in their country of their Cuban and Russian liberators. Recipients of socialist assistance — however worthy according to revolutionary criteria — are vulnerable to changes in the interests of the donors. The revolutions in Laos and Cambodia were delayed because the Vietnamese gave and withdrew assistance in accordance with the progress of their own struggle. Socialist rivalries — for example Chinese support for the FNLA and Cuban and Soviet for the MPLA in Angola — have sometimes helped to create divisions in liberation movements.

In a very real sense the intervention of socialist countries is also limited and shaped by the constraints of balance-of-power politics. In several Latin American countries the Moscow-controlled communist parties have been ambivalent towards armed struggle: fluctuating between support for insurrection and for more 'legitimate' activity in accord with the turns and swings of international politics. The support of socialist countries for the revolutions in former Portuguese Africa was covert and limited in quantity until the international political conjuncture became favourable to larger-scale involvement after the invasion of Angola by South Africa.

Despite the expansion of capital on a world scale there is little semblance of an international superstructure, comparable to the national state. There are instead only *partial* international superstructures: some based on region (the EEC, ASEAN etc); some constituting military alliances between states (NATO, the Warsaw Pact and the moribund SEATO and CENTO); and some with specialised functions (the UN agencies, IMF, World Bank etc). These do relatively little to bind the world system together. Indeed military alliances and regional pacts on the whole deepen the main fractures between blocs. Rather than superstructure it might be more apposite to talk of a 'superstruggle': but for the integrating mechanisms both of the international economy, which incorporates enterprises and states alike in the circuit of capital, and of balance-of-power politics which (at least for the time being) prevents the war of all against all.

Although most statesmen and military leaders subscribe to the concept of a balance of power — and thus make it take on the character of self-fulfilling prophecy — it is thoroughly ambiguous. The nature of the nuclear means of mass destruction on which the balance between the central world powers is based is such that balances computed merely in terms of the numbers of missiles, aircraft and nuclear warheads available to each side make little sense. Further, the very ability to participate depends on a very advanced technology and industrial base. The balance thus expresses the competing interests of the ruling classes of advanced industrial countries and the clientage of those of the third world.

Furthermore, a balance between societies with diverse modes of production is by no means a balance of equivalents. For its equilibrium is constantly disturbed by the contradictory pressures of capitalist and of socialist expansion towards the periphery. Such an international system does not even succeed in providing a political basis for the orderly expansion of capital on an international level; the tools of international economic management having proved woefully inadequate to deal with the current international economic crisis. Balance-of-power politics provides only temporary and largely inadequate solutions to the international pressures which beset the third world. Typically, it is devoted to stabilising the *existing* situation without getting to grips with the substantive issues, the very real contradictions which underlie conflicts such as the Middle East crisis or the wars of national liberation in Southern Africa.

The very severity of the present international crisis in some ways, however, provides favourable opportunities for the modification or destruction of existing relations of international domination: a nuclear stalemate in which great powers can be played off against each other; internal dissent within the large capitalist powers which makes it more difficult for their governments to pursue expansionist foreign policies; economic crisis which fuels this discontent inside capitalist countries, and, further, makes it difficult for them to finance external military ventures or to subsidise arms sales in order to gain political influence. The same crisis is also bringing things to a head in the periphery, concentrating economic grievances and mobilising popular forces (but also increasing the repression by dominant classes).

To the extent that attempts to stabilise the existing pattern of international arrangements merely buy time, in which lines of conflict harden and the international production and diffusion of destructive weapons continues, they may actually increase the ultimate danger. Weapons and military organisations — the means of force — are in the international domain, in that their deployment and/or use is a matter of common danger and common social concern for all mankind. Yet they are still appropriated and controlled by national ruling classes which use or threaten to use them to reproduce their national power and international interests. This makes social control over their use and conditions of lasting peace almost impossible to bring about without major transformation in the structures of international production, power and force. But the risks of the struggle to bring about such transformation impose heavy responsibilities on those who undertake it.

Notes

1. Karl Marx, 'The Eighteenth Brumaire of Louis Bonaparte', in Karl Marx and Frederick Engels, *Selected Works* (Foreign Languages Publishing House, Moscow, 1958), vol. 1, pp. 243-344.

2. Harold Lasswell, 'The garrison State', *American Journal of Sociology*, XLVI (January 1941).

3.8

TECHNOLOGICAL DEPENDENCE

Frances Stewart

Source: *Technology and Underdevelopment*, 2nd edn (Macmillan, London, 1978), pp. 123-40.

Stewart examines the undesirable consequences incurred by developing countries as a result of technological dependence on developed countries. She argues that these costs cannot be effectively reduced by autarky, but only by greater exchange amongst the third world countries themselves.

The undesirable consequences of technological dependence may usefully be classified into four categories:

(i)   cost;
(ii) loss of control over decisions;
(iii) unsuitable characteristics of the technology received;
(iv) lack of effective indigenous scientific and innovative capacity, which is itself a symptom of underdevelopment.

The four categories are interrelated, affecting and reinforcing each other. Each has consequences for the extent and pattern of development.

(i)   Cost

[. . .] The heavy costs of technology transfer for third world countries are in large part due to their situation of technological dependence. In the first place, it is technological dependence that leads to the necessity for the net import of technology and the consequent net payments. Secondly, the situation of technological dependence is responsible for the very weak bargaining position of many developing countries *vis-à-vis* technology suppliers, and consequently for the poor terms exacted.

In the market for technology, bargaining power is of key importance in determining the terms of transfer. This is because the market for technology is, of its nature, imperfect. In a perfect market, competition would reduce the cost of acquiring technology to its marginal cost. But once the technology has been developed, the marginal cost is very low, sometimes approaching zero. The system of commercialisation of technology, consisting of legalised monopolistic practices, like the patent system, product differentiation and trademarks, has permitted the monopolisation or oligopolisation of the market for technology and hence the sale of technology at a price far in excess of its marginal cost.

Commercialisation has thus established a system whereby sellers of technology are able to exact a price in excess of the cost of its communication to buyers. The exact price depends on the maximum the buyers are prepared to pay for the technology, the minimum at which the sellers are prepared to sell it, and the bargaining strength of buyers and sellers.

The maximum price the buyers are prepared to pay depends on their estimation of the value of the technology, and the cost of alternative ways of acquiring the technology, including buying it from other sources or developing it themselves. Their estimates of these are often uncertain — particularly since it is the essence of buying technology that one does not know exactly what one is buying. Estimates are likely to be weaker, and more susceptible to sellers' influence, the weaker the country is technologically. This is one reason why technological dependence tends to lead to a bad bargain. The minimum price the seller is prepared to accept depends on the actual costs of imparting the information and the monetary loss he would incur by imparting it. The latter, which is normally of much greater importance than the costs of communication, consists in the loss in revenue consequent on the dilution of his monopoly power as a result of parting with the technology, and also the potential loss of revenue on sales of the same technology elsewhere in the world, which may result from reducing his price in any particular case. There is a sort of spiral effect which the seller takes into account, as the terms of a technology bargain in one part of the world influence the terms the seller receives elsewhere, and this spiral effect helps determine the minimum price he is prepared to accept in a particular case.

Thus, although the actual cost to the seller of imparting his information may be very low, this may bear little relation to the minimum price he is prepared to accept, because he also takes into account his potential monetary loss from striking a poor bargain. Similarly, although the cost of developing the technology again may be very high, the buyer of the technology is rarely concerned with this price, but more often with whether it is worth acquiring the technology at all, and with alternative sources. None the less, there is often a wide gap between sellers' minimum and buyers' maximum prices, and this is where bargaining becomes important.

Technological dependence makes a high price likely. First, it may rule out the possibility of reproducing the technology oneself. Even where this is a possibility, and indeed even where local technology has already been developed — see section (iv), below — the market structure and the prejudice that favour the use of foreign technology, which stem from technological dependence, tend to lead to an exaggeration of the benefits of foreign technology, and an underestimation of local technical capacity. This raises the price the buyer is prepared to pay for the foreign technology. Secondly, technological dependence reduces technical knowledge on the buyer's side, severely limiting the ability to search for alternative sources, and the ability to estimate realistically the gains from acquiring the technology. Thirdly, it reduces bargaining power in the sense that the buyer has little or nothing to withhold which the seller wants. In trade in technology between advanced countries cross-licence agreements are widespread; such agreements temper the exploitation of monopoly power on the part of the sellers.

Countries differ in their local technical capacity and in their bargaining power *vis-à-vis* technology sellers. They may also differ as between different industries. But in general it remains likely that those countries which are weakest in their own technical capacity are also most technologically dependent, and in the worst position to strike a satisfactory bargain with technology sellers. Comparisons of the terms reached with different countries, at different stages of development, would be instructive in this respect.

The final price agreed on, for any individual technology contract, is likely to be the more unfavourable to the buyer the more widespread technological dependence is. This is because, on the demand side, the more widespread this technological dependence the fewer are likely to be the known alternative technologies. And also, because from the point of view of the seller of technology, the greater the technological dependence among developing countries, the greater the quasi-rents he receives from his technology, and therefore the greater his potential loss should he strike a 'poor' bargain with any individual country, since this might lead to poor bargains elsewhere. Hence, given any degree of technological dependence in a particular country, the price agreed on for technology contracts is likely to be the higher (with both the minimum supply price and the maximum demand price higher) the more prevalent technological dependence is among developing countries generally. Similarly, the cost of acquiring technology in any country is likely to be reduced by a reduction of technological dependence in the world as a whole. Thus, developing countries stand to gain from reduced dependence elsewhere. [. . .]

(ii)   Lack of Control

Economic independence has been defined as a 'situation in which national institutions (including private business and interest groups) have the right, capacity and power to take and implement decisions affecting the national economy and its component units without a *de jure* or *de facto* veto power being held by foreign individuals, enterprises, interest groups or governments'.[1] Economic interdependence between individuals, countries and enterprises is such that complete independence, in this sense, is not a possibility. But there are big differences in the extent of national control over local decision making. At one extreme, with most assets in foreign ownership most of the economic decisions may be made outside the country. This was the situation which many countries faced in the early 1950s. A powerful motive for nationalisation was the desire to secure local economic control. Increasingly, new foreign investment was only permitted a minority shareholding in the ventures to which it contributed, another aspect of the attempt to secure economic control. However, it is becoming increasingly evident that ownership as such means very little so long as countries remain technologically dependent. Technological dependence has as an important consequence a severe dilution of economic control, *irrespective* of the nationality of the ownership of the assets.

Some aspects of an enterprise's operations are outside its control because they are the products of the decisions of other economic units: for example, the price and availability of raw materials may be of this nature. Decisions which normally are within the control of the individual enterprise are those on the quantity and nature of investment, price levels, quantities produced, suppliers and purchasers, the allocation of profits, etc. Technological dependence tends to remove these latter decisions from local control. The extent to which it does so depends on the extent, nature and form of technological dependence. Technological dependence may take the form of foreign-financed investment, using foreign managers; of joint ventures with some foreign managers and finance; and of local ownership with contracts to secure foreign technology.

Clearly foreign investment involves the most complete loss of control. Although countries can and do impose some restrictions on the activities of foreign investors, by its nature foreign investment removes control of all the main economic variables into foreign hands. Localisation of manpower requirements may retain managerial office formally in local hands, but the main decisions are often taken in the head office of the company. Subsidiaries of multinational companies naturally have many of their decisions taken as part of the overall plan for the company as a whole. These include decisions on investment, pricing, profit remittances, sources of inputs and outlets for output. Joint ventures have been advocated as a means of avoiding some of this loss of control. Much depends on how large the foreign minority shareholding is, who the local partner is, and how determined the local partner is to take control. [. . .]

The loss of control resulting from technological dependence weakens the bargaining power of the local firms and hence increases the cost of imported technology. It also makes it more likely that the imported technology will be associated with unsuitable characteristics. By inhibiting local R and D and tying the local firm to further technological developments overseas, the technology contracts often prevent or at least inhibit the local adaptation of the imported technology.

(iii)   Unsuitable Characteristics

Perhaps the most obvious feature of imported technology is that its design is normally originally intended for the *producing* country, and hence its characteristics may be unsuitable for the *importing* country. In trade in technology between rich countries and poor countries unsuitable characteristics are particularly likely to be the consequence. The discussion will not be repeated here. But it must be emphasised that this is an important (perhaps the most important) consequence of technological dependence, where countries rely on imported technology and therefore do not have technology designed for their own conditions and needs. The manifold consequences – on employment, income distribution, etc. – following from the use of inappropriate technology, are also aspects of technological dependence of the poor countries on the advanced countries.

(iv)   Lack of Effective Indigenous Scientific and Innovative Capacity

Technological dependence, of course, is largely the result of the lack of local technology; but it also contributes to the lack of an effective local scientific and technical capacity. It does so in two ways: by inhibiting the process of learning-by-doing in technical development, which is essential for the development of scientific capacity; and by leading to a structure of productive activity, which tends to make the activities of the local scientific and technical institutions either totally irrelevant, or poor images of advanced-country institutions. [. . .]

The trouble is that it is in the nature of technological dependence, as we have described it, that it seems to prevent this process of learning-by-doing from happening – or at least drastically cuts down the scope for it. Foreign licensors or direct investors very often insist on using their usual machine suppliers in the advanced countries; they contract advanced-country engineering designers; they may have exclusive agreements with advanced-country plant contractors, who are then brought in to put up the plant in the developing country. Even if the foreign supplier of process technology is working with a locally-owned firm (through a licence or a joint venture for example) there will not necessarily be any pressure for it to use local skills rather than foreign. Local businessmen also often have strong preferences for foreign engineering firms and contractors — precisely because they also are suspicious of the inexperience of local engineers. In a similar way, local businessmen are often unwilling to use *local* technologies even where they are available, because foreign technologies which are commercially proven, and which are supplied along with experienced technicians and engineers from the foreign supplying firm, are a much less risky proposition. So there are repeatedly cases where local scientific and engineering laboratories in developing countries have been able to develop a technology to the point of commercial production — only to find that local firms prefer to license a precisely similar technique from abroad, in spite of higher financial costs.

Policies Towards Technological Dependence

Two strategies may be distinguished: first, one of *controlling* technology imports, so that the undesirable consequences of technological dependence are modified or offset; secondly, that of making a direct attempt to *reduce* the extent of technology imports. Both policies are made difficult, if not impossible, by the general relationship of dependence of the third world on the advanced countries. Discussion of policies thus reveals a close connection between the somewhat pragmatic view of technological dependence, discussed above, and dependency theories.

Controlling Foreign Technology

During the past half-century two countries succeeded in basing their industrial development on imported technology, and used this technology, successfully, as a basis for their own technological development: these two countries are Japan and Russia. Both show that it is possible to import technology and yet not be swamped by it; lessons from their experience are therefore of particular relevance. These two countries have had three things in common in their policy towards technology imports. First, they maintained a strict control over technology imports and deliberately restricted them to particular areas where they considered the need greatest, and where they would not inhibit local development efforts. Secondly, they allowed technology imports via licensing agreements, but they did not allow (except for special cases in Japan) the imports to be accompanied by foreign investment, with majority foreign shareholding. Thirdly, they adapted the technology they received and rarely introduced it unmodified.

In Japan one-third of total R and D expenditure has been devoted to adapting foreign technology, and the average expenditure devoted to adapting a unit of technology has been greater than the average expenditure devoted to creating a unit of local technology. [. . .]

The experience of Japan and Russia then suggests that a controlled policy towards technology imports can succeed in securing many of the advantages of technology imports while avoiding the worst consequences. However, other countries have set up a similar structure, without securing the same results. India is the obvious example. On paper her policy towards science and technology imports allows only selective imports; she avoids foreign investment wherever possible and negotiates toughly on terms. Yet practice has not mirrored policy. Foreign technology imports have inhibited local science and technology; control has been lost to the foreign licensors; local R and D does not make use of and adapt foreign technology but, on the whole, imitates it. Closer study of all these countries is needed to provide full backing for these claims, and a soundly based explanation. But, tentatively, the paradox may be explained in terms of stage of development and structure of production. Both Japan and Russia were advanced but backward countries, which were in a much better position than India to develop rather than be swamped by foreign technology; and both had rigid controls against the outside world. In contrast, despite the apparatus of import controls, India has close contacts with the advanced countries and until recently has encouraged the import of technology. Vested interests have developed in the production of Western-style products using Western-style technology, and the technology policy is not tough enough to stand up to the interests it would need to counteract to be successful. To be successful, a technology policy must succeed in breaking the ties with advanced-country companies, tastes and products, which technological dependence has built up. This sort of break is the more difficult to achieve the more integrated the ties and the interests that have developed in the system; on the other hand, while in one way it is easier for less developed and less integrated countries to break the ties at an earlier stage of development, it is more difficult in another because they lack the technological capacity to make the break.

Reducing Dependence

The dichotomy posed between controlling foreign technology and reducing dependence may be a false one. Successful control of technology will have, as an important long-term consequence, reduced dependence, as local scientific capacity is developed on the basis of the imports.

There are some differences in policies between the two strategies.

Policies of modifying technology imports are concerned to use foreign technology as the lever or take-off point for local technology, whereas policies aimed at reducing technological dependence would be more concerned to develop local technology as an *alternative* to foreign technology, i.e. to replace foreign technology entirely. This could mean a quite different distribution of imported technology. While modifying foreign technology would tend to distribute local scientific resources more or less *pari passu* with imported technology, so as to adapt and modify and learn from it, a policy of creating a local alternative technology would allow foreign technology only in those areas where a local alternative was out of the question. Modifying foreign technology would make local and foreign R and D complementary in the same industries; a policy of reducing dependence would make them complementary but in different industries. The modifying policy would tend to be less effective than a direct attack on dependence, in terms of reducing overall dependence, because the complementarity of local and foreign R and D would normally require the continued import of foreign technology. Much depends on whether foreign technology really can be controlled in an ideal way, such that local adaptation and learning occurs, eventually to be transformed into local technological independence. This ideal policy sounds very good on paper, making the best of foreign technology without its ill-effects. In practice it may well be an impossible policy for most countries. This is because technology imports are not policy-neutral, so that they can be encouraged/discouraged, selected/rejected in a pre-planned way; once allowed, they establish a hold over policies by changing market and economic conditions, and creating vested interests, which makes them extremely difficult to manage, and indeed may largely reduce the desire to manage them. Perhaps they might be likened to a drug: with addictive drugs, a plan to use them to stimulate the nervous system and incite a feeling of general well-being, and then gradually to stop their use as the system moves to a higher level of well-being without them, sounds excellent — but is extremely difficult to put into practice. The question then is whether technological imports may be managed and are non-addictive, as perhaps the experience of Japan might suggest, or are addictive and unmanageable, as the experience of India might argue. In the former case, a policy of modifying the consequences by a controlled strategy followed by a gradual move towards independence is a possibility. In the latter it is not; and if reduced dependence is an aim, then it must be pursued as such, and not indirectly via controlling the consequences of importing technology. From this point of view, India's policy of developing substitute technology is rational: the only drawback is that it has not been *used* as a substitute in practice; rather the foreign technology has been the substitute. But what is required then is far more extensive prohibition of the use of foreign technology, rather than redistributing scientific and technical resources to make them complementary with foreign imports. Again, however, the possibility of this as a realistic policy depends on how far the foreign technology and the interests to which it gives rise have penetrated in the power structure.

In terms of actual policies, a direct attack on technological dependence would require the minimum import of foreign technology, and the maximum encouragement and use of local technology. How far this 'minimum' or 'maximum' actually took one would depend in part on local technological capacity, and in part on what cost the country was prepared to bear in the short run to achieve independence. There are bound to be heavy short-run costs, in terms of loss of output and incomes, as a country struggles to manage on its own.

It is clear that such a policy is more nearly a possibility for some countries than others. Small countries with neither technicians, experience, nor capital goods capacity are in no position to aim for technological independence, whereas some larger countries have considerable local capacity. This brings us to the question of why *national* independence should, in any case, be an aim. National economic or technological independence has little rationale in terms of the independence of homogeneous interests; nor is it justified from the point of view of economic efficiency. Many national units are far too small to provide a sensible basis for economic or technical autarky. For each nation, big or small, to duplicate the economic and technological efforts of every other is as irrational and inefficient as the economic arrangements of the Zollverein states.

Many of the disadvantages of dependence *vis-à-vis* advanced countries could be eliminated, without incurring the heavy costs of autarky, by greater specialisation and exchange *between third world countries*. Exchange between third world countries would avoid the unequal exchange associated with exchange in technology between advanced and third world countries; it would allow for the development of a more appropriate technology for the third world, and for specialisation in its production; and it would remove the inhibiting effects of advanced technology on learning. Where the import of advanced technology is required, by negotiating jointly third world countries could much increase their bargaining power, reduce the extent and hence cost of multiple collaboration through the third world as a whole, and hence reduce the costs of importing the technology.

If a third world technology policy is to get anywhere a prime need is for institutional machinery to establish technical links between third world countries, exchange information on technical know-how and capacity and provide for bargaining assistance and eventually for joint negotiation. At the moment, as with most other areas of policy, all links are North/ South, not South/South, so that innovations are rarely transferred between third world countries, and nearly always from advanced countries, even where third world countries have suitable technology available. This is partly because of historical ties between advanced countries and ex-colonies; partly because financial ties are almost all in that direction; and partly because the same sort of prejudice that thwarts the use of local technology where foreign is available also acts in favour of developed country technology and against technology from other underdeveloped countries.

Technological dependence can be seen as cause and effect of the general dependency relationship. It is cause in so far as the need to import technology — lacking an indigenous technological base — leads to foreign investment, loss of control and the introduction of advanced-country patterns of consumption and production. An enclave economy, dependent on the advanced countries, and with its main links for inputs, markets, management, finance and technology with the advanced countries, then develops. The situation is self-reinforcing because once advanced-country technology has been introduced it creates a society in its own image, requiring further import of technology to feed the markets which have been created, and to enable the industries to survive and expand. Given a productive structure based on the production of advanced-country products, using advanced-country techniques, the natural consequence is that the local science and technology systems are small and irrelevant, adept at assimilating (unadapted) foreign technology, but lacking independent innovatory force. Yet the weakness of the local scientific/technological base is not only an outcome but also a prime cause of technological dependence, and indeed of dependence generally, because it means that there is no real alternative to the import of foreign technology. There is a vicious circle in which weak technology reinforces dependence, and dependence creates weakness.

Attempts to break out of the cycle tend to be thwarted by the attitudes and interests developed as a result of the dependent relationship. Action on science and technology alone, and on the *terms* of transfer of technology, are likely to be ineffective without more general action on economic dependence, because the political economy resulting from this dependence requires further import of advanced-country technology. But attempts to reorient the whole economy away from the dependent relationship are prevented by the loss in efficiency that would result, in the absence of an effective alternative technology, *and* by local interests that have developed in the continuation of the system. These obstacles were apparent in the policy discussion above. The dependent relationship means that the advanced countries' interests are internalised, inhibiting independent action to counter technological dependence.

Note

1. R.H. Green, in D. Ghai (ed.), *Economic Independence in Africa* (East African Literature Bureau, 1973).

THE RISE AND FUTURE DEMISE OF THE WORLD CAPITALIST SYSTEM: CONCEPTS FOR COMPARATIVE ANALYSIS

Immanuel Wallerstein

Source: *Comparative Studies in Society and History*, vol. 16, no. 4 (1974), pp. 387-415.

Wallerstein examines the functions of states within the capitalist world-economy. He identifies three structural positions – core, peripheral and semi-peripheral – the last of which is essential to the smooth running of the world-economy since it acts as a bridge between core and periphery and a channel for development. He goes on to review historical evidence for this pattern and to project it into the future.

The structural differences of core and periphery are not comprehensible unless we realize that there is a third structural position: that of the semi-periphery. This is not the result merely of establishing arbitrary cutting-points on a continuum of characteristics. Our logic is not merely inductive, sensing the presence of a third category from a comparison of indicator curves. It is also deductive. The semi-periphery is needed to make a capitalist world-economy run smoothly. Both kinds of world-system, the world-empire with a redistributive economy and the world-economy with a capitalist market economy, involve markedly unequal distribution of rewards. Thus, logically, there is immediately posed the question of how it is possible politically for such a system to persist. Why do not the majority who are exploited simply overwhelm the minority who draw disproportionate benefits? The most rapid glance at the historic record shows that these world-systems have been faced rather rarely by fundamental system-wide insurrection. While internal discontent has been eternal, it has usually taken quite long before the accumulation of the erosion of power has led to the decline of a world-system, and as often as not, an external force has been a major factor in this decline.

There have been three major mechanisms that have enabled world-systems to retain relative political stability (not in terms of the particular groups who will play the leading roles in the system, but in terms of systemic survival itself). One obviously is the concentration of military strength in the hands of the dominant forces. The modalities of this obviously vary with the technology, and there are to be sure political prerequisites for such a concentration, but nonetheless sheer force is no doubt a central consideration.

A second mechanism is the pervasiveness of an ideological commitment to the system as a whole. I do not mean what has often been termed the 'legitimation' of a system, because that term has beeen used to imply that the lower strata of a system feel some affinity with or loyalty towards the rulers, and I doubt that this has ever been a significant factor in the survival of world-systems. I mean rather the degree to which the staff or cadres of the system (and I leave this term deliberately vague) feel that their own well-being is wrapped up in the survival of the system as such and the competence of its leaders. It is this staff which not only propagates the myths; it is they who believe them.

But neither force nor the ideological commitment of the staff would suffice were it not for the division of the majority into a larger lower stratum and a smaller middle stratum. Both the revolutionary call for polarization as a strategy of change and the liberal encomium to consensus as the basis of the liberal polity reflect this proposition. The import is far wider than its use in the analysis of contemporary political problems suggests. It is the normal condition of either kind of world-system to have a three-layered structure. When and if this ceases to be the case, the world-system disintegrates.

In a world-empire, the middle stratum is in fact accorded the role of maintaining the marginally-desirable long-distance luxury trade, while the upper stratum concentrates its resources on controlling the military machinery which can collect the tribute, the crucial mode of redistributing surplus. By providing, however, for an access to a limited portion of the suprlus to urbanized elements who alone, in pre-modern societies, could contribute political cohesiveness to isolated clusters of primary producers, the upper stratum effectively buys off the potential leadership of co-ordinated revolt. And by denying access to political rights for this com-mercial-urban middle stratum, it makes them constantly vulnerable to confiscatory measures whenever their economic profits become sufficiently swollen so that they might begin to create for themselves military strength.

In a world-economy, such 'cultural' stratification is not so simple, because the absence of a single political system means the concentration of economic roles vertically rather than horizontally throughout the system. The solution then is to have three *kinds* of states, with pressures for cultural homogenization within each of them — thus, besides the upper-stratum of core-states and the lower stratum of peripheral states, there is a middle stratum of semi-peripheral ones.

The semi-periphery is then assigned as it were a specific economic role, but the reason is less economic than political. That is to say, one might make a good case that the world-economy as an economy would function every bit as well without a semi-periphery. But it would be far less *politically* stable, for it would mean a polarized world-system. The existence of the third category means precisely that the upper stratum is not faced with the *unified* opposition of all the others because the *middle* stratum is both exploited and exploiter. It follows that the specific economic role is not all that important, and has thus changed through the various historical stages of the modern world-system. We shall discuss these changes shortly.

Where then does class analysis fit in all of this? And what in such a formulation are nations, nationalities, peoples, ethnic groups? First of all, without arguing the point now, I would contend that all these latter terms denote variants of a single phenomenon which I will term 'ethno-nations'.

Both classes and ethnic groups, or status-groups, or ethno-nations are phenomena of world-economies and much of the enormous confusion that has surrounded the concrete analysis of their functioning can be attributed quite simply to the fact that they have been analyzed as though they existed within the nation-states of this world-economy, instead of within the world-economy as a whole. This has been a Procrustean bed indeed.

The range of economic activities being far wider in the core than in the periphery, the range of syndical interest groups is far wider there. Thus, it has been widely observed that there does not exist in many parts of the world today a proletariat of the kind which exists in, say, Europe or North America. But this is a confusing way to state the observation. Industrial activity being disproportionately concentrated in certain parts of the world-economy, industrial wage-workers are to be found principally in certain geographic regions. Their interests as a syndical group are determined by their collective relationship to the world-economy. Their ability to influence the political functioning of this world-economy is shaped by the fact that they command larger percentages of the population in one sovereign entity than another. The form their organizations take has, in large part, been governed too by these political boundaries. The same might be said about industrial capitalists. Class analysis is perfectly capable of accounting for the political position of, let us say, French skilled workers if we look at their structural position and interests in the world-economy. Similarly with ethno-nations. The meaning of ethnic consciousness in a core area is considerably different from that of ethnic consciousness in a peripheral area precisely because of the different class position such ethnic groups have in the world-economy.

Political struggles of ethno-nations or segments of classes within national boundaries of course are the daily bread and butter of local politics. But their significance or consequences can only be fruitfully analyzed if one spells out the implications of their organizational activity or political demands for the functioning of the world-economy. This also incidentally makes possible more rational assessments of these politics in terms of some set of evaluative criteria such as 'left' and 'right'.

The functioning then of a capitalist world-economy requires that groups pursue their economic interests within a single world market while seeking to distort this market for their benefit by organizing to exert influence on states, some of which are far more powerful than others but none of which controls the world-market in its entirety. Of course, we shall find on closer inspection that there are periods where one state is relatively quite powerful and other periods where power is more diffuse and contested, permitting weaker states broader ranges of action. We can talk then of the relative tightness or looseness of the world-system as an important variable and seek to analyze why this dimension tends to be cyclical in nature, as it seems to have been for several hundred years.

We are now in a position to look at the historical evolution of this capitalist world-economy itself and analyze the degree to which it is fruitful to talk of distinct stages in its evolution as a system. The emergence of the European world-economy in the 'long' sixteenth century (1450-1640) was made possible by an historical conjuncture: on those long-term trends which were the culmination of what has been sometimes described as the 'crisis of feudalism' was superimposed a more immediate cyclical crisis plus climatic changes, all of which created a dilemma that could only be resolved by a geographic expansion of the division of labor. Furthermore, the balance of inter-system forces was such as to make this realizable. Thus a geographic expansion did take place in conjunction with a demographic expansion and an upward price rise.

The remarkable thing was not that a European world-economy was thereby created, but that it survived the Hapsburg attempt to transform it into a world-empire, an attempt seriously pursued by Charles V. The Spanish attempt to absorb the whole failed because the rapid economic-demographic-technological burst forward of the preceding century made the whole enterprise too expensive for the imperial base to sustain, especially given many structural insufficiencies in Castilian economic development. Spain could afford neither the bureaucracy nor the army that was necessary to the enterprise, and in the event went bankrupt, as did the

French monarchs making a similar albeit even less plausible attempt.

Once the Hapsburg dream of world-empire was over — and in 1557 it was over forever — the capitalist world-economy was an established system that became almost impossible to unbalance. It quickly reached an equilibrium point in its relations with other world-systems: the Ottoman and Russian world-empires, the Indian Ocean proto-world-economy. Each of the states or potential states within the European world-economy was quickly in the race to bureaucratize, to raise a standing army, to homogenize its culture, to diversify its economic activities. By 1640, those in northwest Europe had succeeded in establishing themselves as the core states; Spain and the northern Italian city-states declined into being semi-peripheral; northeastern Europe and Iberian America had become the periphery. At this point, those in semi-peripheral status had reached it by virtue of decline from a former more pre-eminent status.

It was the system-wide recession of 1650-1730 that consolidated the European world-economy and opened stage two of the modern world-economy. For the recession forced retrenchment, and the decline in relative surplus allowed room for only one core state to survive. The mode of struggle was mercantilism, which was a device of partial insulation and withdrawal from the world market of *large* areas themselves hierarchically constructed — that is, empires within the world-economy (which is quite different from world-empires). In this struggle England first ousted the Netherlands from its commercial primacy and then resisted successfully France's attempt to catch up. As England began to speed up the process of industrialization after 1760, there was one last attempt of those capitalist forces located in France to break the imminent British hegemony. This attempt was expressed first in the French Revolution's replacement of the cadres of the regime and then in Napoleon's continental blockade. But it failed.

Stage three of the capitalist world-economy begins then, a stage of industrial rather than of agricultural capitalism. Henceforth, industrial production is no longer a minor aspect of the world market but comprises an ever larger percentage of world gross production — and even more important, of world gross surplus. This involves a whole series of consequences for the world-system.

First of all, it led to the further geographic expansion of the European world-economy to include now the whole of the globe. This was in part the result of its technological feasibility both in terms of improved military firepower and improved shipping facilities which made regular trade sufficiently inexpensive to be viable. But, in addition, industrial production *required* access to raw materials of a nature and in a quantity such that the needs could not be supplied within the former boundaries. At first, however, the search for new markets was not a primary consideration in the geographic expansion since the new markets were more readily available within the old boundaries, as we shall see.

The geographic expansion of the European world-economy meant the elimination of other world-systems as well as the absorption of the remaining mini-systems. The most important world-system up to then outside of the European world-economy, Russia, entered in semi-peripheral status, the consequence of the strength of its state-machinery (including its army) and the degree of industrialization already achieved in the eighteenth century. The independences in the Latin American countries did nothing to change their peripheral status. They merely eliminated the last vestiges of Spain's semi-peripheral role and ended pockets of non-involvement in the world-economy in the interior of Latin America. Asia and Africa were absorbed into the periphery in the nineteenth century, although Japan, because of the combination of the strength of its state-machinery, the poverty of its resource base (which led to a certain disinterest on the part of world capitalist forces), and its geographic remoteness from the core areas, was able quickly to graduate into semi-peripheral status.

The absorption of Africa as part of the periphery meant the end of slavery world-wide for two reasons. First of all, the manpower that was used as slaves was now needed for cash-crop production in Africa itself, whereas in the eighteenth century Europeans had sought to *discourage* just such cash-crop production. In the second place, once Africa was part of the periphery and not the external arena, slavery was no longer economic. To understand this, we must appreciate the economics of slavery. Slaves receiving the lowest conceivable reward for their labor are the least productive form of labor and have the shortest life span, both because of undernourishment and maltreatment and because of lowered psychic resistance to death. Furthermore, if recruited from areas surrounding their workplace the escape rate is too high. Hence, there must be a high transport cost for a product of low productivity. This makes economic sense only if the purchase price is virtually nil. In capitalist market trade, purchase always has a real cost. It is only in long-distance trade, the exchange of preciosities, that the purchase price can be in the social system of the purchaser virtually nil. Such was the slave trade. Slaves were bought at low immediate cost (the production cost of the items actually exchanged) and none of the usual invisible costs. That is to say, the fact that removing a man from West Africa lowered the productive potential of the region was of *zero* cost to the European world-economy since these areas were not part of the division of labor. Of course, had the slave trade totally denuded

Africa of all possibilities of furnishing further slaves, then a real cost to Europe would have commenced. But that point was never historically reached. Once, however, Africa was part of the periphery, then the real cost of a slave in terms of the production of surplus in the world-economy went up to such a point that it became far more economical to use wage-labor, even on sugar or cotton plantations, which is precisely what transpired in the nineteenth-century Caribbean and other slave-labor regions.

The creation of vast new areas as the periphery of the expanded world-economy made possible a shift in the role of some other areas. Specifically, both the United States and Germany (as it came into being) combined formerly peripheral and semi-peripheral regions. The manufacturing sector in each was able to gain political ascendancy, as the peripheral subregions became less economically crucial to the world-economy. Mercantilism now became the major tool of semi-peripheral countries seeking to become core countries, thus still performing a function analogous to that of the mercantilist drives of the late seventeenth and eighteenth centuries in England and France. To be sure, the struggle of semi-peripheral countries to 'industrialize' varied in the degree to which it succeeded in the period before the First World War: all the way in the United States, only partially in Germany, not at all in Russia.

The internal structure of core states also changed fundamentally under industrial capitalism. For a core area, industrialism involved divesting itself of substantially all agricultural activities (except that in the twentieth century further mechanization was to create a new form of working the land that was so highly mechanized as to warrant the appellation industrial). Thus whereas, in the period 1700-40, England not only was Europe's leading industrial exporter but was also Europe's leading agricultural exporter — this was at a high point in the economy-wide recession — by 1900, less than 10 per cent of England's population were engaged in agricultural pursuits.

At first under industrial capitalism, the core exchanged manufactured products against the periphery's agricultural products — hence, Britain from 1815 to 1873 as the 'workshop of the world'. Even to those semi-peripheral countries that had some manufacture (France, Germany, Belgium, the US), Britain in this period supplied about half their needs in manufactured goods. As, however, the mercantilist practices of this latter group both cut Britain off from outlets and even created competition for Britain in sales to peripheral areas, a competition which led to the late nineteenth-century 'scramble for Africa', the world division of labor was reallocated to ensure a new special role for the core: less the provision of the manufactures, more the provision of the machines to make the manufactures as well as the provision of infra-structure (especially, in this period, railroads).

The rise of manufacturing created for the first time under capitalism a large-scale urban proletariat. And in consequence for the first time there arose what Michels has called the 'anti-capitalist mass spirit',[1] which was translated into concrete organizational forms (trade-unions, socialist parties). This development intruded a new factor as threatening to the stability of the states and of the capitalist forces now so securely in control of them as the earlier centrifugal thrusts of regional anti-capitalist landed elements had been in the seventeenth century.

At the same time that the bourgeoisies of the core countries were faced by this threat to the internal stability of their state structures, they were simultaneously faced with the economic crisis of the latter third of the nineteenth century resulting from the more rapid increase of agricultural production (and indeed of light manufactures) than the expansion of a potential market for these goods. Some of the surplus would have to be redistributed to someone to allow these goods to be bought and the economic machinery to return to smooth operation. By expanding the purchasing power of the industrial proletariat of the core countries, the world-economy was unburdened simultaneously of two problems: the bottleneck of demand, and the unsettling 'class conflict' of the core states — hence, the social liberalism of welfare-state ideology that arose just at that point in time.

The First World War was, as men of the time observed, the end of an era; and the Russian Revolution of October 1917 the beginning of a new one — our stage four. This stage was to be sure a stage of revolutionary turmoil but it also was, in a seeming paradox, the stage of the *consolidation* of the industrial capitalist world-economy. The Russian Revolution was essentially that of a semi-peripheral country whose internal balance of forces had been such that as of the late nineteenth century it began on a decline towards a peripheral status. This was the result of the marked penetration of foreign capital into the industrial sector which was on its way to eliminating all indigenous capitalist forces, the resistance to the mechanization of the agricultural sector, the decline of relative military power (as evidenced by the defeat by the Japanese in 1905). The Revolution brought to power a group of state-managers who reversed each one of these trends by using the classic technique of mercantilist semi-withdrawal from the world-economy. In the process of doing this, the now USSR mobilized considerable popular support, especially in the urban sector. At the end of the Second World War, Russia was reinstated as a very strong member of the semi-periphery and could begin to seek full core status.

Meanwhile, the decline of Britain which dates from 1873 was confirmed and its hegemonic role was assumed by the United States. While the US thus rose, Germany fell further behind as a result of its military defeat. Various German attempts in the 1920s to find new industrial outlets in the Middle East and South America were unsuccessful in the face of the US thrust combined with Britain's continuing relative strength. Germany's thrust of desperation to recoup lost ground took the noxious and unsuccessful form of Nazism.

It was the Second World War that enabled the United States for a brief period (1945-65) to attain the same level of primacy as Britain had in the first part of the nineteenth century. United States growth in this period was spectacular and created a great need for expanded market outlets. The Cold War closure denied not only the USSR but Eastern Europe to US exports. And the Chinese Revolution meant that this region, which had been destined for much exploitative activity, was also cut off. Three alternative areas were available and each was pursued with assiduity. First, Western Europe had to be rapidly 'reconstructed', and it was the Marshall Plan which thus allowed this area to play a primary role in the expansion of world productivity. Secondly, Latin America became the reserve of US investment from which now Britain and Germany were completely cut off. Thirdly, Southern Asia, the Middle East and Africa had to be decolonized. On the one hand, this was necessary in order to reduce the share of the surplus taken by the Western European intermediaries, as Canning covertly supported the Latin American revolutionaries against Spain in the 1820s. But also, these countries had to be decolonized in order to mobilize productive potential in a way that had never been achieved in the colonial era. Colonial rule after all had been an *inferior* mode of relationship of core and periphery, one occasioned by the strenuous late-nineteenth-century conflict among industrial states but one no longer desirable from the point of view of the new hegemonic power.

But a world capitalist economy does not permit true imperium. Charles V could not succeed in his dream of world-empire. The Pax Britannica stimulated its own demise. So too did the Pax Americana. In each case, the cost of *political* imperium was too high economically, and in a capitalist system, over the middle run when profits decline, new *political* formulae are sought. In this case the costs mounted along several fronts. The efforts of the USSR to further its own industrialization, protect a privileged market area (Eastern Europe), and force entry into other market areas led to an immense spiralling of military expenditure, which on the Soviet side promised long-run returns whereas for the US it was merely a question of running very fast to stand still. The economic resurgence of Western Europe, made necessary both to provide markets for US sales and investments and to counter the USSR military thrust, meant over time that the Western European state structures collectively became as strong as that of the US, which led in the late 1960s to the 'dollar and gold crisis' and the retreat of Nixon from the free-trade stance which is the definitive mark of the self-confident leader in a capitalist market system. When the cumulated Third World pressures, most notably Vietnam, were added on, a restructuring of the world division of labor was inevitable, involving probably in the 1970s a quadripartite division of the larger part of the world surplus by the US, the European Common Market, Japan, and the USSR.

Such a decline in US state hegemony has actually *increased* the freedom of action of capitalist enterprises, the larger of which have now taken the form of multinational corporations which are able to maneuver against state bureaucracies whenever the national politicians become too responsive to internal worker pressures. Whether some effective links can be established between multinational corporations, presently limited to operating in certain areas, and the USSR remains to be seen, but it is by no means impossible.

This brings us to the seemingly esoteric debate between Liu Shao-Chi and Mao Tse-Tung as to whether China was, as Liu argued, a socialist state, or whether, as Mao argued, socialism was a *process* involving continued and continual class struggle. No doubt to those to whom the terminology is foreign the discussion seems abstrusely theological. The issue, however, is real. If the Russian Revolution emerged as a reaction to the threatened further decline of Russia's structural position in the world-economy, and if fifty years later one can talk of the USSR as entering the status of a core power in a *capitalist* world-economy, what then is the meaning of the various so-called socialist revolutions that have occurred in a third of the world's surface? First let us notice that it has been neither Thailand nor Liberia nor Paraguay that has had a 'socialist revolution' but Russia, China and Cuba. That is to say, these revolutions have occurred in countries that, in terms of their internal economic structures in the pre-revolutionary period, had a certain minimum strength in terms of skilled personnel, some manufacturing, and other factors which made it plausible that, within the framework of a capitalist world-economy, such a country could alter its role in the world division of labor within a reasonable period (say 30-50 years) by the use of the technique of mercantilist semi-withdrawal. (This may not be all that plausible for Cuba, but we shall see.) Of course, other countries in the geographic regions and military orbit of these revolutionary forces had changes of regime without in any way having these characteristics (for example, Mongolia or Albania). It is also to be noted that many of the countries where similar forces are strong or where considerable counterforce is required to keep them from emerging also share this status of minimum strength. I think of Chile or Brazil or Egypt – or indeed Italy.

Are we not seeing the emergence of a political structure for *semi-peripheral* nations adapted to stage four of the capitalist world-system? The fact that all enterprises are nationalized in these countries does not make the participation of these enterprises in the world-economy one that does not conform to the mode of operation of a capitalist market-system: seeking increased efficiency of production in order to realize a maximum price on sales, thus achieving a more favorable allocation of the surplus of the world-economy. If tomorrow US Steel became a worker's collective in which all employees without exception received an identical share of the profits and all stockholders were expropriated without compensation, would US Steel thereby cease to be a capitalist enterprise operating in a capitalist world-economy?

What then have been the consequences for the world-system of the emergence of many states in which there is no private ownership of the basic means of production? To some extent, this has meant an internal reallocation of consumption. It has certainly undermined the ideological justifications in world capitalism, both by showing the political vulnerability of capitalist entrepreneurs and by demonstrating that private ownership is irrelevant to the rapid expansion of industrial productivity. But to the extent that it has raised the ability of the new semi-peripheral areas to enjoy a larger share of the world surplus, it has once again de-polarized the world, recreating the triad of strata that has been a fundamental element in the survival of the world-system.

Finally, in the peripheral areas of the world-economy, both the contin-ued economic expansion of the core (even though the core is seeing some reallocation of surplus internal to it) and the new strength of the semi-periphery have led to a further weakening of the political and hence eco-nomic position of the peripheral areas. The pundits note that 'the gap is getting wider', but thus far no one has succeeded in doing much about it, and it is not clear that there are very many in whose interests it would be to do so. Far from a strengthening of state authority, in many parts of the world we are witnessing the same kind of deterioration Poland knew in the sixteenth century, a deterioration of which the frequency of military coups is only one of many signposts. And all of this leads us to conclude that stage four has been the stage of the *consolidation* of the capitalist world-economy.

Consolidation, however, does not mean the absence of contradictions and does not mean the likelihood of long-term survival. We thus come to projections about the future, which has always been man's great game, his true *hybris*, the most convincing argument for the dogma of original sin. Having read Dante, I will therefore be brief.

There are two fundamental contradictions, it seems to me, involved in the workings of the capitalist world-system. In the first place, there is the contradiction to which the nineteenth-century Marxian corpus pointed, which I would phrase as follows: whereas in the short-run the maximization of profit requires maximizing the withdrawal of surplus from immediate consumption of the majority, in the long-run the continued production of surplus requires a mass demand which can only be created by redistributing the surplus withdrawn. Since these two considerations move in opposite directions (a 'contradiction'), the system has constant crises which in the long-run both weaken it and make the game for those with privilege less worth playing.

The second fundamental contradiction, to which Mao's concept of socialism as process points, is the following: whenever the tenants of privilege seek to co-opt an oppositional movement by including them in a minor share of the privilege, they may no doubt eliminate opponents in the short-run; but they also up the ante for the next oppositional movement created in the next crisis of the world-economy. Thus the cost of 'co-option' rises ever higher and the advantages of co-option seem ever less worthwhile.

There are today no socialist systems in the world-economy any more than there are feudal systems because there is only *one* world-system. It is a world-economy and it is by definition capitalist in form. Socialism involves the creation of a new kind of *world*-system, neither a redistributive world-empire nor a capitalist world-economy but a socialist world-government. I don't see this projection as being in the least utopian but I also don't feel its institution is imminent. It will be the outcome of a long struggle in forms that may be familiar and perhaps in very new forms, that will take place in *all* the areas of the world-economy (Mao's continual 'class struggle'). Governments may be in the hands of persons, groups or movements sympathetic to this transformation but *states* as such are neither progressive nor reactionary. It is movements and forces that deserve such evaluative judgments.

Note

1. Robert Michels, 'The Origins of the Anti-Capitalist Mass Spirit', in *Man in Contemporary Society* (Columbia University Press, New York, 1955), vol. 1, pp. 740-65.

Part 4

PERSPECTIVES AND WORLD POLITICS

INTRODUCTION

Previous sections in this Reader focused on a particular perspective. The three articles in this final section highlight the implications and importance of different perspectives. In particular, they establish links between theory and practice and explore not only what world politics looks like today but also how we can affect what the world might look like tomorrow. The future direction of world politics is in part dependent upon the perspective we are currently employing.

Rothstein concentrates upon the 'Realist' perspective and argues that, despite the existence of competing perspectives, this approach continues to dominate the thinking of those involved in the management of world affairs. In his opinion, this failure to take account of alternative perspectives bodes ill for the future safety of the world. Gilpin looks at three models of the future. His mercantilist, sovereignty-at-bay and dependence models (which correspond closely to the perspectives identified in this Reader) have implications not just for theorizers but also for practitioners. The final article by Cox looks at the demands of the Third World for a New International Economic Order. He, however, identifies five distinct approaches. This serves to remind us that there is nothing sacrosanct about the three perspectives developed in this Reader, and that there is always room for further refinement. Nevertheless, we hope that this final section will convince the reader that the identification of competing perspectives is an important aid to understanding world politics.

4.1

ON THE COSTS OF REALISM

Robert L. Rothstein

Source: *Political Science Quarterly*, vol. LXXXVII, no. 3 (1972), pp. 347-62.

After identifying the chief characteristics of the Realist view of world politics, Rothstein considers what the effect of this view has been upon politicians and diplomats since World War II and points to the dangers inherent in its continuing to dominate the thinking of foreign policy makers.

[The article begins by pointing to the contrast between the declining satisfaction with Realism in academic circles and its continuing attraction for policy makers. It suggests that this contrast can be understood only by recognizing the nature of the Realist vision.]

Realism involved commitment to a set of propositions about international politics which were essentially extrapolations from the diplomatic history of nineteenth-century Europe. They were propositions which the generation of statesmen in Europe after 1919 either had lost or misunderstood: reeducation in the 'perennials' was clearly necessary. The catechism was simple. All states sought, or would seek, power, given the opportunity. It was an essential prerequisite for the achievement of any other goals. Today's enemy could be tomorrow's ally (n.b., not 'friend', for, as Salisbury put it, 'Great Britain has no permanent friends, only permanent interests'). The use of any means was acceptable (atomic weapons created a dilemma, resolved by silence or metaphysical despair), or at least possible, though only one or two might be appropriate at any single moment. The best operator was the man who possessed 'traditional wisdom'; and the man who possessed 'traditional wisdom' was the best operator.

The scenario and the stage directions are very familiar. The metaphor is deliberate, for many Realists considered international politics a great drama in which wise statesmen made 'hard choices' in a bitter but limited struggle for dominance. They were constrained by their own power and their own fallibility, but at the very least they never fell victim to illusions about the 'true' nature of the world. It was a world in which states were involved in an unending struggle with each other (because that was the nature of states in an anarchic world); power was necessary to survive in it or to continue to fight; all states were potential enemies (Realism requires enemies more than it needs friends), but the worst might be avoided by clever diplomacy and by virtue of the fact that all alike shared a similar conception of rational behavior. It was indeed a dramatic picture, and an especially exciting one, for it was a drama of war in which the wartime mind predominated. This made it particularly attractive to an emerging generation of statesmen whose views had been formed as a response to the failure to stop Hitler before it was too late and who were thus predisposed toward a doctrine which would guarantee that the same errors would not be committed against Stalin.

The Realist model of world politics was simple and elegant. An image of states as billiard balls, interacting within a specific arena and according to established rules, became increasingly prevalent. Once the implication of the metaphor was grasped, that there are only a few immutable patterns of behavior in politics – billiard balls, after all, are not very complex phenomena – the principal preoccupation of statesmen became clear. They were to judge, by experience and intuition, the requisite amount of force necessary to move one or another ball in a preferred direction. Purposes, as in wartime where the need for survival and victory dominated everything, could be taken for granted. Individual idiosyncrasies, which might influence choice of purpose, or domestic politics, which might destroy the elegance of the game, could be safely ignored, for they were hardly significant in comparison to the external imperatives imposed by life in the international arena. All states would respond to the same drummer, irrespective of internal differences, because they had no choice if they wished to survive (at any rate, as a Great Power).

Is there something beyond its elegance and simplicity which has made this doctrine so popular, so to speak so 'natural', to the practitioner? The power of fascination of a doctrine ultimately must rest on its apparent ability to provide answers to practical questions. The answers must be attributable to the doctrine, at least in the sense that some connection may safely be posited between successful practitioners and doctrinal commitment. In the case at hand, the ability to make that connection would imply that a substantive distinction exists between a Realist and a non-Realist.

Is it really that easy to distinguish a Realist from a non-Realist? The difficulty is that commitment to the Realists' image of world politics – a world scarred by a permanent quest for power by potentially wicked men – hardly guarantees realistic decisions about the practical world.

Realists and non-Realists may disagree about the permanence of power as the decisive factor in international politics, but they can still reach similar judgments about specific cases. On the other hand, two confessed Realists may reach totally dissimilar conclusions about the same case — in fact, at times, it is difficult to relate an individual Realist's position on policy to his philosophical convictions. Correlating Morgenthau and Kennan on policy with Morgenthau and Kennan on 'Realism' requires a Talmudist's skill and patience, not to say a willingness to suspend disbelief. The difficulty is that reality is so complex and ambiguous that the policies which we choose to call 'realistic' at any particular moment depend to a significant degree on personal predispositions and perspectives.

What this suggests is that Realism involves something more than a temporal perspective on power and the nature of man. It also suggests that lists of characteristics presumably shared by all Realists are irrelevant: statesmen or analysts possessing all the characteristics can act very 'unrealistically' (which we know only after the fact), while others possessing none of the characteristics may act 'realistically' (which we also know only after the fact). The more subtle contention that Realists share an awareness that full security is beyond attainment and that compromise and adjustment of interests are necessary, is more helpful. It implies that Realism involves a state of mind with which to approach problems, rather than the possession of a few characteristics or attachment to the permanent significance of a single operating principle. Nevertheless, some groups have the same sense of the nature of politics and are not considered Realists (for example, some liberals). Moreover, the difficulty of discovering exactly why one policy position is more realistic than another persists.

Various efforts to give Realism an acceptable programmatic content have been inadequate, for the task itself is probably impossible. We can define a Realist arbitrarily as someone who possesses certain characteristics or who believes in certain doctrinal propositions, but there is no way in which we can convincingly relate those characteristics or beliefs to specific choices in the world of action. Realism simply constitutes belief in the wisdom of certain 'eternal verities' about politics, conveniently collected in a few texts and conveniently 'confirmed' by a series of all too recent blunders by non-Realists. The point surely is not that Realism is unimportant or irrelevant. But its real significance has not been in providing a (nonexistent) direct connection between theory and action. Its power and influence over the choice of specific actions has been — and perhaps remains — pervasive, but indirect. It has conditioned the political climate so that some actions seem 'to stand to reason' and others seem naive — by definition. And it has furnished an authentic body of scripture to rationalize 'hard choices', to justify the notion that a democratic foreign policy is inconceivable, and to provide psychic support for the acolyte compelled to lie in defense of his own interpretation of the national interest.

The great hero in the Realist canon has always been the successful diplomat — many of the founders and followers of Realism were frustrated Castlereaghs, or better yet, Metternichs — and the great danger the bumbling amateur. Professionals, after all, could always 'work something out'. The very ambiguity and uncertainty of the relationship between the theory and the choice of specific actions guarantee the supremacy of the diplomat's role. What else but experience and intuition allow the necessary connections to be made? And who but the diplomat is trained (rather, one should say, 'experienced') to make the necessary judgments? It is peculiarly true, then, that the lack of an obvious connection beween the theory and a practical action, and the ensuing necessity of relying on a corps of skilled intermediaries, has made Realism singularly attractive to professional diplomats. [. . .]

Realism presumes a world of similar states: it is a doctrine based upon, and beholden to, the behavioral styles of the traditional Great Power. Totalitarian, revolutionary, underdeveloped, and unstable states — as well as Small Powers, international organizations, and nongovernmental organizations, like the multinational corporation or the Ford Foundation — are all unwelcome anomalies. Such states violate and perhaps destroy the notion of a shared, if tacit, sense of a range of permissible behavior for states. It is not altogether inexplicable that many of the events which have surprised us — both theorists and practitioners — in the last twenty-five or so years have been perpetrated by these new kinds of states: the Nazi-Soviet pact in 1939, Pearl Harbor, the German blitz, Soviet acquisition of a nuclear capability, the Berlin blockade, North Korean aggression and Chinese intervention, Nasser's reaction to US Aswan Dam 'diplomacy', the sputniks, the Berlin wall, the installation of missiles in Cuba, and the more recent internal turmoil in both Indonesia and China. It is not that we failed to predict the exact moment or event; it is that we were neither politically nor psychologically prepared for them to happen at all.

It is important to note that many of these failures resulted from the inability of men trained to deal with concrete contingencies as they arise to understand the actions of men or states committed to an ideological interpretation of world affairs — or at least to an interpretation not derived from the history of the European state system. In addition, a congenital bias against planning made it difficult to deal with those who did have a plan. At any rate, both Realists and practitioners shared a bias toward analyzing and evaluating the world according to habits and precepts drawn from European history.

One other aspect of Realism has made it especially attractive to diplomats and practitioners. Concentrating on interaction between states perceived as billiard balls tends to turn attention away from structural alterations in the international system itself. The systemic environment, in the large, is taken as a constant — that is, as a field fluctuating around a metaphorical balance of power. The result has been a static theory concerned only with creating or preserving an equilibrium. As such, only tactical questions — operator's questions about means, not ends — appear truly interesting. The central preoccupation is never why or where the system is going (it is going no place, by definition), but rather how to preserve the existing order of things. It has meant that the Realists have been very poor guides through the thickets of bipolarity, multipolarity, polycentrism, and the like.

Practitioners generally object strenuously to the notion that they all believe in any single doctrine. They point to the indisputable fact that there are sharp disagreements within the government over major issues like Vietnam and the ABM. This mistakes disagreements about specifics for disagreement about general attitudes and approaches. Anyone who reads the memoirs of former practitioners, or who spends any substantial amount of time talking with them, can attest to the existence of widely shared beliefs and very similar perceptions of what can be taken for granted about the conduct of foreign affairs. These shared beliefs and convictions are not held or expounded with anything like the formal elegance or coherence which one finds in a Morgenthau or Kennan text. Nonetheless, they exist and they reinforce — or repeat — the Realist canon. It may be violently unsettling to the political practitioner, but he does indeed 'speak' theory — of a sort. It would be better for all of us if he were aware of it and understood what it implied.

The Practical Effects of Realism

The extent to which Realism has been elitist and antidemocratic was masked — or ignored — for many years, for the policies which dominated American foreign policy rested on a substantial domestic consensus about the proper way to deal with the Soviet and Chinese threats. Not only the mass public but anyone who disagreed with the conventional wisdom could be disregarded, be they reporters, professors, or 'bleeding hearts' in general. What Realism passed on was a kind of romanticism about both policy – for the 'responsibilities of power' meant that we had a stake as policeman or judge in anything happening anywhere – and the policy-maker – who had to make 'hard choices' in spite of domestic stupidity or indifference. The 'professionals' would give Americans a good and prudent foreign policy even if they had to be tricked into it or misinformed or lied to. In effect, Realism has provided the high tone of necessity for a rather low range of behavior. In this sense, the revelation in the *Pentagon Papers* of a persistent disregard for the democratic process and a persistent fascination with fooling the press and obscuring the truth was entirely predictable.

Realism is also implicitly a conservative doctrine attractive to men concerned with protecting the status quo. It hardly predisposes its followers to look favorably at revolutionary change, for that kind of change threatens all the fences which Realism has erected: it means one might have to deal with some very untraditional states – and 'diplomats' – about some very untraditional issues. It means that disagreement about ends and values might begin to creep into the system, surely an unfortunate development from the point of view of men committed to the notion that only the proper choice of means is ever really at issue.

From one point of view, Realism has always been an eminently sensible doctrine: its emphasis on the virtues of moderation, flexibility, and compromise was an intelligent response to the difficulties and dangers of living in an anarchic world. But from another point of view, Realism has emphasized the necessity for Great Powers to maintain their prestige, status, and credibility. Great Powers, by definition, are compelled to play 'prestige politics', that is to say, a form of politics particularly difficult to compromise or control. Turning the other cheek could be disastrous, or at least imprudent, in a world dominated by the quest for power. In fact, it has always been necessary to use, or to appear to be willing to use, limited amounts of force quickly in order to avoid having to use larger amounts belatedly. This seemingly sensible proposition, so fundamental to a generation who remembered the follies of Chamberlain and Daladier, was very dangerous for men who could remember – or learn – nothing else. Flexibility, moderation, and compromise would have to take a back seat to the necessity of teaching the aggressors a lesson and enhancing the credibility of one's word. An awful lot of 'brinkmanship' and waiting to see if 'the other guy would blink first' could result.

Realism asserts – and it can be neither proved nor disproved – that nothing much can be changed, that the only guide to the future is the past, and that the best interpreter of the way to get there safely is the operator skilled at negotiating limited compromises. It thus gives the 'generalist', the operator armed only with traditional procedural skills, a central role in the conduct of foreign policy. But it is also a conservative and anti-innovative role; as a result, the doctrine has provided a kind of meta-physical justification for the passivity and procedural inertia of the Foreign Service and the State Department, characteristics already built into the policy-making system by incrementalism and the play of bureaucratic politics.

The nature of the role which the practitioner is expected to play also has had a crucial effect on the nature of the training he is expected to undergo. The only unanswered questions are tactical questions about applications. And there is no way to train someone to make correct tactical decisions except 'on the job'. Thus the proper training for the practitioner is never analytical or intellectual; presumably, his proper role is simply to apply known principles to individual cases. That task, which rests on a combination of experience, intuition, and familiarity with the latest details, can be learned only by doing – or, more accurately, by imitating. It is one of the few illustrations of a profession which takes anti-intellectualism as a virtue. In any case, it sharply circumscribes the ability of the practitioner to deal with untraditional events.

The fact that Realism has operated with a strikingly narrow definition of politics also has had a major effect on the behavior of its practitioners. Diplomatic maneuvering to achieve or maintain the gains of 'high politics' became the norm – the analogy with the chessboard, an elegant and intricate arena of play, always seemed appropriate. New developments which undermine the utility of the analogy have to be either ignored or dismissed as irrelevant. Thus the State Department and its denizens have had little influence on a whole range of issues which have dominated foreign policy since World War II: for example, political and economic development in the underdeveloped countries, the relationship between nuclear weapons and political behavior, the control of the arms race, limited and sublimited war, and the erosion of the distinction between foreign and domestic policy. It is misleading to assert, as some critics have done, that these are issues which have been *taken* from the State Department: it is more accurate to say that they have been given away in the apparent hope that they would disappear, or at least not intrude upon the ordered universe of diplomacy.

Realism has the ring of truth to it for men compelled to work in an environment which they can not always understand and can never ade-quately control. It provides a few simple keys which facilitate understanding (if only, inevitably, by oversimplification) and an intellectual justification for the failure to control (for all is unpredictable – although hardly unexpectable). None of this means that Realism has been responsible for, or 'caused', any particular policy choice: it could just as well have been used, for example, to defend going into Vietnam as staying out. What it has done has been to foster a set of attitudes that predisposed its followers to think about international politics in a particularly narrow and ethnocentric fashion, and to set very clear bounds around the kinds of policies which it seemed reasonable to contemplate. And once decisions have been made, it has provided the necessary psychological and intellectual support to resist criticism, to persevere in the face of doubt, and to use any means to outwit or to dupe domestic dissenters.

The Future of Realism

The appeal of Realism is deceptive and dangerous, for it rests on assumptions about state behavior which have become increasingly irrelevant. It treats one time-bound set of propositions as if they were universally applicable, and thus turns everyone's attention to problems of application – to issues of 'how' not 'why'. It is always a doctrine which takes for granted the primacy of foreign policy and the dominance of the security issue defined in terms of simple notions of power. It is, in sum, not only the classic version of a state-centric doctrine but also an affirmation of the rightful dominance of the Great Powers and the autonomy of their foreign policies.

We could treat this discussion as being of only historical interest but for one fact: despite Realism's increasing irrelevance as an interpretation of the external world, its hold over the mind of the practitioner is still formidable. Why this should be so can only be explained by the dominant – and thus exceedingly attractive – role which Realism assigns to the 'generalist' practitioner (who gets a hunting license on all issues in spite of an absence of substantive expertise); and by the more general consideration that all doctrines persist at the practical level much beyond the point they begin to be assailed at the theoretical level. After all, for the practitioner to abandon or question what he considers to be his own particular expertise is to abandon or question the only thing which separates him from outsiders, and that is very threatening.

The greatest danger in this situation is that Realism is becoming even more irrelevant to the international system in the process of emerging. What we may be witnessing is the first systemic revolution occurring without the intervention of general war or the development of a wholly new kind of military technology. The central point is that the traditional security issue is no longer likely to be the dominant consideration in world politics. I am *very* far from asserting that security will no longer be an issue or that it will somehow disappear from the calculations of states — some analysts of the emerging system seem to take this position, at least implicitly, thus acting as if the realm of security and the realm of interdependence were in fact completely autonomous. It is clear, however, that security will be only one of the issues of world politics, albeit a crucial one, for it will have to share prominence with a range of issues heretofore left to technicians or to the play of domestic politics.

The growing interdependence on economic, social, and cultural matters within the state system obviously implies a system in which the autonomy and sovereignty of all the members — great and small — is being eroded. Rational decision-making on such issues requires a degree of international cooperation well beyond anything which has occurred in the field of security. (Even in NATO, for example, the United States always determined strategic questions by itself even though they affected all the allies.) This is particularly true because there is no guarantee that these issues will reduce the degree of conflict in the international system *unless* they are handled in a manner which is minimally satisfactory to all concerned. Interdependence clearly could just as well lead to trade wars and an insane effort to achieve autarchy as it could to increased prosperity and welfare; only a new style of decision-making and a change in basic thought patterns could turn these developments into an opportunity to enhance the degree of cooperation in the system. Finally, it deserves some mention that the security issue itself is becoming (or perhaps one should say, is finally being recognized as) increasingly one involving interdependence, as the recent agreements on the hot line and nuclear accidents attest. It will become even more so if nuclear weapons proliferate and arms technology itself continues to grow in complexity. Even a more mundane, but very critical, security issue like the control of conventional arms cannot be handled by any traditional formula — if it can be handled at all.

The attitudes and predispositions which Realism fosters constitute a classically inappropriate response to these developments. With its overly narrow conception of politics, and with its antiquated notions of sovereignty, Great Power dominance and the autonomy of foreign policy, the Realist response is bound to create conflict and destroy the possibility of working out new forms of cooperation. The potential which these issues have for creating either cooperation or conflict means that they must be deliberately manipulated to encourage cooperation; it may even be necessary to adopt a decision-making style borrowed from domestic politics, or to begin to take functions like planning seriously. We may also be compelled to contemplate other heresies. The Realist mentality would find it virtually impossible to even think about these matters in their proper dimension; worse yet, since Realism presupposes conflict, it is likely to turn the politics of interdependence into another exercise in the politics of security.

4.2

THREE MODELS OF THE FUTURE

Robert Gilpin

Source: *International Organization*, vol. 29, no. 1 (1975), pp. 37-60.

Gilpin outlines three approaches to international economic relations which represent in turn the liberal, Marxist and economic nationalist schools. He presents each model and then outlines a critique of each before presenting what he considers to be the likely future development of international organizations.

Edward Hallet Carr observed that 'the science of economics presupposes a given political order, and cannot be profitably studied in isolation from politics'.[1] Throughout history, the larger configurations of world politics and state interests have in large measure determined the framework of the international economy. Succeeding imperial and hegemonic powers have sought to organize and maintain the international economy in terms of their economic and security interests.

From this perspective, the contemporary international economy was the creation of the world's dominant economic and military power, the United States. At the end of the Second World War, there were efforts to create a universal and liberal system of trade and monetary relations. After 1947, however, the world economy began to revive on the foundations of the triangular relationship of the three major centers of noncommunist industrial power: the United States, Western Europe, and Japan. Under the umbrella of American nuclear protection and connected with the United States through military alliances, Japan and Western Europe were encouraged to grow and prosper. In order to rebuild these industrial economies adjacent to the Sino-Soviet bloc, the United States encouraged Japanese growth, led by exports, into the American market and, through the European Economic Community's (EEC) common external tariff and agricultural policy, also encouraged discrimination against American exports.

Today, the triangular relationship of the noncommunist industrial powers upon which the world economy has rested is in disarray. The signs of decay were visible as early as the middle 1960s, when President John F.

Kennedy's grand design failed to stem the coalescence of an inward-looking European economic bloc and to achieve its objective of an economic and political community extending from Scandinavia to Japan and pivoted on the United States.

Believing that the world trading and monetary system was operating to America's disadvantage, the administration of Richard Nixon took up the challenge with a completely different approach. On 15 August 1971, former President Nixon announced a new foreign economic policy for the United States. In response to the first trade deficit since 1893 and to accelerating attacks on the dollar, the president imposed a surcharge on American imports, suspended the convertibility of the dollar, and took other remedial actions. Subsequently the dollar was devalued twice (December 1971 and February 1973); the world moved toward a system of flexible exchange rates; and intense negotiations were initiated to create a new international monetary and trading system.

A new economic policy was necessary for several reasons. The United States believed an overvalued dollar was adding significantly to its unemployment rate. American expenditures abroad for military commitments, foreign direct investment, and goods and services required, in the 1970s, greater outlays of foreign exchange than the United States could earn or wished to borrow. The US rapprochement with China, its moves toward détente with the Soviet Union, and President Nixon's announcement of the New Economic Policy appeared to signal the end of the political order that American economic and military supremacy had guaranteed; this political order had been the foundation for the post-World War II world economy. All these policy initiatives were efforts to adjust to the growing economic power of America's partners, Europe and Japan, and to the growing military power of its primary antagonist, the Soviet Union. In terms of the present article, these economic and political changes raised the question of whether the interdependent world economy could survive in the changing political environment of the 1970s and beyond.

In this brief article I make no attempt to give a definitive answer to the question. Rather, my purpose is to present and evaluate three models of the future drawn from current writings on international relations. These models are really representative of the three prevailing schools of thought on political economy: liberalism, Marxism, and economic nationalism. Each model is an amalgam of the ideas of several writers who, in my judgment (or by their own statements), fall into one or another of these three perspectives on the relationship of economic and political affairs.

Each model constitutes an ideal type. Perhaps no one individual would subscribe to each argument made by any one position. Yet the tendencies and assumptions associated with each perception of the future are real enough; they have a profound influence on popular, academic, and official thinking on trade, monetary, and investment problems. One, in fact, cannot really escape being influenced by one position or another.

Following the presentation of the three models, I present a critique that sets forth the strengths and weaknesses of each. On the basis of this critique, I draw some general conclusions with respect to the future of international economic organization and the nature of future international relations in general.

The Sovereignty-at-Bay Model

I label the first model *sovereignty-at-bay*, after the title of Raymond Vernon's influential book on the multinational corporation.[2] According to this view, increasing economic interdependence and technological advances in communication and transportation are making the nation state an anachronism. These economic and technological developments are said to have undermined the traditional economic rationale of the nation state. In the interest of world efficiency and domestic economic welfare, the nation state's control over economic affairs will continually give way to the multinational corporation, to the Eurodollar market, and to other international institutions better suited to the economic needs of mankind.

Perhaps the most forceful statement of the sovereignty-at-bay thesis is that of Harry Johnson — the paragon of economic liberalism. Analyzing the international economic problems of the 1970s, Johnson makes the following prediction:

> In an important sense, the fundamental problem of the future is the conflict between the political forces of nationalism and the economic forces pressing for world integration. This conflict currently appears as one between the national government and the international corporation, in which the balance of power at least superficially appears to lie on the side of the national government. But in the longer run economic forces are likely to predominate over political, and may indeed come to do so before the end of this decade. Ultimately, a world federal government will appear as the only rational method for coping with the world's economic problems.[3]

Though not all adherents of the sovereignty-at-bay thesis would go as far as Johnson, and an interdependent world economy is quite conceivable without unbridled scope for the activities of multinational corporations, most do regard the multinational corporation as the embodiment *par excellence* of the liberal ideal of an interdependent world economy. It has taken the integration of national economies beyond trade and money to the internationalization of production. For the first time in history, production, marketing, and investment are being organized on a global scale rather than in terms of isolated national economies. The multinational corporations are increasingly indifferent to national boundaries in making decisions with respect to markets, production, and sources of supply.

The sovereignty-at-bay thesis argues that national economies have become enmeshed in a web of economic interdependence from which they cannot easily escape, and from which they derive great economic benefits. Through trade, monetary relations, and foreign investment, the destinies and well-being of societies have become too inexorably interwoven for these bonds to be severed. The costs of the ensuing inefficiencies in order to assert national autonomy or some other nationalistic goal would be too high. The citizenry, so this thesis contends, would not tolerate the sacrifices of domestic economic well-being that would be entailed if individual nation states sought to hamper unduly the successful operation of the international economy.

Underlying this development, the liberal position argues, is a revolution in economic needs and expectations. Domestic economic goals have been elevated to a predominant position in the hierarchy of national goals. Full employment, regional development, and other economic welfare goals have become the primary concerns of political leadership. More importantly, these goals can only be achieved, this position argues, through participation in the world economy. No government, for example, would dare shut out the multinational corporations and thereby forgo employment, regional development, or other benefits these corporations bring into countries. In short, the rise of the welfare state and the increasing sensitivity of national governments to the rising economic expectations of their societies have made them dependent upon the benefits provided by a liberal world-economic system. [. . .]

The sovereignty-at-bay view also envisages a major transformation of the relationships among developed and underdeveloped countries. The multinational corporations of the developed, industrial economies must not only produce in each other's markets, but the locus of manufacturing industry will increasingly shift to underdeveloped countries. As the economies of developed countries become more service oriented, as their terms of trade for raw materials continue to deteriorate, and as their labor costs continue to rise, manufacturing will migrate to lesser-developed countries. United States firms already engage in extensive offshore production in Asia and Latin America. Western Europe has reached the limits of importing Mediterranean labor, which is the functional equivalent of foreign direct investment. Japan's favorable wage structure and under-valued currency have eroded. With the end of the era of cheap energy and of favorable terms of trade for raw materials, the logic of industrial location favors the underdeveloped periphery. Increasingly, the multi-national corporations of all industrial powers will follow the logic of this manufacturing revolution. Manufacturing, particularly of components and semiprocessed goods, will migrate to lesser-developed countries.

This vision of the future has been portrayed most dramatically by Norman Macrae, in an issue of *The Economist*, who foresees a world of spreading affluence energized perhaps by 'small transnational companies run in West Africa by London telecommuters who live in Honolulu'.[4] New computer-based training methods and information systems will facilitate the rapid diffusion of skills, technologies, and industries to lesser-developed countries. The whole system will be connected by modern telecommunications and computers; the rich will concentrate on the knowledge-creating and knowledge-processing industries. More and more of the old manufacturing industries will move to the underdeveloped world. The entire West and Japan will be a service-oriented island in a labor-intensive global archipelago. Thus, whereas the telephone and jet aircraft facilitated the internationalization of production in the Northern Hemisphere, the contemporary revolution in communications and trans-portation will encompass the whole globe.

'The logical and eventual development of this possibility', according to management consultant John Diebold, 'would be the end of nationality and national governments as we know them'.[5] This sovereignty-at-bay world, then, is one of voluntary and cooperative relations among inter-dependent economies, the goal of which is to accelerate the economic growth and welfare of everyone. In this model, development of the poor is achieved through the transfer of capital, technology, and managerial know-how from the continually advancing developed lands to the lesser-developed nations; it is a world in which the tide of economic growth lifts all boats. In this liberal vision of the future, the multinational corporation, freed from the nation state, is the critical transmission belt of capital, ideas, and growth.

The Dependencia Model

In contrast to the sovereignty-at-bay vision of the future is what may be characterized as the *dependencia* model. Although the analysis underlying the two approaches has much in common, the dependencia model challenges the partners-in-development motif of the sovereignty-at-bay model. Its Marxist conception is one of a hierarchical and exploitative world order. The sovereignty-at-bay model envisages a relatively benevolent system in which growth and wealth spread from the developed core to the lesser-developed periphery. In the dependencia model, on the other hand, the flow of wealth and benefits is seen as moving – via the same mechanisms – from the global, underdeveloped periphery to the centers of industrial financial power and decision. It is an exploitative system that produces affluent development for some and dependent underdevelopment for the majority of mankind. In effect, what is termed transnationalism by the sovereignty-at-bay advocates is considered imperialism by the Marxist proponents of the dependencia model.

In the interdependent world economy of the dependencia model, the multinational corporation also reigns supreme. But the world created by these corporations is held to be far different from that envisaged by the sovereignty-at-bay school of thought. In the dependencia model the political and economic consequences of the multinational corporation are due to what Stephen Hymer has called the two laws of development: the law of increasing firm size, and the law of uneven development. The law of increasing firm size, Hymer argues, is the tendency since the Industrial Revolution for firms to increase in size 'from the *workshop* to the *factory* to the *national* corporation to the *multidivisional corporation* and now to the multinational corporation'.[6] The law of uneven development, he continues, is the tendency of the international economy to produce poverty as well as wealth, underdevelopment as well as development. Together, these two economic laws are producing the following consequence:

a regime of North Atlantic Multinational Corporations would tend to produce a hierarchical division of labor within the firm. It would tend to centralize high-level decision-making occupations in a few key cities in the advanced countries, surrounded by a number of regional sub-capitals, and confine the rest of the world to lower levels of activity and income, i.e., to the status of towns and villages in a new Imperial system. Income, status, authority, and consumption patterns would radiate out from these centers along a declining curve, and the existing pattern of inequality and dependency would be perpetrated. This pattern would be complex, just as the structure of the corporation is complex, but the basic relationship between different countries would be one of superior and subordinate, head office and branch office.[7]

In this hierarchical and exploitative world system, power and decision would be lodged in the urban financial and industrial cores of New York, London, Tokyo, etc. Here would be located the computers and data banks of the closely integrated global systems of production and distribution; the main computer in the core would control subsidiary computers in the periphery. The higher functions of management, research and development, entrepreneurship, and finance would be located in these Northern metropolitan centers. 'Lower' functions and labor-intensive manufacturing would be continuously diffused to the lesser-developed countries where are found cheap pliable labor, abundant raw materials, and an indifference to industrial pollution. This global division of labor between higher and lower economic functions would perpetuate the chasm between the affluent northern one-fifth of the globe and the destitute southern four-fifths of the globe.

The argument of the dependencia thesis is that the economic dependence of the underdeveloped periphery upon the developed core is responsible for the impoverishment of the former. Development and underdevelopment are simultaneous processes; the developed countries have progressed and have grown rich through exploiting the poor and making them poorer. Lacking true autonomy and being economically dependent upon the developed countries, the underdeveloped countries have suffered because the developed have a veto over their development. [. . .]

The Mercantilist Model

A key element missing in both the sovereignty-at-bay and the dependencia models is the nation state. Both envisage a world organized and managed by powerful North American, European, and Japanese corporations. In the beneficial corporate order of the first model and the imperialist corporate order of the second, there is little room for nation states, save as servants of corporate power and ambition. In opposition to both these models, therefore, the third model of the future – the mercantilist model – views the nation state and the interplay of national interests (as distinct from corporate interests) as the primary determinants of the future role of the world economy.

According to this mercantilist view, the interdependent world economy, which has provided such a favorable environment for the multinational corporation, is coming to an end. In the wake of the relative decline of American power and of growing conflicts among the capitalist economies, a new international political order less favorable to the multinational corporation is coming into existence. Whether it is former President Nixon's five-power world (US, USSR, China, the EEC, and Japan), a triangular world (US, USSR and China), or some form of American-Soviet condominium, the emergent world order will be characterized by intense international economic competition for markets, investment outlets, and sources of raw materials.

By *mercantilism* I mean the attempt of governments to manipulate economic arrangements in order to maximize their own interests, whether or not this is at the expense of others. These interests may be related to domestic concerns (full employment, price stability, etc.) or to foreign policy (security, independence, etc.).

This use of the term *mercantilism* is far broader than its eighteenth-century association with a trade and balance-of-payments surplus. The essence of mercantilism, as the concept is used in this article, is the priority of *national* economic and political objectives over considerations of *global* economic efficiency. The mercantilist impulse can take many forms in the contemporary world: the desire for a balance-of-payments surplus; the export of unemployment, inflation, or both; the imposition of import and/or export controls; the expansion of world market shares; and the stimulation of advanced technology. In short, each nation will pursue economic policies that reflect domestic economic needs and external political ambitions without much concern for the effects of these policies on other countries or on the international economic system as a whole.

The mercantilist position in effect reverses the argument of the liberals with respect to the nature and success of the interdependent world economy. In contrast to the liberal view that trade liberalization has fostered economic growth, the mercantilist thesis is that several decades of uninterrupted economic growth permitted interdependence. Growth, based in part on relatively cheap energy and other resources as well as on the diffusion of American technology abroad, facilitated the reintroduction of Japan into the world economy and the development of a closely linked Atlantic economy. Now both cheap energy and a technological gap, which were sources of rapid economic growth and global interdependence, have ceased to exist.

International competition has intensified and has become disruptive precisely because the United States has lost much of its technological lead in products and industrial processes. As happened in Britain in the latter part of the nineteenth century, the United States no longer holds the monopoly position in advanced technologies. Its exports must now compete increasingly on the basis of price and a devalued dollar. As was also the case with Great Britain, the United States has lost the technological rents associated with its previous industrial superiority. This loss of industrial supremacy on the part of the dominant industrial power threatens to give rise to economic conflict between the rising and declining centers of industrial power.

[. . .]. These mercantilist writers tend to fall into the two camps of malevolent and benign mercantilism. Both tend to believe the world economy is fragmenting into regional blocs. In the wake of the relative decline of American power, nation states will form regional economic alliances or blocs in order to advance their interests in opposition to other nation states. International trade, monetary arrangements, and investment will be increasingly interregional. This regionalization of economic relations will replace the present American emphasis on multilateral free trade, the international role of the dollar, and the reign of the American multinational corporation.

Malevolent mercantilism believes regionalization will intensify international economic conflict. Each bloc centered on the large industrial powers – the United States, Western Europe, Japan, and the Soviet Union – will clash over markets, currency, and investment outlets. This would be a return to the lawlessness and beggar-thy-neighbor policies of the 1930s.

Benign mercantilism, on the other hand, believes regional blocs would stabilize world economic relations. It believes that throughout modern history universalism and regionalism have been at odds. The rationale of regional blocs is that one can have simultaneously the benefits of greater scale and interdependence and minimal accompanying costs of economic and political interdependence. Though the material gains from a global division of labor and free trade could be greater, regionalism is held to provide security and protection against external economic and political forces over which the nation state, acting alone, has little influence or control. In short, the organization of the world economy into regional blocs could provide the basis for a secure and peaceful economic order.

A Critique of the Three Models

In this section of the article, I evaluate the three models and draw from each what I consider to be important insights into the nature of contemporary international economic relations. This critique is not meant to cover all the points of each model but only those most directly relevant to this essay.

Sovereignty at Bay

Fundamentally, the sovereignty-at-bay thesis reduces to a question of interests and power: Who has the power to make the world economy serve its interests? This point may be best illustrated by considering the relationship of the multinational corporation and the nation state. In the writings I identified with the sovereignty-at-bay thesis, this contest is held to be most critical.

On one side of this contest is the host nation state. Its primary source of power is its control over access to its territory, that is, access to its internal market, investment opportunities, and sources of raw material. On the other side is the corporation with its capital, technology, and access to world markets. Each has something the other wants. Each seeks to maximize its benefits and minimize its costs. The bargain they strike is dependent upon how much one wants what the other has to offer and how skilfully one or the other can exploit its respective advantages. In most cases, the issue is how the benefits and costs of foreign investment are to be divided between the foreign corporation and the host economy.

The sovereignty-at-bay thesis assumes that the bargaining advantages are and always will be on the side of the corporation. In contrast to the corporation's vast resources and flexibility, the nation state has little with which to bargain. Most nation states lack the economies of scale, indigenous technological capabilities, or native entrepreneurship to free themselves from dependence upon American (or other) multinational corporations. According to this argument, the extent to which nation states reassert their sovereignty is dependent upon the economic price they are willing to pay, and it assumes that when confronted with this cost, they will retreat from nationalistic policies.

In an age of rising economic expectations, the sovereignty-at-bay thesis rests on an important truth: a government is reluctant to assert its sovereignty and drive out the multinational corporations if this means a dramatic lowering of the standard of living, increasing unemployment, and the like. But in an age when the petroleum-producing states, through cooperation, have successfully turned the tables on the multinational corporations, it becomes obvious that the sovereignty-at-bay thesis also neglects the fact that the success of the multinational corporation has been dependent upon a favorable political order. As this order changes, so will the fortunes of the multinationals. [. . .]

Dependencia

The weakness of the dependencia, or ultra-imperialism, model is that it makes at least three unwarranted assumptions. In the first place, it assumes much greater common interest among the noncommunist industrial powers — the United States, Western Europe, and Japan — than is actually the case. Secondly, it treats the peripheral states of Asia, Africa, Latin America, Canada, and the Middle East solely as objects of international economic and political relations. Neither assumption is true. As the first assumption is considered in more detail in the next section, let us consider the second for a moment.

After nearly two centuries, the passivity of the periphery is now past. The Soviet challenge to the West and the divisions among the capitalist powers themselves have given the emerging elites in the periphery room for maneuver. These nationalist elites are no longer ignorant and pliable colonials. Within the periphery, there are coalescing centers of power that will weigh increasingly in the future world balance of power: China, Indonesia, India, Iran, Nigeria, Brazil and some form of Arab oil power. Moreover, if properly organized and led, such centers of power in control over a vital resource, as the experience of the Organization of Petroleum Exporting Countries (OPEC) demonstrates, may reverse the tables and make the core dependent upon the periphery. For the moment at least, a perceptible shift appears to be taking place in the global balance of economic power from the owners of capital to the owners of natural resources.

The third unwarranted assumption is that a quasi-Marxist theory of capitalist imperialism is applicable to the relationship of developed and lesser-developed economies today. Again, I illustrate my argument by considering the role of the multinational corporation in the lesser-developed countries, since its allegedly exploitative function is stressed by almost all dependencia theorists.

The dependencia theory undoubtedly has a good case with respect to foreign direct investment in petroleum and other extractive industries. The oil, copper, and other multinationals have provided the noncommunist industrial world with a plentiful and relatively cheap supply of minerals and energy. The dramatic reversal of this situation by the oil-producing countries in 1973-74 and the steady rise of prices of other commodities support the contention that the producing countries were not getting the highest possible price and possibly not a just price for their nonrenewable resources. But what constitutes the just price for a natural endowment that was worthless until the multinationals found it is not an easy issue to resolve.

With respect to foreign direct investment in manufacturing, the case is far more ambiguous. Even if technological rents are collected, does the foreign corporation bring more into the economy in terms of technology, capital, and access to world markets than it takes out in the form of earnings? The research of Canadian, Australian, and other economists, for example, suggests that it does. They find no differences in the corporate behavior of domestic and foreign firms; on the contrary, foreign firms are given higher marks in terms of export performance, industrial research and development, and other economic indicators. Nonetheless, it would be naive to suggest that no exploitation or severe distortions of host economies have taken place. [. . .]

Mercantilism

It seems to me that mercantilists either ignore or ascribe too little significance to certain primary facts. Although the relative power of the United States has declined, the United States remains the dominant world economy. The scale, diversity, and dynamics of the American economy will continue to place the United States at the center of the international economic system. The universal desire for access to the huge American market, the inherent technological dynamism of the American economy, and America's additional strength in both agriculture and resources − which Europe and Japan do not have − provide a cement sufficient to hold the world economy together and to keep the United States at its center.

Furthermore, the United States can compensate for its loss of strength in one issue area by its continued strength in another. For example, the American economic position has indeed declined relative to Europe and Japan. Yet the continued dependence of Europe and Japan on the United States for their security provides the United States with a strong lever over the economic policies of each.

Thus, the fundamental weakness of the mercantilist model is the absence of a convincing alternative to an American-centered world economy. Western Europe, the primary economic challenger to the United States, remains internally divided; it is as yet unable to develop common policies in such areas as industry and energy or with respect to economic and monetary union. It is merely a customs union with a common agricultural policy. Moreover, like Japan, it continues to be totally dependent upon the United States for its security. As long as both Europe and Japan lack an alternative to their military and economic dependence on the United States, the mercantilist world of regional blocs lacks credibility. [. . .]

Implications for International Organization

What then do these three models and their relative merits tell us about the future of international economic organizations? As a consequence of the relative decline of American power and of other developments treated in this article, there is little reason to believe that many new international institutions will be created, but it is likely that the nature and functioning of existing institutions will be profoundly altered.

In a world of national states, international organizations tend to reflect the power and interests of the dominant states in the international system. From this perspective, the international organizations founded at the end of the Second World War reflected the then predominant states in the system. As the structure of the United Nations reflected the distribution of power between the United States and the Soviet Union, so the so-called Bretton Woods system and the institutions associated with it – the International Monetary Fund (IMF), the World Bank, and subsequently the General Agreement on Trade and Tariffs (GATT) – reflected the power and interests of the dominant world economy, the United States.

In both cases, the relative decline of American power over the past several decades has led to profound modifications of these political and economic institutions. Thus, with the growth of Soviet power in the United Nations Security Council and of the so-called nonaligned bloc in the General Assembly, the United Nation's role in American foreign policy and as an institution have been altered significantly. In terms of the major political issues of the world, the United Nations has moved from center stage to the sidelines. A similar transformation can be seen in the area of international economic institutions. This can be witnessed, for example, in the case of the IMF and the negotiations for the reform of the international monetary system which have taken place outside its aegis.

The transformation of the IMF began in the late 1950s with the gradual weakening of the dollar as an international currency. After 1958 the American balance-of-payments deficit began to assume major proportions. The moderate deficits of the previous decade became severe. A drain began on the large gold hoard the United States had accumulated before and during the Second World War. Between 1957 and 1963, US gold holdings fell from $22.8 billion to $15.5 billion, and foreign dollar holdings (official and private) rose from $15.1 to $28.8 billion. By 1968, American gold holdings fell to $10.9 billion, and foreign dollar holdings rose to $31.5 billion.

As Europeans and others began to turn dollars into gold, it became obvious that the United States could not continue to meet all gold claims.

The immediate American response was to initiate numerous makeshift expedients – the gold pool, currency swap arrangements, the General Arrangements to Borrow, etc. – to reinforce the position of the dollar. Additionally, the United States undertook unilateral measures such as the Interest Equalization Tax (1963), 'voluntary' controls on the export of capital (1965), and, eventually, mandatory controls on foreign direct investment (1968) to stem the outflow of dollars.

Despite these and other measures, monetary crises continued to mount throughout the 1960s. In response to these crises, demands mounted for a fundamental reform of the international monetary system. In the ensuing monetary negotiations, as in trade negotiations, the Western powers divided into three positions. On one side were ranged the United States and Great Britain. On the other stood France. In the middle was West Germany, which attempted to reconcile the Common Market and the Atlantic powers.

Whereas the United States wanted a reform that would ensure the continued privileged position of the dollar, France under de Gaulle wanted a reform that would dethrone the dollar and thus would redistribute economic power in the West. This would allegedly be achieved if the world returned to what de Gaulle believed was the true measure of wealth and guarantor of political independence, namely, gold. A return to the gold standard would not only enhance the power of France, which had replenished its gold reserves, but the United States would have to expend real wealth in order to maintain and/or expand its hegemony. If other nations refused to accept any more dollars and demanded gold, the United States would be forced to bring its payments into balance and to liquidate its global economic and military position. In short, a shift from the dollar to gold as the world's reserve currency would mean a rentrenchment of American power in Europe, Asia, and around the globe.

At the same time that the United States desired to maintain the privileged position of the dollar, the basic instability of the system was appreciated by all. An international monetary system and an expanding trade system that depended upon the deficits of the United States were prone to crisis. From the perspective of most countries, a return to gold was both politically and economically undesirable, however. In the late sixties, therefore, extensive IMF negotiations produced an 'international money' called special drawing rights (SDRs).

The United States had desired the SDRs to relieve the pressure on the dollar while preserving its ultimate reserve role. France wanted nothing less than the reimposition of monetary restraints on the United States. Between the two of them stood West Germany and its desire to hold together the European and Atlantic powers. Due largely to German initiatives, a compromise solution was finally reached, which gave the Americans their SDRs in exchange for greater European voting power in the International Monetary Fund. Thus, while the IMF would have the power to 'issue' SDRs as an international reserve on a limited scale, Europe (if it were united) could exercise a veto over American policy in the IMF.

In short, the internal structure and functioning of the IMF was reconstituted to reflect the distribution of world economic and monetary power. The United States no longer ran the organization. Control over it was now shared by the European powers. Similarly, one can anticipate that the immense growth of Arab monetary balances will lead to a further internal transformation of the IMF. By one method or other, this redistribution of monetary power will be given an institutional form.

Notes

1. Edward Hallet Carr, *The Twenty Years' Crisis 1919-1939* (Macmillan and Company, London, 1951), p. 117.

2. Raymond Vernon, *Sovereignty at Bay* (Basic Books, New York, 1971).

3. Harry G. Johnson, *International Economic Questions Facing Britain, the United States and Canada in the 70's* (British-North American Research Association, June 1970), p. 24.

4. Norman Macrae, 'The Future of International Business', *The Economist*, 22 January 1972.

5. John Diebold, 'Multinational Corporations – Why be Scared of Them?', *Foreign Policy*, no. 12 (Fall 1973), p. 87.

6. Stephen Hymer, 'The Multinational Corporation and the Law of Uneven Development', in Jagdish Bhagwati (ed.), *Economics and World Order – From the 1970's to the 1990's* (The Macmillan Company, New York, 1972), p. 113 and *passim*.

7. Ibid., p. 114.

4.3

IDEOLOGIES AND THE NEW INTERNATIONAL ECONOMIC ORDER: REFLECTIONS ON SOME RECENT LITERATURE

Robert W. Cox

Source: *International Organization*, vol. 33, no. 2 (1979), pp. 257-67.

Cox takes the demand for a New International Economic Order and identifies the links between the theoretical analyses and strategies for action it has provoked. In particular, he identifies five 'opinion clusters' or perspectives which he dubs 'establishment', 'social democratic', 'Third World', 'neo-mercantilist' and 'historical materialist'. Each of these adopts a particular intellectual framework, which defines the way in which the NIEO issue is analyzed and policy options proposed.

What is the NIEO Literature About?

The demand for a New International Economic Order, that can be formally dated from the Algiers conference of the Non-Aligned Countries in 1973 and which has been pursued with the backing of these countries in the United Nations and other international instances, has precipitated a reconsideration of the structure and processes of world political economy among all the principal interests. This has resulted in a large and growing literature that to date, if it has not entirely clarified the problems and issues besetting the world political economy, has at least made it possible to identify certain salient currents of thought about them, each setting forth a mode of analysis and a strategy of action. This review article attempts to survey some of this literature. I take my stand not in some conception of objective science from which to allocate merits and demerits to particular authors, but rather as an observer of the confrontation of ideas, considering the role of ideas in relation to the positions of conflicting forces. The survey cannot claim to be comprehensive, though it does aim to be representative of different perspectives. [. . .]

Ideological analysis is, of course, a critic's weapon and one most effectively used against the prevailing orthodoxies which, when stripped of their putative universality, become seen as special pleading for historically transient but presently entrenched interests. Social science is never neutral. It is, therefore, only fair to warn the reader that my purpose in undertaking this survey was to discover and encourage avenues of enquiry that might in the long run aid towards the transformation of power relations both within and among nations in the direction of greater social equality. Thus, I found the work of some of the radical neo-mercantilists and historical materialists discussed below more potentially valuable (though as yet very inadequately developed) than the more prestigious products of the western academic establishments.

Some preliminary remarks are called for before getting to the books themselves. In the first place, what is the New International Economic Order? Or, more specifically, what, in the broad, is this literature about? A number of answers are possible, all of which are in some measure correct. At a first level, the NIEO is a series of specific demands and considerations embodied in an impressive range and number of official documents adopted by international conferences. The extent of these can be measured by the size of a two-volume collection of official papers compiled by the librarians of the United Nations Institute for Training and Research which includes texts from the Group of 77 and its regional groups and the Non-Aligned Countries as well as from the organizations of the United Nations family (UNITAR, *A New International Economic Order. Selected Documents, 1945-1975*).

At a second level, the NIEO is a negotiation process, broadly speaking, between countries of North and South but taking place through a variety of institutions and forums in which are represented wider or narrower ranges of functional and geographical interests. This negotiation process is concerned with the possibilities of agreement concerning both revised international policies and reformed or new institutions (including the power relationships governing these institutions). No one has yet attempted to plot the inter-institutional complex through which this negotiation process is taking place, though UNITAR and the Ford Foundation have sponsored a team project with Robert W. Gregg as principal investigator to 'describe, explain, and analyze' this aspect.

At a third level, the NIEO has precipitated a debate about the real and desirable basic structure of world economic relations. Though the term 'international' (consciously chosen in preference to 'world' or 'global' by the authors of the demand) connotes a limitation of the issue to relations among countries, the debate cannot be so artificially constrained and has ranged inevitably into domestic and transnational structural issues. Structures here encompass the relationships among regions within countries, among different industries and economic activities, among different modes of production, and among social classes, as well as those among countries of different groupings. This debate brings into focus theories concerned with imperialism, with the causes of underdevelopment, and with the physical limits to growth.

Finally, at a fourth level, the debate becomes one about the form of knowledge appropriate to understanding these issues. In effect, the demand for a NIEO has mobilized a fresh challenge to the intellectual hegemony of liberal economics and its claims to an exclusive 'rationality'. For its critics, economics is an ideology derived from a particular historically determined set of power relations, not a science with absolute and universal scope, and the emergence of new power relations of which the NIEO is one manifestation calls for a reformulating of a more appropriate political economy.

The specific policy and institutional issues that are the subject of diplomatic negotiations and the theoretical and epistemological issues debated in academic seminars and symposia are indeed intimately related. Any general organization of power not only generates institutions and policy mechanisms but also sustains ideas which legitimate it. Such a dominant ideology justifies the existing order of power relations by indicating the benefits accruing (or accruable) to all the principal parties, including in particular the subordinate or less favored. So long as these latter acquiesce in the dominant mode of thought, their demands are likely to be reconcilable within the existing system of power. However, where there is a general challenge to the prevailing structure of power, then the articulation of counter-ideologies becomes a part of the action, and the possibility of reaching reasonably durable agreement on the practical issues of policies and institutions becomes bound up with the possibility of reaching a new consensus on theories and modes of analysis.

Moreover, in the case of the NIEO, there is a considerable overlap in the personnel concerned, on the one hand with the policy negotiations, and on the other hand with the debate about theory. This underlines the practical political importance of the theoretical issues and indeed gives the debate about theory a certain logical priority in that its outcomes would provide the rationale for future policies. Much of the literature to be discussed is the product of actual participants in the negotiations and is thus to be considered as political action, an aspect of a political process (rather than as independent, objective, or scientific analyses made by disinterested observers).

The intellectual participants who are politically active in the NIEO negotiations together with those academics who play a more indirect role can be seen as linked in a series of networks, each of which is mobilizing ideas around a certain partial consensus. There are, of course, disagreements among individuals within a particular network, but these disagreements are within a certain commonality of ideas or a basic common approach. There are also certain individuals who participate in more than one network and who are thus potential hinges or go-betweens. Such individuals might conceivably be important in exploring the possibility of broadening a partial consensus to encompass two or more networks, ultimately towards a new hegemonic ideology. The present state of the literature does not enable one to speculate about the shape of a new hegemony, but it does make it possible to juxtapose the main networks and to place the various authors within this juxtaposition of perspectives or partial consensuses (while recognizing that individual authors may resist assimilation to a school). The political nature of the literature justifies this political mode of analysis.

These networks are not mere constructs of my imagination, classifications of authors whose ideas seem to have a certain community of spirit. Intellectual production is now organized like the production of goods or of other services. The material basis of networks is provided by formal (usually nongovernmental) organizations as mobilizing and coordinating agencies with research directors and funds (from sources sometimes more, sometimes less visible) for commissioning studies, financing conferences, and symposia or informal luncheon discussions. The materially independent scholar is a rarity, though perhaps not quite extinct. The material basis of networks allows for a selection of participants which guarantees a certain homogeneity around a basic core of orthodoxy. However, since the object of the exercise is consensus-building, narrow orthodoxy or exclusiveness would be a self-defeating criterion, and the activators of each network extend their search to those whose ideas reach the outer boundaries of what might ultimately be acceptable. Above and beyond material support, the organized network holds out to the intellectual the prospect of political influence, of being listened to by top decision-makers and even of becoming part of the decision-making team.

Five opinion clusters, some of which are more or less structured networks and some less formally structured orientations or approaches to the issues of North-South relations, can be identified from the literature concerning the NIEO:

1. An 'establishment' perspective that could be characterized as monopolistic liberalism is the dominant view in the industrialized countries. The Trilateral Commission is the most important formal organization co-

ordinating this network. There is no need to embroider upon the variety of articles, journalistic and otherwise, that have underlined the potentially influential nature of this assemblage of political, business, and academic personalities from North America, Western Europe, and Japan including a number of leading members of governments presently in power. The NIEO lies at the center of the Trilateral Commission's concerns and is the subject of several studies commissioned by it. One in particular, *Towards a Renovated International System* by Richard N. Cooper, Karl Kaiser, and Masataka Kosaka, is extremely pertinent. Pierre Uri has written a book called *Development Without Dependence* for the Atlantic Institute for International Affairs that concords broadly with Trilateral views. Several prominent Trilateralists figure in another symposium organized at MIT in May 1976 with the support of the Ford Foundation which has resulted in a volume of papers edited by Jagdish N. Bhagwati. The contributors, while mainly American, include some non-Americans (British, Canadian, Japanese, and Third World). The Council on Foreign Relations, another body whose membership overlaps with the Trilateral Commission, has sponsored, within the framework of its 1980s project, a study by Albert Fishlow, Carlos F. Diaz-Alejandro, Richard R. Fagen, and Roger Hansen entitled *Rich and Poor Nations in the World Economy*. A further study that can be read as having a relationship to this intellectual community, also supported in part by the Ford Foundation as well as by the US National Science Foundation and the Netherlands Government, is the report prepared for the United Nations by Wassily Leontief and others, *The Future of the World Economy*. Basically these documents, whether the emphasis is on 'the management of interdependence' (Trilateral, p. 5) or on 'the correction of the existing economic inequalities among countries' (Leontief, p. 30), take the existing structure of world economy as a starting point and ask what adjustments can be agreed upon by the dominant powers to gain wider acceptability. This is the view from the top.

2. What can be described as a social democratic variant of the establishment view shares with it a basic commitment to the normative preference for a world economy with relatively free movement of capital, goods, and technology as well as an acceptance of the rationality of conventional economics, while putting more stress upon the needs of the poor. It represents, in other words, a broader and somewhat more generous view of the adjustments that can be made without fundamentally disturbing the existing hegemony. The network that is developing ideas consistent with this general perspective is less fully organized than the first one, though key groupings can be identified. The Club of Rome group presided

over by Jan Tinbergen that produced the report *Reshaping the International Order* (or RIO report for short) represents a major statement of this viewpoint. Like the publications mentioned under the first category, this also is the fruit of a collective effort. Tinbergen is a major figure articulating this tendency. The Institute of Development Studies at the University of Sussex has been an important center nourishing and stimulating this current of thought and some people associated with it, now or formerly, have been of influence in shaping relevant programs of the United Nations and other international agencies, the world employment program of the ILO for example. Dudley Seers, Paul Streeten, and Hans Singer, all Sussex alumni, are among these. Hans Singer, who has been influential within the UN secretariat on development assistance policy as well as in an independent academic capacity, has written with Jared Ansari a book intended for undergraduates and for the general reader entitled *Rich and Poor Countries*. From the ILO's world employment program comes a study viewing the future of the world economy from the standpoint of maximizing employment, especially in less developed countries, by Bohuslav Herman, *The Optimal International Division of Labour*, a study given its ideological consecration in a preface by Jan Tinbergen. Gerald Helleiner of the University of Toronto, whose intellectual affinities are with the Sussex group, has edited another symposium, *A World Divided. The Less Developed Countries in the International Economy*. Whereas the Bhagwati book is addressed primarily to rich country policy makers in answer to the question, What response can be given to Third World demands?, the Helleiner book is addressed primarily to Third World policy makers in answer to the question, What Third World strategies towards the First World are most likely to advance Third World development goals? The contributors to the Helleiner symposium are mainly economists from the First World (mostly non-American) who are actively sympathetic with Third World aims (Reginald Green, for instance, has worked directly in the service of the Tanzanian government) together with several Third World economists. By and large, the social democratic perspective is that of First World understanding and sympathy with the Third World. Helleiner and Streeten are both contributors to the Bhagwati volume and though more at home in the second may be regarded as examples of potential links between the first two networks. Some contributors to the Helleiner symposium should also be assimilated into the following perspectives.

3. There is a category of more or less official Third World representatives who have formalized a continuing network, the Third World Forum. I do

not wish to suggest here that there is a single Third World viewpoint. The range of opinion among spokesmen for countries in the Third World is much wider than that to be found among participants in this network, diversified as it is. Yet there is a body of thought-engaged-in-action that corresponds to the French adjective *tiers-mondiste* − a form of radical perspective shaped less by abstract analytical categories then by existential political struggle. Mahbub ul Haq, a senior official of the World Bank who was formerly responsible for economic planning in Pakistan at the time of General Ayoub, places the origin of this grouping at the Stockholm conference on the environment in 1972. In his book *The Poverty Curtain. Choices for the Third World*, which is a kind of personal memoir of the evolution of thinking of a Yale-trained Third World economic policy maker, he indicates how this organization grew out of informal discussions he had with Gamani Corea (of UNCTAD), Enrique Iglesias (of ECLA) and Samir Amin (of the UN Institute in Dakar for Development Planning), all of them high level international officials and Third World intellectuals. The purpose, according to Mahbub ul Haq, was 'intellectual self-reliance, both at the national and at the international level, which could give some form and substance to our [i.e., the Third World's] aimless search for appropriate development strategies at home and to our disorganized efforts to co-ordinate our negotiating positions abroad' (Mahbub ul Haq, p. 84). The Third World Forum took shape during 1972-73 at a time when the Third World countries' claims seemed to have been set aside by the First World in its concern with its own internal economic problems. The network was already in being when the succession of events of 1973, including the oil crisis, gave a new momentum to the Third World. President Echeverria of Mexico both gave his country a leading role in promoting the NIEO at the United Nations and put his personal support behind the Third World Forum, and the Third World Forum was not unassociated with his bid for the Secretary-Generalship of the UN. If since that time the Third World Forum seems to have been less active, its function may be revived through the proposal for a more formal Third World secretariat. From outside the circle of Third World economic negotiators, but still within the orbit of senior international officials, comes another recent book: Albert Tévoédjre's *La pauvreté, richesse des peuples* (an English edition is in preparation) by the director of the ILO's International Institute for Labour Studies, a national of Benin (formerly Dahomey).

Ideologically, the Third World network of policy intellectuals shares the ambivalence of official Third World positions. Some, like Mahbub ul Haq himself, have impeccable liberal economics credentials, though experience with the practical problems of Third World development has

led them to abandon faith in the market in favor of government intervention. Others, like Samir Amin, have a Marxist background. One senses
a constant tension between intellectual analysis that leans towards a
rejection of western models (and thus implicitly of the institutions that
embody these models, such as the World Bank) and a hope for support
from the western economies (which would be delivered through these
same institutions), and tension also between a conviction that social and
political revolution is a necessary condition for real development in the
Third World and an unwillingness to allow First World economists and
officials to use the ineffectiveness of existing governmental measures as
an excuse for placing conditions of surveillance on resource transfers to
the Third World. The ambivalence is acute in personal terms as these
intellectuals, whose thinking tends to take a radical bent, are aware that
their political influence depends upon the support of governments that
cannot share their views. They face in an acute form the dilemma of the
intellectual who seeks power and influence with power as an opportunity
to put his ideas into practice, while knowing in his heart that the very
power he solicits will be the contradiction of his goals.

4. My fourth category can be designated neo-mercantilist. Unlike the first
three it does not have a formal network, though at least one group of
American policy thinkers, the group associated with the magazine *Com-
mentary*, some of whose members have also enjoyed support from the
Lehrman Institute in New York, may be seen as constituting something
of a network within a much larger and more amorphous cluster. Whereas
most of the authors in the first three categories considered here are in one
way or another active in the negotiating process over NIEO policy issues,
the neo-mercantilist works we have to consider here are those of individual
observer-critics, not policy intellectuals.

The neo-mercantilist sees economic policy as an instrument of political
goals — politics leads and economics follows. (In de Gaulle's phrase,
l'intendance suivra.) Economic theory that makes an abstraction of
economic behavior from politics is therefore to be rejected (as biased and
misleading) in favor of a revival of political economy. The world is to be
understood, not in terms of a market equilibrium model, but in terms of
an organization of power: a world system in which economic processes
are among the major manifestations of power.

Right-wing and Left-wing neo-mercantilisms can be distinguished. The
coming to power of the Trilateral Commission in the United States with
the Carter election in effect displaced tendencies towards a Right-wing
mercantilism observable in the Kissinger-Nixon administration. The vision

of a reunified Trilateral world as the anchor of a liberal world economy replaced the notion of a pentagonal organization of world power that seemed likely to become one of competing economic blocs. Kautsky's ultra-imperialism seemed to triumph over Lenin's rival imperialisms. Among the books considered here, the Right of neo-mercantilism in the United States is represented by Robert W. Tucker's *The Inequality of Nations.* He distrusts Trilateralism and argues for the defense of American power in a world in which the balance of power among nations has not ceased to operate. The Left of neo-mercantilism recognize the same basic framework of power, but write from a standpoint of sympathy with those who are challenging dominant power in the world economy. Two recent works are worth noting.

Michael Hudson, an unconventional American radical, has written *Global Fracture. The New International Economic Order.* This is a sequel to his earlier *Superimperialism*, in which he argued that the United States had organized a dominant imperial system in which government financial management played the crucial role. *Global Fracture* dates the decline of this empire from the crises of 1973 and the gradual emergence of a world of competing blocs (the US sphere receding to the American hemisphere, a Western Europe-Arab-African complex, a Japanese sphere in Southeast Asia, the Soviet sphere, and China — each with its own center-periphery dialectic). Its title and its message are in pointed contrast to the *Global Reach* of Barnet and Muller: powerful governments, not multinational corporations, are the dominant forces. The other book, intended as an academic textbook more than as a contribution to public debate, is *La dialectique de la dépendence* by André Tiano, representing a French tradition of economic thought in which the state has always been a principal actor, and which has never (like most Anglo-Saxon economics) been able to ignore Marxian analysis but has remained in constant dialogue with it. 'La réalité internationale qu'il convient d'expliquer', Tiano writes at the beginning of his book, 'n'est pas économique, politique, juridique, culturelle ou démographique. C'est un "système" qui dans une connaissance idéale ne se plie à aucune fragmentation disciplinaire' (Tiano, p. 11). One of the modern greats of French economics, Francois Perroux, recently said (*Le Monde*, 27 June 1973), in a phrase consistent with Tiano's approach, 'Il n'y a pas de sosie en économie . . . la loi est celle de l'inégalité' (There are no identical actors in economics . . . the law is that of inequality), by which he meant that the notion of a homogeneous market composed of numerous anonymous and roughly similar buyers and sellers is a misleading fiction, since economic actors are unequal in power and the only valid way of representing their interactions is by a model depicting the structure of their power relations.

5. The historical materialist current of thought likewise disdains the economics of liberalism as a mode of comprehending the issues posed by the NIEO, but, in distinction to neo-mercantilism which focuses upon the state, historical materialism directs attention in the first instance to the production process. I prefer the term historical materialism to Marxism in this context, since Marxism carries so many conflicting connotations of doctrinal orthodoxies and political lines. In regard to the Third World and the problem of development, historical materialism is now a broad intellectual current within which a vigorous debate is taking place. Like neo-mercantilism, it is fragmented into a variety of groups and individuals, constituting an informal community of discourse rather than a formally organized network. Its members know and recognize each other and debate their differences in preference to engaging in polemics with those who do not share their own basic orientation. Like the neo-mercantilists considered here, the historical materialists are observer-critics generally far removed from influence upon current negotiations over international economic policies. (Samir Amin is a notable exception as a participant in the Third World network and link between it and the historical materialist current.)

The historical materialist position on development most familiar to those outside this school is that of Gunder Frank: the notion of a single all-embracing world capitalist system in which development at the center generates underdevelopment in the peripheries. Immanuel Wallerstein's refinement of this notion has also become fairly widely recognized. Less known by English-language readers is the work of Christian Palloix whose thesis of the internationalization of capital seems consistent with the Frank-Wallerstein approach insofar as it envisages a globally unifying capitalist mode of production, but is inconsistent with Frank and Wallerstein in rejecting the center-periphery polarity with its implication that the revolutionary potential for transforming the system will come from the Third World. Some seminars by Palloix given during the summer of 1977 at the Autonomous University of Mexico have been published as *Travail et production* and are considered here.

Quite different is the approach of those who see not one big capitalist mode of production, but rather a dominant capitalist mode articulated with other non-capitalist modes. The difference in viewpoints is not likely to be resolvable by refinements of deductive reasoning or further exegesis of the sacred texts (though many efforts are still being devoted to this form of Marxist scholasticism), but only by further study and observation of the actual development of production processes, especially in the Third World. One of the major contributors to the articulation of the modes of production notion, P.P. Rey, has recently republished *Les Alliances de Classes* (first published in 1973, though written in 1969), and Aidan Foster-Carter has written for the *New Left Review* (January-February 1978) a critical review of this literature in 'The Modes of Production Controversy'.

The central historical problem in the historical materialist perspective is how the world system may be transformed. One focus of interest is upon the crisis at the center – what the European Left has for several years been calling *la crise*. Paul Sweezy's recent article in the *Monthly Review* (April 1978), 'The Present Global Crisis of Capitalism', deals with this. The other focus of interest is in the peripheries. Samir Amin's article in the same journal (Summer 1977), 'Self-reliance and the New International Economic Order', argues that the present drive to promote industrialization in the Third World by the peripheral bourgeoisies is likely to lead only to a new phase of imperialism (based on export by the periphery of cheap manufactured goods) and that the only hope for a new international order would be if the Third World were to act collectively through mutual support of self-reliant projects and by reducing the flow of raw material exports to the rich countries thereby forcing the center to adjust to a less unequal international division of labor. Some historical materialist viewpoints (by Arghiri Emmanuel and Tamás Szentes in particular) are included in a special number of the *International Social Science Journal* 4 (1976) devoted to the NIEO.

Implicit though not developed in Amin's analysis is the question of the class structure of the peripheral countries and how this conditions the way they link into the world economy. The possibility of Samir Amin's preferred scenario depends upon the emergence of an autonomous 'national' class in the Third World countries, whereas most Marxist analyses have pointed to the creation of local bourgeoisies dependent upon international capital. Hartmut Elsenhans has argued the possibility in certain cases of the coming to power of a 'state class' that could be the author of a national development strategy. Samir Amin's pessimistic scenario is, on the other hand, supported by studies on the multinational corporation. Two which can be related to the historical materialist perspective are Norman Girvan's *Corporate Imperialism: Conflict and Expropriation*, and a case study of one Canadian-based minerals multinational, *Falconbridge. Portrait of a Canadian Mining Multinational*, by John Deverall and the Latin American Working Group.

By considering this selection of recent literature under the five categories indicated above, it is possible to see, for each category or perspective, an intellectual framework or ideology that serves to define a particular problematic peculiar to that perspective. The internal debate within each of the five tendencies also gives an indication of the range of options in the negotiation process that may be seen as feasible from each of the main positions. Finally, since theory and practice are fused in regard to the NIEO, each intellectual position reveals a view of the structure of world power and a strategy of alliances or potential alliances.

INDEX